THE COMPLETE
OUTDOOR BUILDER

**Creative Publishing
international**

Copyright © 2009
Creative Publishing international, Inc.
400 First Avenue North, Suite 300
Minneapolis, Minnesota 55401
1-800-328-0590
www.creativepub.com

Printed in China

10

Library of Congress Cataloging-in-Publication Data

The complete outdoor builder : from arbors to walkways : 150 DIY projects.
     p. cm.
  At head of title: Black & Decker
  Includes bibliographical references and index.
  Summary: "Shows homeowners how to build up, expand, refresh and
accessorize their outdoor spaces using the most contemporary techniques,
tools, and materials while following the most up-to-date codes"--Provided
by publisher.
  ISBN-13: 978-1-58923-483-3 (soft cover : alk. paper)
  ISBN-10: 1-58923-483-9 (soft cover : alk. paper)
  1. Garden structures--Design and construction--Amateurs' manuals.
I. Black & Decker Corporation (Towson, Md.) II. Title: Black & Decker.

  TH4961.C655 2009
  690'.89--dc22

2009028983

President/CEO: Ken Fund

Home Improvement Group

Publisher: Bryan Trandem
Managing Editor: Tracy Stanley
Senior Editor: Mark Johanson
Editor: Jennifer Gehlhar

Creative Director: Michele Lanci-Altomare
Senior Design Managers: Jon Simpson, Brad Springer
Design Manager: James Kegley

Lead Photographer: Joel Schnell
Shop Manager: James Parmeter
Shop Assistant: Charlie Boldt

Production Managers: Laura Hokkanen, Linda Halls

Page Layout Artist: Danielle Smith

The Complete Outdoor Builder
Created by: The Editors of Creative Publishing international, Inc., in cooperation with Black & Decker.
Black & Decker® is a trademark of The Black & Decker Corporation and is used under license.

NOTICE TO READERS

For safety, use caution, care, and good judgment when following the procedures described in this book. The publisher and Black & Decker cannot assume responsibility for any damage to property or injury to persons as a result of misuse of the information provided.

The techniques shown in this book are general techniques for various applications. In some instances, additional techniques not shown in this book may be required. Always follow manufacturers' instructions included with products, since deviating from the directions may void warranties. The projects in this book vary widely as to skill levels required: some may not be appropriate for all do-it-yourselfers, and some may require professional help.

Consult your local building department for information on building permits, codes, and other laws as they apply to your project.

BLACK&DECKER®

THE COMPLETE OUTDOOR BUILDER

From Arbors to Walkways 150 DIY Projects

Creative Publishing
international
www.creativepub.com

Contents

Introduction

Many homeowners and do-it-yourselfers narrow their focus to the interior of their homes as they dream and plan for upcoming projects. However, the area outside of your home is a perfect place to exercise your creativity and is overflowing with possibilities. Whether your front steps simply need a makeover or you think a new greenhouse or shed would give you the extra space you need to fully explore your hobbies, *The Complete Outdoor Builder* has the ideas and know-how to help you turn your plans into realities.

Whether you're new to outdoor home improvement or a seasoned veteran, start with the "Planning" section, which covers essential information about seeking permits, how to estimate and order materials for outdoor construction, and the tools, codes, and challenges of outdoor building. This section also includes insight on how to draw plans to help you ensure that your project ends up as exquisite in real life as it is when you imagine it.

The next sections each cover a different area of outdoor construction, from "Pathways & Patios" to "Porches" and "Sheds & Outbuildings." Projects as simple as building walkways, sidewalks, and patios or as complex as constructing a children's play area from lumber and basic tools are all included in these sections. Pay careful attention to the first few pages of each, which will cover basic techniques to help you complete your project with ease.

After that, be grand in your ambitions and tackle projects both familiar and challenging. If your needs are practical, perhaps you should review how to pour a concrete patio, install a panel fence, or build a children's timberframe sandbox. If you're ready for a larger project, why not build that deck you've been wanting to sit on, screen your porch, or build a service shed for firewood or yard implements. Perhaps, however, you feel like your yard needs dressing up—perfect! Use our plans to construct a garden pond and fountain, a backyard putting green, or a beautiful brick archway over your front drive. The projects in this book include lists of the tools and materials you'll need, the lumber you'll need to purchase, and in some cases, the entire plans for a large-scale projects.

Whatever your ambitions, *The Complete Outdoor Builder* has the tools, expertise, ideas, and simple how-to instructions with large, easy-to-understand photographs to guide you from start to finish. Even if you're a beginner, you'll find many projects here that are well within your abilities. And remember, with each new project you tackle, you'll acquire new skills and gain the confidence to take on larger ones. So what are you waiting for? Start making your backyard dreams a reality today.

Planning

Homeowners no longer think of their yards as great expanses of lawn, but as outdoor living spaces. Permanent outdoor structures can add to the beauty and function of these outdoor rooms. For example, a deck can provide additional space for entertaining or relaxing, a wall can provide privacy and texture, and a walkway or path can unify areas.

But before you can begin building, you have to organize your ideas and create a plan for materials, tools, inspections, measuring, and construction. Proper planning will help you create an outdoor project that is beautiful now and will last for years to come—an important consideration, since landscaping contributes about 30 percent to your home's total value.

This opening section will provide you with all the information you need in order to plan and design the projects of your choice. We'll look at new and standard materials for outdoor projects—including wood, metal, plastic, manufactured and natural stone, and concrete—and show you how to estimate and order supplies. You will find information on basic and specialty tools and a discussion of the common types of hardware and fasteners used for outdoor projects. We'll also review the basics of building codes, including permits and inspections. And to ensure you get the results you want, we'll show you the techniques you'll need to design your own projects.

By following these planning strategies, you will save time and money and enjoy your outdoor home for years to come.

IN THIS CHAPTER:

- Building Materials
  - *Lumber*
  - *Metals & Plastics*
  - *Cast Blocks*
  - *Natural Stone*
  - *Concrete*
  - *Mortar*
- Estimating & Ordering Materials
- Basic Tools
- Power & Rental Tools
- Masonry Tools
- Fasteners & Hardware
- Codes & Courtesies
- Measuring
- Challenges
- Drawing Plans

Bark mulch

Cedar bark wood chips

Teak

Cedar lattice

Redwood

Pine

Wood *is the most common, and arguably the most versatile, of building materials. Carefully choose lumber that is appropriate for your project.*

Building Materials

The building materials you choose should reflect both the function and the appearance of your outdoor project. Materials impact not only the style, but the durability, maintenance requirements, and overall cost of a project. Wood, stone, and brick are traditional favorites, but the versatility and ease of installation you get with PVC vinyl, metal, and concrete make them attractive options for certain applications.

Lumber

Wood remains the most common building material in outdoor construction, and it is usually less expensive than stone or brick. Its versatility lends itself to just about any project, from the plain and practical to the elegant and ornate. It is ideal for decks and walkways, fences and retaining walls, pergolas and screens, outdoor furniture, and of course, outbuildings. And it is beautiful, blending with most architectural styles. It looks especially attractive in settings surrounded by trees.

Most home centers and lumberyards carry a wide selection of dimension lumber, as well as convenient preassembled fence panels, posts, pickets, rails, balusters, floorboards, stringers, and stair railings. Inspect all lumber for flaws, sighting along each board to check for warping, twisting, or loose knots. Boards used for structural parts should have only small knots that are tight and ingrown. Inspect the end grain also. Lumber with a vertical grain will cup less as it ages. Return any boards with serious flaws.

Framing lumber—typically pine or pressure-treated pine—comes in a few different grades: Select Structural (SEL STR), Construction (CONST) or Standard (STAND), and Utility (UTIL). For most applications, Construction Grade No. 2 offers the best balance between quality and price. Utility grade is a lower-cost lumber suitable for blocking and similar uses but should not be used for structural members. Board lumber, or *finish* lumber, is graded by quality and appearance, with the main criteria being the number and size of knots present. "Clear" pine, for example, has no knots.

The most important consideration in choosing lumber is its suitability for outdoor use. Select a wood that is not prone to rot or insect attack. Three types are generally recommended: heart cedar, heart redwood, and pressure-treated lumber. Redwood and cedar are attractive, relatively soft woods with a natural resistance to moisture and insects—ideal qualities for outdoor applications. "Heart" or "heartwood" varieties will be identified on the grade stamp. In both redwood and cedar, heartwood has better resistance to decay than lighter-colored sapwoods.

Western red cedar (WRC) or incense cedar (INC) for decks should be heartwood (HEART) with a maximum moisture content of 15 percent (MC15).

Pressure-treated pine is stronger and more durable than redwood or cedar and is more readily available and less expensive in many areas. Although this lumber has a noticeable green color due to its preservative, the wood can either be stained or left to weather to a pleasing gray.

Plywood designated as exterior-grade is made with layers of cedar or treated wood and a special glue that makes it weather-resistant. Always cover exposed plywood edges to prevent water intrusion.

Some homeowners shy away from pressure-treated lumber, due to the chemicals used to treat it. Despite popular fears, the chemicals in pressure-treated pine do not easily leach into the soil, nor are they easily absorbed through the skin. In fact, it can be argued that pressure-treated lumber is actually a good environmental choice because it lasts longer in projects, thereby reducing the harvest of new trees. When using pressure-treated lumber, however, take some commonsense precautions: avoid

prolonged skin contact by wearing gloves and protective clothing, and avoid breathing the dust by wearing a particle mask.

If you live in an arid climate, such as in the Southwest, you can use untreated pine lumber because wood will not rot if its moisture content is less than 20 percent. However, it's always a good idea to use pressure-treated lumber for deck posts or any other framing members that are in contact with the ground.

Teak and white oak are hardwoods usually reserved for top-of-the-line outdoor furniture. These woods have a dense cell structure that makes them resistant to water penetration. However, because these woods are expensive, they generally aren't practical to use for large structures, such as decks or fences. They are better suited for accent pieces, such as benches or large planters.

Remember that although treated woods do resist rot, they will not last indefinitely without regular maintenance. They should have a fresh coat of stain or sealer every two years to maintain durability and appearance. Sealing cut edges of lumber—including pressure-treated wood—will prevent rotting of the end grain.

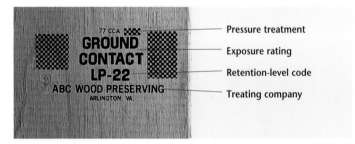

Pressure-treated lumber stamps list the type of preservative and the chemical retention level, as well as the exposure rating and the name and location of the treating company.

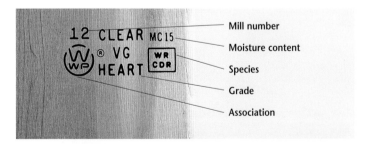

Cedar grade stamps list the mill number, moisture content, species, lumber grade, and membership association. Western red cedar (WRC) or incense cedar (INC) for decks should be heartwood (HEART) with a maximum moisture content of 15% (MC15).

Apply a coat of sealer-preservative or staining sealer to all sides of outdoor structures. Make sure sealer is applied to all end-grain. Even pressure-treated lumber is vulnerable to moisture and rot.

Chain link

Landscape
edging

Landscape
fabric

Prefabricated
plastic stones,
lattice, and
decking

Metals & Plastics

Plastic and aluminum products have become popular alternatives to traditional outdoor building materials, because they are low maintenance, versatile, and easy to install. Though these materials are typically more expensive than wood and other alternatives, their durability makes them attractive options.

Plastics are now available in several colors, and they can be used in most applications where wood is appropriate. They can be found in fencing and timbers for use in decks, walkways, fences, and arbors. PVC vinyl and fiberglass reinforced plastic (FRP) are becoming popular choices for fencing and decking materials. Many styles and sizes are available, and they are strong, versatile, and require no maintenance. Materials are often sold as kits, making installation easy. Before choosing PVC, check manufacturers' specifications on expansion and contraction variances to see if it is suitable for your project.

Composite materials blend together wood fibers and recycled plastics to create a rigid product that, unlike wood, will not rot, splinter, warp, or crack. These boards can be cut to size with a circular saw and do not require painting or staining.

Metal is often used in outdoor applications, such as in fencing and gates. Aluminum offers a sturdy, lightweight, waterproof material that is available in a variety of designs, ranging from the simple to the elaborate. Availability may be limited, so check with local building centers. Galvanized chain-link steel has long been a popular choice for fencing, because it is relatively maintenance free and can be used to create a secure outdoor wall at a reasonable price. Options such as vinyl-coated mesh and color inserts can increase privacy and boost style. Traditional wrought iron, though more expensive and less common today, is used for fencing, railings, and patio furniture to add a touch of elegance.

Copper pipe is a unique and unexpected material that is well suited to temperature swings and water exposure, making it ideal for outdoor use. This metal is inexpensive and available at nearly any home center or hardware store.

Although many of these materials may be more expensive initially, they often carry lifetime warranties, which can make them more economical than wood over time. Before choosing any alternative building material, check on restrictions with your local building department.

Metals and plastics are replacing more traditional materials, as they have minimal maintenance and allow environmentally conscientious consumers to use recycled products.

Cast Blocks

Manufactured stone is often designed to resemble natural stone, but it offers distinct advantages over the real thing. Greater uniformity makes installation easier, and it is often less expensive than natural alternatives.

Although poured concrete isn't as attractive as natural stone, new masonry techniques help it rival natural stone for visual appeal. Brick, concrete, and glass block are available in a growing variety of sizes and styles, providing the flexibility to build distinctive, reasonably priced outdoor structures. Many of these products are well-suited to do-it-yourselfers, because their weights are manageable and installation is easy.

Decorative concrete block can be used to make screen walls and is available in many colors. A decorative block wall is one of the most economical choices for a stone landscape wall.

Concrete paver slabs, available in several shapes and sizes, can be used for laying simple walkways and patios. They are available in a standard finish, a smooth aggregate finish, or can be colored and molded to resemble brick. Concrete paver slabs are relatively inexpensive and quite easy to work with. They're usually laid in a bed of sand and require no mortar. Their surface is generally finished so the smooth gravel aggregate is exposed, but they are also available in plain pavers and aggregate.

Paver bricks resemble traditional kiln-dried clay bricks, but are more durable and easier to install. Paver bricks are available in a variety of colors and geometric shapes for paving patios, walkways, and driveways. Many varieties are available in interlocking shapes that can be combined with standard bricks to create decorative patterns, such as herringbone and basket weave. Paver bricks have largely replaced clay bricks for landscape use and can be set into a bed of sand for patios and driveways, where mortar is not required.

Edging blocks are precast in different sizes for creating boundaries to planting areas, lawns, loose-fill paths, and retaining walls.

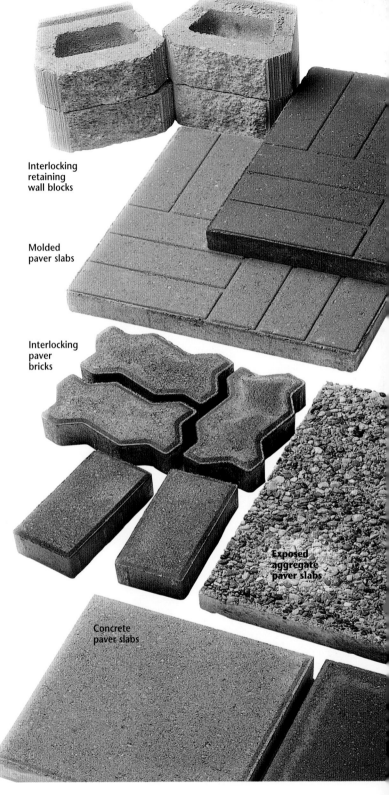

Interlocking retaining wall blocks

Molded paver slabs

Interlocking paver bricks

Exposed aggregate paver slabs

Concrete paver slabs

Brick and concrete block *are available in a growing variety of sizes and styles, allowing you to build distinctive outdoor structures.*

Natural Stone

Natural stone is one of the finest building materials you can use. It offers beautiful color and texture, along with unmatched durability and elegance, making it a classic building material for landscape floors, ornamental walls, retaining walls, and walkways. Because of its beauty, it is also a choice material for decorative features, such as rock gardens, ponds, fountains, and waterfalls.

These virtues come at a price, however: Natural stone is one of the more expensive building materials you can select, and it can be heavy and difficult to work with.

Natural stone includes a wide range of materials, from microscopic sands to enormous boulders and carefully cut granite, marble, limestone, slate, and sandstone. It is sold in many forms, so you'll have to choose what type, form, texture, and shade to use for your project.

Fieldstone, sometimes called river rock, is any loose stone gathered from fields, dry river beds, and hillsides. It is often used to build retaining walls, ornamental garden walls, and rock gardens, where it creates an informal, natural look. When split into smaller pieces, fieldstone can be used in projects with mortar. When cut into small pieces, or quarried stone, fieldstone is called cobblestone, a common material in walks and paths.

Ashlar, sometimes called wall stone, is quarried stone—such as granite, marble, or limestone—that has been smooth-cut into large blocks, ideal for creating clean lines with thin mortar joints. Cut stone works well for stone garden walls, but because of its expense, its use is sometimes limited to decorative wall caps.

Flagstone is large slabs of sedimentary rock with naturally flat surfaces. Limestone, sandstone, slate, and shale are the most common types of flagstone. It is usually cut into pieces up to three inches thick, for use in walks, steps, and patios. Smaller pieces—less than 16" square—are often called steppers.

Veneer stone is natural or manufactured stone cut or molded for use in nonload-bearing, cosmetic applications, such as facing exterior walls or freestanding concrete block walls.

Rubble is irregular pieces of quarried stone, usually with one split or finished face. It is widely used in wall construction.

Each type of stone offers a distinctive look, as well as a specific durability and workability. Often the project dictates the form of stone to use. Ask your local stone supplier to suggest a stone that meets your cost, function, and workability needs.

NOTE: You may find different terms used for various types of stone. Ask your supply yard staff to help you.

Fieldstone is stone gathered from fields, dry river beds, and hillsides. It is used in wall construction.

Flagstone is large slabs of quarried stone cut into pieces up to 3" thick. It is used in walks, steps, and patios.

A stone yard is a great place to get ideas and see the types of stone that are available. This stone yard includes a display area that identifies different types of stone and suggests ways they can be used.

Concrete

Poured concrete has long been a favorite for driveways, walkways, and patios because of its exceptional strength, but new tinting and surface finishing techniques give concrete a decorative look that makes it attractive for landscaping. It's much less expensive than natural stone, and because it's poured while in a semi-liquid state, it can be formed into curves and other shapes, such as landscape ponds or fountains. Using simple tools, you can even finish concrete to simulate brick pavers or flagstone.

Concrete is made up of a mixture of portland cement, sand, coarse gravel, and water. Premixed bags of dry concrete are available at home centers and are easy and efficient to use.

Mix concrete in a wheelbarrow for smaller projects, or rent a power mixer to blend larger amounts of cement, gravel, sand, and water quickly. Buy ready-mixed concrete for large jobs.

Timing and preparation are the most important factors in working with concrete. Concrete will harden to its final form, regardless of whether you have finished working with it. Start with smaller-scale projects until you're comfortable working with concrete. A concrete walkway is a good starter project. Recruit helpers when you're ready to take on a large project.

Premixed concrete products contain all the components of concrete. Just add water, mix, and pour.

To mix concrete ingredients in a wheelbarrow, use a ratio of 1 part portland cement (A), 2 parts sand (B), and 3 parts coarse gravel (C).

Mortar

Masonry mortar is a mixture of portland cement, sand, and water. Ingredients, such as lime and gypsum, are added to improve workability or control "setup" time.

Every mortar mixture balances strength, workability, and other qualities. Make sure to use the mortar type that best suits your needs:

Type N is a medium-strength mortar for above-grade outdoor use in nonload-bearing (freestanding) walls, barbecues, chimneys, soft stone masonry, and tuck pointing.

Type S offers high-strength mortar for exterior use at or below grade. It is generally used in foundations, brick-and-block retaining walls, driveways, walks, and patios.

Type M is a very high strength specialty mortar for load-bearing exterior stone walls, including stone retaining walls and veneer applications.

Glass Block Mortar is a specialty white Type S mortar for glass block projects. Standard gray Type S mortar is also acceptable for glass block projects.

Refractory Mortar is a calcium aluminate mortar that does not break down with exposure to high temperatures; it is used for mortaring around firebrick in fireplaces and barbecues. Chemical-set mortar will cure even in wet conditions.

To mix mortar, always read and follow the manufacturer's specifications on the mortar mix package.

Ingredients for mixing your own mortar include portland cement, sand, and water. For high temperature, add refractory mix.

15

Estimating & Ordering Materials

Whether pouring a small slab or building an elaborate archway, it is important to estimate the dimensions of your project as accurately as possible. This will allow you to create a complete and concise materials list and help eliminate extra shopping trips and delivery costs.

Begin compiling a materials list by reviewing your building plans. These plans should include scaled plans that will make estimating easier.

Once you have developed a materials list, add 10 percent to the estimate for each item. This will help you manage small oversights and allow for waste when cutting.

The cost of your project will depend upon which building materials you choose. But because some materials may not be readily available in your area, plan your projects and place orders accordingly. Lumber, stone, manufactured stone, and alternate materials, such as metals and plastics, can vary widely in price. It's unfortunately true that the most attractive building materials are usually the most expensive as well.

In addition to lumber, fasteners, hardware, hand tools, and power tools, many home centers also carry masonry tools and materials, such as concrete, mortar, and stucco mix, typically in premixed bags. Consider the scale of your project before buying concrete or stucco by the bag, however. For large projects, you may want to hire a ready-mix supplier to deliver fresh concrete.

If you plan on working with specialty or alternative materials, such as vinyl fencing or composite decking, many home centers will have a select range of styles and sizes onhand. Contacting manufacturers directly will lead to greater choices of products, and you will be able to place an order directly with them or be directed to a retailer near you.

Local building suppliers can be a great asset to do-it-yourselfers. The staff can offer professional advice, and yards often carry the tools and other materials necessary to complete your project. Often you can receive help in designing your project and advice on estimating the materials, applicable local building codes, and regional climate considerations.

Many centers also offer coordinating services for landscapers and contractors to work with you. You may also find class offerings in masonry construction or other techniques to help you develop the skills to complete your project.

Local brick and stone suppliers will often help you design your project and advise you about estimating materials, local building codes, and climate considerations.

HOW TO ESTIMATE MATERIALS

Sand, gravel, topsoil (2" layer)	surface area (sq. ft.) ÷ 100 = tons needed
Standard brick pavers for walks (2" layer)	surface area (sq. ft.) × 5 = number of pavers needed
Standard bricks for walls and pillars (4 × 8")	surface area (sq. ft.) × 7 = number of bricks needed (single brick thickness)
Poured concrete (4" layer)	surface area (sq. ft.) × .012 = cubic yards needed
Flagstone	surface area (sq. ft.) ÷ 100 = tons needed
Interlocking block (2" layer)	area of wall face (sq. ft.) × 1.5 = number of stones needed
Ashlar stone for 1-ft.-thick walls	area of wall face (sq. ft.) ÷ 15 = tons of stone needed
Rubble stone for 1-ft.-thick walls	area of wall face (sq. ft.) ÷ 35 = tons of stone needed
8 × 8 × 16" concrete block for freestanding walls	height of wall (ft.) × length of wall (ft.) × 1.125 = number of blocks needed

AMOUNT OF CONCRETE NEEDED (CUBIC FEET)

Number of 8"-Diameter Footings	Depth of Footings (feet) 1	2	3	4
2	¾	1½	2¼	3
3	1	2¼	3½	4½
4	1½	3	4½	6
5	2	3¾	5¾	7½

Amount of Concrete Needed (cubic feet)	Dry Ingredients for Self-mix: 94-lb. bags of portland cement	Cubic feet of sand	Cubic feet of gravel	60-lb. bags of premixed dry concrete
1	⅙	⅓	½	2
2	⅓	⅔	1	4
3	½	1	1½	6
4	⅔	1⅓	2	8
5	1	2	3	10
10	2	4	6	20

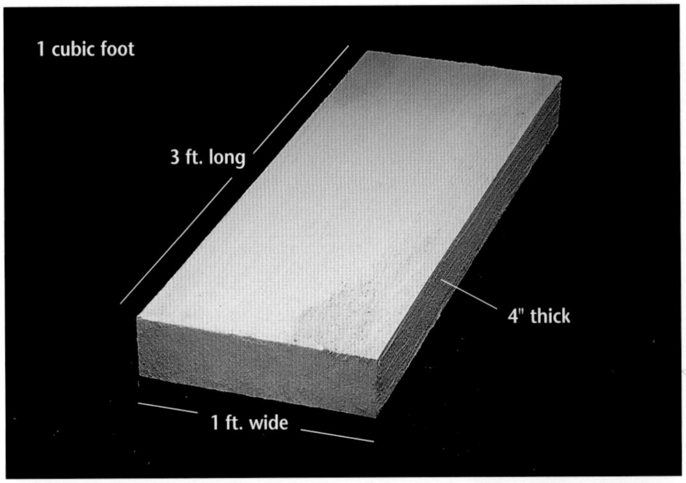
1 cubic foot
3 ft. long
4" thick
1 ft. wide

Measure the width and length *of the project in feet, then multiply the dimensions to get the square footage. Measure the thickness in feet (4" thick equals ⅓ ft.), then multiply the square footage times the thickness to get the cubic footage. For example, 1 ft. × 3 ft. × ⅓ ft. = 1 cu. ft. Twenty-seven cubic feet equals one cubic yard.*

CONCRETE COVERAGE

Volume	Thickness	Surface Coverage
1 cu. yd.	2"	160 sq. ft.
1 cu. yd.	3"	110 sq. ft.
1 cu. yd.	4"	80 sq. ft.
1 cu. yd.	5"	65 sq. ft.
1 cu. yd.	6"	55 sq. ft.
1 cu. yd.	8"	40 sq. ft.

Level

Quick clamp

Cat's paw

Chisel

Mason's string

Tape measure

Shovel

Trowel

Hoe

Rubber mallet

Caulk gun

Mason's hammer

Combination square

Flat pry bar

Line level

Metal snips

Rafter square

Scratch awl

Pipe clamp

Compass

Ratchet wrench & sockets

22-oz. claw hammer

Plumb bob

Chalk line

Putty knife

Framing square

Clamshell posthole digger

Basic Tools

The right tool always makes the job easier. As a homeowner, you may already own many of the tools needed for the projects in this book. If you don't have the necessary tools, you can borrow them, rent them, or buy them.

If you decide to purchase new tools, invest in the highest-quality products you can afford. High-quality tools perform better and last longer than less expensive alternatives. Metal tools should be made from high-carbon steel with smoothly finished surfaces. Hand tools should be well balanced and have tight, comfortably molded handles.

Quality tools may actually save you money over time, because you eliminate the expense of replacing worn out or broken tools every few years.

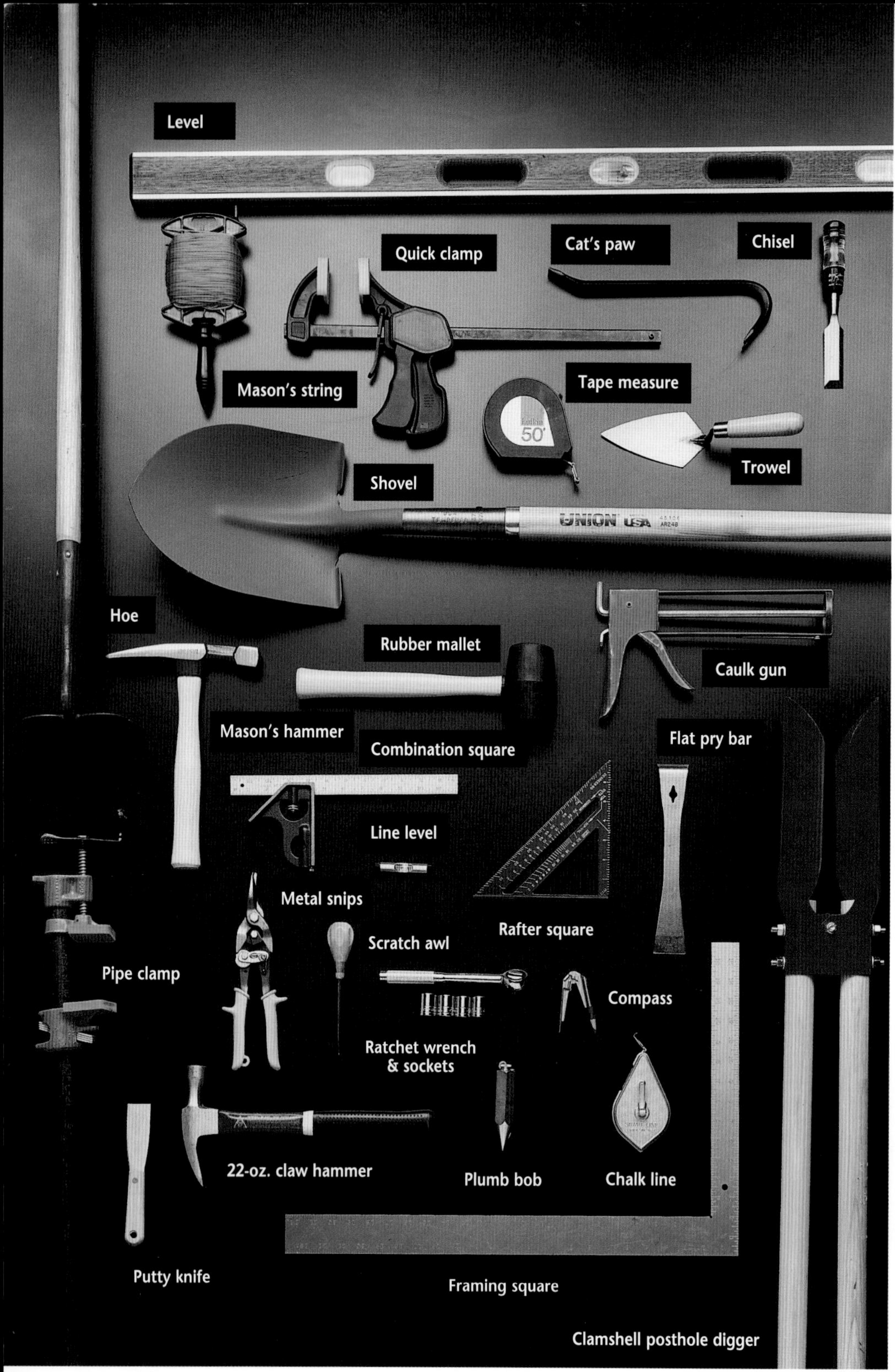

Hand tools for outdoor building should be rated for heavy-duty construction. Always purchase the highest quality tool you can afford; there is no substitute for quality.

Power & Rental Tools

Outdoor building projects and landscaping work often require the use of power tools and specialty tools.

Home centers will have the common power tools you will require in stock, but if your project demands a tool that you will only use once or that is expensive, consider renting. Many home centers now have rental equipment on site. Also check your local rental center outlets for tool availability.

When renting, always read the owner's manual and operating instructions to prevent damage to tools and personal injury. Some rental centers also provide training and assistance on specialty tools.

To ensure your safety, always use a ground-fault circuit-interrupter (GFCI) extension cord with power tools, and wear protective gear, such as work glasses, particle masks, and work gloves when sawing or handling pressure-treated lumber and masonry products.

Power tools include: *power miter saw (A), 14.4-volt cordless trim saw with a 5⅜"-blade (B), reciprocating saw with 6" and 8" blades (C), cordless drill/driver (D), jigsaw (E), ½" hammer drill and bits (F).*

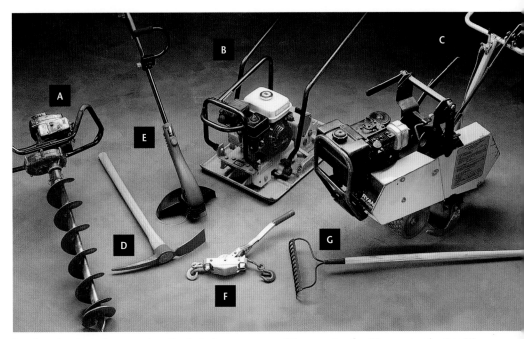

Landscaping tools for preparing sites include: *power auger (A), power tamper (B), power sod cutter (C), pick (D), weed trimmer (E), come-along (F), garden rake (G).*

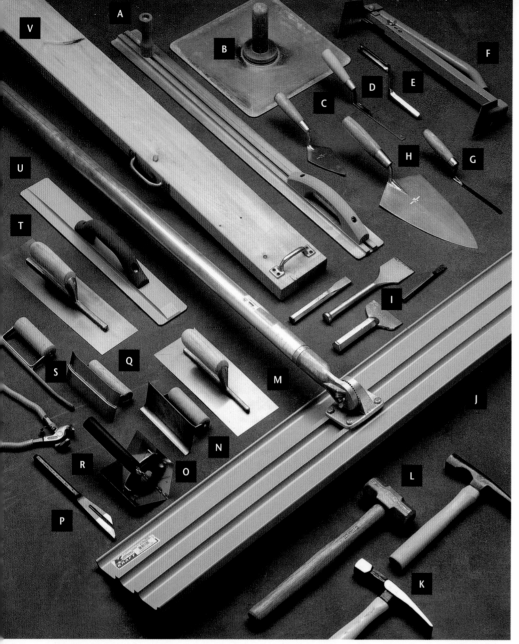

Masonry Tools

Masonry work involves two steps: preparing the site and laying the concrete. To work effectively with masonry products, you will have to buy or rent some special-purpose tools.

You may want to purchase some smaller landscaping tools, including a pick for excavating hard or rocky soil; a weed trimmer for removing brush and weeds before digging; a posthole digger for digging just one or two holes; a come-along for moving large rocks and other heavy objects without lifting; and a garden rake for moving small amounts of soil and debris.

To lay concrete you will need trowels, floats, edgers, and jointers. These are hand tools used to place, shape, and finish concrete and mortar. Chisels are used to cut and fit brick and block. You can also equip your circular saw with blades and your power drill with bits designed for use with concrete and brick.

Always make sure you have the necessary safety equipment on hand before you start a masonry project, including gloves and protective eye wear.

Mason's tools include: a darby (A) for smoothing screeded concrete; mortar hawk (B) for holding mortar; pointing trowel (C) for tuck-pointing stone mortar; wide pointing tool (D) for tuck-pointing or placing mortar on brick and block walls; jointer (E) for finishing mortar joints; brick tongs (F) for carrying multiple bricks; narrow tuck-pointer (G) for tuck-pointing or placing mortar on brick and block walls; mason's trowel (H) for applying mortar; masonry chisels (I) for splitting brick, block, and stone; bull float (J) for floating large slabs; mason's hammers (K) for chipping brick and stone; maul (L) for driving stakes; square-end trowel (M) for concrete finishing; side edger (N) and step edger (O) for finishing inside and outside corners of concrete; joint chisel (P) for removing dry mortar; control jointer (Q) for creating control joints; tile nippers (R) for trimming tile; sled jointer (S) for smoothing long joints; steel trowel (T) for finishing concrete; magnesium or wood float (U) for floating concrete; screed board (V) for screeding concrete.

Fasteners & Hardware

Because you will be building outdoor structures, the connecting hardware, fasteners, and materials you use must hold up to extreme weather conditions. The better the materials, the longer the life of the structure.

Any metal-connecting hardware and fasteners, including nails and screws, should be made from rust-resistant material, such as galvanized steel, aluminum, or stainless steel. Galvanized fasteners should be triple-dipped in zinc to resist corrosion. Although galvanized metals will not stain treated wood, they may react with natural chemicals in cedar and redwood, causing staining. Stainless steel fasteners won't cause staining in any wood, but they are expensive.

Seal screwheads set in counterbored holes with silicone caulk to prevent water damage. Also be aware that when combining dissimilar metals, you will need a plastic spacer to prevent the electrochemical reaction known as galvanic action from occurring, which causes corrosion.

A common type of hardware you'll find throughout this book is the metal anchor, used to reinforce framing connections. Most of the anchors called for in the various projects (and all of the anchors in the sheds and outbuilding projects) are commonly available at lumberyards and home centers. If you can't find what you need on the shelves, look through the manufacturer's catalog, or visit their website (see page 523). Always use the fasteners recommended by the manufacturer.

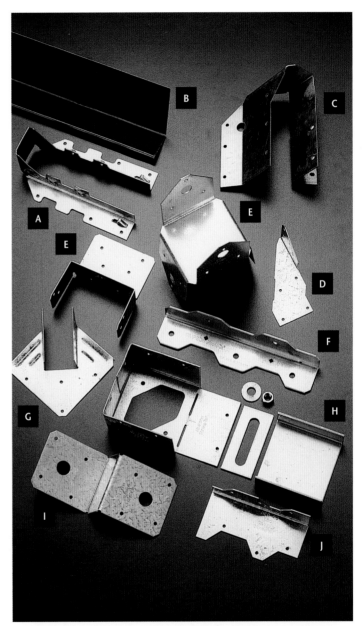

Metal connectors commonly used include: joist hanger (A), flashing (B), angled joist hanger (C), rafter tie (D), post-beam caps (E), stair cleat (F), hurricane tie (G), post anchor with washer and pedestal (H), joist tie (I), angle bracket (J).

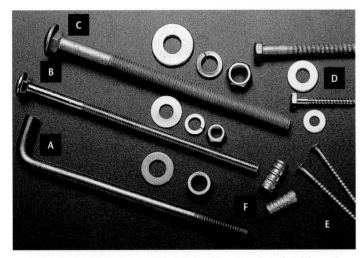

Common types of fasteners include: J-bolt with nut and washer (A), carriage bolts with washers and nuts (B, C), galvanized lag screws and washers (D), corrosion-resistant deck screws (E), masonry anchors (F).

Always talk with your neighbors when planning an outdoor project. *Not only will this ensure that you agree upon details such as property lines, it may also enable you to combine resources or expenses.*

Codes & Courtesies

Almost anytime you build—whether indoors or out—there are local regulations you'll have to consider. Building codes, zoning ordinances, and permits are the legal issues you'll have to contend with, but you should also consider neighborhood standards and the impact your project will have on neighboring properties.

Building codes govern the materials and construction methods of your project to ensure safety, and zoning laws govern the size, location, and style of your structure to preserve aesthetic standards. Permits and inspections are required to ensure your plans meet all local building and zoning restrictions.

Requirements and restrictions vary from one municipality to another, so check the codes for your area. If your plans conflict with local codes, authorities will sometimes grant a variance, which allows you to compromise the strict requirements of the code.

Consult with your local building inspection department early in your planning process to determine if your project requires a permit and whether you must submit plans for approval. The permit process can take several weeks or months, so checking early can help you avoid unnecessary delays or changes to your plans. Then fill out the necessary forms, pay any applicable fees, and wait for your approval.

In the meantime, it's a good idea to discuss your plans with neighbors. A fence, wall, or gate on or near a property line is as much a part of your neighbors' landscapes as your own. The tall hedge you have planned for privacy, for example, may cast a dense shadow over your neighbor's sunbathing deck. The simple courtesy of apprising your neighbors of your plans can help you avoid strained relationships or even legal disputes.

You may find that discussing your plans with neighbors reaps unexpected rewards. For instance, you and your neighbor may decide to share labor and expenses by landscaping both properties at once. Or you may combine resources on a key feature that benefits both yards, such as a stone garden wall or shade tree. When several neighbors put their heads together to create an integrated landscape plan for their yards, the results benefit everyone. Individual landscapes look larger when the surrounding yards share a complementary look and style.

In addition, check with your local utility companies to pinpoint the locations of any underground electrical, plumbing, sewer, or telephone lines on your property. The locations of these features can have an obvious impact on your plans, if your project requires digging or changes to your property's grade. There is no charge to have utility companies locate these lines, and it can prevent you from making an expensive or life-threatening mistake. In many areas, the law requires that you have this done before digging any holes.

On the following pages, you'll find some common legal restrictions for typical landscape projects.

FENCES

• **Height:** The maximum height of a fence may be restricted by your local building code. In some communities, backyard fences are limited to 6 ft. in height, while front yard fences are limited to 3 ft. or 4 ft.—or prohibited altogether.

• **Setback:** Even if not specified by your building code, it's a good idea to position your fence 12" or so inside the official property line to avoid any possible boundary disputes. Correspondingly, don't assume that a neighbor's fence marks the exact boundary of your property. For example, before digging an elaborate planting bed up to the edge of your neighbor's fence, it's best to make sure you're not encroaching on someone else's land.

• **Gates:** Gates must be at least 3 ft. wide. If you plan to push a wheelbarrow through it, your gate width should be 4 ft.

DRIVEWAYS

• **Width:** Straight driveways should be at least 10 ft. wide; 12 ft. is better. On sharp curves, the driveway should be 14 ft. wide.

• **Thickness:** Concrete driveways should be at least 6" thick.

• **Base:** Because it must tolerate considerable weight, a concrete or brick paver driveway should have a compactable gravel base that is at least 6" thick.

• **Drainage:** A driveway should slope ¼" per foot away from a house or garage. The center of the driveway should be crowned so it is 1" higher in the center than on the sides.

• **Reinforcement:** Your local building code probably requires that all concrete driveways be reinforced with iron rebar or steel mesh for strength.

SIDEWALKS & PATHS

• **Size of sidewalks:** Traditional concrete sidewalks should be 4 to 5 ft. wide to allow two people to comfortably pass one another, and 3 to 4" thick.

• **Width of garden paths:** Informal pathways may be 2 to 3 ft. wide, although steppingstone pathways can be even narrower.

• **Base:** Most building codes require that a concrete or brick sidewalk be laid on a base of compactable gravel at least 4" thick. Standard concrete sidewalks may also need to be reinforced with iron rebar or steel mesh for strength.

• **Surface & drainage:** Concrete sidewalk surfaces should be textured to provide a nonslip surface and crowned or slanted ¼" per foot to ensure that water doesn't puddle.

• **Sand-set paver walkways:** Brick pavers should be laid on a 3"-thick base of sand.

STEPS

• **Proportion of riser to tread depth:** In general, steps should be proportioned so that the sum of the depth plus the riser, multiplied by two, is between 25 and 27". A 15" depth and 6" rise, for example, is a comfortable step (15 + 12 = 27), as is an 18" depth and 4" rise (18 + 8 = 26).

• **Railings:** Building codes may require railings for any stairway with more than three steps, especially for stairs that lead to an entrance to your home.

CONCRETE PATIOS

• **Base:** Concrete patios should have a subbase of compactable gravel at least 4" thick. Concrete slabs for patios should be at least 3" thick.

• **Reinforcement:** Concrete slabs should be reinforced with wire mesh or a grid of rebar.

Fences should be set back at least 1 ft. from the formal property lines.

Driveways should be at least 10 ft. wide to accommodate vehicles.

Walkways should crown in the center to provide water runoff.

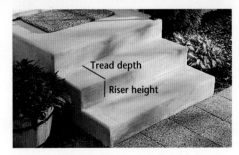

Concrete steps should use a comfortable tread depth and riser height.

23

Concrete patios require reinforcement with steel mesh or rebar.

Frost line

Mortared garden walls need to be supported by concrete footings.

A pool requires a protective fence to keep neighborhood children and animals from falling in.

GARDEN WALLS

• **Footings:** Mortared brick or stone garden walls more than 4 ft. in height often require concrete footings that extend below the winter frost line. Failure to follow this regulation can result in a hefty fine or a demolition order, as well as a flimsy, dangerous wall.

• **Drainage:** Dry-set stone garden walls installed without concrete footings should have a base of compactable gravel at least 6" thick to ensure the stability of the wall.

SWIMMING POOLS

• **Fences:** Nearly all building codes require a protective fence around swimming pools to keep young children and animals away from the water.

• **Location:** In some areas, building codes require that below-ground swimming pools be at least 10 ft. away from a building foundation.

SHEDS

• **Permits:** Sheds greater than 120 sq. ft. generally require a permit, but temporary buildings generally do not. Additionally, if you live in a city or a suburban association, there may be restrictions on where and how you may build a shed. If you live in a rural community, you may not need a permit if the shed will not house humans or animals.

• **Site:** Choose a location that enhances your property in all seasons. Consider setback requirements, yard grade, drainage, sun exposure, foliage, and the shed's function.

• **Size:** Choose a shed size based on what will be housed in the shed and how much room is needed to maneuver objects inside. Most sheds are built with a 3 to 4 ratio, 6-ft. wide by 8-ft. long, for example.

• **Style:** Zoning laws may dictate acceptable shed styles for your area. Try to choose a design that blends with existing home and neighborhood architecture.

• **Foundation:** The type of foundation you will need will depend on the shed's size and purpose, as well as the climate and soil conditions in your region. Cost and local building codes may also play a role in foundation type.

PORCHES

• **Permits:** Permits are required for any additions to a home. Have all gas or electrical elements added to the porch inspected before walls or floors are closed up and finished. In some areas, inspections may also be required for the footings, framing, and insulation.

• **Slope:** When building an open porch, slope floors away from the home to permit water runoff, and construct a roof overhang of 16" to enjoy the porch in the rain.

• **Cost:** To reduce costs, build a porch on a wooden deck, rather than on a concrete slab.

• **Foundation:** Always prime and paint wood support members before installation, including the ends, to prevent rot.

FIRE PITS & BARBECUES

• **Clearance:** Requirements vary by municipality, but in general, permanent open fire or barbecue pits are not permitted less than 25 ft. from your home, garage, shed, wood pile, or wooden fences.

• **Diameter:** Most cities limit the size of a fire or barbecue pit to 3 ft. in diameter, but check with your building or fire department for local requirements. The pit must be ringed with a noncombustible material, such as stone, clay, concrete, or driveway pavers. Some cities may even require a ring of sand around the pit to prevent grass fires.

• **Permits:** An inspector from the fire department will visit your site and determine whether the pit meets local safety codes. If your built-in barbecue will incorporate gas lines or electrical outlets or fixtures, additional permits and inspections will be required. If the pit passes inspection, you will be issued a recreational burning permit for a fee.

• **Burning:** Most localities do not permit burning rubbish or waste. The use of flammable or combustible liquid accelerants is generally prohibited in fire pits. Some may even restrict the size of cut wood that may be burned.

• **Safety:** Most cities require an adult present at a pit fire until all flames are extinguished. If conditions are too windy or dry, or produce excess smoke, you may be asked to extinguish all flames. A connected garden hose or other extinguisher must be near the site.

RETAINING WALLS
• **Height:** For do-it-yourself construction, retaining walls should be no more than 4 ft. high. Higher slopes should be terraced with two or more short retaining walls.

• **Batter:** A retaining wall should have a backward slant (batter) of 2 to 3" for dry-set stones; 1 to 2" for mortared stones.

• **Footings:** Retaining walls higher than 4 ft. must have concrete footings that extend down below the frost line. This helps ensure the stability of the wall.

PONDS
• **Safety:** To ensure child safety, some communities restrict landscape ponds to a depth of 12 to 18", unless surrounded by a protective fence or covered with heavy wire mesh.

DECKS
• **Structural members:** Determining the proper spacing and size for structural elements of a deck can be a complicated process, but if you follow these guidelines, you will satisfy code requirements in most areas:

BEAM SIZE & SPAN

Beam size	Maximum spacing between posts
Two 2 × 8s	8 ft.
Two 2 × 10s	10 ft.
Two 2 × 12s	12 ft.

JOIST SIZE & SPAN

Joist size	Maximum distance between beams (Joists 16" apart)
2 × 6	8 ft.
2 × 8	10 ft.
2 × 10	13 ft.

• **Decking boards:** Surface decking boards should be spaced so the gaps between boards are no more than ¼" wide.

• **Railings:** Any deck more than 24" high requires a railing. Gaps between rails or balusters should be no more than 4".

• **Post footings:** Concrete footings should be at least 8" in diameter. If a deck is attached to a permanent structure, the footings must extend below the frost line in your region.

*A **series of short retaining walls,** rather than one tall wall, is the best way to handle a slope.*

***Railing balusters** are required by building code to be spaced no more than 4" apart to keep small children from slipping through or being trapped between them.*

***Sheds** larger than 120 square feet may require a permit, but temporary structures typically do not.*

Measure and document the features of your yard to create a rough yard survey.

Measuring

You will have to accurately measure and note the features of your yard on a rough sketch, called a yard survey. From this survey, you can draw a detailed scale drawing, called a site plan. The sketch for the yard survey can be rough, but the measurements must be exact.

If possible, enlist someone to help you take these measurements. If you haven't already done so, ask your local utility companies to mark buried utility lines.

You will also have to mark your property lines. If you don't have a plot drawing (available from the architect, developer, contractor, or possibly, the previous owner) or a deed map (available from city hall, county courthouse, title company, or mortgage bank) that specifies property lines, hire a surveyor to locate and mark them. File a copy of the survey with the county as insurance against possible boundary disputes in the future.

THE YARD SURVEY

Accurate yard measurements are critical for estimating quantities and cost of materials. To sketch your survey, follow these steps:

Step A: Sketch your yard and all its main features on a sheet of paper. Assign a key letter to each point. Measure all straight lines and record the measurements on a notepad.

Step C: Plot irregular boundaries and curves, such as shade patterns or low-lying areas that hold moisture after a rainfall. Plot these features by taking a series of perpendicular measurements from a straight reference line, such as the edge of your house or garage.

Step B: Take triangulated measurements to locate other features, such as trees that don't lie along straight lines. Triangulation involves locating a feature by measuring its distance from any two points whose positions are known.

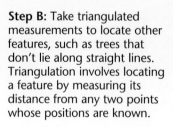

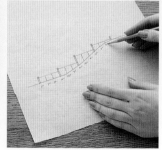

Step D: Sketch elevations to show slopes. Measure the vertical drop of a slope using different-sized stakes and string. Connect the string to the stakes so it is perfectly horizontal. Measure the distance between the string and ground at 2-ft. intervals along the string.

Challenges

Planning an outdoor project often involves dealing with obstacles in your chosen path. You may have to go around a tree or rock outcropping, handle a hill or grade change, cross a depression, or work around buried electric, telephone, gas, cable, and water lines on your property.

You can easily cope with such challenges by removing the interference, when possible, or relocating or rerouting your structure. Contact local utility companies to locate and mark lines before you draw up plans. Law requires that these companies inspect your site on request and mark the location of buried lines.

Another option is to incorporate obstacles into your project layout. For example, on a hillside, step a fence down in level sections, or follow the contour of the slope. If a tree is in your path, try adapting your structure to incorporate the tree's current size and future growth. For example, plan a deck to flow around a large shade tree.

Rocks can be dealt with in much the same way. Incorporate boulders into wall design, or use them as focal points along a pathway.

Redwood fence photo courtesy of California Redwood Association

Board, louver, basket-weave, and panel fences are good choices for stepped fences that accommodate a change in grade. More geometric in shape, they can also be more difficult to design and build.

Inset framing makes it possible to save mature trees when building a deck. Keeping trees and other landscape features intact helps preserve the value and appearance of your property.

Drawing Plans

Not every project needs extensive plans and maps, but the more steps there are to the construction process, the more important it is to carefully consider all the details. Good plans make it possible to efficiently complete a project. Plotting the location of an outdoor structure on paper makes it much easier to determine a realistic budget, make a materials list, and develop a practical work schedule.

From your yard survey, create a site map, or scale drawing, that establishes the position of all elements of the existing site on paper. A site map is an overhead view of your yard and is the basis for the finished project design.

A scale of ⅛" = 1 ft. is common for site maps and project plans. At this scale, you'll be able to map a yard as big as 60 × 80 ft. on a sheet of 8½ × 11" drafting paper; or an 80 × 130 ft. yard on an 11 × 17" sheet. If your yard is too large to fit on one sheet of paper, simply tape several sheets together.

On a copy of the site map, locate and draw your project's layout. Consider how to handle obstacles like large rocks, trees, and slopes. Be sure to take into account local setback regulations and other pertinent building codes. Also make determinations for posts, footings, and accessibility to your structure.

Depending on the complexity of your project, your final plans may also include several different scale drawings, each showing a different aspect. You may create a bubble plan, a final design, and several working plans. An elevation chart may also be helpful if you have significant slope to contend with.

A bubble plan, or zone plan, is a rough sketch that indicates how the new project or projects will be laid out on your site. Draw several variations of your ideas. Even experienced professional designers go through as many as a dozen bubble plans before settling on a favorite. To save time, sketch ideas on photocopies of a tracing of your site map.

For the final design drawings, illustrate all the features of the new project in color. A final design drawing requires careful, detailed work. Expect some trial and error as you transform your bubble plan into a polished drawing.

Strive to integrate your new projects into your existing or planned landscape, establishing a continuous flow from your project to your landscape. Disguise unavoidable straight lines, such as property lines and walkways, by incorporating flowing planting beds or walls that have curved borders.

Also strive for a feeling of continuity between the various rooms of your outdoor home. Many people use lawn grass as the unifying element. Repeated use of building materials or shrubbery and flowers can also provide unity.

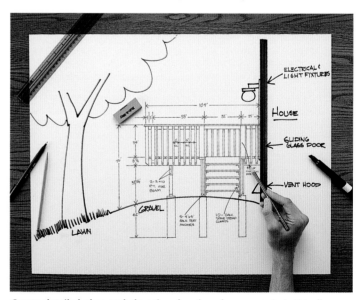

Experiment with project ideas by sketching different designs on separate sheets of tissue paper.

Create detailed plan and elevation drawings for your project. List all dimensions on the drawing, and indicate size, type, and quantities of lumber and hardware needed.

The best plans are the result of playful exploration and fearless trial and error. Take your time, experiment with many different layouts, and don't be afraid to make mistakes and changes.

Once you've worked out the details and decided on a final layout, convert the scale dimensions from the site map to actual measurements. From this information, draw up a materials estimate, adding 10 percent to compensate for errors and oversights.

An elevation plan shows a side view of your planned project. It's not always necessary to draw the entire structure when making an elevation drawing. If you're planning a fence or garden wall on a flat yard, for example, you can draw the elevation for a small section that represents the construction pattern for the entire structure.

Before you begin your project, there is one more set of plans to complete: the working plans. Working plans for a project serve the same function as blueprints for a building. A working plan is a bare-bones version of a plan drawing and elevation that includes only the measurements and specifications needed to actually construct the project.

Working plans help you estimate the amounts of materials you'll need and make it easier to schedule and organize work. Unless your project is very simple, it's a good idea to create several working plans: a demolition plan, a resurfacing plan, a building plan, and a re-landscaping plan. If your projects are quite large, you will want to create separate plans for each part of your overall project plan.

DECIMAL EQUIVALENTS

Converting actual measurements to scale measurements often produces decimal fractions, which then must be converted to ruler measurements. Use this chart to determine equivalents.

Decimal	Fraction
.0625	$\frac{1}{16}$
.125	$\frac{1}{8}$
.1875	$\frac{3}{16}$
.25	$\frac{1}{4}$
.3125	$\frac{5}{16}$
.375	$\frac{3}{8}$
.4375	$\frac{7}{16}$
.5	$\frac{1}{2}$
.5625	$\frac{9}{16}$
.625	$\frac{5}{8}$
.6875	$\frac{11}{16}$
.75	$\frac{3}{4}$
.8125	$\frac{13}{16}$
.875	$\frac{7}{8}$
.9375	$\frac{15}{16}$

Test different bubble plans *in your yard by outlining the walls with rope or a hose and by positioning cardboard cutouts to represent stepping stones and walkways.*

Hang tarps or landscape fabric *over a stake-and-string frame to get a sense of the size of the structure and its impact on the landscape.*

Walkways, Patios & Steps

Pathways and patios transform your yard into a series of living spaces by providing a suitable surface for each room's intended purpose and activities.

By their nature, these outdoor floors must withstand heavy use and the stresses caused by seasonal weather. You will have to carefully select materials, keeping in mind the style and purpose of the area as well as the climate in your region.

There are a variety of materials available. Brick, stone, concrete, wood, and gravel can be used alone or in combinations to create attractive, durable outdoor surfaces. Look for ways to repeat materials used elsewhere in your landscape or house. For example, if you have an attractive wood fence, use the same type of wood to create a boardwalk that flows through your flower beds or garden. Or if your home has a distinctive brick façade, repeat the brick element in a matching brick paver patio or walkway.

The projects in this section illustrate the basics of paving with gravel, stone, brick, concrete, and wood. With an understanding of these techniques, you can easily complete projects as demonstrated or create variations. Many of the projects include suggestions for other materials, applications, or techniques you can apply to the basic principles.

IN THIS CHAPTER:

- Loose-fill Pathway
- Stepping Stone Path
- Flagstone Walkway
- Mortared Flagstone
- Concrete Walkway
  - *Simulating Flagstone in Concrete*
  - *Simulating Brick & Stone in Concrete*
  - *Acid Staining Concrete*
  - *Coloring Concrete*
- Garden Steps
- Brick Paver Landing
- Brick Paver Patio
- Exposed Aggregate Patio
- Tiled Patio
- Tiled Step Landing

Loose-fill Pathway

Walkways and paths serve as hallways between heavily used areas of your yard. In addition to directing traffic, paths create visual corridors that direct the eye to attractive features or areas.

A loose-fill pathway is a simple, inexpensive alternative to a concrete or paved path. Lightweight loose materials, such as gravel, crushed rock, bark, or wood chips, are used to "pave" a prepared pathway surface. Because the materials are not fixed within the path, edging is installed around the perimeter of the pathway to hold them in place. In addition to using standard

preformed plastic edging, you can fashion edging from common hardscape building materials, such as wood, cut stone, and brick pavers. For professional-looking results, repeat a material used in the exterior of the house or other landscape structures in the pathway edging. Select loose-fill materials that complement the color and texture of your edging.

Our loose-fill project uses brick edging set in soil, which works well for casual, lightly traveled pathways. However, this method should be used only in dense, well-drained soil. Bricks set in loose or swampy soil won't hold their position.

Loose-fill materials are available at most home and garden stores. Many stores sell these materials prebagged, which makes transporting and applying them easier. Aggregate supply companies also sell crushed rock and pea gravel in bulk, which is often a less expensive option. If you buy loose-fill material in bulk, it may be easier to have the supplier deliver it than to transport it yourself.

As you prepare to build a path, consider how it will normally be used, keeping in mind that loose-fill pathways are best suited to light-traffic areas. Also think about how the path will fit into the overall style and shape of your landscape. Curved pathways create a soft, relaxed look that complements traditional landscape designs, while straight or angular paths fit well in contemporary designs. You may want to strategically place the path to lend depth to an area or highlight an interesting element.

TOOLS & MATERIALS

- Rope or garden hose
- Spade
- Rake
- Trowel
- Trenching spade or hoe
- Rubber mallet
- Brick pavers
- Landscape fabric
- Loose-fill material

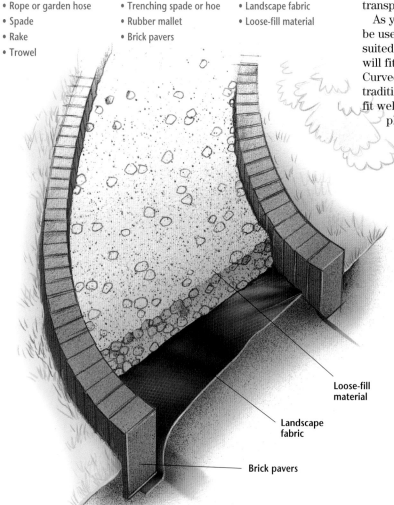

Loose-fill material

Landscape fabric

Brick pavers

A. *Dig narrow trenches for the edging on both sides of the excavated path site. Check the depth with a brick paver.*

HOW TO CREATE A LOOSE-FILL PATHWAY

Step A: Excavate the Path

1. Lay out the shape of the path with a rope or garden hose, then use a spade to excavate the area to a depth of 3". Rake the site smooth.

2. Dig narrow edging trenches along both edges of the path site, using a trenching spade or hoe. Make the trenches about 2" deeper than the path.

3. Test the trench depth with a brick paver placed on end in the trench—the top of the brick should stand several inches above ground. If necessary, adjust the trench to bring the bricks to the correct height.

Step B: Add Landscape Fabric

Line the trench with strips of landscape fabric, overlapping the strips by at least 6". Push the ends of the landscape fabric into the edging trenches.

Step C: Set the Bricks

1. Set the bricks into the edging trenches. Arrange them side by side, with no gaps between bricks.

2. Using a trowel, pack soil behind and beneath each brick. Adjust bricks as necessary to keep rows even.

Step D: Spread the Loose-fill Material

1. Spread the loose-fill material, adding material until it sits slightly above ground level. Level the surface using a garden rake.

VARIATION: CHILDREN'S PLAY AREA

Using the same techniques shown here for building a path, you can pave the floor of an outdoor room with loose-fill material.

Loose-fill paving, especially pea gravel or sand, works well in a children's play area (pages 454 to 463).

2. Tap the bricks lightly on the inside faces to help set them into the soil. Inspect and adjust the bricks yearly, adding new loose-fill material as necessary.

B. *Place strips of landscape fabric over the path and into the edging trenches, overlapping sections by 6".*

C. *Install bricks end to end and flush against each other in the trenches, then pack soil behind and beneath each brick.*

D. *Fill the pathways with loose-fill material. Tap the inside face of each brick paver with a mallet to help set them permanently in the ground.*

Stepping Stone Path

Laying stepping stones creates a practical and appealing way to traverse a garden. With stepping stones providing foot landings, you are free to put pretty much any type of infill between the stones. Gravel, smooth stones, ceramic toads—if you don't have to walk on it, anything goes. Some people place stepping stones on individual footings over ponds and streams, making water the temporary infill that surrounds the stones. The infill does not need to follow a narrow path bed, either. Steppers can be used to cross a broad expanse of gravel, such as a Zen gravel panel, or a smaller graveled opening in an alpine rock garden.

HOW TO MAKE A PEBBLED STEPPING STONE PATH

1. Excavate and prepare a bed for the path as you would for the loose-fill pathway (pages 32 to 33), but use coarse building sand instead of compactable paver-base. Screed the sand flat

2" (5 cm) below the top of the edging. Do not tamp the sand. You may use any edging material you like. Low-profile plastic landscape edging is a good choice because it does not compete with the pathway.

2. Position the stepping stones in the coarse sand bedding, spacing them based on the average slow-walk stride of the people who will use the path. Orient the stones to create a pleasing composition. Staggering them in a left/right fashion is a common practice. Strive for a layout that's both comfortable to walk and attractive to look at. They can be in a fairly regular, left/right pattern or arranged into clusters for a more interesting appearance. Add or remove sand beneath the steppers until they are stable and even with one another.

3. Pour in a layer of the larger infill stones (2"-dia. river rock is seen here). Smooth the stones with a garden rake. They should be below the tops of the stepping stones. Reserve about one-third of the larger diameter rocks.

1. *Excavate the pathway site and prepare a foundation (as shown on pages 32 to 33). Substitute coarse building sand for compactable gravel. Strike the sand to a consistent depth with a notched 2 × 4.*

2. *Level the stones by adding and removing sand until they are solidly seated. On flat runs, you should be able to rest a flat 2 × 4 on three stones at once, making solid contact with each. It is much easier to pack sand under stones if you moisten the sand first. Also moisten the sand bed to prevent sand from drifting.*

4. Add the smaller diameter infill, which will migrate down and fill in around the larger infill rocks. To help settle the rocks, you can tamp lightly with a hand tamper, but don't get too aggressive—the larger rocks will fracture fairly easily.

5. Scatter the remaining larger diameter infill stones across the infill area so they float on top of the other stones. Eventually, they will sink down lower in the pathway, and you will need to lift and replace them selectively to maintain the original appearance.

DESIGN TIP

Move from a formal area to a less orderly area of your yard by creating a pathway that begins with closely spaced steppers on the formal end and gradually transforms into a mostly-gravel path on the casual end, with only occasional clusters of steppers.

3. *If you're using two or more sizes of infill, start by spreading out a layer of the largest diameter rock.*

4. *Add the smallest size infill stones last, spreading them evenly so you do not have to rake them much.*

5. *Place the remaining larger-diameter infill stones around the surface of the walkway to enhance the visual effect of the pathway.*

Flagstone Walkway

Natural flagstone is an ideal material for creating landscape floors. It's attractive and durable and blends well with both formal and informal landscapes. Although flagstone structures are often mortared, they can also be constructed with the sand-set method. Sand-setting flagstones is much faster and easier than setting them with mortar.

There are a variety of flat, thin sedimentary rocks that can be used for this project. Home and garden stores often carry several types of flagstone, but stone supply yards usually have a greater variety. Some varieties of flagstone cost more than others, but there are many affordable options. When you buy the flagstone for your project, select pieces in a variety of sizes from large to small. Arranging the stones for your walkway is similar to putting together a puzzle, and you'll need to see all the pieces. When you're ready to begin the project, sort the stones by size, and spread them out so that you can see each one.

The following example demonstrates how to build a straight flagstone walkway with wood edging. If you'd like to build a curved walkway, select another edging material, such as brick or cut stone. Instead of filling gaps between stones with sand, you might want to fill them with topsoil and plant grass or some other ground cover between the stones.

TOOLS & MATERIALS

- Basic tools (page 18)
- Work Gloves
- Line level
- Circular saw with masonry blade
- Power drill
- Masonry chisel
- Stakes & string
- Rubber mallet
- Pencil
- Sod cutter (optional)
- Landscape fabric
- Sand
- 2 × 6 pressure-treated lumber
- Galvanized screws
- Compactable gravel
- Flagstone pavers
- Water

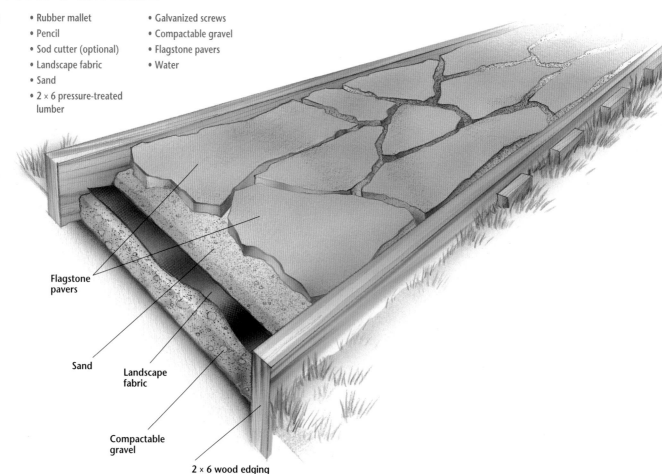

Flagstone pavers

Sand

Landscape fabric

Compactable gravel

2 × 6 wood edging

HOW TO BUILD A FLAGSTONE WALKWAY

Step A: Prepare the Site & Install the Edging

1. Lay out, excavate, and prepare the base for the walkway. Remove the stakes and string when the base is complete.

2. Form edging by installing 2 × 6 pressure-treated lumber around the perimeter of the pathway.

3. Drive stakes on the outside of the edging, spaced 12" apart. The tops of the stakes should be below ground level. Drive galvanized screws through the edging and into the stakes.

Step B: Arrange the Stones

1. Test-fit the stones over the walkway base, finding an attractive arrangement that limits the number of cuts needed. The gaps between the stones should range between ⅜ and 2" wide.

A. Drive 12" stakes outside the 2 × 6 pressure-treated edging, then attach them together with galvanized screws.

B. Test-fit the flagstones inside the edging, mark them for cutting, then set them aside in the same arrangement.

C. Spread a 2" layer of sand over the landscape fabric and smooth it out with a screed board made from a notched 2 × 6.

2. Use a pencil to mark the stones for cutting, then remove the stones and place them beside the walkway in the arrangement.

3. Score along the marked lines with a circular saw and masonry blade set to ⅛" blade depth. Set a piece of wood under the stone, just inside the scored line. Use a masonry chisel and hammer to strike along the scored line until the stone breaks.

Step C: Make a Sand Base

1. Lay strips of landscape fabric over the walkway base, overlapping the strips by 6". (If you plan to grow grass or another ground cover between the stones, skip this step.)

2. Spread a 2" layer of sand over the landscape fabric. Make a "screed board" for smoothing the sand from a short 2 × 6, notched to fit inside the edging (see INSET). The depth of the notches should equal the thickness of the stones.

3. Pull the screed from one end of the walkway to the other, adding sand as needed to create a level base.

Step D: Lay the Flagstones

1. Beginning at one corner of the walkway, lay the flagstones onto the sand base. Repeat the arrangement you created in Step B, with ⅜- to 2"-wide gaps between stones.

2. If necessary, add or remove sand to level the stones, then set them by tapping them with a rubber mallet or a length of 2 × 4.

Step E: Add Sand Between the Stones

1. Fill the gaps between the stones with sand. (Use topsoil, if you're going to plant grass or ground cover between the stones.)

2. Pack sand into the gaps, then spray the entire walkway with water to help settle the sand.

3. Repeat #2 until the gaps are completely filled and tightly packed with sand.

D. *Lay the flagstones in the sand base leaving a gap between stones. Use a rubber mallet to set them in place.*

E. *Pack the gaps between the stones and the edging with sand, then lightly spray the entire walkway with water.*

Mortared Flagstone

With its permanent, solid finish, mortared flagstone tends toward a more formal patio setting than sandset stone. It also has a cleaner feel because there's no sand to get kicked up out of the joints. Yet the mortared application offers the same organic appeal and dramatic lines of any natural flagstone surface. If you'd like to go a step further toward a formal look, you can use cut flagstone, installing it with the same basic steps shown here, but working with a grid layout instead of a random arrangement.

TOOLS & MATERIALS

- Paint roller with extension pole
- Work Gloves
- Stone cutting and dressing tools
- Tape measure
- Tools for mixing mortar
- Mason's trowel
- Rubber mallet
- 4 ft. level
- Straight 2 × 4
- Grout bag
- Stiff-bristled brush
- Jointing tool
- Whisk broom
- Latex concrete
- bonding agent
- Flagstone
- Mortar
- Acrylic fortifier
- Plastic sheeting
- Stone sealer (optional)

Mortared flagstone benefits from the organic appeal of natural flagstone, without the sand between joints, which can be messy.

A. Thoroughly clean the concrete slab, then apply a concrete bonding agent.

B. Arrange stones on the patio for an accurate dry-run layout.

OPTION: If desired, let outer stones extend beyond the edges of the slab.

The proper base for mortaring flagstone is a structurally sound concrete slab. If you're covering an old concrete patio, inspect the slab for signs of structural problems. Wide cracks and uneven surfaces indicate shifting soil or an insufficient subbase. This movement most likely will continue, leading to cracks in your new stone surface. You should remove the old slab and pour a new one or consider sand-setting the stone over the slab.

One of the advantages of mortared stone is that edging along the patio border is optional. Edging is not needed to contain the patio surface, as it is with a sandset application. This gives you the option of leaving the edges of the patio rough to enhance the natural appearance or even to hang the outer stones over the edges of the slab, to help conceal the concrete below.

HOW TO BUILD A MORTARED FLAGSTONE PATIO
Step A: Clean & Prepare the Slab
1. Thoroughly clean the concrete slab. As mentioned, the slab must be in good structural condition, but minor surface flaws are acceptable.

2. After all repairs have cured completely and the cleaned surface is dry, apply a latex bonding agent over the entire area that will be mortared. This helps the mortar adhere to the old concrete. Follow the manufacturer's instructions carefully.

Step B: Dry-lay the Stones
1. After the bonding agent has set up per the manufacturer's directions, dry-lay the stones on the patio to find a pleasing arrangement. Work outward from the center, and space the stones between ½ and 1" apart. Distribute smaller and larger stones evenly throughout the patio to avoid a lopsided layout.

2. Mark stones for cutting, as needed. Make the cuts when you're confident in the layout.

3. Complete the dry run, cutting stones along the patio edge to accommodate edging treatments, or leave the stones uncut to retain their natural shape.

Option: Overhanging the Outer Stones
For a more rustic or natural appearance, allow stones to overhang the edges of the slab below. Thick stones (4" or so) may be able to overhang as much as 6", provided that the slab supports ⅔ of the stone. For thinner stones, or stones of inherently weak species, don't overhang more than 2 or 3".

Step C: Begin the Mortaring
1. Starting near the center of the patio, set aside some of the stones, maintaining their relative positions in the dry-run layout.

2. Mix a stiff batch of mortar. Use the mortar type recommended by your stone supplier, based on the type of stone and the local climate.

C. *Move some of the stones aside, then apply mortar for setting the first few stones.*

D. *Bed the first stone into the mortar, then check it for level.*

E. *Add mortar and stones to complete the surface, checking for level as you go.*

F. *Fill the joints with mortar, using a grout bag for a neat application.*

G. *Smooth the mortar joints flush with the stone surfaces (INSET), and then let the mortar cure completely. After a week, seal the stone, if desired.*

3. Spread a 2"-thick layer of mortar over a workable small area of the slab, using a mason's trowel or concrete float.

Step D: Set the First Stone

1. Firmly press the first large stone into the mortar in its original position in the dry-run layout.

2. Tap the stone with a rubber mallet or the handle of a trowel to set it into the mortar.

3. Use a 4-ft. level and straight 2 × 4 to check the stone for level. Make any necessary adjustments by tapping with the mallet until the stone is level.

Step E: Lay the Remaining Stones

1. Using the first stone as a reference for the overall height of the patio surface, continue laying stones into the mortar, working outward from the center of the slab and adding mortar as needed. Maintain ½ to 1" mortar joints, and do not let stones touch in the final layout.

2. Check for level as you work, using the level and 2 × 4. First check each stone for level as you bed it, then make sure the stone is roughly level with all neighboring stones. If a stone is too high, tap with the mallet to lower it; if too low, remove the stone and add mortar underneath, then re-bed the stone. Remove any spilled mortar from the stone surfaces before it dries, using a wet brush or broom.

3. After all the stones are laid, let the mortar set up for at least a full day before walking on the patio.

Step F: Grout the Mortar Joints

1. Mix a small batch of mortar, adding acrylic fortifier to the mix to make the mortar more elastic.

2. Load a grout bag with mortar. Use the bag to fill the joints between the stones, being careful not to spill mortar onto the stone faces. Do not overfill the joints. For large joints, pack the bottoms of the joints with gravel to conserve mortar and increase the strength of the joints.

3. Wipe up any spills using a brush and sponge.

Step G: Tool the Mortar & Seal the Stone

1. Once the mortar is stiff enough to hold your thumbprint (without mortar sticking to your thumb), smooth the joints with a whisk broom, jointer, or other finishing tool. Rake the joints just enough so the mortar is flush with the stone faces. This prevents water from pooling on the surface and makes the patio easier to clean.

2. Cover the patio with plastic sheeting and let the mortar cure for 3 to 4 days, then remove the plastic and clean the stones with water and a stiff-bristled brush.

3. After a week, apply a stone sealer, if desired, following the manufacturer's directions.

Concrete Walkway

Pouring a concrete walkway is one of the most practical projects you can master as a homeowner. Once you've excavated and poured a walkway, you can confidently take on larger concrete projects, such as patios and driveways.

Poured concrete sidewalls are practical and extremely durable. A frost footing is not required, but you will need to remove sod and excavate the site. The depth of the excavation varies from project to project and depends on the thickness of the concrete, plus the thickness of the sand or compactable gravel subbase. The subbase provides a more stable surface than the soil itself and an opportunity for water to run off so it does not pool directly under the walkway.

TOOLS & MATERIALS

- Line level
- Work Gloves
- Hammer
- Shovel
- Sod cutter
- Wheelbarrow
- Tamper
- Drill
- Level
- Screed board
- Straightedge
- Mason's string
- Mason's float
- Mason's trowel
- Edger
- Groover
- Stiff-bristle broom
- Garden stakes
- 2 × 4 lumber
- Screws (2½", 3")
- Concrete mix or crack-resistant concrete mix
- Concrete sealer
- Isolation board
- Compactable gravel
- Construction adhesive
- Garden hose
- Masonry hoe
- Spade
- Miter saw
- Plastic sheeting

CONCRETE TIP

Fiber-reinforced and air-entrained, crack-resistant concrete is recommended for concrete subjected to freezing and thawing to prevent scaling.

Poured concrete sidewalks are a clean, finished way to bridge the gap between your outdoor spaces.

TIPS FOR BUILDING A CONCRETE SIDEWALK

Use a sod cutter to strip grass from your pathway site. Available at most rental centers, sod cutters excavate to a very even depth. The cut sod can be replanted in other parts of your lawn.

Install stakes and strings when laying out straight walkways, and measure from the strings to ensure straight sides and uniform excavation depth.

OPTIONS FOR DIRECTING WATER OFF WALKWAYS

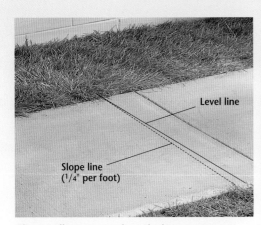

Level line

Slope line
(¹/₄" per foot)

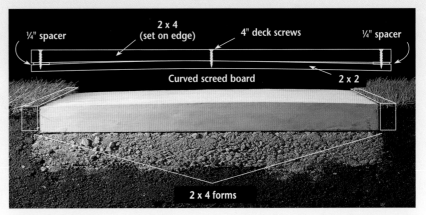

¼" spacer   2 x 4 (set on edge)   4" deck screws   ¼" spacer

Curved screed board   2 x 2

2 x 4 forms

Slope walkways away from the house to prevent water damage to the foundation or basement. Outline the location of the walkway with level mason's strings, then lower the outer string to create a slope of ¼" per foot.

Crown the walkway so it is ¼" higher at the center than at the edges. This will prevent water from pooling on the surface. To make the crown, construct a curved screed board by cutting a 2 × 2 and a 2 × 4 long enough to rest on the walkway forms. Butt them together edge to edge and insert a ¼" spacer between them at each end. Attach the parts with 4" deck screws driven at the center and the edges. The 2 × 2 will be drawn up at the center, creating a curved edge. Screed the concrete with the curved edge of the screed board facing down.

HOW TO BUILD A CONCRETE WALKWAY

1. *Select a rough layout, including any turns. Stake out the location and connect the stakes with mason's strings. Set the slope, if needed. Remove sod between and 6" beyond the lines, then excavate the site with a spade to a depth 4" greater than the thickness of the concrete walkway, following the slope lines to maintain consistent depth.*

2. *Pour a 5" layer of compactable gravel as a subbase for the walkway. Tamp the subbase until it compacts to an even 4"-thick layer.*

3. *Build and install 2 × 4 forms set on edge. Miter-cut the ends at angled joints. Position them so the inside edges are lined up with the strings. Attach the forms with 3" deck screws, then drive 2 × 4 stakes next to the forms at 3-ft. intervals. Attach the stakes to the forms with 2½" deck screws. Use a level to make sure forms are level or set to achieve the desired slope. Drive stakes at each side of angled joints.*

4. *Glue an isolation board to the steps, house foundation, or other permanent structures that adjoin the walkway using construction adhesive.*

5. *Prior to placing concrete, it is necessary to dampen the gravel subbase. Spray the subbase using a water hose until saturated but do not leave standing water.*

6. *Mix, then pour concrete into the project area. Use a masonry hoe to spread it evenly within the forms.*

7. *After pouring all of the concrete, run a spade along the inside edges of the form, then rap the outside edges of the forms with a hammer to help settle the concrete.*

8. *Build a curved screed board and use it to form a crown when you smooth out the concrete.* NOTE: *A helper makes this easier.*

9. *Smooth the concrete surface with a wood float. The goal is to smooth it, not to level it. (You should maintain the slight crown created by the curved screed board.)*

10. *Shape the edges of the concrete by running an edger along the forms. Smooth out any marks created by the edger using a float. Lift the leading edge of the edger and float slightly as you work.*

11. *Cut control joints in the concrete after the concrete sets up, but before it hardens.*

CONTROL JOINTS

- Control joints are designed to allow for concrete expansion, contraction, and movement.

- Control joints can be made using a grooving tool.

- Control joints tell the concrete where to crack as it shrinks during the hardening process, which is called hydration.

- Control joints made by a grooving tool must be a minimum of one-fourth the depth of the slab (for example, 1" deep for a 4"-thick slab).

- Control joint spacing formula: Slab thickness (in inches) × 2.5 = joint placement interval (in feet). For example, 4" thick × 2.5 = 10 ft.

- Keep the slab as square as possible.

12. *Create a textured, nonskid surface by drawing a clean, stiff-bristled broom across the surface once the surface is thumbprint hard. Avoid overlapping broom marks.*

13. *Keep concrete damp by spraying periodically with a fine water mist or cover with plastic sheeting for five to seven days.*

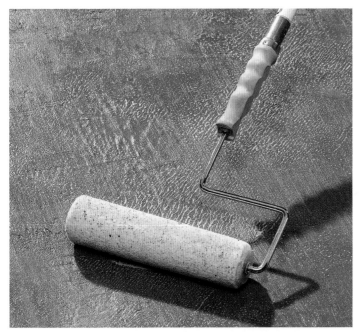

OPTION: *Apply acrylic cure and seal with a garden sprayer or roller to eliminate the need for water curing and to seal the concrete for a more durable surface.*

14. *Remove the forms, then backfill the space at the sides of the walkway with dirt or sod.*

Simulating Flagstone in Concrete

Carving joints in a concrete walk is an easy way to simulate the look of natural flagstones and add interest to an otherwise undistinguished path.

TOOLS & MATERIALS

- Concrete mix
- Concrete tint
- 2 × 4 lumber
- Circular saw or handsaw
- 3" deck screws
- Level
- Screed board
- Jointing tool or curved ¾" copper pipe
- Magnesium float
- Concrete sealer

By tinting the concrete before pouring it and carving the joints, you can create a walk that resembles a tightly laid flagstone path, hence the name false flagstone, often given to this age-old finishing technique.

Start by studying some flagstone paths in your neighborhood and sketching on paper the look you want to re-create. This way, you can also get an idea of the color to aim for when tinting the concrete mix. Keep in mind the color of your house and landscaping, and experiment with tint until you find a complementary hue. For directions on pouring a concrete walk, turn to the walkway project on pages 44 to 47.

HOW TO SIMULATE FLAGSTONE IN A CONCRETE WALKWAY

Step A: Tint & Pour the Concrete

1. Mix concrete and a tinting agent, following the manufacturer's instructions.

2. Pour the concrete into forms (pages 44 to 47), and smooth the surface with a screed board and magnesium float.

Step B: Create Flagstone Pattern

Cut shallow lines in the concrete, using a jointing tool or a curved copper pipe.

Step C: Refloat the Surface

1. Refloat the surface, using a magnesium float. Once the concrete has cured, remove the forms.

2. Protect the surface with a clear concrete sealer, following the manufacturer's instructions.

A. Pour concrete into forms, and smooth the surface with a screed board and magnesium float.

B. Cut shallow lines in the concrete, using a jointing tool or a curved copper pipe.

C. Refloat the surface, and remove the forms once the concrete has cured. Protect the surface with a clear concrete sealer.

Simulating Brick & Stone in Concrete

A well-made walkway or garden path not only stands up to years of hard use, it enhances the natural landscape and complements a home's exterior features. While traditional walkway materials like brick and stone have always been prized for both appearance and durability, most varieties are quite pricey and often difficult to install. As an easy and inexpensive alternative, you can build a new concrete path using manufactured forms. The result is a beautiful pathway that combines the custom look of brick or natural stone with all the durability and economy of poured concrete.

Building a path is a great do-it-yourself project. Once you've laid out the path, mix the concrete, set and fill the form, then lift off the form to reveal the finished design. After a little troweling to smooth the surfaces, you're ready to create the next section—using the same form. Simply repeat the process until the path is complete. Each form creates a section that's approximately 2 feet square using one 80 pound bag of premixed concrete. This project shows you all the basic steps for making any length of pathway, plus special techniques for making curves, adding a custom finish, or coloring the concrete to suit your personal design.

TOOLS & MATERIALS

- Excavation and site preparation tools
- QUIKRETE® Walkmaker form
- Wheelbarrow or mixing box
- Shovel
- Level
- Margin trowel or finishing trowel
- Concrete mix or crack-resistant concrete mix
- Liquid cement color
- Plastic sheeting
- Polymer-modified jointing sand
- Compactable gravel

Basket Weave Brick

Country Stone Pattern

Running Bond Brick

European Block Brick

Walkmaker® molds are available in four decorative patterns, shown here: Basket Weave Brick, Running Bond Brick, Country Stone, and European Block Brick.

ESTIMATING CONCRETE FOR YOUR PROJECT

For Basket Weave Brick, Running Bond Brick, and European Block Brick patterns:				For Country Stone Pattern (interlocks so each section is approx. 1 ft. 9 in.):			
Length of walk	# of Poured Sections	# of 80-lb. Bags of Concrete	# of 60-lb. Bags of Concrete	Length of walk	# of Poured Sections	# of 80-lb. Bags of Concrete	# of 60-lb. Bags of Concrete
2 ft.	1	1	2	2 ft.	1	1	2
4 ft.	2	2	3	3 ft. 9 in.	2	2	3
6 ft.	3	3	4	5 ft. 6 in.	3	3	4
10 ft.	5	5	7	9 ft.	5	5	7
16 ft.	8	8	11	16 ft.	9	9	12
24 ft.	12	12	16	23 ft.	13	13	18
30 ft.	15	15	20	30 ft.	17	17	23

HOW TO CREATE A WALKMAKER® PATH

1. *Prepare the project site by leveling the ground, removing sod or soil as needed. For a more durable base, excavate the area and add 2 to 4" of compactable gravel. Grade and compact the gravel layer so it is level and flat.*

2. *Mix a batch of concrete for the first section, following the product directions (see page 53 to add color, as we have done here). Place the form at the start of your path and level it, if desired. Shovel the wet concrete into the form to fill each cavity. Consolidate and smooth the surface of the form using a concrete margin trowel.*

3. *Promptly remove the form, and then trowel the edges of the section to create the desired finish (it may help to wet the trowel in water). For a nonslip surface, broom the section or brush it with a stiff brush. Place the form against the finished section and repeat steps 2 and 3 to complete the next section. Forms can be rotated to vary pattern.*

4. *After removing each form, remember to trowel the edges of the section to create the desired finish. Repeat until the path is finished. If desired, rotate the form 90° with each section to vary the pattern. Damp-cure the entire path for 5 to 7 days.*

HOW TO CREATE A CURVED WALKWAY WITH FAUX MORTAR JOINTS

1. After removing the form from a freshly poured section, reposition the form in the direction of the curve and press down to slice off the inside corner of the section (photo left). Trowel the cut edge (and rest of the section) to finish. Pour the next section following the curve (photo right). Cut off as many sections as needed to complete the curve.

2. Sprinkle the area around the joint or joints between pavers with polymer-modified jointing sand after the concrete has cured sufficiently so that the sand does not adhere. Sweep the product into the gap to clean the paver surfaces while filling the gap.

3. Mist the jointing sand with clean water, taking care not to wash the sand out of the joint. Once the water dries, the polymers in the mixture will have hardened the sand to look like a mortar joint. Refresh as needed.

FILLING JOINTS

Use jointing sand in place of play sand to simulate mortar joints. Sweep the polymer-modified sand into the joints, mist with water, and the sand will harden in place.

Acid Staining Concrete

Acid staining is a permanent color treatment for cured concrete that yields a translucent, attractively mottled finish that's well suited to patios. Unlike paint, which is a surface coating, acid stain is a chemical solution that soaks into the concrete pores and reacts with minerals in the concrete to create the desired color. The color doesn't peel or wear, but it won't hide blemishes or discoloration in the original concrete surface. Some colors of stain may fade in direct sunlight, so be sure to choose a color guaranteed by the manufacturer not to fade.

To apply an acid stain, follow the manufacturer's directions carefully. Here is a typical process:

1. Thoroughly clean the concrete and let dry. Then, wearing protective clothing and eyewear, load the stain into a plastic bucket or all-plastic pump sprayer. Apply stain with a brush or sprayer. Always brush to a wet edge to prevent dark lap marks. Sprayed-on stain may be left alone for a highly mottled finish or brushed or mopped for less mottling.

2. Allow surface to dry, and then remove residual stain with rags or a broom. Rinse. Stain may be reapplied for a darker shade, or another color may be added for accents.

3. Allow stain to dry, according to the manufacturer's directions, and then apply a water-based concrete sealer using a brush or roller. For faster results, use a hand-pump sprayer.

NOTE: Always test stain in an inconspicuous area before applying it to your primary surface.

Always seal acid-stained concrete for a polished, finished appearance.

HOW TO ACID STAIN CONCRETE

1. *Use a paintbrush to apply stain using long, even strokes. Minimize brush strokes.*

2. *Once stain has absorbed, remove residual stain with rags.*

3. *Apply a sealer using a hand-pump sprayer.*

Coloring Concrete

Coloring concrete is a great way to add depth and beauty to a concrete slab. Together with stamps, colored concrete can successfully mimic many other patio surfaces. To achieve vibrant colors, use white Portland cement in the concrete mix.

Dry pigment colors the surface of poured concrete. Not only is it easy to work with, but it is also used and trusted by professionals. You simply dust the powder over the concrete prior to final floating, and then finish with a magnesium float. To achieve an even color, you may want to dust and then spot dust again. Make sure you follow the manufacturer's instructions, and avoid overworking the concrete with the float. Overworking concrete may cause bleed water to rise and dilute the color and leads to rapid deterioration of the surface.

1. Once you have poured the concrete (see pages 44 to 47), smooth the surface and then add the pigment.

2. Following the manufacturer's instructions, dust the powdered pigment over the entire concrete surface, throwing out handfuls of the powdered pigment so that it disperses and leaves an even, fine dusting. As you become more comfortable with the product, you'll be able to work faster and cover larger areas at a time by throwing out handfuls of the dry pigment.

3. Float the concrete surface using a magnesium float.

After a concrete slab has been colored and floated, there may still be color inconsistencies. This actually adds depth to a stamped surface, creating a more realistic emulation of stone or brick. Left unstamped, it is also a desirable finished style.

Dust the powdered pigment over the entire concrete surface, following the manufacturer's instructions. Then float the surface using a magnesium float.

COLORING YOUR CONCRETE PATH

Coloring gives molded concrete a more natural-looking finish and is great for blending your path or walkway into your landscape design. Adding colorant to the concrete mix is the easiest method and produces consistent results:

1. For every two 60-lb. or 80-lb. bags of dry concrete mix, first blend one 10-oz. bottle of liquid cement color with 5 quarts of clean water. Mix the liquid into the dry concrete until the color is uniform. Add more clean water as needed to achieve the desired consistency.

2. After placing and finishing the path sections, cure the concrete carefully to produce the best color quality. If curing conditions will be less than ideal, apply concrete sealer to ensure slow, even curing and good coloring.

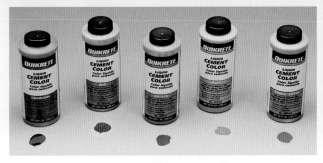

Garden Steps

If you have a steep slope in a high-traffic area of your yard, adding garden steps makes the slope safer and more manageable. Or, if your yard has a long, continuous hill, you can add several sets of steps to get the same results. In addition to making your landscape more accessible, garden steps make your yard more attractive by creating visual interest.

Garden steps are built into an excavated portion of a slope or hill, flush with the surrounding ground. You can build steps from almost any hardscape material: stone, brick, concrete, wood, or even interlocking block. Our version uses two materials: wood and concrete. The design is simple—the steps are formed by a series of wood frames made from 5 × 6 landscape timbers. The frames are stacked on top of one another, following the run of the slope. After the frames are set in place, they're filled with concrete and given a finished texture.

The exact dimensions of the frames you build will depend on the height of your slope, the size of the timbers you're using, and how wide and deep the steps must be. Gradual slopes are best suited to a small number of broad steps. Steeper slopes require a larger number of narrower steps. To keep the stairs easy to use, the risers should be no more than 6 inches high, and the depth of the frame, also called the tread depth, should be at least 11 inches.

To plan for your steps, first drive a tall stake into the ground at the bottom of the slope and adjust it until it's plumb. Then drive a shorter stake at the top of the slope. Position a straight 2 × 4 against the stakes, with one end touching the ground next to the top stake. Adjust the 2 × 4 so it's level, then attach it to the stakes with screws (see diagram at left). Measure from the ground to the bottom of the 2 × 4 to find the total vertical rise of the stairway. Divide the total rise by the actual thickness of the timbers to find the number of steps required. Round off fractions to the nearest whole number.

Measure along the 2 × 4, between the stakes, to find the total horizontal span. Divide the span by the number of steps to find the tread depth. If the tread depth comes out to less than 11 inches, revise the step layout to extend it.

TOOLS & MATERIALS

- Level
- Reciprocating saw
- Hand tamp
- Power drill
- Spade bit
- Hammer
- Wheelbarrow
- Shovel
- Garden rake
- Stiff-bristled broom

- Sod cutter (optional)
- 12" spikes
- 2 × 4 scrap
- 5 × 6 Landscape timber
- Measuring tape

- Stakes & string
- ¾" pipe
- Plastic sheeting
- Concrete
- Compactable gravel

Concrete

5 × 6 landscape timbers

Compactable gravel

HOW TO BUILD GARDEN STEPS

A. *Arrange the timbers to form the step frame and end nail them together using 12" spikes. Use a reciprocating saw to cut timbers.*

B. Outline the area for the steps with stakes and string, then measure the height of the slope. Position the stakes at the front edge of the bottom step and the back edge of the top step.

C. Excavate the area for the first step, and install the first step frame. Create a flat bed with a very slight forward slope, dropping about ⅛" from back to front. Tamp the soil down firmly using a hand tamp. Set the timber frame into the excavation area and check for level. Using a spade bit, drill two 1" guide holes in the front timber and the back timber, 1 ft. from the ends. Anchor the steps to the ground by driving a 2½-ft. length of ¾" pipe through each guide hole until the pipe is flush with the timber.

D. Excavate the area for the next step, and assemble the frame. Stake the second frame to the first with 12" spikes. Drill guide holes and drive two pipes through the back timber to anchor the second frame in place.

E. Cover the completed framework with plastic. Pour and smooth a 2" layer of compactable gravel in each frame.

F. Shovel concrete into the first frame, then work it with a garden rake to remove air bubbles. Screed the concrete using a 2 × 4. Smooth cracks in between the concrete and timbers using and edging tool.

G. Texture the surface of the concrete by drawing a stiff-bristled broom across it in one sweeping motion while the concrete is still wet. Brush only once to avoid overlap. Remove plastic. When hardened, mist with water and then cover with plastic. Allow to cure for one week.

Brick Paver Landing

The entry area is the first detail that visitors to your home will notice. Create a memorable impression by building a brick paver landing that gives any house a warmer, more formal appearance. You can also add a special touch to the landing by building a permanent planter next to it using matching brick.

Remember that when adding an adjoining structure, like a planter, you must create a separate building base and be sure to include an isolation joint so the structure is not connected to the landing area or to the house. An isolation joint will allow the structures to move independently from one another, minimizing the risk of damage to either.

In many cases, a paver landing like the one shown here can be built directly over an existing sidewalk. Make sure the sidewalk is structurally sound and free from major cracks. Pavers are often cast with spacing flanges on the sides, but these are for sand-set projects. Use a spacing guide, like a dowel, when setting pavers in mortar.

HOW TO BUILD A BRICK PAVER LANDING
Step A: Prepare the Site

1. Dry lay the pavers onto the concrete surface and experiment with the arrangement to create a layout that uses whole bricks, if possible.

TOOLS & MATERIALS

- Tape measure
- Mason's hoe
- Mason's trowel
- Level
- Straightedge
- Mortar bag
- Jointing tool
- Coarse rag
- Brick pavers
- Isolation board
- Construction adhesive
- Type S mortar
- Plastic sheeting

Build a brick paver landing over an existing sidewalk or over excavated ground.

A. *Mix a batch of mortar and dampen the concrete slightly. If the landing will abut an adjoining structure, secure an isolation board in place.*

2. Attach an isolation board to the foundation with construction adhesive to prevent the mortar from bonding with any adjoining structures. Mix a batch of mortar, then dampen the concrete slightly.

Step B: Lay the Border Pavers

1. Lay a bed of mortar for three or four border pavers, starting at one end or corner. Level off the bed to about ½" in depth with a trowel.

2. Lay the border pavers, buttering an end of each paver with mortar as you would a brick. Set the pavers into the mortar bed, pressing them down so the bed is ⅜" thick.

3. Cut off excess mortar from the tops and sides of pavers. Use a level to make sure the pavers are even across the tops. Also, make sure that mortar joints are uniform in thickness.

4. Finish the border section next to the foundation, and check with a level to make sure the row is even in height.

5. Trim off any excess mortar, then fill in the third section, leaving the front edge of the project open to provide easier access for laying the interior field pavers.

Step C: Set the Field Pavers

1. Apply a ½"-thick bed of mortar between the border pavers in the work area closest to the foundation. Because mortar is easier to work with when fresh, mix and apply the mortar in small sections (no more than 4 sq. ft.).

2. Begin setting pavers in the field area, without buttering the edges. Check the alignment with a straightedge, and adjust the pavers' heights as needed, making sure the mortar joints are uniform in width.

3. Fill in the rest of the pavers to complete the pattern in the field area. Apply mortar beds in small sections. Then add the final border sections.

Step D: Mortar the Joints

1. Every 30 minutes add mortar to the joints between the pavers until the joints are level with the tops of the pavers. Use a mortar bag to deliver the mortar into the joints.

2. Smooth and shape the mortar joints with a jointing tool. Tool the full-width "running" joints first, then tool the joints at the ends of the pavers.

3. Let the mortar dry for a few hours, then remove any residue by scrubbing the pavers with a coarse rag and water.

4. Cover the walkway with plastic and let the mortar cure for at least two days. After removing the plastic, do not walk on the pavers for at least one week.

B. *Lay the border pavers, buttering an end of each paver with mortar. Use a level to make sure the pavers are even across the tops.*

C. *Set the pavers in the field area, without buttering the edges. Apply mortar beds in small sections—no more than 4 sq. ft.*

D. *Use a mortar bag to fill mortar joints between pavers. Smooth with a jointing tool, making sure the joints are even with the tops of the pavers.*

Brick Paver Patio

Brick pavers are versatile and durable, and they come in a variety of shapes, patterns, and colors, making them an excellent material for creating walkways and patios. They convey an impression of formality, quickly dressing up your landscape. It's best to use concrete pavers rather than traditional clay bricks, as concrete pavers have self-spacing lugs that make them easy to install.

The easiest way to build a patio or walkway with brick pavers is to set them in sand. With this method, the pavers rest on a 1 inch layer of sand spread over a prepared base. Pavers are then arranged over the sand, and the joints between them are densely packed with more sand. The sand keeps the pavers in place, but it still allows them to shift as the ground contracts and expands with temperature changes.

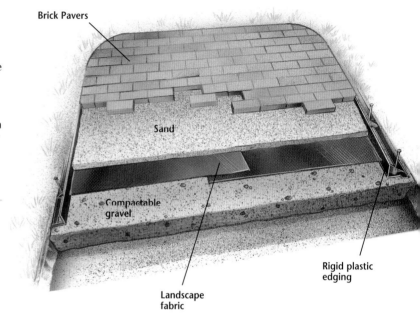

Brick Pavers

Sand

Compactable gravel

Landscape fabric

Rigid plastic edging

TOOLS & MATERIALS

- Tape measure
- Carpenter's level
- Shovel
- Line level
- Rake
- Hand tamper
- Tamping machine

- Stakes
- Mason's string
- Compactable gravel subbase
- Rigid plastic edging
- Landscape fabric
- Sand

- Pavers
- 1"-thick pipes
- Galvanized spikes
- Garden hose
- 2 × 4
- Mallet
- Circular saw

HOW TO BUILD A SAND-SET PATIO WITH BRICK PAVERS

1. Lay out and excavate for the patio, using the same techniques as for a concrete walkway. Cut strips of landscape fabric and lay them over the base, overlapping each strip by at least 6". Install rigid plastic edging around the edges of the patio, anchored with galvanized spikes (Inset). For curves and rounded patio corners, use rigid edging with notches on the outside flange (Inset).

2. Remove strings, then place 1"-thick pipes or wood strips over the landscape fabric, spaced every 6 ft. to serve as depth spacers for laying the sand base.

3. Spread a 1" layer of sand over the landscape fabric, using a garden rake to smooth it out. The sand should just cover the tops of the depth spacers. Water the layer of sand thoroughly, then lightly pack it down with a hand tamper.

4. Screed the sand to an even layer by resting a long 2 × 4 on the spacers and drawing it across the sand, using a sawing motion. Fill footprints and low areas with sand, then water, tamp, and screed again.

5. Lay the first border paver in one corner of the patio, making sure it rests firmly against the plastic edging. Lay the next paver snug against the first. Set the pavers by tapping them into the sand with a mallet. Use the depth of the first paver as a guide for setting the remaining pavers in a 2-ft. section.

6. After each section is set, use a long level to make sure the pavers are flat. Make adjustments by tapping high pavers deeper into the sand or by removing low pavers and adding a thin layer of additional sand underneath them.

7. *Continue installing 2-ft.-wide sections of the border and interior pavers. At rounded corners, install border pavers in a fan pattern with even gaps between the pavers. Gentle curves may accommodate full-sized border pavers, but for sharper bends, you'll need to mark and cut wedge-shaped border pavers to fit. Use a circular saw with a masonry blade to cut the pavers. Lay the remaining interior pavers.*

8. *Use a 2 × 4 to check that the entire patio is flat. Adjust any uneven pavers by tapping them with the mallet or by adding more sand beneath them.*

9. *Spread a ½" layer of sand over the patio, then use the tamping machine to compress the entire patio and pack the sand into the joints.*

10. *Sweep up the loose sand, then soak the patio area thoroughly to settle the sand in the joints. Let the surface dry completely. If necessary, spread and pack sand over the patio again until all the joints are tightly packed.*

INSTALLATION VARIATIONS FOR BRICK PAVERS

Dry mortar: (Shown at right) Installation is similar to sand-set patio, but joints are ⅜" wide and are packed with a mixture of sand and mortar, soaked with water, and finished with a jointing tool. A dry-mortar patio has a more finished masonry look than a sand-set patio, but the joints must be repaired periodically.

Wet mortar: This method often is used when pavers are installed over an old concrete patio or sidewalk. Pavers can be laid in much the same fashion as stone tiles over a concrete patio slab. Joints are ½" wide. Wet mortar installation can also be used with flagstone. For edging on a wet-mortar patio, use rigid plastic edging or paver bricks set on end.

After the mortar has been packed into the joints and wetted, finish the joints with a jointing tool.

Common Paving Patterns for Standard Brick Pavers

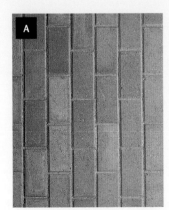 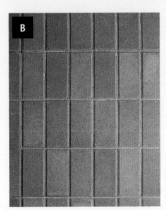  

Standard brick pavers can be arranged in several different patterns, including: (A) running bond, (B) jack-on-jack, (C) herringbone, and (D) basket-weave. Jack-on-jack and basketweave patterns require fewer cut pavers along the edges. Standard pavers have spacing lugs on the sides that automatically set the joints at the right width.

Exposed Aggregate Patio

Concrete is an inexpensive material for creating durable, low-maintenance outdoor floors. It can be formed into almost any shape or size, making it an ideal choice for walkways, driveways, and patios.

The patio in our project is divided into four even quadrants separated by permanent forms. This construction method makes it possible to complete the project in four easy stages—you can pour, tool, and screed each quadrant separately.

An isolation joint separates the patio from the foundation of the house, so footings aren't necessary. When calculating the depth of the base, remember to maintain adequate clearance between the top of the patio and the door threshold. The top of the patio should be at least 2" below the house sill or threshold, so the concrete has room to rise and fall without suffering damage from frost heave.

Concrete may be left as is or finished with a variety of techniques to give the surface an attractive texture or pattern. For this project, we added color and texture with a layer of seeding aggregate.

TOOLS & MATERIALS

- Basic tools (page 18)
- Tape measure
- Circular saw or handsaw
- Wheelbarrow
- Masonry hoe
- Spade
- Hammer

- Wood float
- Concrete edger
- Stiff-bristled brush
- Stakes & string
- Pressure-treated 2 × 4s
- 2½" galvanized deck screws

- Masking tape
- Wire mesh
- Bolsters
- Concrete
- Seeding aggregate
- Plastic sheeting
- Exposed aggregate sealer
- Garden hose

HOW TO CONSTRUCT A CONCRETE PATIO

Step A: Prepare the Surface & Build the Forms

1. Excavate the site and prepare a base of compactable gravel for drainage. Lay out the shape with stakes and string.

2. Measure and cut pressure-treated 2 × 4s for the permanent form outlining the entire patio.

3. Lay the boards in place, using the strings as guides. Fasten the ends with 2½" deck screws.

4. Temporarily stake the forms at 2-ft. intervals, then use a 2 × 4 and a level to make sure the frame is level.

Step B: Divide the Form into Quadrants

1. Measure, mark, and cut the 2 × 4s that divide the patio into quadrants. Attach these pieces to the frame with toenailed deck screws.

2. Drive deck screws halfway into the inside faces of all the forms, spacing them every 12". These exposed screws will act as tie rods between the poured concrete and the forms.

3. Cover the tops of the forms with masking tape to protect them when you pour the concrete.

Step C: Pour the Concrete for the First Quadrant

1. Cut reinforcing wire mesh to fit inside each quadrant, leaving 1" clearance on all sides. Use bolsters to raise the mesh off the base, making sure it remains at least 2" below the top of the forms.

2. Mix the concrete in a wheelbarrow, then pour it into the first quadrant. Use a masonry hoe to spread the concrete evenly in the form.

3. Screed the concrete with a straight 2 × 4 that is long enough to reach across a quadrant.

4. Slide a spade along the inside edges of the form, then rap the outer edges with a hammer to settle the concrete into the quadrant.

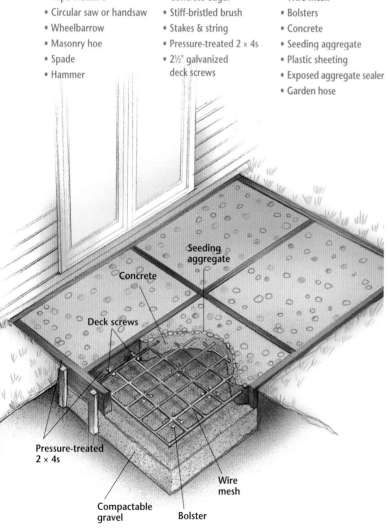

Seeding aggregate

Concrete

Deck screws

Pressure-treated
2 × 4s

Compactable
gravel

Bolster

Wire
mesh

Step D: Embed the Aggregate & Pour Remaining Quadrants

1. Sprinkle handfuls of seeding aggregate evenly over the wet concrete.

2. Use a float to embed the aggregate, making sure that the aggregate is firmly embedded, but still visible.

3. Tool the edges of the quadrant with a concrete edger, then use a wood float to smooth out any marks left by the tool. Cover the seeded concrete with plastic so it doesn't cure too quickly as you pour and finish the remaining quadrants.

4. Pour concrete into and finish the remaining quadrants, one at a time, using the same technique.

Step E: Complete the Finish & Seal the Concrete

1. After the water has evaporated from the concrete surface, mist it with water, then scrub it with a stiff-bristled brush to expose the aggregate.

2. Remove the tape from the forms, then replace the plastic and let the concrete cure for one week. After the concrete has cured, rinse and scrub the aggregate again to remove any remaining residue.

3. Wait three weeks, then seal the patio surface with exposed-aggregate sealer. Apply the sealer according to the manufacturer's directions.

A. Build a permanent form around the patio perimeter and temporarily stake it into place, using a level as you work. B. (INSET) Install the 2 × 4s that divide the patio into four quadrants, and attach them to the frame with deck screws.

C. Pour concrete into the first quadrant and screed the concrete smooth with a 2 × 4 that rests on top of the form.

D. Sprinkle handfuls of seeding aggregate evenly over the surface of the wet concrete and embed it with a float.

E. Mist the surface of the concrete with water and scrub it with a stiff-bristled brush to expose the aggregate.

Exterior tile is available in a wide variety of colors and styles; choose the style that best matches or complements your home's exterior.

New subbase
Building paper
Old patio

Tiled Patio

It's easy to create a beautiful tiled patio. If you have ever laid ceramic or vinyl tile inside your house, you already have valuable experience that will help you lay patio tile. The project layout and application techniques are quite similar.

The patio tiling project shown here is divided into two separate projects: pouring a new subbase and installing patio tile. If your existing patio is in good condition, you will not need to pour a new subbase. If you do not have a concrete slab in the project area already, you will have to pour one. In that case, skip step A through step E and refer to pages 358 to 360.

Make sure you purchase exterior tile for your patio project. Exterior tile is designed to withstand freezing and thawing better than interior tile. A wide variety of styles and colors are available to choose from. Try to select colors and textures that match or complement other parts of your house and yard.

If you have never laid tile before, here are some helpful tips for laying a tiled patio:

• Rent a wet saw from your local rental store for cutting tiles or use a tile cutter. For curved cuts, use tile nippers.

• Do not mortar more area than you can tile in 15 to 20 minutes.

Start with smaller sections, then increase the size as you get a better idea of your working pace.

• Add a latex-fortified grout additive so excess grout is easier to remove. Also, because patio tile will absorb grout quickly and permanently, remove all excess grout from the surface before it sets. It is a good idea to have helpers when working on large areas.

TOOLS & MATERIALS

- Basic hand tools (page 18)
- Shovel
- Mortar box
- Hand tamper
- Magnesium float
- Concrete edger
- Utility knife
- Trowel or putty knife
- Measuring tape
- Tile marker
- Chalk line
- Carpenter's square
- Straightedge
- Square-notched trowel

- Rubber mallet
- Tile cutter or wet saw
- Tile nippers
- Needlenose pliers
- Caulk gun
- 2 × 4 and 2 × 2 lumber
- Deck screws (2½", 3")
- ⅜" stucco lath
- Heavy gloves
- 30# building paper
- Dry floor-mix concrete
- Plastic sheeting
- Dirt
- Roofing cement
- Tile

- Tile spacers
- Dry-set mortar
- ¼"-diameter caulking backer rod
- Grout
- Latex-fortified grout additive
- Grout float
- Grout sponge
- Coarse cloth or abrasive pad
- Latex tile caulk
- Caulk tint
- Grout sealer
- Tile sealer

A. *Adjust the form height by setting stucco lath on the surface, then place a 2 × 2 spacer on top of the lath (their combined thickness should equal the thickness of the subbase).*

HOW TO INSTALL A TILED PATIO

Step A: Install Subbase Form Boards

1. Dig a trench 6" wide and no more than 4" deep around the patio to create room for 2 × 4 forms. Clean dirt and debris from the exposed sides of the patio.

2. Cut and fit 2 × 4 frames around the patio (pages 62 to 63), joining the ends with 3" deck screws. Cut wood stakes from 2 × 4s and drive them next to the forms at 2-ft. intervals.

3. Set stucco lath on the surface, and then set a 2 × 2 spacer on top of the lath to establish the subbase thickness. NOTE: Wear heavy gloves when handling metal, such as stucco lath.

4. Adjust the form boards so the tops are level with the 2 × 2. Screw the stakes to the forms with 2½" deck screws.

Step B: Prepare the Site

1. Remove the 2 × 2 spacers and stucco lath, then lay strips of 30# building paper over the patio surface, overlapping seams by 6", to create a bond-breaker for the new surface.

2. Crease the building paper at the edges and corners, making

B. *Build temporary 2 × 2 forms to divide the project into working sections. The forms also provide rests for the screed board used to level and smooth the fresh concrete.*

sure the paper extends past the tops of the forms. Make a small cut in each corner of the paper for easier folding.

3. Lay strips of stucco lath over the building paper, overlapping seams by 1". Keep the lath 1" away from the forms and the wall. Use aviation snips to cut the lath.

4. Build temporary 2 × 2 forms to divide the project into 3- to 4-ft. sections. Screw the ends of the 2 × 2s to the form boards so the tops are level.

Step C: Place Concrete in the First Section

1. Mix dry floor-mix concrete according to the manufacturer's directions using either a mortar box or a power mixer. The mixture should be very dry so it can be pressed down into the voids in the stucco with a tamper.

2. Fill one section with the concrete, up to the tops of the forms. Tamp the concrete thoroughly with a lightweight tamper to force it into the voids in the lath and into the corners.

3. Drag a straight 2 × 4 across the tops of the forms to screed the concrete surface level. Use a sawing motion as you progress to create a level surface and fill any voids in the concrete. If voids or hollows remain, add more concrete and smooth it off.

4. Use a magnesium float to smooth the surface of the concrete. Apply very light pressure and move the float back and forth in an arching motion. Tip the lead edge up slightly to avoid gouging the surface.

Step D: Fill Remaining Sections

1. Pour and smooth out the next section. Float the section then remove the 2 × 2 temporary forms between the two sections.

2. Fill the void left behind with fresh concrete. Float the concrete until it is smooth and level and blends into the section on each side.

3. Pour and finish the remaining sections one at a time using the same techniques.

Step E: Finish the Subbase

1. Let the concrete dry until pressing the surface with your finger does not leave a mark, then cut contours around the edges of the subbase with a concrete edger. Tip the lead edge of the edger up slightly to avoid gouging the surface. Using a float, smooth out any marks left by the edger.

2. Cover the concrete with sheets of plastic, and weigh down the edges. Let the concrete cure for at least three days, or according to the manufacturer's directions.

3. After curing is complete, remove the plastic, disassemble and remove the forms, and trim off the building paper around the sides of the patio using a utility knife.

4. Apply roofing cement to two sides of the patio, using a trowel or putty knife to fill and seal the seam between the old and new surfaces. To provide drainage for moisture between the layers, do not seal the lowest side of the patio.

C. *Level off the surface of the concrete by dragging a straight 2 × 4 across the top, with the ends riding on the forms.*

D. *Pour and smooth out the next working section. After floating this section, remove the 2 × 2 temporary form between the two sections and fill with fresh concrete.*

5. After the roofing cement dries, shovel dirt or ground cover back into the trench around the patio.

Step F: Dry Lay the Tile

1. Dry lay one row of tile vertically and one horizontally on the subbase, so they intersect at the center of the patio. Use tile spacers between tiles to represent joints. Keep the tiles ¼ to ½" away from the house to allow for expansion.

2. Adjust the tile to create a layout that minimizes tile cutting. Shift the rows of tiles and spacers until the overhang is equal at each end and any cut portions are less than 2" wide.

3. With the layout set, mark the subbase at the joint between the third and fourth row out from the house, then measure and mark it at several more points along the subbase. Snap a chalk line to connect the marks.

4. Use a carpenter's square and a long, straight board to mark end points for a second reference line perpendicular to the first. Mark the points next to the dry-laid tile so the line falls on a joint location. Snap a chalk line that connects the points.

Step G: Place First Legs of Tile

1. Mix a batch of dry-set mortar in a bucket, according to the manufacturer's directions.

2. Spread mortar evenly along both legs of the first quadrant near the house, using a square-notched trowel. Apply enough mortar for four tiles along each leg.

E. *After curing is complete, remove the plastic, disassemble and remove the forms, and trim off the building paper around the sides. Apply roofing cement to two sides of the subbase.*

F. *Adjust the tile to create a layout that minimizes tile cutting. Shift the rows of tiles and spacers until the overhang is equal at each end and any cut portions are less than 2" wide.*

G. *Set the first tile in the corner of the quadrant where the lines intersect, adjusting until it is exactly aligned with both reference lines. Position the next tile along one arm of the quadrant, fitting it neatly against the spacer.*

3. Use the edge of the trowel to create furrows in the mortar. Apply enough mortar to completely cover the area under the tiles without covering up the reference lines.

4. Set the first tile in the corner of the quadrant where the lines intersect, pressing down lightly and twisting slightly from side to side. Adjust the tile until it is exactly aligned with both reference lines.

5. Rap the tile gently with a rubber mallet to set it into the mortar. Rap evenly across the entire surface area. Be careful not to break the tile or completely displace the mortar beneath the tile.

6. Set plastic spacers at the corner of the tile that faces the working quadrant.

7. Position the next tile into the mortar bed along one arm of the quadrant. Make sure the tiles fit neatly against the spacers. Rap the tiles with the mallet to set it into the mortar, then position and set the next tile on the other leg of the quadrant. Make certain the tiles align with the reference lines.

8. Fill out the rest of the tiles in the two mortared legs of the quadrant. Use the spacers to maintain uniform joints between tiles. Wipe off any excess mortar before it dries.

Step H: Fill the First Quadrant

1. Apply a furrowed layer of mortar to the field area of the first quadrant, and then set tiles into it. Save any cut tiles for last. Use a wet saw or a tile cutter for cutting. For curved cuts, use tile nippers.

2. Place several tiles at once, and then set them all with the rubber mallet at one time.

3. As you finish the quadrant, use a needlenose pliers to carefully remove the plastic spacers before the mortar hardens—usually within one hour. Clean all excess mortar from the tiles before it hardens.

Step I: Fill the Remaining Quadrants

1. Apply mortar and fill in tiles in the remaining quadrants, beginning with the next quadrant against the house. Use the same techniques used for the first quadrant.

2. Use a straightedge to check the tile joints occasionally. If any of the joint lines are out of alignment, compensate for the misalignment over several rows of tiles.

3. After all the tiles for the patio are set, make sure all spacers are removed and any excess mortar has been cleaned from the tile surfaces. Cover the project area with plastic for three days to allow the mortar to cure properly.

Step J: Create Expansion Joints

After three days, remove the plastic and insert strips of ¼"-diameter caulking backer rod into the joints between quadrants and over any control joints, to keep grout out of these joints.

Step K: Grout the Joints

1. Mix a batch of tile grout to the recommended consistency. TIP: Add latex-fortified grout additive so excess grout is easier to remove. Use a damp sponge to wipe off grout film.

2. Start in a corner and spread a layer of grout onto a 25-sq.-ft. or less area of the tile surface.

H. Set tiles into the field area of the first quadrant, saving any cut tiles for last. Cut tile using a wet saw or a tile cutter. For curved cuts, use tile nippers.

I. Fill in the remaining quadrants, using a straightedge to check joints occasionally. If any of the joint lines are out of alignment, compensate over several rows of tiles. After all tiles are set, remove spacers.

3. Use a rubber grout float to spread the grout and pack it into the tile joints. Scrape diagonally across the joints, holding the float in a near-vertical position. Make sure to scrape off excess grout from the surface of the tile so the tile does not absorb it.

4. Use a damp sponge to wipe the grout film from the surface of the tile. Rinse the sponge out frequently with cool water, and be careful not to press down so hard around joints that you disturb the grout. Wash grout off of the entire surface.

Step L: Finish & Seal the Tile

1. Let the grout dry for four hours, and then poke it with a nail to make sure it has hardened. Use a cloth to buff the surface to remove any remaining grout film. Use a coarse cloth, such as burlap, or an abrasive pad to remove stubborn grout film.

2. Remove the caulking backer rod from the tile joints, then fill the joints with caulk tinted to match the grout color.

3. Apply grout sealer to the grout lines using a sash brush or small sponge brush. Avoid spilling over onto the tile surface with the grout sealer. Wipe up any spills immediately.

4. After one to three weeks, seal the surface with tile sealer. Follow the manufacturer's application directions, using a paint roller with an extension pole.

Caulking backer rod

J. *After three days, remove plastic sheeting and insert strips of caulking backer rod into the joints between quadrants and control joints.*

K. *Mix a batch of tile grout to the recommended consistency and use a grout float to pack it into tile joints.*

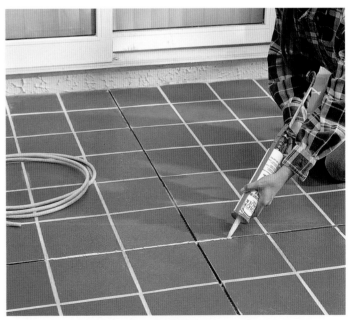

L. *Remove the caulking backer rod, then fill the joints with caulk that is tinted to match the grout color. Apply grout sealer, then seal the entire surface with tile sealer after one to three weeks.*

Tiled Step Landing

In addition to the traditional tricks for improving your home's curb appeal—landscaping, fresh paint, pretty windows—a tiled entry makes a wonderful, positive impression. To be suitable for tiling, stair treads must be deep enough to walk on safely. Check local building codes for specifics, but most require that treads be at least 11" deep (from front to back) after the tile is added.

Before you start laying any tiles, the concrete must be free of curing agents, clean, and in good shape. Make necessary repairs and give them time to cure. An isolation membrane can be applied before the tile. This membrane can be a fiberglass sheet or it can be brushed on as a liquid to dry. In either case, it separates the tile from the concrete, which allows the two to move independently and protects the tile from potential settling or shifting of the concrete.

Choose exterior-rated, unglazed floor tile with a skid-resistant surface. Tile for the walking surfaces should be at least ½" thick. Use bullnose tiles at the front edges of treads (as you would on a countertop) and use cove tiles as the bottom course on risers.

TOOLS & MATERIALS

- Pressure washer
- Masonry trowel
- 4-foot level
- Straightedge
- Tape measure

- Tile cutter or wet saw
- Tile nippers
- Square-notched trowel
- Needle-nose plier
- Grout float

- Grout sponge
- Caulk gun
- Isolation membrane
- Tile spacers
- Plastic sheeting

- Thin-set mortar
- Field tile
- Bullnose tile
- Grout
- Latex tile caulk

- Grout sealer
- 2 × 4 lumber
- Carpet scrap
- Cold chisel or
  flat-head screwdriver

- Wire brush
- Broom
- Notched trowel
- Latex bonding adhesive
- Chalk or marker

Tiled steps are inviting and safer for your guests. Choose skid-resistant surfaced tile for the longest-lasting walking surface.

HOW TO TILE CONCRETE STEPS

1. Use a pressure washer to clean the surface of the concrete. (Use a washer with at least 4,000 psi and follow manufacturer's instructions carefully to avoid damaging the concrete with the pressurized spray.)

2. Dig out rubble in large cracks and chips using a small cold chisel or flathead screwdriver. Use a wire brush to loosen dirt and debris in small cracks. Sweep the area or use a wet/dry vacuum to remove all debris.

3. Fill small cracks and chips with masonry patching compound using a masonry trowel. Allow the patching compound to cure according to manufacturer's directions.

4. If damage is located at a front edge, clean it as described above. Place a board in front and block the board in place with bricks or concrete blocks. Wet the damaged area and fill it with patching compound. Use a masonry trowel to smooth the patch and then allow it to cure thoroughly.

5. Test the surface of the steps and stoop for low spots, using a 4-foot level or other straightedge. Fill any low spots with patching compound and allow the compound to cure thoroughly.

6. *Spread a layer of isolation membrane over the concrete using a notched trowel. Smooth the surface of the membrane using the flat edge of a trowel. Allow the membrane to cure according to manufacturer's directions.*

7. *The sequence is important when tiling a stairway with landing. The primary objective is to install the tile in such a way that the fewest possible cut edges are visible from the main viewing position. If you are tiling the sides of concrete steps, start laying tile there first. Begin by extending horizontal lines from the tops of the stair treads back to the house on the sides of the steps. Use a 4-foot level.*

8. *Mix a batch of thinset mortar with latex bonding adhesive and trowel it onto the sides of the steps, trying to retain visibility of the layout lines. Because the top steps are likely more visible than the bottom steps, start on top and work your way down.*

9. *Begin setting tiles into the thinset mortar on the sides of the steps. Start at the top and work your way downward. Try to lay out tile so the vertical gaps between tiles align. Use spacers if you need to.*

10. *Wrap a 2 × 4 in old carpet and drag it back and forth across the tile surfaces to set them evenly. Don't get too aggressive here—you don't want to dislodge all of the thinset mortar.*

11. *Measure the width of a riser, including the thickness of the tiles you've laid on the step sides. Calculate the centerpoint and mark it clearly with chalk or a high visibility marker.*

12. *Install the tiles on the stair risers. Because the location of the tops of the riser tiles affects the positioning of the tread and landing tiles, you'll get the most accurate layout if the riser tiles are laid first. Start by stacking tiles vertically against the riser. (In some cases, you'll only need one tile to reach from tread to tread.) Add spacers. Trace the location of the tread across the back of the top tile to mark it for cutting.*

13. *Cut enough tiles to size to lay tiles for all the stair risers. Be sure to allow enough space for grout joints if you are stacking tiles.*

14. *Trowel thinset mortar mixed with bonding adhesive onto the faces of the risers. In most cases, you should be able to tile each riser all at once.*

15. *Lay tiles on the risers. The bottom tile edges can rest on the tread, and the tops of the top tiles should be flush with or slightly lower than the plane of the tread above.*

16. Dry-lay tile in both directions on the stair landing. You'll want to maintain the same grout lines that are established by the riser tiles, but you'll want to evaluate the front-to-back layout to make sure you don't end up with a row of tiles that is less than 2" or so in thickness.

17. Cut tiles as indicated by your dry run, and then begin installing them by troweling thinset adhesive for the bullnose tiles at the front edge of the landing. The tiles should overlap the top edges of the riser tiles, but not extend past their faces.

18. Set the first row of field tiles, maintaining an even gap between the field tiles and the bullnose tiles. Set the remaining field tiles.

19. Add the last row of tiles next to the house and threshold, cutting them as needed so they are between ¼ and ½" away from the house.

20. *Install tiles on the stair treads, starting at the top tread and working your way downward. Set a bullnose tile on each side of the centerline and work your way toward the sides, making sure to conceal the step side tiles with the tread tiles.*

21. *Fill in the field tiles on the stair treads, being sure to leave a gap between the back tiles and the riser tiles that's the same thickness as the other tile gaps. Allow thinset mortar to cure for a few days.*

22. *Apply grout in the gaps between tiles using a grout float. Wipe away the grout after it clouds over. Cover with plastic in the event of rain.*

23. *After a few weeks, seal the grout lines with an exterior-rated grout sealer.*

24. *Select (or have prepared) a pretinted caulk that's the same color as your grout. Fill the gap between the back row of tiles and the house with caulk. Smooth with a wet finger if needed.*

Fences & Walls

Crawling across a rolling field or guarding a suburban home, a fence or wall defines space and creates a backdrop for the enclosed landscape. Its materials, style, shape, and colors set a tone that may even tell you something about what you'll find on the other side.

Traditional picket fences conjure up images of cottage gardens and children playing. Post and rail fences often surround rustic landscapes or pastures; long expanses of a white board fence can make you believe there might be horses over the next hill. Privacy fences, such as board and stringer, or security fences, such as chain link, produce images of swimming pools sparkling in the sun.

Landscape walls can serve many purposes: They can define property boundaries, separate living areas within the yard, and screen off unpleasant views or utility spaces. Durable masonry walls, such as glass block, concrete block, stone, or stone veneer, can introduce new textures and patterns into your landscape, while living walls, like the framed trellis wall, can provide beautiful backdrops for your favorite vines or lush border gardens.

Using simple building techniques, the projects in this section offer a wide variety of choices for practical, visually appealing fences and walls. Properly constructed, the fences or walls you build should last decades with little maintenance.

IN THIS CHAPTER:

Fence Lines

Fence installations begin with plotting the fence line and marking post locations. Make a site map and carefully measure each post location. The more exact the posthole positions, the less likely it is that you'll need to cut stringers and siding to special sizes.

For walls, determine the outside edges of the footings along the entire site, as for a fence line. Then plot right angles to find the ends and inside edges of the footings.

Laying out a fence or wall with square corners or curves involves a little more work than for a straight fence line. The key in both instances is the same as for plotting a straight fence line: measure and mark accurately. This will ensure proper spacing between the posts and accurate dimensions for footings, which will provide strength and support for each structure.

TOOLS & MATERIALS

- Stakes & mason's string
- Line level
- Tape measures
- Circular saw
- Drill
- Masking tape
- 1 × 4, 2 × 4 lumber
- Permanent marker
- Screw gun
- Galvanized nails or screws

HOW TO LAY OUT A STRAIGHT FENCE LINE

Step A: Determine your exact property lines. Plan your fence line with the locally required setback (usually 6 to 12") from the property line, unless you and your neighbor have come to another agreement. Draw a site map. It should take all aspects of your landscape into consideration, with the location of each post marked. Referring to the site map, mark the fence line with stakes at each end or corner-post location.

Step B: Drive a pair of wood stakes a couple of feet beyond each corner or end stake. Screw a level crossboard across the stakes about 6" up from the ground on the highest end of the fence run. Draw a mason's line from the first batter board down the fence line. Level the line with a line level and mark the height of the line against one stake of the second batter board pair. Attach a level batter board to these stakes at this height and tie the string to the cross board so it is taut.

Step C: To find the on-center spacing for the gateposts, combine the width of the gate, the clearance necessary for the hinges and latch hardware, and the actual width of one post (the actual width of a 4 × 4 is 3½"). Mark the string with a "V" of masking tape to indicate the center point of each gatepost.

Step D: To mark remaining posts, refer to your site map, and then measure and mark the line post locations on the string with marks on masking tape. Remember that the marks indicate the center of the posts, not the edges.

Use a pair of wood stakes and some mason's line to plot the rough location of your fence or wall. Then, for greater accuracy, install batter boards to plot the final location.

HOW TO INSTALL BATTER BOARDS

First pair of stakes

Crossboard

Second pair of stakes

Line from first pair of stakes

Post location

1. *To install batter boards, drive a pair of short wood stakes a couple of feet beyond each corner or end of the rough planned fence line. Screw a level cross board across one pair of stakes, about 6" up from the ground on the higher end of the fence run. Loosely tie a mason's line to the middle of the cross board.*

2. *Stretch the mason's line from the first pair of batter boards to the pair of stakes at the opposite end or corner of the run. Attach a line level to the string, draw it tight against a stake and raise or lower the string until the line is level. Mark this height line on the stake and tie the string to the cross board.*

3. *Measure out from the starting points of the fence line and mark post locations directly onto the layout lines using pieces of masking tape (don't forget to allow for the post widths of your posts—see tips below).*

TIPS FOR SPACING LINE POSTS AND GATE POSTS

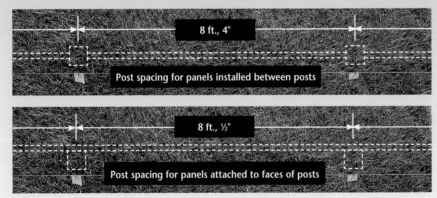

8 ft., 4"

Post spacing for panels installed between posts

8 ft., ½"

Post spacing for panels attached to faces of posts

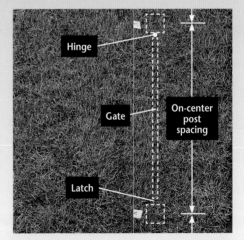

Hinge

Gate

On-center post spacing

Latch

If your fence panels will be installed between fence posts (top photo) and you are using 4 × 4" wood posts, add 4" to the length of the fence panels and use that distance as the on-center span between posts (the 4 × 4" posts are actually only 3½" wide but the extra ½" created by using the full 4" dimension will create just the right amount of "wiggle room" for the panel). If panels will be attached to the post faces, add ½" to the actual panel width to determine post spacing.

To find the on-center spacing of gateposts, add the gate width, the clearance needed for hinge and gate hardware, and the actual diameter of one post.

Laying Out Right Angles

If your fence or wall will enclose a square or rectangular area, or if it joins a building, you probably want the corners to form 90-degree angles. There are many techniques for establishing a right angle when laying out an outdoor project, but the 3-4-5-triangle method is the easiest and most reliable. It is a simple method of squaring your fence layout lines, but if you have the space, use a 6-8-10 or 9-12-15 triangle. Whichever dimensions you choose, you'll find it easier to work with two tape measures to create the triangle.

HOW TO LAY OUT A RIGHT ANGLE

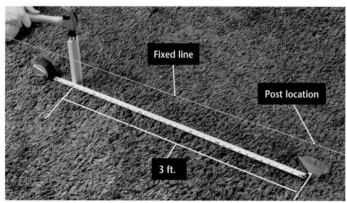

1. Drive a pair of stakes along a known fence line and run a line that crosses the corner post location (this line should stay fixed as a reference while you square the crossing line to it). Drive a stake 3 ft. out from the corner post location, on the line you don't want to move. You will adjust the other line to establish the right angle.

2. Draw one tape measure from the post location roughly at a right angle to the fixed line. Draw the tape beyond the 4 ft. mark and lock it.

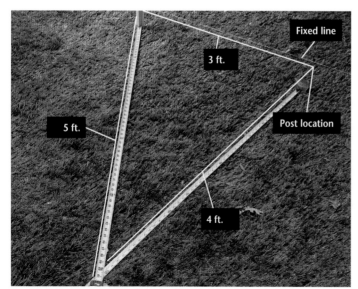

3. Angle the second tape measure from the 3-ft. stake toward the 4 ft. mark on the first tape measure. The two tapes should intersect at 5 ft. and 4 ft.

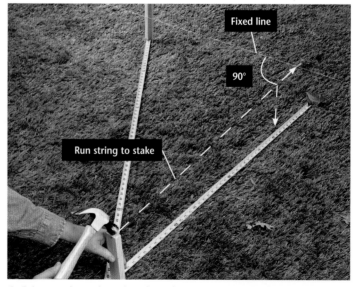

4. Drive a stake at the point where the tape measure marks intersect. Run a line for this stake to another driven past the post location to establish perpendicular layout lines. The string tied to the second stake should pass directly over the post location.

Posts

Even among professional landscapers you'll find widely differing practices for setting fence posts. Some take the always-overbuild approach and set every post in concrete that extends a foot past the frostline. Others prefer the impermanence, adjustability, and drainage of setting posts in packed sand or gravel. Some treat the post ends before setting the posts, others don't bother. The posts may be set all at once, prior to installing the stringers and siding; or, they may be set one-at-a-time in a build-as-you-go approach. Before deciding which approach is best for your situation, it's a good idea to simply walk around your neighborhood and see how the posts for similar fences are installed, then assess which posts seem to be holding up the best.

Another area of dispute is at which point in the process posts should be cut to length (height). While there are those who advocate cutting all posts before installation and then aligning them in the ground before setting them (especially when installing chain link), the most reliable method is to trim the posts to height with a circular saw or hand saw after they are set in the ground and the concrete has dried.

Taking the time to make sure posts are vertical and positioned precisely is perhaps the most important aspect of a successful fencebuilding project.

TOOLS & MATERIALS

- Plumb bob
- Stakes & strings
- Hand maul
- Power auger or post-hole digger
- Colored plastic
- Waxed paper

- Shovel
- Coarse gravel
- Carpenter's level
- Concrete
- Nails
- Wheelbarrow
* Circular saw

- Mason's trowel
- Pressure-treated cedar or redwood 4 × 4 posts
- Scrap lengths of 2 × 4
- Masking tape
- Screws
- Drill

HOW TO SET FENCE POSTS

1. Set batter boards at both ends of the fence line. String a mason's line between the batter boards and level it. Mark post locations on the string with masking tape. according to your plan.

2. Transfer the marks from the string to the ground, using a plumb bob to pinpoint the post locations. Pin a piece of colored plastic to the ground with a nail at each post location.

Depth gauge

3. Dig post holes using a clamshell-type post-hole digger (left photo) or a rented power auger (right photo). Post-hole diggers work well for most situations, but if your holes are deeper than 30" you'll need to widen the hole at the top to operate the digger, so consider using a power auger. Make a depth gauge by tacking a board onto a 2 × 4 at the hole depth from the end of the 2 × 4. As you dig, check the depth with the gauge. If you'll be filling the post hole with concrete, widen the bottoms of the holes with your post-hole digger to create bell shapes. This is especially important in states where the ground freezes.

81

Original position of line

4. *Reset the mason's string as a guide for aligning posts. If you want the post to be in exactly the same spot it was laid out, shift the string half the thickness of the post. Pour a 6" layer of gravel into each hole for improved drainage. Position each post in its hole.*

OPTION: *For full concrete footings in frost-heave prone soils, cut 8"-dia. concrete forming tubes into 18" sections to collar the posts near grade level and prevent the concrete from spreading. Holes tend to flare at the top, giving concrete footings a lip that freezing ground can push against.*

5. *Align your post along one line or two (if it's a corner post). Brace the post on adjacent sides with boards screwed to wood stakes. Adjust to plumb in both directions, anchoring each brace to the post with screws when plumb. As you plumb the post, keep the post flush against the line. Set the remaining posts the same way.*

MIXING CONCRETE

If you've never filled post holes with concrete before, you will be amazed at how much it takes to fill a hole. A 12"-dia. hole that's 36" deep will require around three cubic feet of concrete—or, about six 60-pound bags of dry mix. If you're installing 10 posts, that's 60 bags. This is yet another reason why setting posts one at a time is a good idea—you can spread out the heavy labor of mixing concrete in wheelbarrow or mortar tub. If you'll be needing more than one cubic yard (27 cubic feet) consider having ready-mix concrete trucked in. But make sure all your posts are braced and set and have at least two wheelbarrows and three workers on hand.

6. *Mix concrete in a wheelbarrow and tamp into the hole with a 2 × 4 to pack the concrete as tightly as you can. Recheck the post alignment and plumb as you go, while correction is still possible. TIP: Mask the post with waxed paper near the collaring point of the concrete to keep the visible portion of the post clean. Remove the waxed paper before the concrete sets up.*

Form a rounded crown *of concrete with your trowel just above grade to shed water.*

7. *For reasonably level ground, draw a mason's string from end post to end post at the height the posts need to be cut (for custom fences, this height might be determined by your shortest post). Mark each post at the string. Carry the line around each post with a pencil and speed square.*

8. *Wait at least a day for the concrete to set up and then clamp a cutting guide to the posts (a speed square is perfect). Cut along the trim line on each face of each with a circular saw to trim your posts. (this is a great time to use a cordless circular saw). In most cases, you'll want to add a post cap later to cover the end grain.*

Poured Footings

Footings provide a stable, level base for brick, block, stone, and poured concrete structures. They distribute the weight of the structure evenly, prevent sinking, and keep structures from moving during seasonal freeze-thaw cycles.

The required depth of a footing is usually determined by the frost line, which varies by region. The frost line is the point nearest ground level where the soil does not freeze. In colder climates, it is likely to be 48" or deeper. Frost footings (footings designed to keep structures from moving during freezing temperatures) should extend a minimum of 6 to 12" below the frost line for the area.

Footings are required for concrete, stone, brick, and block structures that adjoin other permanent structures or that exceed the height specified by local codes. Slab footings, which are typically 8" thick, may be recommended for low, freestanding structures built using mortar or poured concrete. Before starting your project, ask a building inspector about footing recommendations and requirements for your area.

OPTIONS FOR FORMING FOOTINGS

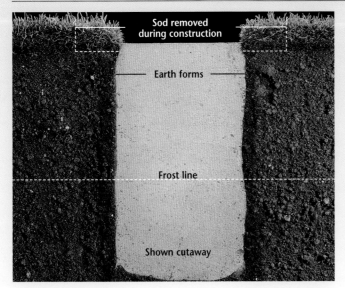

For poured concrete, use the earth as a form. Strip sod from around the project area, then strike off the concrete with a screed board resting on the earth at the edges of the top of the trench.

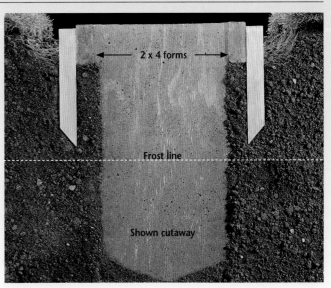

For brick, block, and stone, build level, recessed wood forms. Rest the screed board on the frames when you strike off the concrete to create a flat, even surface for stacking masonry units.

TIPS FOR BUILDING FOOTINGS

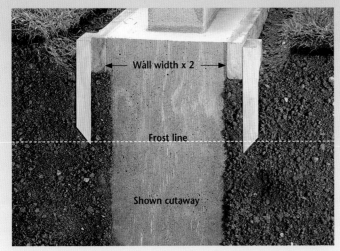

Make footings twice as wide as the wall or structure they will support. They also should extend at least 12" past the ends of the project area.

Add tie-rods if you will be pouring concrete over the footing. Before the concrete hardens, press 12" sections of rebar 6" into the concrete. The tie-rods will anchor the footing to the structure it supports.

HOW TO POUR A FOOTING

1. *Make a rough outline of the footing using a rope or hose. Outline the project area with stakes and mason's string.*

2. *Strip away sod 6" outside the project area on all sides, then excavate the trench for the footing to a depth 12" below the frost line.*

3. *Build and install a 2 × 4 form frame for the footing, aligning it with the mason's strings. Stake the form in place, and adjust to level.*

VARIATION: *If your project abuts another structure, such as a house foundation, slip a piece of asphalt-impregnated fiber board into the trench to create an isolation joint between the footing and the structure. Use a few dabs of construction adhesive to hold it in place.*

4. Make two #3 rebar grids to reinforce the footing. For each grid, cut two pieces of #3 rebar 8" shorter than the length of the footing, and two pieces 4" shorter than the depth of the footing. Bind the pieces together with 16-gauge wire, forming a rectangle. Set the rebar grids upright in the trench, leaving 4" of space between the grids and the walls of the trench. Coat the inside edge of the form with vegetable oil or commercial release agent.

5. Mix and pour concrete so it reaches the tops of the forms. Screed the surface using a 2 × 4. Float the concrete until it is smooth and level.

6. Cure the concrete for one week before you build on the footing. Remove the forms and backfill around the edges of the footing.

Board & Stringer Fence

If you want a high-quality, well-built wood fence, a board-and-stringer fence may be the best answer. This fence style is constructed from a basic frame with at least two rails, called *stringers*, that run parallel to the ground between posts to form the framework. Vertical boards, called siding, are attached to the framework created by the stringers.

A board-and-stringer fence is well-suited for yards of almost any contour.

We used dog-eared siding in this project, but these construction methods can be used with many siding patterns. Spend a little time looking at magazines and driving through your favorite neighborhoods—you're certain to find a siding style that appeals to you and suits your property.

HOW TO BUILD A BOARD & STRINGER FENCE
Step A: Trim the Posts & Add the Top Stringers
1. Lay out the fence line (page 80) and install the posts (page 82). Let the concrete cure at least two days.
2. On each post, measure up from the ground to a point 12" below the planned fence height. Snap a level chalk line across all posts at this height. Trim the posts using a reciprocating saw.
3. Cut a 2 × 4 to 72" for the top stringer. Coat the ends of the stringers with sealer and let them dry.
4. Place the stringers flat on top of the posts, centering the joints over each post. Attach the stringers to the posts using 3" galvanized deck screws.

Step B: Install the Remaining Stringers
1. Measuring down from the top of each post, mark lines at 24" intervals to mark the locations for the other stringers in this bay.
2. At each mark, attach a 2 × 4 fence bracket to the inside face of the post, flush with the outside edge, using 4d box nails.

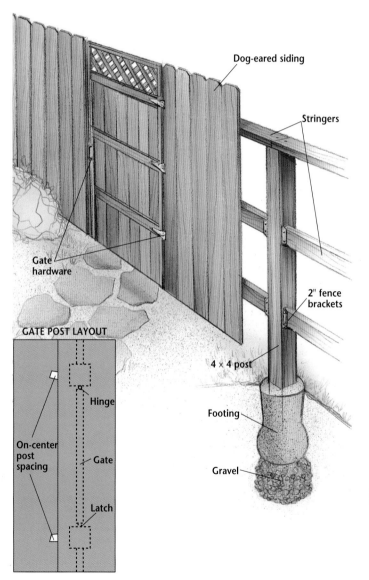

Dog-eared siding

Stringers

Gate hardware

2" fence brackets

4 × 4 post

Footing

Gravel

GATE POST LAYOUT

Hinge

On-center post spacing

Gate

Latch

A. Trim the posts and attach the cut stringers on top of the posts with 3" galvanized deck screws.

TOOLS & MATERIALS

- Tools & materials for setting posts
- Tape measure
- Chalk line
- Line level
- Reciprocating saw or handsaw
- Paintbrush
- Hammer
- Drill

- Level
- Wood sealer/protectant or paint
- Pressure-treated lumber:
  4 × 4s, 10 ft.
  2 × 4s, 8 ft.
  1 × 6s, 8 ft.
- Galvanized deck screws (2", 3")

- Galvanized 2 × 4 fence brackets
- Galvanized box nails (4d, 6d)
- ⅛" piece of scrap wood
- Prefabricated gate & hardware
- Wood scraps for shims

B. *Attach the fence brackets to the inside faces of the posts. Position the stringers in the brackets, then nail them in place.*

3. Position a 2 × 4 between each pair of brackets. Hold or tack the board against the posts, and scribe the back side along the edges of the posts.

4. Cut the stringers ¼" shorter than marked, so they will slide into the brackets easily. Coat the cut ends of the stringers with sealer and let them dry.

5. Nail the stringers into place using 6d galvanized box nails. If the stringers are angled to accommodate a slope, bend the bottom flanges of the brackets to match the angles of the stringers.

Step C: Attach the Siding

1. Beginning at an end post, measure from the ground to the top edge of the top stringer and add 8½". Cut a 1 × 6 to this length and seal its edges.

2. Position the 1 × 6 so that its top extends 10½" above the top stringer, leaving a 2" gap at the bottom. Make sure the siding board is plumb, then attach it to the post and rails with 2" galvanized deck screws.

3. Measure, cut, and attach the remaining siding to the stringers. Leave a gap of at least ⅛" between boards using pieces of scrap wood for spacers. If necessary, rip boards at the ends of the fence to make them fit.

Step D: Hang the Gate

1. Attach three hinges to the gate frame, evenly spaced and parallel to the gate edge.

2. Shim the gate into position between the gate posts. Drill pilot holes and attach the hinges to the gate post using the screws provided with the hinge hardware.

3. On the opposite side, attach the latch hardware to the fence and to the gate.

4. Open and close the gate to make sure the latch works correctly. Make adjustments if necessary. Paint the fence or coat with sealer.

C. *Measure and cut the siding to size. Attach the siding to the framework, spacing them at least ⅛" apart.*

D. *Attach the hinges according to the manufacturer's directions, then hang the gate and install the latch hardware.*

Panel Fence

Panel fences are one of the easiest, quickest types of fences you can build. They're also reasonably priced and ideal for yards that are flat or have a steady, gradual slope.

Preassembled fence panels come in a wide variety of popular styles. The one disadvantage is that not all panels are as well built as you might like. Shop around to find well-constructed panels made of high-quality materials. Be sure to choose and purchase your panels before setting your posts, so you canspace the posts accurately.

Although you can trim panels to fit between the posts if necessary, doing that can be difficult. Try to plan a layout that uses only full-sized panels.

If the fence line includes a slope, decide whether to contour or step the fence and plan accordingly.

Panel fences can be very simple or beautifully ornate. For best results, choose a fence panel size that will blend in with your home's style and add elegant detail.

TOOLS & MATERIALS

- Tools and materials for setting posts
- Pressure-treated, cedar, or redwood 4 × 4 posts
- Prefabricated fence panels
- Corrosion-resistant fence brackets

- Post-hole digger
- Concrete
- Pieces of scrap wood
- 4d corrosion-resistant nails
- 1" corrosion-resistant deck screws
- Post caps

- Prefabricated gate & hardware
- Corrosion-resistant casing nails
- Circular saw
- Drill
- 2 × 4
- Level

HOW TO BUILD A WOOD PANEL FENCE
Dig Holes, Brace End Post

Lay out the fence line and mark the post-hole locations. Space the holes to fit the panels you've purchased, adding the actual post diameter (3½" for 4" nominal posts) plus ¼" for brackets to the length of a panel. Measure spacing for stepped fences on a level line, not along the slope.

Dig the first two holes of a run and tamp gravel into the hole bottoms for drainage. Position, plumb, and stake the end post, adding a forming tube at the top of the hole if needed. Set your bracing so it won't interfere with the first panel. If you're renting an auger, you may want to dig all your holes at once, otherwise, digging as you go leaves room for spacing adjustment if needed. Use a stake to hold your alignment line out of the way while digging.

1. Lay out the fence line and mark the post-hole locations (INSET photo). Space the holes to fit the panels you've purchased. To the length of a panel, add the actual post diameter (3½" for 4" nominal posts) plus another ¼" for brackets.

2. Dig a post hole at a corner or an end post location. A clam-shell type post-hole digger is a good choice for holes up to 30" deep. Make a depth gauge from scrap wood to measure the hole depth as you dig.

3. Set, plumb, and brace the first post; then run one of the stringers along the fence line as a reference for digging the next post hole.

4. Fill your first post hole with concrete unless you are setting posts in gravel or sand. Tamp the wet concrete with an old 2 × 4 to pack it into the post hole.

5. Attach three evenly spaced and centered fence brackets to the first post and trim fence post to desired height.

6. Set the first fence panel into the brackets, level it, and attach the end to the brackets with deck screws or joist hanger nails.

Top trim line

Story pole for marking bracket positions

7. Position a post in the next post hole and clamp the unattached end of the fence panel to the post (you may need to tack a clamping block to the post rail first). Mark the positions of the rails onto the post. Unclamp the fence panel and remove the post from the hole.

8. Attach the fence brackets according to the marks made in the previous step. For the remaining posts, create a story pole to use as a gauge for marking consistent bracket locations and a top trim line. Trim the post to length before inserting it back into the hole.

9. Plumb the post perpendicular to the fence line, making sure the panel is level. Brace the post, recheck for plumb and level, and then set the post the same way you set the first one.

Fill your first post hole with concrete and tamp it into the post hole with the end of a 2 × 4.

Set the First Panel

Nail three, evenly spaced and centered fence brackets to the first post and trim fence post to desired height. The bottom of the fence needs to be at least 2" off the ground. Transfer your bracket spacing and cutoff line to a 1 × 4 gauge board with a marker. Bend down the bottom tabs on the top two brackets.

Level the panel in the brackets, supporting the loose end against the ground with blocking. Nail the brackets to the panel. For extremely gradual slopes, you may follow a mason's line that follows the actual grade instead of trying to establish true level.

Set the second post in its hole, and mark the position of the bottom bracket. Use your gauge board to mark the locations of the other brackets and post tops. Unless your fence needs to step up or down a slope, carry your measurements around the post with a speed square and mark the locations of the brackets for the next section as well.

Remove the post and attach the brackets. Trim the post top to height. Set the post in the hole and insert the stringers in the brackets. Plumb the post, make sure the panel is level, and then attach the brackets to the fence panel.

Plumb the post perpendicular to the fence line with a single staked brace screwed to the post face so it will not interfere with the installation of the brackets for setting the next panel. Set the post in concrete or tamped dirt and gravel.

Attach Remaining Posts & Panel Sections

Repeat steps 2 through 4 down the line. For a stepped fence, establish a consistent step height or determine the step-up or step-down height one panel at a time. Backfill end post and gatepost holes with concrete. Backfill the line and corner posts with concrete or tamped dirt and gravel. Allow three days for concrete to cure before removing braces.

Hang the gate (see Basic Gates section on page 152 for more information on selecting and installing gates). Attach the post caps or finials to the post tops with galvanized casing nails or deck screws. Paint, stain, or seal the fence.

10. *Finish installing the posts and panels. You can continue to fill the holes with concrete one at a time, or wait and fill them all once the posts are all positioned and braced.*

TIP

When installing a gate, attach the hinges to the gate first. For maximum strength, the hinges should be located at stringer locations on fence panels, especially if you are using strap hinges like the ones shown here. Once the hinges are attached, prop the gate into position and attach the free hinge leaves to the gate post. (A gate post should always be set in concrete—even if the other posts are loose set in gravel, sand or dirt.)

11. *Attach post caps or finials and seal, stain or paint your new fence.*

Picket Fence

For generations, the stereotypical dream home has been a vine-covered cottage surrounded by a white picket fence. But these days, the diversity in designs and styles of this classic American fence make it adaptable to any home, from a three-story Victorian to a modest rambler.

The charm of a picket fence lies in its open and inviting appearance. The repetitive structure and spacing create a pleasing rhythm that welcomes family and friends while maintaining a fixed property division.

Traditionally, picket fences are 36 to 48" tall. Our version is 48" tall, the posts are spaced 96" on-center, and the pickets are spaced 1¾" apart. It's important that the spacing appear to be consistent. Using a jig simplifies that process, and, if necessary, you can spread any extra space across many pickets to mask the discrepancy.

Picket fences are traditionally white; however, matching your house's trim color or stain can be an eye-catching alternative. You'll need to apply two coats of paint or stain. If you prime and paint all the materials before construction, apply the second coat after the fence is completed to cover any marks, smudges, and nail or screw heads.

There are a number of picket styles to choose from. Most building centers carry a variety, or you can design your own by simply creating a template. If you need a large quantity of pickets or want to use an intricate design, contact a cabinet shop in your area—the time saved may be worth the added expense.

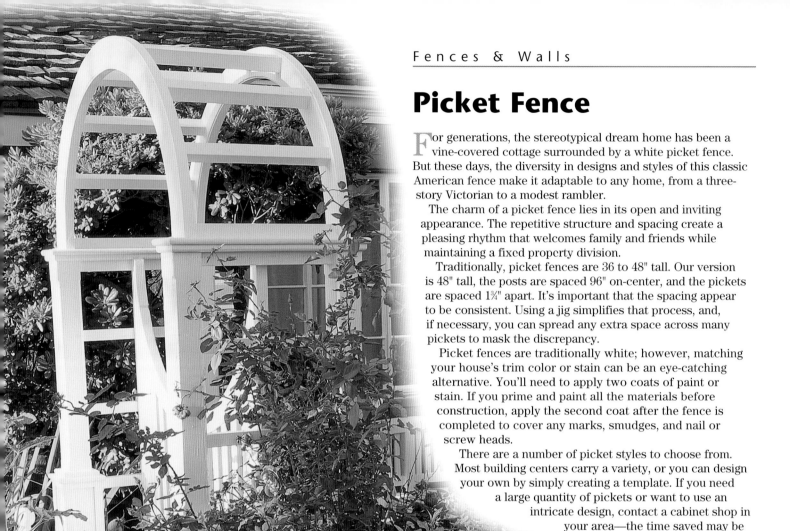

Although picket fences are traditionally white, matching your fence to your house's trim or stain color is an eye-catching alternative.

TOOLS & MATERIALS

- Tools & materials for setting posts
- Circular saw
- Jigsaw
- Paintbrush and roller
- Tape measure
- Reciprocating saw or handsaw

- Spring clamps
- Framing square
- Drill and bits
- Pressure-treated lumber:
  1 × 4s, 8 ft. (9 per bay)
  2 × 4s, 8 ft. (2 per bay)
  4 × 4s, 8 ft. (2 per bay)
- Paint, stain, or sealer

- 16d galvanized nails
- 1½" galvanized deck screws
- Fence post finials
- Mason's string and stakes
- Hammer
- Straightedge

HOW TO BUILD A PICKET FENCE

Step A: Prepare the Materials

1. Lay out the fence line with stakes and mason's string (pages 78 to 79). Space the post locations every 96" on-center.

2. Count the 4 × 4 posts and estimate the number of pickets you'll need to complete the project. Since it's likely you'll make a cutting error or two, estimate enough lumber to compensate.

3. If you're creating your own pickets, cut 1 × 4s to length. (Our design calls for 46" pickets.) Cut simple, pointed pickets with a circular saw. For more elaborate designs, like the one shown here, make a template, then use a jigsaw to cut the pickets.

4. Apply the first coat of paint, stain, or sealer.

Step B: Set the Posts

1. Set the posts (pages 82 to 83). Allow the concrete footings to cure for two days.

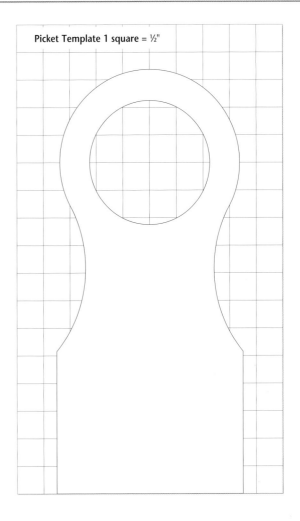

Picket Template 1 square = ½"

A. *Mark the fence line and calculate the number of posts and pickets required. Cut pickets using a template and a jigsaw.*

Cutting List

Each 96" bay requires:

Part	Type	Size	Qty.
Posts	4 × 4	78"	2
Pickets	1 × 4	46"	18
Stringers	2 × 4	92½"	2
Jig	1 × 4	1¾ × 46"	1

2. Measure up 48" from the base of each post and mark cutting lines.

3. Trim the posts along the cutting lines, using a reciprocating saw or handsaw.

Step C: Build the Framework

1. On each post, measure and mark a line 6" down from the top of the post to indicate the upper stringer position and 36½" from the top to indicate the lower stringer.

B. *Set the posts, then mark cutoff lines and trim them to 48" above ground level.*

2. At the upper stringer marks on the first two posts, clamp an 8-ft. 2 × 4 with the top edge of the 2 × 4 flush with the mark. Scribe the post outline on the back of the stringer at each end. Remove and cut the upper stringer to size, using a circular saw.

3. Position the upper stringer between the two posts, set back ¾" from the face of the posts. Toenail the stringer into place with 16d galvanized nails.

4. Repeat #2 and #3 to install the remaining stringers, both upper and lower.

Step D: Space & Hang the Pickets

1. To compensate for slope or shorter sections, calculate the picket spacing: Decide on the number of pickets you want between posts. Multiply that number by the width of a single

PICKET SPACING EXAMPLE

18 (pickets) × 3½" (picket width) = 63" (total picket width).

92½" (space between posts) – 63" = 29½" (unoccupied space).

29½" ÷ 19 (18 pickets + 1) = 1¾" (space between pickets).

NOTE: Not all calculations will work out evenly. If your figures come out uneven, make slight adjustments across the entire fence section.

C. *Mark the stringer position on the posts, then scribe and cut the stringer to size. Toenail the stringer in place (INSET).*

D. *Calculate the picket spacing and make a spacing jig. Position the first picket and secure it with 1½" galvanized deck screws. Using the spacing jig, position and install the remaining pickets.*

picket. This is the total width of pickets between the posts. Subtract that number from the total distance between the posts. The remainder equals the unoccupied space. Divide that number by the number of pickets plus 1 (the number of spaces that will exist between the posts). The resulting number equals the picket spacing.

2. To make a spacing jig, rip a 1 × 4 to the spacing size—1¾" in this project. Attach a scrap of wood to one end of the board as a cleat.

3. Draw a reference mark on each picket, 6" down from the peak.

4. Place a picket flat against the stringers and slide it flush against the post. Adjust the picket until the reference line is flush with the top edge of the upper stringer. Drill pilot holes and attach the picket, using 1½" deck screws.

5. Hang the jig on the upper stringer and hold it flush against the attached picket. Position a new picket flush against the jig and attach it. Reposition the jig and continue along the fence line.

Step E: Apply Finishing Details

1. Attach fence post finials for detail. Use a straightedge to draw lines from corner to corner on the top of the post to determine the center. Drill a pilot hole where the lines intersect and screw a finial into the center of each post.

2. For painted fences, apply the second coat.

E. *Determine the center of the post tops, drill pilot holes, and screw in fence post finials.*

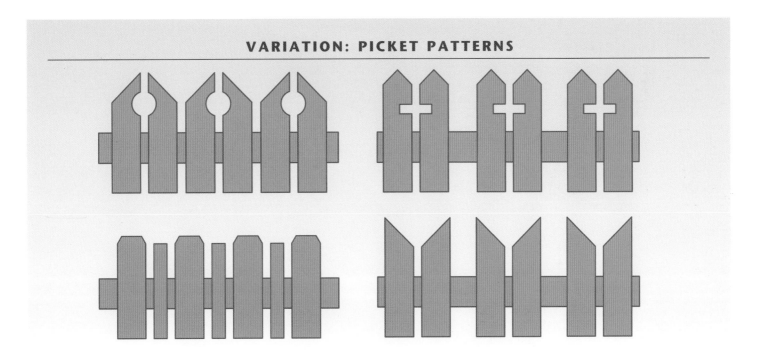

VARIATION: PICKET PATTERNS

Post & Rail Fence

Post-and-rail construction can be used to build fences in a surprising range of styles, from a rustic split-rail fence to the more genteel post-and-rail fence.

Because they use so little lumber, post-and-rail fences are very efficient for confining a large area. In most cases you can (and probably should) build this fence by setting the posts in gravel-and-dirt footings. This method is common in some regions, but isn't appropriate everywhere. Set fence posts in concrete if required by the building codes in your area.

One other note: if you don't want to cut mortises, most lumberyards offer premortised posts and tapered stringers that are designed for building split-rail fences.

Post-and-rail fences, which are typically painted, but can be stained and sealed, require more lumber and more upkeep than split-rail fences, but in certain settings nothing else will do.

HOW TO BUILD A MORTISED RAIL FENCE
Step A: Prepare the Posts
1. Plot the fence line and dig the post holes.

2. From the top of each post, measure and mark points 6" and 26½" down the center. Outline 2"-wide by 4"-tall mortises at each mark, using a cardboard template.

Step B: Cut the Mortises
1. Drill a series of 1" holes inside each mortise outline, drilling through the backside if necessary. Drill only halfway through for end posts, and halfway through on adjacent sides for corner posts.

2. Remove the remaining wood from the mortises with a hammer and chisel.

Step C: Shape the Tenons
1. Snap a straight chalk line down the sides of the stringers.

2. On one end, draw a straight line from the chalk line mark at the edge, to the center of the timber using a combination square.

3. At the center, draw a 1½"-long line perpendicular to the first, extending ¾" from each side. From each end of this line, draw perpendicular lines up to the edge of the timber. You will have outlined a rough, 1½ × 1½" square tenon end.

*A **split-rail fence**, pictured here, is an inexpensive and attractive way to fence off a large area of land.*

TOOLS & MATERIALS

- Tools & materials for plotting a fence line (page 78)
- Cardboard
- Chalk line
- Tape measure
- Shovel
- Combination square
- Drill with 1"-bit
- 2" wood chisel
- Hammer
- Reciprocating saw with a 6"-wood blade
- Rubber mallet
- Lumber
- Coarse gravel

A. *Outline the mortise on the first fence post according to the dimensions in the illustration above. Use a cardboard template to lay out the mortise shape.*

4. Measure and mark 3½" down from the end stringer for the tenon length.

5. Rough-cut the tenons using a reciprocating saw with a 6"-wood blade. If necessary, shape the tenons with a hammer and chisel to fit the mortises.

Step D: Set Posts & Attach Stringers

1. Fill the post holes with 6" of gravel, and insert the first post. Because each post is cut to size, make sure the post top measures 36" from the ground. If it sits too high, lay a board over the post top and tap down with a rubber mallet. If it's too low, add more gravel. Leave 6" of clearance between the position of the bottom stringer and the ground.

2. Begin to fill the post hole with gravel and dirt. Every few inches, tamp the dirt around the post with the end of your shovel and check the post for plumb.

3. Place the next post in the post hole without setting it. Insert the tenons of the stringers into the mortises of the first, set post. Insert the other ends of the stringers to the unset post. Adjust the post to fit the stringers if necessary.

4. Plumb the post and then pack the post hole with gravel, then dirt to set it. Repeat this procedure of setting a post, then attaching the stringers. Alternate the stringers so the tenons of one stringer face upward and the tenons of the next stringer face downward, creating a tight fit in the mortise. Plumb each post as you work.

B. *Remove as much waste wood as you can in the mortise area by drilling 1"-dia. holes all the way through. Square the mortises with a wood chisel.*

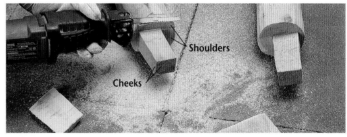

C. *Using a reciprocating saw, make cheek cuts then shoulder cuts to create tenons on the ends of the rails.*

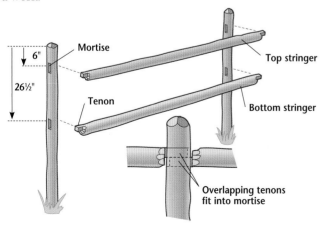

D. *Assemble the entire fence with the posts loose set in the post holes. Once all the rails are in place, square and plumb each section and then pack the posts in more tightly or set in concrete.*

Composite Fence

HOW TO INSTALL A COMPOSITE FENCE

The following instructions offer general information on installing a fence system with hollow posts that fit over 4×4 posts. The specific model shown is "Seclusions" manufactured by Trex. Refer to the manufacturer's instructions for whichever fence type you purchase.

Step A: Obtain Materials, Locate Posts

1. Obtain your materials and mark your exact post locations. This particular fence required 96" on-center spacing of line posts.

2. Position gateposts correctly. For this fence, on-center gatepost spacing equals the width of the gate, plus 1" plus the post width.

Step B: Dig Postholes, Set Posts

1. Slip composite post sleeves over 4×4 pressure-treated posts. The posts do not need to reach to the full height of the sleeves, but they should extend into the concrete footing and well up into the sleeve. Set your posts in 30" holes on 6" of pea gravel.

Be meticulous with post spacing, alignment, and plumbing. The rails are difficult to cut down and cannot be lengthened.

2. Set posts to the manufacturer- specified height as well. Fences stepped down a hill need to be set higher above the grade.

3. Tamp wet concrete mix into your post holes with a 2×4, to within 2 or 3" inches of the top of the hole. Let cure for two to three days before removing your bracing.

Step C: Install the Brackets

1. Screw the bottom bracket to the post with the fasteners provided. The manufacturer of the system shown here provides a template for attaching the brackets that sets the bottom stringer 2" up from the ground.

2. Measure up from the bottom bracket to establish the position of the top bracket according to manufacturer specifications.

3. For a level fence or a fence that follows the contour of the land, all bottom brackets are set the same height above grade.

4. For a stepped fence, attach the brackets for a fence section to the up-slope post first. Draw a level line from the bottom of the lower bracket to position the lower bracket on the downhill post.

Step D: Install Bottom Rails

1. Slide the two bottom rail sides over the aluminum bottom rail insert. For short sections, the composite part of the rail may

---

TOOLS & MATERIALS

- Tools & materials for setting posts
- Cordless drill or screwdriver
- Level
- Composite fencing materials

- Construction adhesive
- Circular saw
- Jigsaw
- Hacksaw
- Hammer
- Pea gravel
- Clamps

- Concrete
- 2×4
- Picket screws
- 8d galvanized casting nails
- Wood glue

New composite fencing systems offer a broader range of colors and employ installation techniques that are more familiar to DIYers than most vinyl fencing.

1. *Lay out the fence line with batter boards and strings and then begin digging post holes at the post locations. Start at an end or corner.*

be cut down with a carbide tooth circular saw blade. Cut the aluminum insert with a nonferrous metal cutting blade in your circular saw.

2. Place the bottom rail onto the lower brackets. Attach each side of the rail insert to its bracket with a screw provided for the purpose.

Step E: Install Pickets

1. Notch first picket in each 8 ft. section in order to avoid upper bracket assembly. Secure the picket to the post with three of the picket screws, evenly spaced.

2. Insert each C-shaped picket into the bottom rail so it opposes and interconnects with the last. Continue until you reach the far post. A full section of our fence used 19 pickets and would require less if it's been cut down.

3. Notch the upper corner of the last picket to clear the bracket. Secure the last picket to the post the same way you attached the first picket, with three evenly spaced screws into the post.

Step F: Install Top Rail, Post Caps, and Gate

1. Place the top rail over the pickets and upper brackets. Screw the rail to each bracket with a rail-to-bracket screw.

2. Install the post caps with 8d galvanized casing nails or glue it on with exterior-rated adhesive.

3. Install gate according to manufacturer instructions.

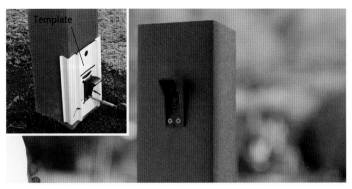

3. *Set all posts and check post heights with a mason's line or laser level. Trim to uniform height if needed. Attach hanger brackets according to manufacturer's directions—some will supply alignment templates (INSET photo).*

4. *Assemble the bottom stringer. Since composite material is not structurally rated, systems use either metal or wood reinforcement. Assemble the stringers (here, composite cladding is threaded over both faces of an aluminum rail).*

2. *Insert 4 × 4 pressure-treated wood posts into composite post sleeves and set the posts in concrete. Plumb, level, and brace the posts as with vinyl posts.*

5. *If stringers are too long or if you need to reduce the size of section to fit a small bay, cut the rail with a saw appropriate to the material (a hacksaw or a circular saw with a nonferrous metal blade may be used to cut aluminum). The composite components may be cut with a circular saw or power miter saw and a panel-cutting blade.*

6. Rest the clad rail stringers onto the post brackets and check with a level. If necessary, remove the stringer and adjust the bracket height.

7. Attach each side of the rail insert to its bracket with a screw provided for the purpose.

8. The initial siding strip fits inside the upper bracket and is screwed to the fence post.

9. Begin installing the interlocking (INSET photo) siding strips. Trim off the corner of the first infill picket in each section in order to avoid upper bracket assembly. Set the siding into the lower stringer channel and secure the first strip to its post with screws provided by the manufacturer.

10. Continue filling in with the interlocking siding strips.

11. *Trim the upper corner of the last picket to clear the bracket. Secure last picket to the post like the first, with three evenly spaced screws into the post.*

12. *Place the top rail over the pickets and upper brackets.*

13. *From above, screw the top rail to each bracket with a rail-to-bracket screw.*

14. *Install the post caps with 2"-galvanized casing nails or with a multi-purpose wood glue, such as Gorilla Glue or Liquid Nails. Faceted pyramid caps and flat-topped caps are available.*

Chain Link Fence

If you're looking for a strong, durable, and economical way to keep pets and children in—or out—of your yard, a chain link fence may be the perfect solution. Chain link fences require minimal maintenance and provide excellent security. Erecting a chain link fence is relatively easy, especially on level property. Leave contoured fence lines to the pros. For a chain link fence with real architectural beauty, consider a California-style chain link with wood posts and rails.

A 48"-tall fence—the most common choice for residential use—is what we've demonstrated here. The posts, fittings, and chain link mesh, which are made from galvanized metal, can be purchased at home centers and fencing retailers. The end, corner, and gate posts, called *terminal posts*, bear the stress of the entire fence line. They're larger in diameter than line posts and require larger concrete footings. A footing three times the post diameter is sufficient for terminal posts. A properly installed stringer takes considerable stress off the end posts by holding the post tops apart.

The fittings are designed to accommodate slight alignment and height differences between terminal posts and line posts. Tension bands, which hold the mesh to the terminal posts, have one flat side to keep the mesh flush along the outside of the fence line. The stringer ends hold the top stringer in place and keep it aligned. Loop caps on the line posts position the top stringer to brace the mesh.

When the framework is in place, the mesh must be tightened against it. This is done a section at a time with a winch tool called a *come-along*. As you tighten the come-along, the tension is distributed evenly across the entire length of the mesh, stretching it taut against the framework. One note of caution: It's surprisingly easy to topple the posts if you over-tighten the come-along. To avoid this problem, tighten just until the links of the mesh are difficult to squeeze together by hand.

To stiffen the fabric along the bottom, you may add a tension wire close to the ground before installing the fabric. This is more important on vinyl-coated chain link, which is more flexible.

Chain link fences are effective and economical. They also work well if your yard includes slight slope changes.

TOOLS & MATERIALS

- Tools & materials for setting posts
- Tape measure
- Mason's string
- Stakes
- Chalk
- Shovel

- Wrench & pliers
- Hacksaw or pipe cutter
- Come-along (fence stretcher)
- Galvanized terminal and line posts
- Concrete

- Galvanized fittings (see diagram)
- Bolts & nuts for chain link fence assembly
- Galvanized chain link mesh
- Dirt

HOW TO INSTALL A CHAIN LINK FENCE

Set the Posts

Mark the fence location with stakes and mason's string. Measure and mark the post locations every 96" on center.

Dig post holes 30" down or below the frost line, whichever is deeper. Line posts should be 6" wide but terminal (end, corner, and gate) posts should be 8" wide and belled even wider at the bottoms. You may adjust line post holes along (but not out of) the fence line to avoid obstacles.

Set the terminal posts in concrete, but leave the top of the concrete about 3" down from grade level. Each terminal post should be 50" above the ground or 2" above the fence height. Plumb each post and brace it on adjacent sides with staked braces taped securely to post. Make sure gate posts are spaced for your gate and gate hardware. Pack dirt over concrete.

Mark each terminal post 46" above grade. Run a mason's string at this level as a line-post height reference. Run another mason's string along the outside face of the terminal posts near the ground. Adjust line post holes now if needed.

Set line posts along (but not touching) bottom mason's line. Keep the post tops about 46" above grade, but if they diverge from your height line, make sure they do so gradually and evenly. Divergence will bring the fabric into the ground or cause gaps at the bottom. Plum each post and brace it on adjacent sides.

Site down the posts to check for dips and bumps. Fill the line post holes with concrete to about 3" below grade. Pack dirt over the concrete and allow to cure for a day or two.

Attach the Fittings

Add a fourth tension band at the bottom, oriented like the others, if you will be using a tension wire.

For corner posts, use six tension bands—two bands in each location with flat sides to the outside of the fence and pointing away from each other. Add two more opposing bands to the bottom for a tension wire.

Attach the Top Stringer

Start at one section, between two terminal posts, and feed the nontapered end of a top stringer piece through the loop caps, toward a terminal post. Insert the nontapered end into the cup

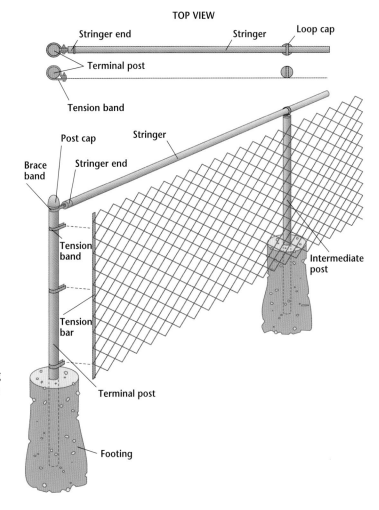

TOP VIEW

Stringer end · Stringer · Loop cap · Terminal post · Tension band

Post cap · Stringer · Brace band · Stringer end · Tension band · Tension bar · Intermediate post · Terminal post · Footing

of the stringer end. Make sure the stringer is snug. If necessary, loosen the brace band bolt and adjust it.

Continue to feed pieces of top stringer through the loop caps, fitting the nontapered ends over the tapered ends. Use a sleeve to join two nontapered ends, if necessary.

To fit the last piece of top stringer in the section, measure from where the taper begins on the previous piece to the inside back wall of the stringer end cup. Cut a piece of top stringer to size using a hacksaw or pipe cutter. Connect the nontapered end to the tapered end of the previous stringer. Loosen the brace band bolt and insert the cut end to the stringer end assembly. Make sure the fittings remain snug. Repeat for each section of the fence.

Apply Tension Wire and Fabric

Add a tension wire to the fence between lower tension bands according to manufacturer's instructions. You will need a wire grip for your come-along.

Weave a tension bar through the end row of the mesh. Secure the tension bar to the tension bands on the terminal post with bolts and nuts. Make sure the bolt heads face the outside of the fence.

Pull the mesh taut along the fence line by hand, moving towards the terminal post at the other end. Set the mesh on end and lean it against the posts as you go.

Stretch the Chain Link Mesh

Weave the spread bar for a come-along through the mesh, approximately 48" from the final terminal post. Hook the spread bar of the come-along to the tension bar. Attach the other end of the come-along to the terminal post, roughly in the middle.

Tighten the come-along until you can't squeeze the diamonds together with one hand. Make sure to keep the top of the mesh lined up, so that the peaks of the links rise about 1" above the top stringer.

1. Set the posts and brace them into position so they are plumb. Chain link fence posts should be set in concrete.

2. Place three tension bands on every gate and end post. Place the first band 8" from the top, the second 24" from the top, and the third 8" off the ground. Make sure the flat side of each tension band faces the outside of the fence and points into the fence bay.

3. For a corner, place two brace bands 3" from the top of the post. Attach stringer ends with the angle side up to the upper brace band and the angle side down to the lower band.

4. Top each terminal post with a post cap and each line post with a loop cap. Make sure the loop cap openings are perpendicular to the fence line, with the offset side facing the outside of the fence line.

Pull the remaining chain link mesh tight to the terminal post by hand and insert a tension bar where the mesh meets the tension braces.

Remove any excess mesh by bending back both knuckle ends of one zig-zag strand in the mesh. Spin the strand counter-clockwise so it winds out of the links, separating the mesh into two.

Secure the tension bar to the tension bands with bolts and nuts, with the bolt heads facing the outside of the fence.

Use tie wire spaced every 12" to attach the mesh to the top stringer and line posts. Use hog rings and hog ring pliers to attach the fabric to the tension wires. Repeat for each section.

5. *Cut the last piece of top stringer in a section to size. Adjust the brace band and stringer end to fit it in place.*

6. *To fit the last piece of top stringer in the section, measure from where the taper begins on the previous piece to the inside back wall of the stringer end cup. Cut a piece of top stringer to fit.*

7. *Weave a tension bar through the chain link mesh and attach it to the tension braces with bolts.*

8. *Use a come-along to stretch the mesh taut against the fence. The mesh is tight enough when the links are difficult to squeeze together by hand.*

Brick & Cedar Fence

This elegant fence is not nearly as difficult to construct as it looks. It does, however, require some time and effort and will make use of both your carpentry and masonry skills. There are also quite a few necessary materials, which does increase the expense. But when the project is complete, you'll have an attractive, durable structure that will be the envy of the neighborhood.

The 72" brick pillars replace the posts of most fences. The footings need to be 4" longer and wider than the pillar on each side, 16 × 20" for this project.

To maintain an even ⅜" mortar joint spacing between bricks, create a story pole using a 2 × 2 marked with the spacing. After every few courses, hold the pole against the pillar to check the joints for a consistent thickness. Also make sure the pillars remain as plumb, level, and square as possible. Poor pillar construction greatly reduces strength and longevity of the pillars.

Attaching the stringers to the pillars is much easier than you may imagine. Fence brackets and concrete screws are available that have as much holding power as lag bolts and anchors.

Although other brands are available, we used ¼"-diameter concrete screws. The screws come with a special drill bit to make sure the embedment holes are the right diameter and depth, which simplifies the process for you.

The part of this project that looks the trickiest is creating the arched top of the cedar-slat fence sections. It can be achieved relatively easily by using a piece of PVC pipe. With the ends anchored, the pipe is flexible enough to bend into position and rigid enough to hold the form of the arch so it can be traced.

HOW TO BUILD A BRICK & CEDAR FENCE
Step A: Install the Footings

1. Measure and mark the fence line with stakes and mason's string.

2. Determine the center of each pillar location along the fence line. To space the pillars at 96" edge to edge, drop a plumb bob 12" in from the end of the fence line and then every 116". Place a stake at each pillar location.

A brick and cedar fence is the type of upgrade that will make your outdoor space the most distinctive on the block.

TOOLS & MATERIALS

- Tools & materials for pouring footings
- Tape measure
- Level
- Plumb bob
- Wheelbarrow or mortar box
- Mason's trowel
- Jointing tool
- Aviation snips
- Drill
- Circular saw
- Hammer
- Jigsaw
- Shovel

- Standard modular bricks (4 × 2⅔ × 8", 130 per pillar)
- 2 × 2 lumber, 10 ft.
- Chalk
- Type N mortar mix
- ¼" wooden dowel & vegetable oil
- ¼" wire mesh
- Capstone or concrete cap
- Wood scraps (⅜"-thick, ½"-thick)
- 2 × 6 fence brackets (6 per bay)
- Concrete

- 1¼" countersink concrete screws
- Concrete drill bit
- Pressure-treated lumber:
  1 × 6 × 8 ft. (16 per bay)
  2 × 6 × 8 ft. (3 per bay)
- 1½" stainless steel deck screws
- 1½" finish nails (3)
- 96"-length of flexible ¼" PVC pipe
- Stakes & mason's string
- 1½" finish nails

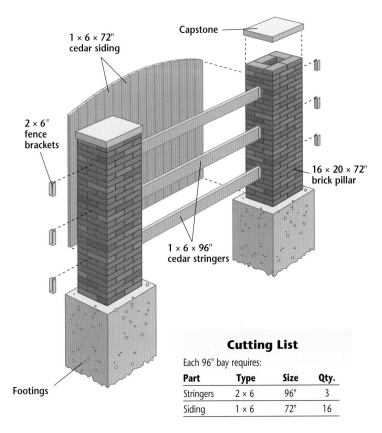

3. Outline 16 × 20" pillar footings at each location, then dig the trenches and pour the footings. Let the footings cure for two days.

Step B: Lay the First Course

1. On a flat work surface, lay out a row of bricks, spaced ⅜" apart. Mark the identical spacing on a 2 × 2 to create a story pole.

2. Dry-lay the first course of five bricks—center them on the footing, leaving ⅜" spaces between them. Mark reference lines around the bricks with chalk.

Cutting List

Each 96" bay requires:

Part	Type	Size	Qty.
Stringers	2 × 6	96"	3
Siding	1 × 6	72"	16

A. *Pour footings that are 4" longer and wider than the pillars on each side. This project calls for 16 × 20" footings (see page 84).*

B. *Trowel a bed of mortar inside the reference lines and lay the first course. Create a weep hole in the mortar with a dowel to ensure the drainage of any moisture that seeps into the pillar.*

3. Set the bricks aside and trowel a ⅜"-layer of mortar inside the reference lines. Set a brick into the mortar with the end aligned with the reference lines. Set a level on top of the brick, then tap the brick with the trowel handle until it's level.

4. Set the rest of the bricks in the mortar, buttering the mating ends with mortar. Use the reference lines to keep the bricks aligned, and make sure they are plumb and level.

5. Use a pencil or dowel coated with vegetable oil to create a weep hole in the mortar of the first course of bricks, so that any moisture that seeps into the pillar will drain away.

C. *Lay each new course so the bricks overlap the joints of the previous course. Use a jointing tool after every five courses to smooth the firm mortar joints.*

D. *Lay the final course over a bed of mortar and wire mesh, with an additional block added to the center. Fill the joints with mortar, and work them with a jointing tool as soon as they become firm.*

Step C: Lay the Subsequent Courses

1. Lay the second course, rotating the pattern 180°, so the joints of the first course are overlapped by the bricks of the second course.

2. Lay the subsequent courses, rotating the pattern 180° with each course. Use the story pole and a level to check the faces of the pillar after every other course. Use the story pole after every few courses to make sure the mortar joints are consistent.

3. After every fourth course, cut a strip of ¼" wire mesh and place it over a thin bed of mortar. Add another thin bed of mortar on top of the mesh, then add the next course of brick.

4. After every five courses, use a jointing tool to smooth the joints when they have hardened enough to resist minimal finger pressure.

Step D: Lay the Final Course

1. For the final course, lay the bricks over a bed of mortar and wire mesh. After placing the first two bricks, add an extra brick in the center of the course. Lay the remainder of the bricks to fit around it.

2. Fill the remaining joints, and work them with the jointing tool as soon as they become firm.

3. Build the remaining pillars. Use the story pole to maintain identical dimensions and a 96" length of 2 × 2 to keep the spacing between pillars consistent.

Step E: Install the Top Cap

1. Select a capstone 3" longer and wider than the top of the pillar. Mark reference lines on the bottom of the capstone to help you center it.

2. Spread a ½"-thick bed of mortar on top of the pillar. Center the capstone on the pillar using the reference lines. Strike the

E. *Spread a ½"-thick bed of mortar on top of the pillar, and center the cap, using the reference lines.*

mortar joint under the cap so it's flush with the pillar. If mortar squeezes out of the joints, press ⅜"-thick wood scraps into the mortar at each corner to support the cap. Remove the scraps after 24 hours and fill the gaps with mortar.

Step F: Attach the Stringers

1. On the inner face of each pillar (the face perpendicular to the fence line), measure down from the top and use chalk to mark at 18", 36", and 60".

2. At each mark, measure in 6¾" from the outside face of the pillar and mark with the chalk. Position a 2 × 6 fence bracket at the point where the reference marks intersect. Mark the screw holes on the pillar face, two or three per bracket.

3. Drill 1¾"-deep embedment holes at each mark, using the bit provided with the concrete screws. The hole must be ¼" deeper than the length of the screw.

4. Align the fence bracket screw holes with the embedment holes, and drive the 1¼" concrete screws into the pillar. Repeat for each pillar, attaching three fence brackets on each side of each line pillar.

5. Measure the distance from a fence bracket of the first pillar to the corresponding fence bracket of the next to determine the exact length of the stringers. If necessary, mark and then cut a cedar 2 × 6 to length using a circular saw.

6. Insert a 2 × 6 stringer into a pair of fence brackets and attach it with 1½" stainless steel screws. Repeat for each stringer.

Step G: Cut the Section Arch

1. Cut 1" off the ends of the cedar 1 × 6s to create a square edge.

2. On a large, flat surface, such as a driveway, lay out 16 1 × 6s, with approximately ½" of space between them and the cut ends flush.

3. On the two end boards, measure up from the bottom and mark 64". Tack a 1½" finish nail into each mark, 2" from the edge of the board.

4. Draw a line connecting the nails. Measure and mark the center (48" from the edge in our project). At the center, mark a point 6" above the original line. This mark indicates the height of the arch.

5. Place a 96"-long piece of flexible PVC piping against the two nails. At the mid-point, bend the PVC pipe until it meets the height mark. Tack a 1½" finish nail behind the PVC pipe to hold it in place, then trace along the PVC pipe to form the arch. Cut the arch using a jigsaw along the marked line.

Step H: Attach the Siding

1. Run a mason's string 2" above the bottom of the fence line as a guide.

2. Attach the siding to the stringers, using 1½" stainless steel deck screws. Maintain a 2" gap at the bottom of the fence, and make sure the boards are plumb. Use ½" scraps of wood as spacing guides between boards.

3. Repeat for each section of fence.

F. Attach 2 × 6 fence brackets to the pillars, using 1¼" concrete screws.

G. Align cedar slats for a 96" section, and tack two nails on opposite sides, 64" from the bottom. Deflect a piece of PVC pipe against the nails, 6" up from the middle, and trace the arch.

H. Attach the cedar slats to the stringers with 1½" stainless steel deck screws. Maintain their order to properly form the arch top.

111

Brick Archway

Building an arch over a pair of pillars, especially over a driveway or sidewalk entrance, adds luxury and elegance to your estate. This impressive decorative masonry is a seemingly challenging task made easier with a simple, semi-circular form that you can build yourself using 2× lumber, plywood, and wallboard screws. Continue to dress up your pillars by installing a wrought-iron gate between them or adding a brick flower box in front of the entrance. Plant crawling vines and coax them over the brick archway for a dramatic, old-world effect.

Build the arch over new or existing pillars by laying bricks along the form's curved edge. Select bricks equal in length to those used in the pillars. If building new pillars (pages 108 to 110, Step A through Step E), use the colors and textures of your home exterior and landscape to guide your choice of brick. Brickyards sell mortar tint to complement the color of your bricks. Once you settle on the amount of tint to add to the mortar, record the recipe so you can maintain a consistent color in every batch.

Careful measurements are essential for success in this project, so take your time layout out each brick according to your measurements.

A brick archway is a relatively easy project that adds instant elegance to any driveway or walkway entrance.

TOOLS & MATERIALS

- Joint chisel
- Mason's hammer
- Pry bar
- Jigsaw
- Circular saw
- Drill
- Compass
- Level
- Mason's string
- Trowel
- Jointing tool
- Tuck-pointer
- Plywood (¾", ¼")
- Wallboard screws (1", 2")
- Bricks
- Type N mortar mix
- Lumber (2 × 4, 2 × 8)
- Shims
- Rubber mallet
- Tape measure
- Pencil/pen

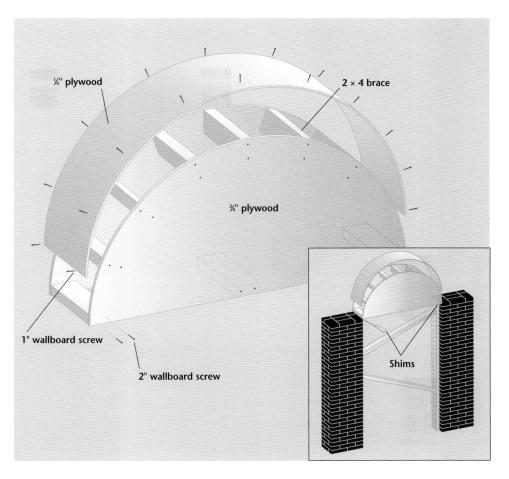

HOW TO BUILD THE ARCH FORM

1. Determine the distance between the inside edges of the tops of your pillars. Divide the distance in half, and then subtract ¼". Use this as the arch radius.

2. Mark a point at the center of a sheet of ¾" plywood. Use a pencil and a piece of string to scribe the circle on the plywood using the radius calculated above. Cut out the circle with a jigsaw. Then mark a line through the center point of the circle and cut the circle in half with a jigsaw or a circular saw.

3. Construct the form by bracing the two semicircles using 2" wallboard screws and 2 × 4s. To calculate the length of the 2 × 4 braces, subtract the combined thickness of the plywood sheets—1½"—from the width of the pillars and cut the braces to length. Cover the top of the form with ¼" plywood, attached with 1" wallboard screws.

4. If your pillars are capped, remove the caps before building an arch. Chip out the old mortar from underneath using a hammer and joint chisel. With a helper nearby to support the cap, use a pry bar and shims to remove each cap from the pillar.

HOW TO BUILD A BRICK ARCH
Step A: Mark Brick Spacing on Form

1. Center a brick at the peak of the form. Set a compass to the width of one

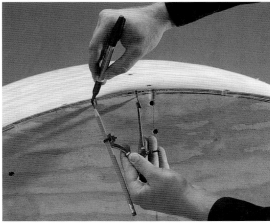

A. *Mark reference lines along the form using a compass.*

B. *Cut two 2 × 8 braces, ½" shorter than pillar height, and prop one against each pillar with 2 × 4 cross braces.*

brick plus ¼". Place the compass point at one edge of the brick and mark the form with the pencil.

2. Place the compass point on the new mark and make another mark along the curve. Continue to make marks along the curve until less than a brick's width remains.

3. Divide the remaining width by the number of compass marks, and increase the compass setting by the amount. Use a different color to make the final reference marks to each side of the peak.

4. Extend the pencil lines across the curved surface of the form and onto the far edge.

Step B: Mount the Form to the Pillars

1. Cut two 2 × 8 braces, ½" shorter than pillar height. Prop one brace against each pillar with 2 × 4 cross braces.

2. Place shims on top of each 2 × 8 to raise the form so its bottom is even with the tops of the pillars. Rest the plywood form on the braces.

Step C: Lay the First Course

1. Mix mortar and trowel a narrow ⅜" layer on top of one pillar. Place one brick, and then rap the top with a trowel handle to settle it.

C. *Place five bricks, then tack a string to the center point of the form on each side, and use the strings to check each brick's alignment.*

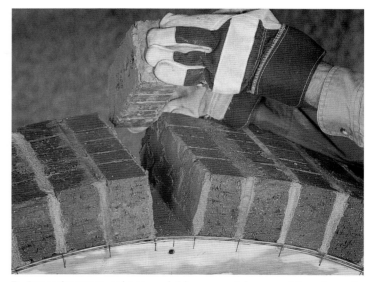

D. *Butter the center, or keystone, brick as accurately as possible and ease it into place. Smooth the remaining joints with a jointing tool.*

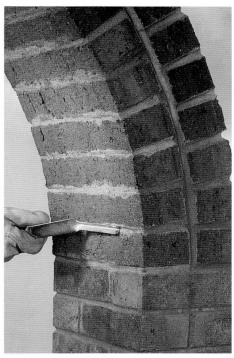

E. *Lay the second course halfway up each side of the area. Dry-lay several more bricks on one side— using shims as substitutes for mortar joints—to check the amount of space remaining. Remove the shims and lay the final bricks.*

F. *Leave the form in place for a week, misting occasionally. Remove the braces and form, then tuck-point the joints on the underside of the arch.*

2. Butter the bottom of each subsequent brick, and place it in position.

3. Place five bricks, then tack a string to the center point of the form on each side, and use the strings to check each brick's alignment. Switch to the other side of the form and place five more bricks to balance the weight on the form.

4. Continue to place bricks on alternate sides of the form until the space for one brick remains. Take care not to dislodge other bricks as you tap a brick into position.

5. Smooth previous joints with a jointing tool as they become firm.

Step D: Place the Keystone in the First Course

Butter the final brick in the first course, the center brick or *keystone*, as accurately as possible and ease it into place. Smooth the remaining joints with a jointing tool.

Step E: Lay the Second Course

1. Lay a bed of mortar over the first course, and then lay the second course halfway up each side. Maintain the same mortar joint thickness as in the first layer. Some of the joints will be staggered, adding strength to the arch.

2. Dry-lay several more bricks on one side—using shims as substitutes for mortar joints—to check the amount of space remaining.

3. Remove the shims and lay the final bricks with mortar. Smooth the joints with a jointing tool.

Step F: Tuck-point the Underside of the Arch

Leave the form in place for one week, misting occasionally. Carefully remove the braces and form. Tuck-point and smooth the joints on the underside of the arch.

Stone & Rail Fence

This 36-inch-tall, rustic stone-and-rail fence is constructed in much the same way as the brick-and-cedar fence, but with stone rather than brick and simple 2 × 4 rails rather than siding.

Each pillar requires a footing that extends 6 inches beyond its base in all directions. Carefully plan the layout and sort the stones before you begin setting them. If necessary, use a stone cutter's chisel and a maul to trim stones or cut them to size.

TOOLS & MATERIALS

- Tools & materials for pouring footings
- Tape measure
- Level
- Wheelbarrow or mortar box
- Mason's trowel
- Jointing tool
- Stiff-bristle brush
- Drill
- Stone cutter's

- chisel & maul
- Paintbrush & roller
- Type M mortar
- Stones of various shapes and sizes
- Wood shims
- 2 × 4" fence brackets (6 per bay)
- 1¼" countersink concrete screws
- Concrete drill bit

- Rough-cut cedar 2 × 4" × 8 ft. (3 per bay)
- Paint, stain, or sealer
- 1½" galvanized deck screws
- Chalk
- Circular saw
- Mason's string & stakes
- Wood shims
- Jointing tool

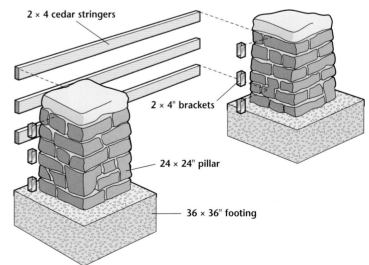

2 × 4 cedar stringers

2 × 4" brackets

24 × 24" pillar

36 × 36" footing

HOW TO BUILD A STONE & RAIL FENCE

Step A: Dry-lay the First Course

1. Plot the fence line with stakes and mason's string. For 72" bays between 24 × 24" pillars, measure and mark 18" in from the end of the fence line and then every 96" on-center.

2. Outline, dig, and pour 36 × 36" concrete footings. Let the concrete cure for two days.

3. Sort individual stones by size and shape. Set aside suitable tie stones for corners and the largest stones for the base.

4. Dry-lay the outside stones in the first course to form a 24 × 24" base centered on the footing.

5. Use chalk to trace a reference outline on the footing around the stones, then set them aside.

Step B: Mortar the First Course

1. Trowel a 1"-thick bed of mortar inside the reference outline, then place the stones in the mortar, in the same positions as in the dry run.

2. Fill in the center with small stones and mortar. Leave the center slightly lower than the outer stones.

3. Pack mortar between the outer stones, recessing it roughly 1" from the faces of the stones.

Step C: Lay the Subsequent Courses & Tool the Joints

1. Set each subsequent course of stone in a bed of mortar laid over the preceding course, staggering the vertical joints.

2. On every other course, place tie stones that extend into the pillar center. Use wood shims to support large stones until the mortar sets. Build each pillar 36" tall, using a level to check for plumb as you work.

3. When the mortar sets enough to resist light finger pressure, smooth the joints with a jointing tool. Keep the mortar 1" back from the stone faces.

4. Remove any shims and fill the holes with mortar. Remove dry spattered mortar with a dry, stiff-bristle brush.

Step D: Lay the Capstones & Attach Stringers

1. Lay a 1"-thick bed of mortar on the pillar top and place the capstones. Smooth the joints as in Step C.

2. Mist with water regularly for one week, as the mortar cures.

3. On the inner face of each pillar, measure up from the footing and mark with chalk at 12", 21", and 30".

4. At each mark, measure in 6" from the outside face of the pillar and mark, then line up the top and side edges of a 2 × 4" fence bracket where these two marks intersect. Mark the screw holes on the pillar, then drill a 1½"-deep embedment hole at each mark using the drill bit provided with the concrete screws.

5. Align the bracket screw holes with the embedment holes, and attach with the 1¼" countersink concrete screws. Repeat for each bracket.

6. Measure the distance from a fence bracket on one pillar to the corresponding bracket on the next for the stringer size. Mark and cut 2 × 4s to size, using a circular saw.

7. Paint, stain, or seal each stringer, and allow to dry.

8. Insert stringers into the fence brackets and attach them using 1½" galvanized deck screws.

117

Framed Trellis Wall

This simple design creates a sophisticated trellis wall that would work in many settings. Part of its appeal is that the materials are inexpensive and the construction remarkably simple.

It can be used as an accent wall, a backdrop to a shallow garden bed, or a screen to block a particular view. As a vertical showcase for foliage or flowers, it can support a wide display of colorful choices. Try perennial vines such as golden clematis (*Clematis tangutica*) or trumpet creeper (*Campsis radicans*). Or, for spectacular autumn color, plant Boston ivy (*tricuspidata*). If you prefer annual vines, you might choose morning glories (*Ipomoea tricolor*) or a black-eyed susan vine (*Thunbergia alata*). The possibilities go on and on—just make sure that the plants you select are well-suited to the amount of sunlight they'll receive.

Depending on the overall look you want to achieve, you can paint, stain, or seal the wall to contrast with or complement your house or other established structures. Well-chosen deck post finials can also help tie the wall into the look of your landscape.

This project creates three panels. If you adapt it to use a different number of panels, you'll need to revise the list of materials.

TOOLS & MATERIALS

- Tools & materials for setting posts
- Tape measure
- Framing square
- Hammer
- Chalk line
- Line level
- Paintbrush & roller

- Reciprocating saw or handsaw
- Drill
- Caulk gun
- Nail set
- Paint, stain, or sealer
- 10d galvanized casing nails

- Galvanized finish nails (4d, 6d)
- Construction adhesive
- Pressure-treated lumber (see Cutting List)
- Deck post finials (4)

Cutting List

Part	Type	Size	Qty.
Posts	4 × 4	10 ft.	4
Stringers	2 × 4	48"	6
Back frame			
Top & bottom	1 × 4	41"	6
Sides	1 × 4	72"	6
Front frame			
Top & bottom	1 × 4	48"	6
Sides	1 × 4	65"	6
Stops			
Top & bottom	1 × 1	48"	12
Sides	1 × 1	70½"	12
Lattice panels	4 × 8	48 × 72"	3
Post caps	1 × 6	4½ × 4½"	4

HOW TO BUILD A FRAMED TRELLIS WALL
Step A: Set the Posts

1. Mark the post positions 4 ft. apart, as indicated in the diagram at right. Dig holes and set the posts. It's important to maintain the 4-ft. spacing between posts as accurately as possible.

2. On the first post, measure and mark a point 77" from the ground. Using a framing square, draw a level line across the post at the mark. Tack a nail in place along the line, and tie a chalk line to it. Stretch the chalk line to the opposite post, then use a line level to level it. Remove the line level and snap a line across all four posts.

3. On each post, measure down 75" from the chalk line and draw a line across the post, using a framing square.

4. Mark a line 10" above the chalk line. Trim off the posts along these lines using a reciprocating saw or handsaw. Paint, stain, or seal the posts, including the cut ends.

A. *Set posts and let the concrete dry thoroughly. Snap level chalk lines to indicate the positions for the stringers. At the line for the top stringer, measure up 10" and draw a cutting line on each post.*

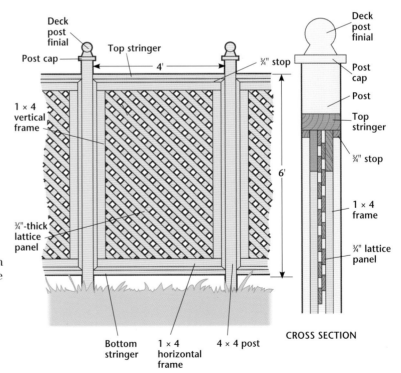

CROSS SECTION

119

TIP: EASY TIES

Tying vines requires a material that's both strong and gentle—strong enough to support the vine and gentle enough not to damage the tendrils.

Old, 100% cotton t-shirts make terrific, inexpensive ties that can go into the compost bin for further recycling when the growing season is over.

Starting at the bottom, cut around the shirt in a continuous spiral about 1½" wide. When you reach the armholes, begin making straight cuts from the edge of one sleeve to the edge of the other. One shirt usually produces 15 to 20 yards of tying material.

Step B: Prepare Pieces & Position Stringers

1. Cut the stringers, back and front frame pieces, stops, lattice panels, and post caps as indicated on the Cutting List on page 119. Paint, stain, or seal these pieces.

2. Transfer the level lines to the inside face of the posts using a framing square.

3. Working between the two center posts, position the top stringer; make sure the top of the stringer is even with the marked line. Attach the stringer, toenailing it with 10d galvanized casing nails. Align the bottom stringer with the marked line and secure it in the same way.

Step C: Add Stops to the Back of the Fence Frame

Position a 1 × 1 stop flush with the back edge of the stringer and post. Drill pilot holes approximately every 8", then drive 6d galvanized finish nails through the stop and into the fence frame.

Step D: Set up the Back Frame

1. On a level work surface, position the pieces of the back frame to form a 4 × 6-ft. rectangle with butted joints. Measure the opposite diagonals. Adjust the frame until these measurements are equal, ensuring that the frame is square.

2. Run a bead of construction adhesive around the center of the back frame. Set the lattice panel in place, making sure it's square within the frame.

Step E: Attach the Front Frame

Set the front frame in place, with the joints butted in the opposite direction of those on the back frame. Square the frame as described in Step D, then secure the frame with 4d galvanized finish nails driven every 6". Sink the nails, using a nail set. Let the adhesive cure according to manufacturer's directions.

B. *Transfer the level lines to the inside of the posts using a framing square. Install the first set of stringers between the center posts, even with the marked lines.*

C. *Add the stops to the back side of the fence frame. Drill pilot holes and nail the stops in place with 6d galvanized finish nails.*

Step F: Install the Framed Lattice Panel

1. Set the panel in place between the center posts, positioned firmly against the stops.

2. Position 1 × 1 stops around the front edges of the frame. Push the stops in until they hold the panel snugly in place. Drill pilot holes approximately every 6" and drive 6d galvanized finish nails through the stops and into the fence frame.

Step G: Complete the Wall

1. Repeat Steps B through F to install the left and right panels.

2. Set a post cap over each post, positioned so that the overhang is equal on all sides. Nail the trim in place using 6d galvanized finish nails.

3. On top of each post cap, draw diagonal lines from corner to corner, forming an "X". Drill a pilot hole through the center of each "X", then install a deck post finial in each hole.

D. Set up the pieces of the back frame, butting the joints. Square the frame, then apply a bead of construction adhesive along the center of the frame. Carefully set the lattice panel in place.

E. Set the front frame in place, butting the pieces in the opposite direction of the back frame. Drive 4d galvanized finish nails every 6" to secure the front frame to the lattice panel and back frame.

F. Set the panel in place between the center pair of posts. Add stops on the front side, then drill pilot holes and nail the stops in place, using 6d galvanized nails.

G. Install the remaining panels and add post caps to the posts. Add a deck finial to each post.

Mortared Block Wall

Block walls can be built fairly quickly because of the size of the individual blocks. Still, the same patience and attention to detail involved in laying blocks are required. Check your work often, and don't be afraid to back up a step or two to correct your mistakes.

This section features a concrete block wall laid up one course at a time. Make sure you have a sturdy, level footing before you start.

TOOLS & MATERIALS

- Trowel
- Chalk line
- Level
- Mason's string
- Line blocks
- Jointing tool
- Mortar mix (Type S or N)
- 8 × 8" concrete blocks
- Stakes
- Cap blocks
- Wire reinforcing strips

Mortared concrete block walls *are durable, economical, and provide privacy and security. Add decorative blocks, as shown here, or cover with a veneer to add style to the utilitarian look.*

MASON MIX CALCULATOR

Number of bags required to lay blocks ⅜" joint (9mm)

Number of Blocks (8 x 8 x 16")	10	15	25	30	50	100	125	500	1000
80-lb Bags (36.3 kg)	1	2	3	3	5	9	11	42	84

HOW TO MAKE A CONCRETE BLOCK WALL

1. Dig trenches and pour footings twice as wide as the proposed wall (reference page 84).

TIP

Dampen the block before placing mortar for improved bond strength.

2. Dry-lay the first course, leaving a ⅜" gap between blocks. Draw reference lines on the concrete base to mark the ends of the row, extending the lines well past the edges of the block. Use a chalk line to snap reference lines on each side of the base 3" from the blocks. These reference lines will serve as a guide when setting the blocks into mortar.

3. Dampen the concrete slab or footing with water, and dampen the blocks if necessary. Mix mortar and place a layer of mortar on to the footing for the first two blocks at one end of the layout. The mortar should be firm enough to support the weight of the first block course.

4. Set a combination corner block into the mortar bed. Press it into the mortar to create a ⅜"-thick bed joint. Hold the block in place and cut away the excess mortar (save excess mortar for the next section of the mortar bed). Check the block with a level to make sure it is level and plumb. Make any necessary adjustments by rapping on the high side with the handle of a trowel. Be careful not to displace too much mortar.

5. Drive a stake at each end of the project and attach one end of a mason's string to each stake. Thread a line level onto the string and adjust the string until it is level and flush with the top of the corner block. Place a mortar bed and set a corner block at the other end. Adjust the block so it is plumb and level, making sure it is aligned with the mason's string.

6. Place a mortar bed for the second block at one end of the project: butter one end of a standard block and set it next to the corner block, pressing the two blocks together so the joint between them is ⅜" thick. Tap the block with the handle of a trowel to set it, and adjust the block until it is even with the mason's string. Be careful to maintain the ⅜" joint.

7. Install all but the last block in the first course, working from the ends toward the middle. Align the blocks with the mason's string. Clean excess mortar from the base before it hardens.

VARIATION

Apply mortar to the flanges on each side of the block.

8. *Butter the flanges on both ends of a standard block for use as the closure block in the course. Slide the closure block into the gap between blocks, keeping the mortar joints an even thickness on each side. Align the block with the mason's string.*

9. *Apply a 1"-thick mortar bed for the half block at one end of the wall, then begin the second course with a half block.*

TIP

Buttering a concrete block involves laying narrow slices of mortar on the two flanges at the end of the block. It is not necessary to butter the valley between the flanges unless the project calls for it.

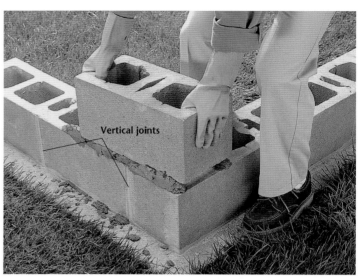

10. *Set the half block into the mortar bed with the smooth surfaces facing out. Use the level to make sure the half block is plumb with the first corner block, then check to make sure it is level. Adjust as needed. Install a half block at the other end.*

VARIATION: *If your wall has a corner, begin the second course with a full-sized end block that spans the vertical joint formed where the two walls meet. This layout creates and maintains a running bond pattern for the wall.*

11. *Attach a mason's string for reference, securing it either with line blocks or a nail. If you do not have line blocks, insert a nail into the wet mortar at each end of the wall, then wind the mason's string around and up to the top corner of the second course, as shown above. Connect both ends and draw the mason's string taut. Place a mortar bed for the next block, then fill out the second course using the mason's string as a reference line.*

OPTION: *When building stack bond walls with vertical joints that are in alignment, use wire reinforcing strips in the mortar beds every third course (or as required by local codes) to increase the strength of the wall. The wire should be completely embedded in the mortar.*

12. *Smooth (strike) the fresh mortar joints with a jointing tool when mortar is thumbprint hard, and remove any excess mortar. Tool the horizontal joints first, then the vertical joints. Cut off excess mortar using a trowel blade. When the mortar has set but is not too hard, brush any excess mortar from the block faces. Continue building the wall until it is complete.*

13. *Install a wall cap on top of the wall to cover the empty spaces and create a finished appearance. Set the cap pieces into mortar beds, then butter an end with mortar. Level the cap, then tool to match the joints in the rest of the wall.*

VARIATION: APPLYING STONE VENEER

If a mortared block wall fits into your plans, but you don't like the appearance, you can set stone veneer over the finished wall.

Start by attaching wire lath to the entire surface of the wall, using self-tapping masonry anchors.

Next, apply a ½"-thick layer of mortar over the lath. Scratch grooves into the damp mortar, using the trowel tip. Let the mortar dry overnight.

Apply mortar to the back of each veneer piece, then press it onto the wall with a twisting motion. Start at the bottom of the wall and maintain a ½" gap between pieces. Let the mortar dry for 24 hours.

Fill the joints with fresh mortar, using a mortar bag. Use a V-shaped jointing tool to finish the joints.

Stone veneer can dress up the surface of a block wall. Veneer, which is lightweight and easy to handle, is available in many styles and colors. Shaped end and corner pieces greatly simplify the process of setting it.

127

Interlocking Block Retaining Wall

Retaining walls are often used to level a yard or to prevent erosion on a hillside. In a flat yard, you can build a low retaining wall and fill in behind it to create a raised planting bed. Terraced retaining walls work well on steep hillsides. Two or more short retaining walls are easier to install and more stable than a single, tall retaining wall. Construct the terraces so each wall is no higher than 3 ft. (91 cm).

While retaining walls can be built from many materials, including pressure-treated timbers and natural stone, interlocking concrete blocks have become a very popular choice. Typically made from concrete, interlocking retaining wall blocks are rather inexpensive, very durable, and DIY-friendly. Several styles of interlocking block are available at building centers and landscape materials suppliers. Most types have a split-face finish that combines the rough texture of cut stone with the uniform shape and size of concrete blocks. Some have cast flanges or tongues and grooves to create a mechanical bond that holds the walls together. Other types do not interlock, but have flat surfaces that need to be bonded with rock and stone adhesive.

Interlocking block weighs up to 80 pounds (35 kg) each, so it is a good idea to have helpers when building a retaining wall. Suppliers offer substantial discounts when interlocking block is purchased in large quantities, so you may be able to save money if you coordinate your own project with those of your neighbors.

Structural features for all retaining walls include the following: a compactable gravel subbase to make a solid footing for the wall, crushed stone backfill and a perforated drain pipe to improve drainage behind the wall, and landscape fabric to keep the loose soil from washing into and clogging the gravel backfill.

When building retaining walls, pay special attention to drainage. Your wall can be damaged if water saturates the soil behind it, so make sure you include the proper drainage gravel and drain pipes or tile. You may need to dig a drainage swale before building in low-lying areas.

Be sure to check your local codes for maximum wall height restrictions and for minimum property line setback. Also have your public utility company visit your property and flag any utility lines that are in or near the project area.

Interlocking block retaining walls are manufactured with the DIYer in mind. They are available as prefit designs to eliminate cuts and they come in natural stone looks.

TOOLS & MATERIALS

- Wheelbarrow
- Shovel
- Garden rake
- Line level
- Hand tamper
- Plate compactor
- 3-lb. maul
- Masonry chisel

- Retaining wall block
- Eye protection
- Hearing protection
- Work gloves
- Level
- Circular saw with masonry blade
- Tape measure
- Marking pencil

- Caulk gun
- Stakes
- Mason's string
- Landscape fabric
- Compactable gravel
- Perforated drain pipe
- Backfill gravel
- Construction adhesive

HOW TO BUILD AN INTERLOCKING BLOCK RETAINING WALL

1. Excavate the hillside as necessary. Allow 12" (30 cm) of space for crushed stone backfill between the back of the wall and the hillside. Use stakes to mark the front edge of the wall. Connect the stakes with mason's string, and use a line level to check for level. The base of the trench must always remain at least 6" (15 cm).

2. Line the excavation with strips of landscape fabric cut 3 ft. longer than the planned height of the wall. Make sure all seams overlap by at least 6" (15 cm).

3. Spread a 4" (10 cm) layer of compactable gravel over the bottom of the excavation as a subbase and pack it thoroughly.

OPTIONS FOR POSITIONING A RETAINING WALL

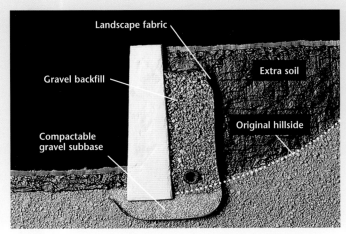

Increase the level area above the wall by positioning the wall well forward from the top of the hill. Fill in behind the wall with extra soil, which is available from sand-and-gravel companies.

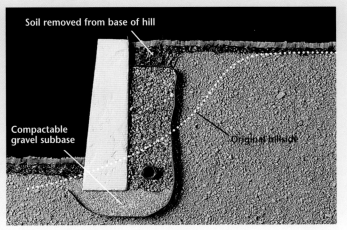

Keep the basic shape of your yard by positioning the wall near the top of the hillside. Use the soil removed at the base of the hill to fill in near the top of the wall.

TIPS FOR BUILDING RETAINING WALLS

Backfill with crushed stone and install a perforated drain pipe about 6" (15 cm) above the bottom of the backfill. Vent the pipe to the side or bottom of the retaining wall, where runoff water can flow away from the hillside without causing erosion.

Make a stepped trench when the ends of a retaining wall must blend into an existing hillside. Retaining walls often are designed so the ends curve or turn back into the slope.

A rented plate compactor works better than a hand tamper for packing the subbase. The compacted base must be flat in order for the wall to be level, so check it frequently with a level.

4. Lay the first course of block, aligning the front edges with the mason's string. When using flanged block, some manufacturers recommend that you place the first course upside down and backward. Check frequently with a level and adjust, if necessary, by adding or removing subbase material below the blocks.

5. Lay the second course of block according to manufacturer's instructions, checking to make sure the blocks are level. Lay flanged block with the flanges tight against the underlying course. Add 3 to 4" (8 to 10 cm) of gravel behind the block, and pack it with a hand tamper.

6. Make half-blocks for the corners and ends of a wall, and use them to stagger vertical joints between courses. Score full blocks with a circular saw and masonry blade, then break the blocks along the scored line with a maul and chisel.

NOTE: Some manufacturers sell precast half-blocks so you do not have to create your own.

7. Add and tamp crushed stone, as needed, to create a slight downward pitch (about ¼" [6 mm] of height per foot [30 cm]) leading to the drain pipe outlet. Place the drain pipe on the crushed stone, 6" (15 cm) behind the wall, with the perforations face down. Make sure the pipe outlet is unobstructed. Lay courses of block until the wall is about 18" (46 cm) above ground level, staggering the vertical joints. Fill behind the wall with crushed stone, and pack it with the hand tamper. Lay the remaining courses of block, except for the cap row, backfilling with crushed stone and packing with the tamper as you go.

8. Before laying the cap block, fold the end of the landscape fabric over the crushed stone backfill. Add a thin layer of topsoil over the fabric, then pack it thoroughly with a hand tamper. Fold any excess landscape fabric back over the tamped soil.

9. Apply stone and rock adhesive to the top course of block, then lay the cap blocks. Use topsoil to fill in behind the wall and to fill in the base at the front of the wall. Install sod or plants, as desired.

1. *Lay out the wall location with stakes and string and excavate as needed.*

2. *Line the trench with landscape fabric and pin or stake it temporarily at the highpoint.*

3. *Place a 4" (10 cm)-thick layer of compactable gravel in the trench and compact it with a plate compactor.*

4. Begin laying the first course. Check for level frequently.

5. Lay the second course of block on top of the starter course making sure the vertical seams are staggered. Backfill with drainage rock as you work.

6. Cut half-blocks for corners on alternating courses.

7. Lay perforated drain pipe at a slight slope behind the wall and cover with drainage rock.

8. Fold the landscape fabric back against the drainage rock and then backfill over the fabric with black dirt.

9. Install the wall cap blocks using stone and rock adhesive if recommended by the manufacturer.

Poured Concrete Wall

Building vertically with poured concrete introduces a whole new dimension to this ever-versatile material. And as much as walls may seem more challenging than slabs or casting projects, the basic building process is just as simple and straightforward. You construct forms using ordinary materials, then fill them with concrete and finish the surface. While tall concrete walls and load-bearing structures require careful engineering and professional skills, a low partition wall for a patio or garden can be a great do-it-yourself project.

The first rule of concrete wall building is knowing that the entire job relies on the strength of the form. A cubic foot of concrete weighs about 140 pounds, which means that a three-foot-tall wall that is six inches thick weighs 210 pounds for each linear foot. If the wall is 10 feet long, the form must contain over a ton of wet concrete. And the taller the wall, the greater the pressure on the base of the form. If the form has a weak spot and the concrete breaks through (known in the trades as a *blowout*), there's little chance of saving the project. So be sure to brace, stake, and tie your form carefully.

This project shows you the basic steps for building a three-foot-high partition wall. This type of wall can typically be built on a poured concrete footing or a reinforced slab that's at least four inches thick. When planning your project, consult your local building department for specific requirements such as wall size, footing specifications, and metal reinforcement in the wall. NOTE: This wall design is not suitable for retaining walls, tall walls, or load-bearing walls.

The footing should be at least 12" wide (twice the wall thickness) and at least six inches thick (1× wall thickness), and it must extend below the frost line (or in accordance with the local building code).

TOOLS & MATERIALS

- Drill and ⅛" bit
- Hacksaw or reciprocating saw
- Pliers
- Level
- Power mixer
- Shovel
- Concrete trowel
- Lumber (2 x 4", 2 x 2", 1 x 2")

- Nails (16d, 8d)
- ¾" exterior-grade plywood
- #3 rebar
- 8-gauge tie wire
- Wood screws or deck screws
- Vegetable oil or commercial release agent
- Concrete mix

- Plastic sheeting
- Quick-setting cement (mixed with concrete acrylic fortifier) or fast-set repair mortar
- Hammer
- Concrete power mixer (rented)
- Edger
- Scrap wood pieces
- Shovel

In any setting, a poured concrete wall offers clean, sleek lines and a reassuringly solid presence. You can leave the wall exposed to display its natural coloring and texture. For a custom design element, you can add color to the concrete mix or decorate any of the wall's surfaces with stucco, tile, or other masonry finishes.

WALL FORM CONSTRUCTION

Pull wire

Spacer

³/₄" plywood

2 x 4 frame

2 x 2 frame for stop board

#3 rebar

Stake

³/₄" plywood stop board

Concrete footing

Stake

Diagonal bracing

A wall form is built with two framed sides (much like a standard 2 x 4 stud wall) covered with ³/₄" plywood. The two sides are joined together at each end by means of a stop board, which also shapes the end of the finished wall. The form is braced and staked in position. Tie wires prevent the sides of the form from spreading under the force of the concrete. Temporary spacers maintain proper spacing between the sides while the form is empty; these are pulled out once the concrete is placed.

HOW TO CREATE A POURED CONCRETE WALL

1. *Build the frames for the form sides from 2 x 4 lumber and 16d nails. Include a stud at each end and every 16" in between. Plan an extra 2¼" of wall length for each stop board. For walls longer than 8 ft., build additional frames.*

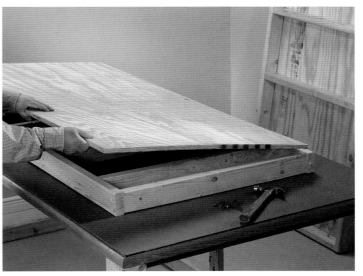

2. *Cut one piece of ³/₄" plywood for each side frame. Fasten the plywood to frames with 8d nails driven through the plywood and into the framing. Make sure the top edges of the panels are straight and flush with the frames.*

133

3. *Drill holes for the tie wires: At each stud location, drill two pairs of ⅛" holes evenly spaced, and keep the holes close to the stud faces. Drill matching holes on the other form side. See page 84 to prepare a poured footing for the wall.*

4. *Cut #3 rebar at 34", for each rebar anchor in the footing. Cut rebar for three horizontal runs, 4" shorter than the wall length. Tie the short pieces to the footing anchors using 8-gauge tie wire, then tie the horizontal pieces to the verticals, spacing them 12" apart and keeping their ends 2" from the wall ends. To make a 90° turn, bend the bars on one leg of the wall so they overlap the others by 24".*

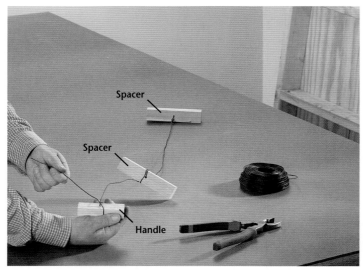

Spacer

Spacer

Handle

5. *Cut 1 x 2 spacers at 6", one piece for each set of tie wire holes. These temporary spacers will be used to maintain the form width. Tie each pair of spacers to a pull wire, spacing them to match the hole spacing. Then attach a piece of scrap wood to the end of the pull wire to serve as a handle.*

6. *Set the form sides in place. Install the stop boards with 2 x 2 frames for backing; fasten the frames to the form sides with screws. Tie a loop of wire through each set of tie wire holes, and position a spacer near each loop. Use a stick to twist the loop strands together, pulling the form sides inward, tight against the spacers.*

BUILDING ON A CONCRETE SLAB

A standard, reinforced 4"-thick concrete slab can be a suitable foundation for a low partition wall like the one shown in this project. The slab must be in good condition, with no significant cracks or changes in level, and you should place the wall several inches away from the slab edge to ensure adequate support.

To anchor the new wall to the slab and provide lateral stability, you'll need to install rebar anchors in the slab, following the basic steps shown here. But before going ahead with the project, be sure to have your plans approved by the local building department.

Mark the locations for the rebar anchors along the wall center: position an anchor 4" from each end of the wall and every 24" in between. At each location, drill a 1½"-diameter hole straight down into the concrete using a hammer drill and 1½" masonry bit (above, left). Make the holes 3" deep. Spray out the holes to remove all dust and debris using an air compressor with a trigger-type nozzle. Cut six pieces of #4 rebar at 16". Mix exterior-use anchoring cement to a pourable consistency. Insert the rods into the holes, then fill the hole with the cement (above, right). Hold the rods plumb until the cement sets (about 10 minutes). Let the cement cure for 24 hours.

SECURING BRACES ON A CONCRETE SLAB

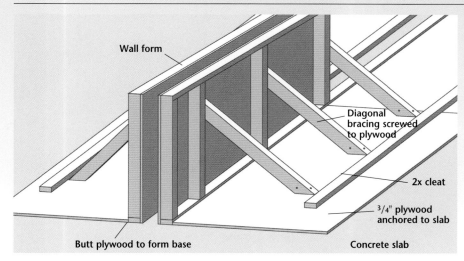

Wall form

Diagonal bracing screwed to plywood

2x cleat

³/4" plywood anchored to slab

Butt plywood to form base

Concrete slab

Fasten sheets of ¾" plywood to the slab as an anchoring surface for form braces. Fasten the plywood with a few heavy-duty masonry screws driven into the slab. Butt the sheets against the bottom of the form to provide the same support you'd get from stakes. Screw diagonal form bracing directly to the plywood. You can also add a cleat behind the braces for extra support.

7. Make sure the form is centered over the footing. Check that the sides are plumb and the top is level. Secure the form with stakes and braces. Install a diagonal brace at each stud location, and stake along the bottom of the form sides every 12". Fasten all stakes and braces to the form framing with screws. For long walls, join additional side pieces with screws for a tight joint with no gapping along the plywood seam. Brace the studs directly behind the joint point between sections. Coat the insides of the form with a release agent. If building on a slab (above, right), construct the form and then attach as a unit (see page 135).

8. Mix the first batches of concrete in a power mixer, being careful not to add too much water—a soupy mix results in weakened concrete.

9. Place the concrete in the forms. Start at the ends and work toward the center, filling the form about halfway up (no more than 20" deep). Rap on the forms to settle out air bubbles and then fill to the top. Remove the spacers as you proceed.

10. Use a shovel to stab into the concrete to work it around the rebar and eliminate air pockets. Continue to rap the sides of the forms with a hammer or mallet to help settle the concrete against the forms.

11. Screed the top of the wall flat with a 2 x 4, removing spacers as you work. After the bleed water disappears, float or trowel the top surface of the wall for the desired finish. Round over the edges of the wall with an edger, if desired.

12. Cover the wall with plastic and let it cure for two or three days. Remove the plastic. Sprinkle with water on hot or dry days to keep concrete from drying too quickly.

13. Cut the loops of tie wire and remove the forms. Trim the tie wires below the surface of the concrete, and then patch the depressions with quick-setting cement or fast-set repair mortar. Trowel the patches flush with the wall surface.

TIP

To achieve a consistent wall color and texture, apply heavy-duty masonry coating with acrylic fortifier using a masonry brush.

Dry Stone Wall

Many homeowners—especially dedicated gardeners—dream of using low stone walls to form the boundaries of their yards or gardens. Sadly, many of them think those stone walls are destined to remain merely dreams. If you're one of those people, you'll be happy to know that you don't have to hire a professional mason or learn to throw mortar in order to build a durable stone wall.

You can construct a low stone wall without mortar using a centuries-old method known as *dry laying*. With this technique, the wall is actually formed by two separate stacks that lean together slightly. The position and weight of the two stacks support each other, forming a single, sturdy wall.

While dry walls are simple to construct, they do require a fair amount of patience. The stones must be carefully selected and sorted by size and shape. They must also be correctly positioned in the wall so that weight is distributed evenly. Long, flat stones work best. A quarry or aggregate supply center will have a variety of sizes, shapes, and colors to choose from. For this project, you'll need to purchase a number of stones in these four sizes:

- **Shaping:** half the width of the wall
- **Tie:** the same width as the wall
- **Filler:** small shims that fit into cracks
- **Cap:** large, flat stones, wider than the wall

Because the wall relies on itself for support, a concrete footing is unnecessary, but the wall must be at least half as wide as it is tall. This means some stones may need to be shaped or split to maintain the spacing and structure of the wall.

To shape a stone, score its surface using a circular saw outfitted with a masonry blade. Place a mason's chisel on the cut and strike it with a hand sledge until the stone breaks. Always wear safety glasses when cutting or shaping stone.

Stone walls built without mortar are a time-tested, attractive option for low, perimeter walls. They are especially lovely surrounding gardens, or as a decorative path accompaniment.

TOOLS & MATERIALS

- Tools & materials for plotting a fence line (page 78)
- Shovel
- Circular saw with masonry blade

- Hand sledge
- Mason's chisel
- 4-ft. level
- Mason's trowel
- Safety glasses

- Stones of various shapes and sizes
- Capstone
- Type M mortar
- Rough-textured rag
- Work gloves

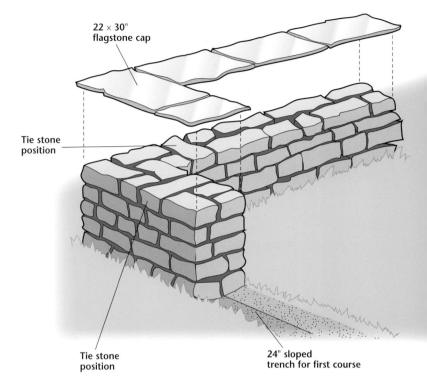

22 × 30" flagstone cap

Tie stone position

Tie stone position

24" sloped trench for first course

HOW TO BUILD A DRY STONE WALL

Step A: Dig the Trench

1. Sort the stones by size and purpose, placing them in piles near the building site.

2. Lay out the wall site with stakes and mason's string. Measure the diagonals to make sure the outline is square, and use a framing square to make sure the corners are square. Adjust if necessary.

3. Dig a 24"-wide trench, 4 to 6" deep, along the site. Create a slight "V" shape by sloping the sides toward the center. The center of the trench should be about 2" deeper than the sides.

Step B: Build the First Course

1. Lay pairs of shaping stones in two rows along the bottom of the trench. Position them flush with the edges of the trench and sloping toward the center. Use stones similar in height. If stones have uneven surfaces, position them with the uneven sides facing down.

A. Sort the stones by size and purpose. After planning the wall location, dig a V-shaped trench for the wall.

B. Lay the first course of shaping stones in the trench, adjusting them so that they slope toward each other. At corners, stagger the stones so the seams between stones are not aligned.

C. *Build up the corner two courses high, with tie stones across the width of each just before they meet. Lay the rest of the course, working from the corner to the end of the wall.*

D. *Add the third course of stone over the second using tie stones every 36", checking periodically with a level.*

E. *Once all the courses are in place, mortar the capstones to the top course of stone, then seal all the gaps between them.*

2. Form a corner by laying the last stone of the outer row so it covers the end of the stone in the outer row of the adjacent wall course. Lay the inner row in the same manner.

3. Fill any significant gaps between the shaping stones with filler stones.

Step C: Build Up the Corners

1. Lay the stones for the second course corner so they cover the joints of the first course corner. Use the same steps as forming the first course corner. Use stones that have long, square sides.

2. Build up the corner two courses high. Place tie stones across the width of each wall just before the corner.

3. Build the wall ends in this same way. Use stones of varying lengths so that each joint is covered by the stone above it.

4. Wedge filler stones into any large gaps.

Step D: Fill the Subsequent Courses

1. Lay the second course using shaping stones. Work from the corner to the end of the wall. Make sure to stagger the joints; stones of varying lengths will help offset them.

2. If necessary, shape or split the final stones of the course to size with a masonry saw or hand sledge and chisel. Carefully place the stones without disrupting the others.

3. For the third course, place tie stones every 36". Lay shaping stones between the tie stones and continue to place filler stones into any cracks on the surface or sides of the wall.

4. Continue laying courses, maintaining a consistent height along the wall and adding tie stones to every third course. Build up the corners first, and then build the courses with shaping stones, working from the corner to the end. Check for level as you go.

Step E: Set the Capstones

1. When the wall is approximately 36" high, check it for level.

2. Apply mortar to the center of the wall using a trowel. Keep the mortar at least 6" from the edges.

3. Center the capstones over the wall and set them as close together as possible.

4. Carefully fill the cracks between the capstones with mortar. Let any excess mortar dry until crumbly, then brush it off. After two or three days, scrub off any residue using water and a rough-textured rag.

VARIATION: SLOPES AND CURVES

If slope is an issue along your wall site, you can easily step a dry stone wall to accommodate it. The key is to keep the stones level so they won't shift or slide with the grade and to keep the first course below ground level. This means digging a stepped trench.

Lay out the wall site with stakes and mason's string. Dig a trench 4 to 6" deep along the entire site, including the slope. Mark the slope with stakes at the bottom where it starts and at the top where it ends.

Begin the first course along the straight-line section of the trench, leading up to the start of the slope. At the reference stake, dig into the slope so a pair of shaping stones will sit level with the rest of the wall.

To create the first step, excavate a new trench into the slope, so that the bottom is level with the top of the previous course. Dig into the slope the length of one-and-a-half stones. This will allow one pair of stones to be completely below the ground level and one pair to span the joint where the new trench and the stones in the course below meet.

Continue creating steps, to the top of the slope. Make sure each step of the trench section remains level with the course beneath. Then fill the courses, laying stones in the same manner as for a straight-line wall. Build to a maximum height of 36", and finish by stepping the top to match the grade change, or create a level top with the wall running into the slope.

If you'd like a curved wall or wall segment, lay out each curve. Then dig the trench as for a straight wall, sloping the sides into a slight "V" toward the center.

Lay the stones as for a straight wall, but use shorter stones; long, horizontal stones do not work as well for a tight curve. Lay the stones so they are tight together, off-setting the joints along the entire stretch. Be careful to keep the stone faces vertical to sustain the curve all the way up the height of the wall.

If the wall goes up or downhill, step the trench, the courses, and the top of the wall to keep the stones level.

To build a curved wall, lay out the curve using a string staked to a center point, and dig the trench and set stones as for a straight wall.

Mortared Stone Wall

The classic look of a mortared stone wall adds a sense of solidity and permanence to a landscape that nothing else can match. Although building a mortared wall takes more work than building a dry-laid one, in some cases the tailored look of mortared stone is just what's needed.

Plan and position your wall carefully—making changes requires a sledgehammer and a fair amount of sweat. Before you begin work, check local building codes for regulations regarding the size and depth of the footings as well as construction details. And remember, in most communities any building project that requires a footing requires a building permit.

Plan to make your wall no more than 18" wide. Purchase a generous supply of stone so that you have plenty to choose from as you fit the wall together. Laying stone is much like putting a jigsaw puzzle together, and the pieces must fit well enough that gravity and their weight—rather than the strength of the mortar—will hold the wall together. Your stone supplier can help you calculate the tonnage necessary for your project.

Add a mortared stone wall for a tailored, permanent structure that divides spaces clearly, yet maintains its organic appeal.

TOOLS & MATERIALS

- Tools & materials for pouring footings
- Stakes & string
- Line level
- Tape measure
- Wheelbarrow or mortar box
- Masonry chisel
- Chalk
- Mason's trowel
- Batter gauge
- 4-ft. level
- Jointing tool
- Stiff-bristle brush
- Stones of various shapes and sizes
- Type N mortar
- ⅜" wood shims
- Spray bottle

A. *Pour footings and let them cure. Dry-fit stones to follow the mason's string guides, staggering the joints (see page 84).*

HOW TO BUILD A MORTARED STONE WALL

Step A: Pour the Footings & Dry-fit the First Course

1. Plot the wall line with stakes and mason's string, then pour the footings. Let the concrete cure for 48 hours, then remove the forms and backfill around the footings. Let the footings cure for a week.

2. Sort the stones by size and shape. Set aside long, thin stones for tie stones. Using stakes, string, and a line level, set up a guide for the height of the first course of the wall.

3. Using larger stones, dry-fit the first course. Center a tie stone on the cement slab, extending from the front to the back. Lay out 3 to 4 ft. of the wall at a time, leaving ½ to ¾" between stones. Chisel or cut the stones as necessary.

4. Trace the outline on the footing with chalk. Remove the stones and set them aside, following the layout you have established.

Step B: Lay the First Course

1. Mix a batch of mortar, following manufacturer's directions. Mist the first 3 to 4 ft. of the footing with water, and then lay a 2"-thick mortar bed on the area.

2. Working along one side of the first course, set stones into the mortar bed. Wiggle each stone after you set it in place, then use the handle of a trowel to tap it down, just firmly enough to remove any air bubbles from the mortar bed.

3. Set the other side of the first course in the mortar bed. Fill the center with smaller stones and mortar; leave the center slightly lower than the outer edges. If you need to reposition a stone, wash off the mortar before resetting it.

4. Pack mortar between the stones, keeping the mortar about 1" from the face of the wall.

5. Continue setting 3 to 4 ft. of the wall at a time until you've completed the entire first course.

Step C: Add Successive Courses

1. Adjust the string and line level to indicate the height of the next course.

2. Dry-fit the second course, 3 to 4 ft. at a time; add a tie stone at the beginning of each section. Stagger the vertical joints by setting one stone over two and two over one.

3. Set the stones aside in the layout you have established. Lay a 2" bed of mortar over the first course, then replace the stones. Check the slope with a batter gauge, and use wood shims to support large stones so their weight doesn't displace the mortar. Keep the side relatively plumb, checking with a 4-ft. level.

4. When the mortar is set enough to resist light finger pressure (about 30 minutes), smooth the joints using a jointing tool. Keep the mortar 1" back from the faces of the stones. Remove the shims and fill the holes. Remove dry spattered mortar with a dry, stiff-bristle brush.

Step D: Add the Capstones

1. Create a level, 1"-thick mortar bed on top of the wall. Center flat stones over the wall and tap them into the mortar.

2. Fill the spaces between stones with mortar. Tool the joints when the mortar is dry enough to resist light finger pressure.

B. *Apply mortar to the footing and set the stones in position, according to the layout. If necessary, use wood shims to keep the stones in position.*

C. *Add courses, staggering the vertical joint. Fill between the two sides of the courses with smaller stones and mortar.*

D. *Center flat cap stones on top of the wall, setting them in a level bed of mortar.*

Stone Moon Window

You can build circular openings into brick or stone walls using a single semicircular wood form (page 113). Moon windows can be built to any dimension, although lifting and placing stones is more difficult as the project grows larger, while tapering stones to fit is a greater challenge as the circle gets smaller. To minimize the need for cutting and lifting stone, we built this window two feet in diameter atop an existing stone wall. Before doing this, you'll need to check with your local building inspector regarding restrictions on wall height, footings, and other design considerations. You may need to modify the dimensions to conform with the local building code.

Make sure to have at least one helper on hand. Building with stone is always physically demanding, and steps such as installing the brace and form require a helper.

TOOLS & MATERIALS

- Circular saw
- Drill
- Tape measure
- Level
- Mortar box
- Trowels
- Jointing tool or tuck-pointer
- Stone chisel
- Plywood (¼", ¾")
- Wallboard screws (1", 2")
- Tapered shims
- Lumber (2 × 4, 2 × 8)
- 4 × 4 posts
- Type M mortar (stiff mix)
- Ashlar stone
- Nails
- Chalk
- Mason's string
- Shims

Building a beautiful stone moon window isn't as difficult as you might think. With a semicircular wood form and good masonry skills, you can easily add this charming landscape feature to the stone walls in your yard.

HOW TO BUILD A STONE MOON WINDOW

Step A: Dry-lay the Stones

1. Build a plywood form, following the instructions on page 111.

2. For the top of the circle, select stones with sides that are squared off or slightly tapered.

3. Dry-lay the stones around the outside of the form, spacing them with shims that are roughly ¼" thick at their narrow end.

4. Number each stone and a corresponding point on the form, then set the stones aside.

5. Turn the form around and label a second set of stones for the bottom of the circle. Use letters to label the bottom set of stones instead of numbers to avoid confusion.

Step B: Set the First Stone

1. Prepare a stiff mix of Type M mortar.

2. Lay a ½"-thick mortar bed on top of the wall for the base of the circle. Center the stone that will be at the base of the circle in the mortar.

Step C: Build the Form Support

1. Construct a sturdy scaffold to hold the plywood arch form in place. Use pairs of 2 × 4s nailed together to create the legs and horizontal supports of the bracing structure (see diagram on right).

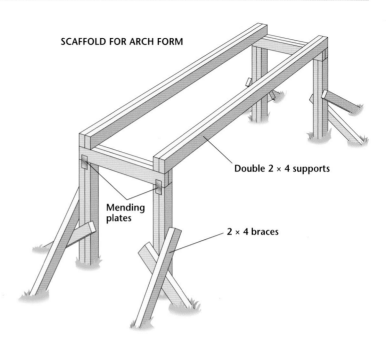

SCAFFOLD FOR ARCH FORM

Double 2 × 4 supports

Mending plates

2 × 4 braces

A. *Dry-lay the stones along the arch form using ¼" shims as spacers. Number the stones and the form at corresponding points.*

B. *Set the first stone in a ½"-thick mortar bed at the base of the window circle.*

C. *Build a 2 × 4 scaffold for the arch form. Position the form on the first stone, level the scaffold, and brace the legs with 2 × 4s.*

D. *Install the lower course of stones in a bed of mortar, building up the rest of the wall as you work. Check the alignment using a mason's line.*

E. *Invert the arch form, reattaching it so it will complete the top half of the window. Check to make sure it is level before fastening to the scaffold.*

2. Set the form on top of the stone at the base of the circle and check it for level in both directions. Adjust the braces as required.

3. Screw the braces to the form, so the edges are at least ¼" in from the edges of the form.

Step D: Lay the Lower Course

1. Extend the mortar bed along the wall and add stones. Butter one end of each stone, and tap them into place with a trowel. Keep the joint width consistent with the existing wall, but set the depth of new joints at about 1", to allow for tuck-pointing.

2. Attach mason's string at the center of the front and back of the form. Use the strings to check the alignment of each stone.

3. Stagger the joints as you build upward and outward. Alternate large and small stones for maximum strength and a natural look. Smooth joints that have hardened enough to resist minimal finger pressure.

4. Dress stones with large bumps or curves if necessary, so the sides are roughly squared off.

Step E: Position the Form for the Upper Course

1. Invert the form on the top of the wall in preparation for laying the top half of the circle. The bottom edge of the form should be set roughly ½" higher than the top of the lower half of the circle.

2. Check the braces for level (both lengthwise and widthwise). Adjust them as necessary, and reattach them to the posts.

Step F: Lay the Upper Course

1. Lay stones around the circle as for the lower course. Work from the bottom up and alternate from one side of the form to the other to balance the weight on the form. The top stone, or *keystone*, will be laid last.

2. If mortar oozes from the joints, insert temporary shims between joints. Remove the shims after two hours, and pack the voids with mortar.

3. Once the keystone is in place, smooth the remaining joints. Let the wall set up overnight, and then mist it several times a day for a week.

Step G: Tuck-point Inside of Circle

1. After a week, remove the form. Remove any excess mortar from the joints inside the circle.

2. Mist lightly, and then tuck-point all joints with stiff mortar so they are of equal depth.

3. Once the joints reach a putty-like consistency, tool them with a jointing tool. Let the mortar harden overnight. Mist the wall for five more days.

F. *Lay the stones around the circle, working from the bottom up, so the keystone is laid last. If necessary, use wood shims to prevent mortar from seeping out of the joints.*

G. *Mist the stones lightly and tuck-point each joint with stiff mortar, then tool them, using a jointing tool.*

Brick Garden Wall

Patience, care, and good technique are the key elements to building brick structures that have a professional look. Start with a sturdy, level footing, and don't worry if your initial bricklaying attempts aren't perfect. Survey your work often and stop when you spot a problem. As long as the mortar's still soft, you can remove bricks and try again.

This section features one method of brick wall construction: laying up the ends of the wall first, then filling in the interior bricks. Laying one course at a time is an alternate method that achieves excellent results.

TOOLS & MATERIALS

- Gloves
- Trowel
- Chalk line
- Level
- Line blocks
- Mason's string
- Jointing tool

- Mortar (Type S or N)
- Brick
- Wall ties
- Rebar (optional)
- ⅜"-diameter dowel

- Pencil
- Straightedge
- Circular saw
- Stiff-bristle brush
- Wall caps

Buttering is a term used to describe the process of applying mortar to the end of a brick or block before adding it to the structure being built. Apply a heavy layer of mortar to one end of a brick, then cut off the excess with a trowel.

MASON MIX CALCULATOR

Number of bags required to lay blocks ⅜" joint (9mm)

Number of Bricks (Standard)	30	50	75	100	180	250	400	800	1500
80-lb Bags (36.3 kg)	1	2	3	3	5	7	11	22	41

HOW TO BUILD A DOUBLE-WYTHE BRICK WALL

1. Dry-lay the first course by setting down two parallel rows of brick spaced ¾ to 1" apart. Use a chalk line to outline the location of the wall on the slab. Draw pencil lines on the slab to mark the end of each brick. Test-fit the spacing with a ⅜"-diameter dowel, then mark the locations of the joint gaps to use as a reference after the spacers are removed. See page 84 for preparing a poured footing for the wall.

2. Dampen the concrete slab or footing with water, and dampen the bricks or blocks if necessary. Mix mortar and place a layer of mortar onto the footing for the first two bricks of one wythe at one end of the layout. Butter the inside end of the first brick, then press the brick into the mortar, creating a ⅜" mortar bed. Cut away excess mortar.

3. Plumb the face of the end brick using a level. Tap lightly with the handle of the trowel to correct the brick if it is not plumb. Level the brick end to end. Butter the end of a second brick, then set it into the mortar bed, pushing the dry end toward the first brick to create a joint of ⅜".

4. Butter and place a third brick using the chalk lines as a general reference, then use a level to check for level and plumb. Adjust any bricks that are not aligned by tapping lightly with the trowel handle.

5. Lay the first three bricks for the other wythe parallel to the first wythe. Level the wythes, and make sure the end bricks and mortar joints align. Fill the gaps between the wythes at each end with mortar.

6. *Cut a half brick, then throw and furrow a mortar bed for a half brick on top of the first course. Butter the end of the half brick, then set the half brick in the mortar bed, creating a ⅜" joint. Cut away excess mortar. Make sure bricks are plumb and level.*

7. *Add more bricks and half bricks to both wythes at the end until you lay the first bricks in the fourth course. Align bricks with the reference lines. NOTE: To build corners, lay a header brick at the end of two parallel wythes. Position the header brick in each subsequent course perpendicular to the header brick in the previous course (INSET).*

8. *Check the spacing of the end bricks with a straightedge. Properly spaced bricks form a straight line when you place the straightedge over the stepped end bricks. If bricks are not in alignment, do not move those bricks already set. Try to compensate for the problem gradually as you fill in the middle (field) bricks (step 10) by slightly reducing or increasing the spacing between joints.*

9. *Every 30 minutes, stop laying bricks and prepare to smooth out all the untooled mortar joints with a jointing tool. Mortar joints should be smoothed when mortar is thumbprint hard. Do the horizontal joints first, then the vertical joints. Cut away any excess mortar pressed from the joints using a trowel. When the mortar has set but is not too hard, brush any excess mortar from the brick faces.*

Line block

10. *Build the opposite end of the wall with the same methods as the first using the chalk lines as a reference. Stretch a mason's string between the two ends to establish a flush, level line between ends—use line blocks to secure the string. Pull the string until it is taut. Begin to fill in the field bricks (the bricks between ends) on the first course using the mason's string as a guide.*

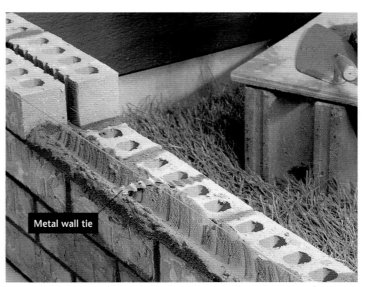

11. Lay the remaining field bricks. The last brick, called the closure brick, should be buttered at both ends. Center the closure brick between the two adjoining bricks, then set in place with the trowel handle. Fill in the first three courses of each wythe, moving the mason's string up one course after completing each course.

12. In the fourth course, embed metal wall ties into the mortar bed of one wythe and on top of the brick adjacent to it. Space the ties 2 to 3 ft. apart, every three courses. For added strength, set metal rebar into the cavities between the wythes and fill with thin mortar.

13. Lay the remaining courses, installing metal ties every third course. Check with mason's string frequently for alignment, and use a level to make sure the wall is plumb and level.

14. Lay a furrowed mortar bed on the top course, and place a wall cap on top of the wall to cover empty spaces and provide a finished appearance. Remove any excess mortar. Make sure the cap blocks are aligned and level. Fill the joints between cap blocks with mortar.

Basic Gates

If you understand the basic elements of gate construction, you can build a sturdy gate to suit almost any situation. The gates shown here illustrate the fundamental elements of a well-built gate.

To begin with, adequate distribution of the gate's weight is critical to its operation. Because the posts bear most of a gate's weight, they're set at least 12" deeper than fence posts. Or, depending on building codes in your area, they may need to be set below the frost line in substantial concrete footings.

However they're set, the posts must be plumb. A sagging post can be reinforced by attaching a sag rod at the top of the post and running it diagonally to the lower end of the next post. Tighten the knuckle in the middle until the post is properly aligned. A caster can be used with heavy gates over smooth surfaces to assist with the weight load.

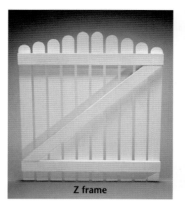

Z frame

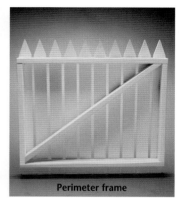

Perimeter frame

Build your own gate *to blend in with or complement your home's exterior. A gate is not only a charming addition, it also can alert you that visitors are arriving or keep pets and kids in the yard.*

The frame also plays an important part in properly distributing the gate's weight. The two basic gate frames featured here are the foundation for many gate designs. A Z-frame gate is ideal for a light, simple gate. This frame consists of a pair of horizontal braces with a diagonal brace running between them. A perimeter-frame gate is necessary for a heavier or more elaborate gate. It employs a solid, four-cornered frame with a diagonal brace.

In both styles, the diagonal brace must run from the bottom of the hinge side to the top of the latch side, to provide support and keep the gate square.

There are a multitude of hinge, latch, and handle styles available. Whichever you choose, purchase the largest hinges available that are in proportion with your gate and a latch or handle appropriate for the gate's purpose.

TOOLS & MATERIALS

- Tape measure
- Level
- Framing square
- Circular saw
- Paintbrush
- Drill
- Spring clamps

- Jigsaw
- Combination square
- Pressure-treated lumber as needed (1 × 2, 2 × 4)
- Paint, stain, or sealer
- Hinge hardware

- Gate handle or latch
- Galvanized deck screws (2", 2½")
- Hammer and nails
- Fence siding
- Wood scraps

A. *Make sure the gate posts are plumb, then measure the distance between them and calculate the dimensions of the gate.*

HOW TO BUILD A Z-FRAME GATE
Step A: Calculate the Width & Cut the Braces

1. Check both gate posts on adjacent sides for plumb, using a level. If a post is not plumb, reinforce it with a sag rod. When both posts are plumb, measure the opening between them.

2. Consult the packaging on your hinge and latch hardware for the clearance necessary between the frame and gate posts. Subtract this figure from the measurement of the opening. The result will be the finished width of the gate. Cut 2 × 4s to this length for the frame's horizontal braces.

3. Paint, stain, or seal the lumber for the frame as well as the siding for the gate, and let it dry completely.

Step B: Attach the Diagonal Brace

1. On the fence, measure the distance from the bottom of the upper stringer to the top of the lower stringer. Cut two pieces of scrap 2 × 4 to this length to use as temporary supports.

2. Lay out the frame on a flat work surface placing the temporary supports between the braces. Square the corners of the frame using a framing square.

3. Place a 2 × 4 diagonally from one end of the lower brace across to the opposite end of the upper brace. Mark and cut the brace, using a circular saw.

4. Remove the temporary supports, and toenail the brace into position using 2½" galvanized deck screws.

B. *Place a 2 × 4 diagonally across the temporary frame, from the lower corner of the hinge side to the upper corner of the latch side, and mark the cutting lines.*

C. Align the end boards of the siding flush with the edge of the frame and attach with screws. Using a spacer, position and attach the remaining siding to the frame.

D. Shim the gate into place. Mark the position of the hardware on the gate and gate posts, drill pilot holes, and attach the hardware.

Step C: Apply the Siding

1. Position the frame so the diagonal brace runs from the bottom of the hinge side to the top of the latch side, then plan the layout of the siding to match the position and spacing of the fence siding. If the final board needs to be trimmed, divide the difference and trim two boards instead. Use these equally trimmed boards as the first and last pieces of siding.

2. Clamp a scrap 2 × 4 flush against the bottom brace as a placement guide. Align the first and last boards, flush with the ends of the braces. Attach these two boards to the horizontal braces using pairs of 2" galvanized deck screws.

3. Attach the rest of the siding, using spacers as necessary.

Step D: Hang the Gate

1. Shim the gate into position and make sure it will swing freely. Remove the gate.

2. Measure and mark the hinge positions on the gate. Drill pilot holes, and secure the hinges to the gate using the screws provided with the hardware.

3. If your latch hardware doesn't include a catch, add a stop on the latch-side post. Clamp a 1 × 2 in place, then shim the gate back into position, centered within the opening. Use a level to make sure that the gate is level and plumb and that the stop is properly positioned. Drill pilot holes and secure the stop to the post using 2" galvanized deck screws.

4. With the gate shimmed into position, mark the hinge-side post to indicate the hinge screw locations, then drill pilot holes. Fasten the hinges to the post, using the screws provided with the hardware.

5. Install the latch hardware to the opposite gate post and the catch to the gate, according to the manufacturer's instructions.

HOW TO BUILD A PERIMETER FRAME GATE

Step A: Build the Gate Frame

1. Determine the gate width and cut the horizontal braces, as for a Z-frame gate (page 155, Step A).

2. On the fence line, measure the distance from the bottom of the upper stringer to the top of the lower stringer. Cut two pieces of 2 × 4 to this length for the vertical braces.

3. Paint, stain, or seal the lumber for the gate and siding, then let it dry thoroughly.

4. Position the pieces of the frame and measure from one corner to the diagonally opposite corner. Repeat at the opposite corners. Adjust the pieces until these measurements are equal, which indicates that the frame is square. Secure each joint using 2½" galvanized deck screws.

Step B: Attach the Diagonal Brace

1. Position the frame on a 2 × 4 set on edge, running diagonally from the lower corner of the hinge-side to the opposite latch-side corner. Support the frame with 2 × 4 scraps underneath the opposing corners, if necessary.

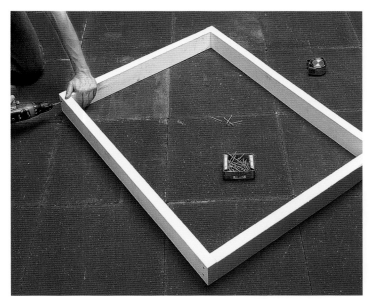

A. *Determine the lengths of the horizontal and vertical braces of the frame. Lay out the frame, check it for square, and secure the joints with 2½" galvanized deck screws.*

B. *Scribe the opposite corners of the frame on the 2 × 4 diagonal brace. Cut the brace, using a circular saw with the blade adjusted for the appropriate bevel angle. Toenail the brace in place.*

2. Make sure the frame is square, and scribe the corners of the frame on the board. Transfer the cut marks to the face of the 2 × 4, using a combination square. Cut with a circular saw, making sure to set the saw blade to the appropriate bevel angle.

3. Toenail the brace into position using 2½" galvanized deck screws.

Step C: Attach the Siding

1. Lay out the siding on the frame, making sure that the diagonal brace runs up from the bottom hinge-side corner to the opposite top latch-side corner. Use wood scraps the same width as the gaps between the pickets in the fence for spacing. If a board must be ripped to fit, divide the difference and rip the first and last boards to the same width.

2. Measure down from the top of the first and last boards and mark the height they will rise above the upper horizontal brace. Align the boards flush with the edges of the vertical braces, with the reference marks meeting the top edge of the upper horizontal brace. Attach each end board to each horizontal brace with 2" galvanized deck screws.

3. Clamp a scrap 2 × 4 flush against the bottom of the end boards as a guide. Align the rest of the siding with the scraps used for spacing. Attach each board with 2" galvanized nails.

4. Paint, stain, or seal the gate and allow it to dry thoroughly. Mount the hardware and hang the gate as you would a Z-frame gate (page 154, Step D).

C. *Secure the first and last siding boards to the frame, aligning them flush with the edges. Using scrap wood as spacers, attach the remaining siding.*

Chain Link Gate

Chain link fences are usually installed more for practical reasons than for aesthetic ones and that is reflected in the appearance of both the fencing and the gates. Like their counterpart fencing, chain link gates are very easy to install once you understand how the pieces fit together.

If you are installing a brand new chain link fence, start with the gate if you can. Set the gate post in a belled concrete footing, making sure it is level and plumb. You can set the fence post at the other side of the gate post at the same time, or you may choose to wait until you've hung the gate so you know precisely where to locate the post. Then, once the gate is installed, you can install the chain link fence to go with it (the section showing how to install chain link fencing is on pages 104 to 107).

You'll find a fair number of design choices if you buy from a fencing contractor or fencing supplier. The fencing contractor can custom-build a gate if you'd like, too—ask them to show you some samples of their work. If you shop at a large building center, you'll be lucky to find more than a small handful of options.

The most important consideration when choosing a chain link gate is that the gate should match the color and style of the chain link fabric in the fence, as with this black-coated chain link.

HOW TO INSTALL A CHAIN LINK GATE

1. Set fence posts in concrete spaced far enough apart to allow for the width of the gate plus required clearance for the latch. Position the female hinges on the gate frame as far apart as possible. Secure with nuts and bolts (orient nuts toward the inside of the fence).

2. Set the gate on the ground in the gate opening, next to the gate post. Mark the positions of the female hinges onto the gate post. Remove the gate and measure up 2" from each hinge mark on the gate post. Make new reference marks for the male hinges.

3. Secure the bottom male hinge to the gate post with nuts and bolts. Slide the gate onto the bottom hinge. Then, lock the gate in with the downward-facing top hinge.

4. Test the swing of the gate and adjust the hinge locations and orientations, if needed, until the gate operates smoothly and the opposite side of the gate frame is parallel to the other fence post. Tighten the hinge nuts securely.

5. Attach the gate latch to the free side of the gate frame, near the top of the frame. Test to make sure the latch and gate function correctly. If you need to relocate a post because the opening is too large or too small, choose the latch post, not the gate post.

Trellis Gate

This trellis gate is a grand welcome to any yard. But don't let its ornate appearance fool you—the simple components create an impression far beyond the skills and materials involved in its construction.

This gate is best suited to a location where it will receive plenty of sunlight to ensure an abundant canopy of foliage. Choose perennials rather than annuals, since they will produce more luxurious growth over time. Heirloom roses are a good choice, providing a charming complement to the gate's old-fashioned look and air of elegance.

Larger, traditional styles of hardware that showcase well against the painted wood will also enhance the gate's impressive presentation. The hardware and the millwork that we used are available at most building centers, but you might want to check architectural salvage shops. They may have unique styles that add another touch of character to the piece.

As with most of our projects, you can alter the dimensions of this project to fit an existing opening. Just recalculate the materials and cutting lists, and make sure you have enough lumber to accommodate the changes.

With a few simple, cleverly utilized components, you can build this impressive entryway to your home without overwhelming time or expense.

TOOLS & MATERIALS

- Tape measure
- Circular saw
- Paintbrush
- Bar clamps
- Drill
- Carpenter's level
- Framing square
- Jigsaw
- Spring clamps
- Pressure-treated lumber
  (see Cutting List)
- Paint, stain, or sealer
- Galvanized deck screws
  (1¼", 1½", 2", 2½")
- Stakes & string
- 24" pressure-treated stakes (4)
- Galvanized lag screws (2", 3")
- Cardboard or posterboard
- Sandpaper
- Victorian millwork brackets (4)
- Galvanized 6d finish nails
- Hinge hardware
- Gate handle
- Flexible PVC pipe
- ⅝"-thick plywood scraps
  (for spacers)
- Pencil

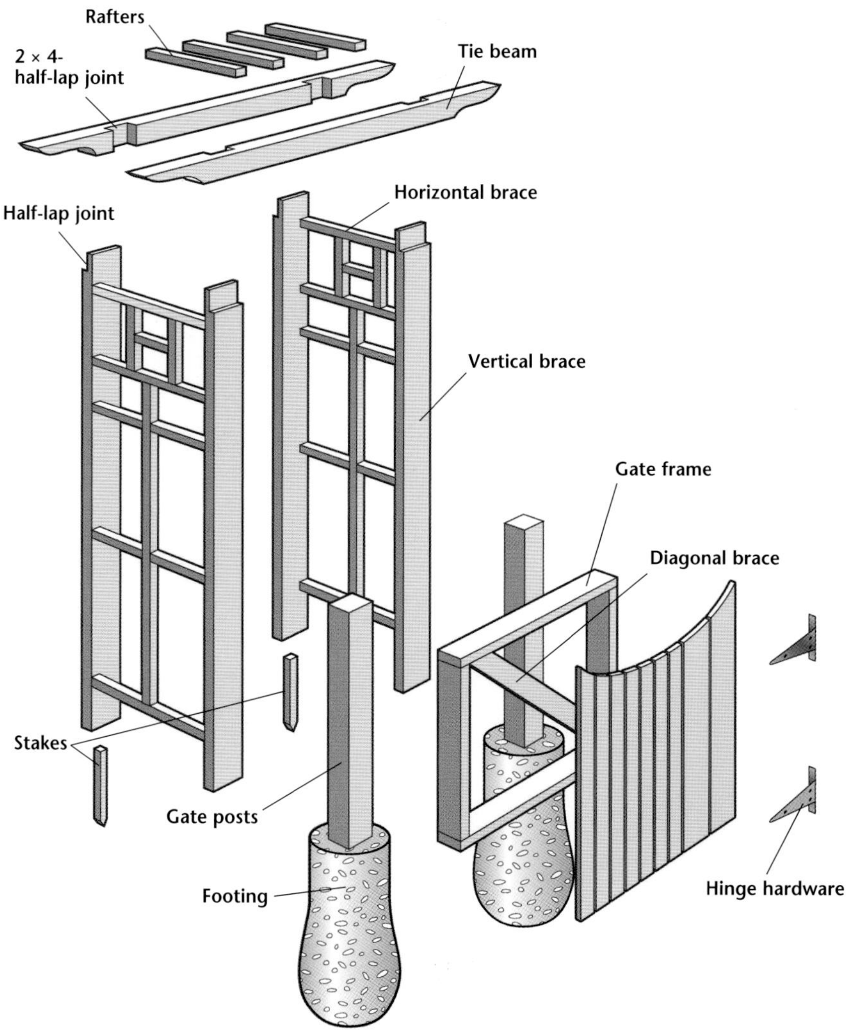

Cutting List

Part	Type	Length	Number
Frames			
Horizontal braces	2 × 2	12"	2
	2 × 2	15¾"	8
	2 × 2	33"	6
Vertical braces	2 × 2	17"	4
	2 × 2	54½"	2
	2 × 4	87½"	4
Stop	1 × 2	46½"	1
Top			
Tie beams	2 × 4	72¾"	2
Rafters	2 × 2	33"	4
Gate			
Horizontal braces	2 × 4	40½"	2
Vertical braces	2 × 4	32¾"	2
Diagonal brace	2 × 4	49½"	1
Siding	1 × 4	45¼"	7
	1 × 6	45¼"	2

Rafters · 2 × 4-half-lap joint · Tie beam · Half-lap joint · Horizontal brace · Vertical brace · Gate frame · Diagonal brace · Stakes · Gate posts · Footing · Hinge hardware

A. *Cut and lay out the pieces for each side of the trellis frame, then secure each joint with 2½" galvanized deck screws.*

HOW TO BUILD A TRELLIS GATE
Step A: Assemble the Trellis Frames

1. Measure the opening between the gate posts and determine the finished size of your gate and trellis. Compare your dimensions to the ones in the Cutting List on page 159 and make any necessary adjustments. (The tie beams for the trellis should be about 32" longer than the width of the gate.) Cut the lumber for the trellis and gate.

2. Paint, stain, or seal the pieces on all sides and edges. Let them dry thoroughly.

3. Lay out one side of the trellis, following the diagram on page 159. Mark the cutting lines and cut the joints, then set the frame back together. When you're satisfied with the layout and sure the frame is square, secure the joints using two 2½" galvanized deck screws in each joint.

4. Repeat #2 and #3 to build the remaining trellis frame.

Step B: Anchor the Frame to the Gate Posts

1. Referring to the diagram on page 159 and to your own gate measurements, mark the positions of the trellis frame on the ground, using stakes and string. Make sure the layout is square

B. *Position the trellis frames, clamping them against the gate posts. Attach the frame to the posts with 3" galvanized lag screws.*

C. *Square the trellis frames, then secure the free end of each frame to stakes using 2" galvanized lag screws.*

by measuring from corner to corner and adjusting the stakes until these diagonal measurements are equal.

2. Set one trellis frame into position, with the inside face of the frame flush with the inside face of the gate post. Drive a 24" pressure-treated stake behind the opposite side of the frame to hold the trellis in position. Drill three evenly spaced pilot holes through the frame and into the gate post. Attach the frame to the post using 3" galvanized lag screws.

3. Repeat #1 and #2 to attach the other trellis frame to the opposite post.

Step C: Secure the Free Sides of the Frames

1. Check the position of the free sides of the frames and measure the diagonals to ensure that the layout is square.

2. Clamp each frame to its stake and check the frame for level. Adjust as necessary. When the trellis frame is level, drill pilot holes and attach the frames to the stakes using 2" lag screws.

Step D: Install the Tie Beams

1. Using the grid method or a photocopier, enlarge the pattern at right, and transfer it to a large piece of cardboard. Cut out the pattern, then trace the shape onto the ends of each 2 × 4 tie beam.

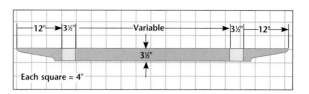

2. Cut the beams to shape using a jigsaw. Mark and cut the lap joints as described in step A. Sand the cut surfaces, then touch them up with paint, stain, or sealer, and let them dry.

3. Position a tie beam flush with the top of the post. Clamp the beam into place and drill pilot holes through it and into each post. Drive five 1½" galvanized deck screws into each joint to attach the tie beam to the posts.

4. Repeat #2 and #3 to install the remaining tie beam.

Step E: Attach the Rafters

Hold a 2 × 2 in position between the tie beams, flush with the tops of the beams and centered between the ends of the trellis

D. *Cut 2 × 4s using the grid pattern for tie beams. Dado each to accommodate the trellis frame post tops, then clamp into position and attach with five 1½" galvanized deck screws at each joint.*

E. *Attach four evenly spaced 2 × 2s between the tie beams for rafters using 2½" galvanized deck screws.*

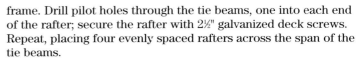

frame. Drill pilot holes through the tie beams, one into each end of the rafter; secure the rafter with 2½" galvanized deck screws. Repeat, placing four evenly spaced rafters across the span of the tie beams.

Step F: Add the Trim

Set a millwork bracket into place at each of the corners between the tie beams and the trellis frame posts. Drill pilot holes and secure the brackets using finish nails.

Step G: Build the Gate Frame

1. Lay out the parts of the gate frame and measure from one corner to the diagonally opposite corner. Repeat at the opposite corners. Adjust the pieces until these measurements are equal and the frame is square. Secure each joint using 2½" galvanized deck screws.

2. Position a 2 × 4 so that it runs from the bottom of the hinge side of the frame to the first horizontal brace on the latch side. Mark the angle of the cutting lines, then cut the brace to fit using a circular saw. Use 2½" galvanized deck screws to secure the brace into position.

F. Add millwork brackets at each corner where the tie beams and the trellis frame posts meet. Secure with finish nails.

G. Lay out the gate frame pieces, check for square, and secure the joints with 2½" galvanized deck screws. Mark and cut the brace, then screw it in place using 2½" galvanized deck screws.

H. Clamp a 2 × 4 across the bottom of the gate frame as a guide, then attach the siding. Begin with two 1 × 6s on the hinge side, then finish with 1 × 4s. Use scraps of ⅜" plywood as spacers.

Step H: Add the Siding

1. Clamp a 2 × 4 across the bottom of the frame to act as a reference for the length of the pickets. Position the siding flush with the lower edge of the clamped 2 × 4.

2. Align the right edge of a 1 × 6 flush with the right edge of the frame. Drill pilot holes and attach the siding to the frame using 1½" galvanized deck screws.

3. Set scraps of ⅝" plywood in place as spacers, then add a second 1 × 6. Continuing to use the ⅝" plywood as spacers, cover the remainder of the frame with 1 × 4 siding.

Step I: Hang the Gate

1. Measure and mark the hinge positions on the gate. Drill pilot holes and drive screws to secure the hinges to the gate.

2. On the handle-side post, clamp a 1 × 2 in place to act as a stop for the gate. Shim the gate into position, centered within the opening. Use a carpenter's level to make sure that the gate is level and plumb and that the stop is properly positioned. Mark the position of the stop and set the gate aside. Drill pilot holes and secure the stop to the post using 2½" galvanized deck screws.

3. With the gate shimmed back into position, mark the hinge-side post to indicate the hinge screw locations, then drill pilot holes. Fasten the hinges to the post, using the screws provided with the hinge hardware.

Step J: Shape the Siding & Add the Gate Handle

1. Cut a piece of flexible PVC pipe 52½" long (or 12" longer than the width of your gate). Clamp the PVC pipe at the top of the outside edges of the last piece of siding on each side of the gate.

2. Tack a nail just above the first horizontal brace of the frame at the center of the gate. If this happens to be between two pieces of siding, set a scrap behind the siding to hold the nail. Adjust the PVC pipe until it fits just below the nail and creates a pleasing curve.

3. Trace the curve of the PVC pipe onto the face of the siding. Remove the pipe and cut along the marked line using a jigsaw. Sand the tops of the siding and repair the finish as necessary.

4. Mark the handle location on the gate. Drill pilot holes and secure the handle using the screws provided by the manufacturer.

I. Clamp a 1 × 2 to the latch-side gate post and secure with 1½" galvanized deck screws.

J. Clamp the ends of a length of PVC pipe at each end of the gate top. Deflect the pipe down to create the curve and trace. Cut to shape using a jigsaw.

Decks

A deck is the perfect way to create a comfortable and practical outdoor living space, whether for cookouts with family and friends or time alone with a cup of coffee and the Sunday paper.

A great deck design makes the best possible use of available outdoor space while meshing gracefully with the beauty and functionality of your home. Decks provide options for almost every space configuration—from wraparound decks that take advantage of small yards by using the space surrounding the house, to detached decks located anywhere in the yard.

This section begins with important information on working with your local building officials and codes to prepare you for obtaining a building permit before you begin construction.

Next, you will find basic deck building techniques showing you how to lay out and install the deck you have designed on paper. Step-by-step instructions explain how to build each component of a basic deck: ledgers, footings, posts, beams, joists, decking, stairs, and railings. The specific tools and materials required for each of these techniques are listed. Also, information regarding the recent trends in alternative decking materials, such as plastic/wood composites and PVC vinyl, are discussed, complete with full how-to steps.

Everything is here to help you design, plan, and build a cost-effective deck that will provide years of enjoyment. All you have left to do now is choose from one of the seven popular designs included here and begin planning your new deck.

IN THIS CHAPTER:

- **Basic Techniques**
  - *Construction Codes*
  - *Determining Lumber Size*
  - *Understanding Loads*
  - *Step-by-Step Overview*
  - *Installing a Ledger*
  - *Locating Post Footings*
  - *Digging & Pouring Footings*
  - *Installing Flashing*
  - *Installing Posts*
  - *Installing Beams*
  - *Hanging Joists*
  - *Laying Decking*
- *Building Stairs*
- *Installing Railings*
  - *Composite Railing*
  - *Glass-panel Railing*
  - *Steel Cable Railing*
  - *Fasteners & Hardware*
- Second-story Walkout Deck
- Ground-level Walkout Deck
- Casual Curve Deck
- Wraparound Deck
- Low-profile Deck
- Platform Deck
- Multi-level Deck

Basic Techniques

Construction Codes

Most decks are relatively simple structures, but even a basic deck project must conform to the requirements of building codes in your area. In fact, virtually every aspect of your new deck—from its location on your property to the design you choose and the materials you buy to build it—all must meet stringent guidelines for safety. Codes vary to some degree from state to state, but they are based on general regulations established by the International Residential Code. Your local building inspector can provide you with a list of the relevant deck codes and help you interpret them so you can create code-compliant plans for your deck project. You may also want to download a free PDF copy of the "Prescriptive Residential Deck Construction Guide" (see Resources, page 523).

The next few pages will provide a survey of some of the more common code requirements for decks, although it is by no means comprehensive. Use this section as a way to familiarize yourself with the code requirements you will probably face as you plan and build your new deck.

Footing diameter and depth is determined by your building official, based on the estimated load of the deck and on the composition of your soil. In regions with cold winters, footings must extend below the frost line. Minimum diameter for concrete footings is 8".

Metal flashings must be used to prevent moisture from penetrating between the ledger and the wall.

Beams may overhang posts by no more than 1 ft. Some local building regulations require that, wherever possible, beams should rest on top of posts, secured with metal post-beam caps.

Engineered beams, such as a laminated wood product or steel girder, should be used on decks with very long joist spans, where standard dimension lumber is not adequate for the load. Engineered beams for decks must be rated for exterior use.

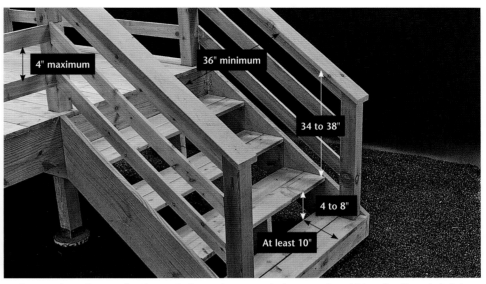

Railings are usually required by local codes for decks more than 30" above the ground and must usually be at least 36" in height. Bottom rails must be positioned with no more than 4" of open space below them. Balusters, whether vertical or horizontal, can be spaced no more than 4" apart.

Stairs must be at least 36" wide. Vertical step risers must be between 4 and 8" and uniform in height within a staircase. Treads must have a horizontal run of at least 10" and be uniform in size within a staircase. Stair railings should be 34 to 38" above the noses of the step treads, and there should be no more than 6" of space between the bottom rail and the steps. The space between the rails or balusters should be no more than 4".

Code violation. The International Building Code no longer allows joists to straddle the sides of a post fastened with through bolts, as shown here. It no longer endorses structural posts made of 4 × 4 lumber: 6 × 6 is the minimum size. Railing posts may be 4 × 4.

Beam assemblies. Deck beams made of 2× lumber must be fastened together with staggered rows of 10d galvanized common nails or #10 wood screws. If the wood components that make up the beam are spliced together, stagger the splices and locate them over beams for added strength.

167

Post-to-beam attachment. *Deck posts, regardless of length or size of deck, should be made of minimum 6 × 6 structural lumber. Notch the posts so that beams can bear fully in the notch, and attach them with pairs of ½-in.-dia. galvanized through bolts and washers. Or, you can mount beams on top of posts with galvanized post cap hardware.*

Ledgers and rim joists. *When a ledger is fastened to a rim joist, the house siding must be removed prior to installation. Either ½-in.-dia. lag screws or through-bolts with washers can be used to make the connections.*

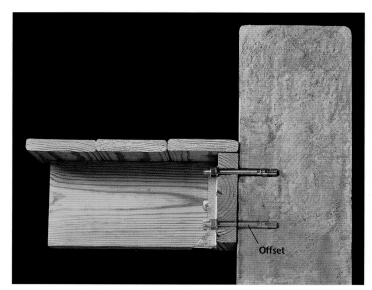

Offset

Ledgers and concrete walls. *Ledgers fastened to solid concrete must be attached with bolts and washers driven into approved expansion, epoxy, or adhesive anchors.*

Ledgers and block walls. *When fastening ledgers to hollow concrete block walls, the block cells in the ledger attachment areas must be filled with concrete or grout. Secure the attachment bolts to the wall with approved epoxy anchors with washers.*

No notched railing posts. *Code no longer allows deck railing posts to be notched where they attach to the deck rim joists. Railing posts should be fastened to rim joists with pairs of ½-in.-dia. through bolts and washers. In some cases, hold-down anchor hardware may also be required.*

Stair lighting. *Deck stairs must be illuminated at night from a light located at the top of the landing. The light can be switch-controlled from inside the house, motion-controlled, or used in conjunction with a timer switch.*

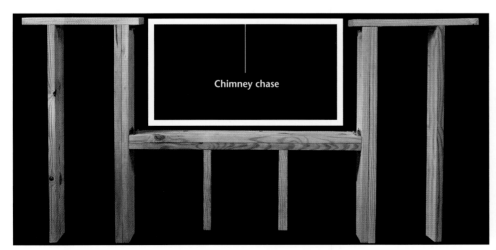

Chimney chase

Chimney chases & bays. *When framing a deck around a chimney or bay window, a suitable double header must be added where the ledger is spliced to accommodate the obstruction. The header can span a maximum of 6 ft.*

Rim joist connections. *Attach rim joists to the end of each joist with five #10 (3" min.) wood screws. Secure decking to the top of rim joists with #10 × 3-in. minimum wood screws, spaced every 6 in.*

Determining Lumber Size

A deck has seven major structural parts: the ledger, decking, joists, one or more beams, posts, stairway stringers, and stairway treads. To create a working design plan and choose the correct lumber size, you must know the span limits of each part of the deck. The ledger is attached directly to the house and does not have a span limit.

A span limit is the safe distance a board can cross without support from underneath. The maximum safe span depends on the size and wood species of the board. For example, 2×6 southern pine joists spaced 16" on-center can safely span 9'9", while 2×10 joists can span 16'1".

Begin planning by first choosing the size and pattern for the decking. Use the tables on the opposite page. Then determine the size and layout of the joists and beams, using the information and span tables on page 171. In general, a deck designed with larger-size lumber, like 2×12 joists and beams, requires fewer pieces because the boards have a large span limit. Finally, choose the stair and railing lumber that fits your plan, again using the tables on the opposite page.

Use the design plans to make a complete list of the quantities of each lumber size your deck requires. Add 10 percent to compensate for lumber flaws and construction errors. Full-service lumberyards have a fine lumber selection, but prices may be higher than those at home improvement centers. The quality of lumber at home centers can vary, so inspect the wood and hand-pick the pieces you want or add a larger percentage to compensate for lumber flaws. Both lumberyards and home centers will deliver lumber for a small fee, and you can usually return unused, uncut lumber if you keep your receipts.

Meet or exceed all lumber size codes. For example, use lumber that is at least 6 × 6" for all deck posts, regardless of the size of the deck or the length of the post.

DIMENSION & SPAN LIMIT TABLES FOR DECK LUMBER

Nominal vs. Actual Lumber Dimensions: *When planning a deck, remember that the actual size of lumber is smaller than the nominal size by which lumber is sold. Use the actual dimensions when drawing a deck design plan.*

Nominal	Actual
1 × 4	¾" × 3¾"
1 × 6	¾" × 5¾"
2 × 4	1½" × 3½"
2 × 6	1½" × 5½"
2 × 8	1½" × 7¼"
2 × 10	1½" × 9¼"
2 × 12	1½" × 11¼"
4 × 4	3½" × 3½"
6 × 6	5¼" × 5¼"

Recommended Decking Span Between Joists: *Decking boards can be made from a variety of lumber sizes. For a basic deck use 2 × 4 or 2 × 6 lumber with joists spaced 16" apart.*

Decking Boards	Recommended Span
1 × 4 or 1 × 6, laid straight	16"
1 × 4 or 1 × 6, laid diagonal	12"
2 × 4 or 2 × 6, laid straight	16"
2 × 4 or 2 × 6, laid diagonal	12"
2 × 4, laid on edge	24"

Minimum Stair Stringer Sizes: *Size of stair stringers depends on the span of the stairway. For example, if the bottom of the stairway lies 7 feet from the deck, build the stringers from 2 × 12s. Stringers should be spaced no more than 36" apart. Use of a center stringer is recommended for stairways with more than three steps.*

Span of Stairway	Stringer Size
Up to 6 ft.	2 × 10
More than 6 ft.	2 × 12

Recommended Railing Sizes: *Sizes of posts, rails, and caps depend on the spacing of the railing posts. For example, if railing posts are spaced 6 feet apart, use 4 × 4 posts and 2 × 6 rails and caps.*

Space Between Railing Posts	Post Size	Cap Size	Rail Size
2 to 3 ft.	2 × 4	2 × 4	2 × 4
3 to 4 ft.	4 × 4	2 × 4	2 × 4
4 to 6 ft.	4 × 4	2 × 6	2 × 6

CHART 1: MAXIMUM SPANS FOR VARIOUS JOIST SIZES

Size	Southern Pine			Ponderosa Pine			Western Cedar		
	12" OC	16" OC	24" OC	12" OC	16" OC	24" OC	12" OC	16" OC	24" OC
2 × 6	10 ft. 9"	9 ft. 9"	8 ft. 6"	9 ft. 2"	8 ft. 4"	7 ft. 0"	9 ft. 2"	8 ft. 4"	7 ft. 3"
2 × 8	14 ft. 2"	12 ft. 10"	11 ft. 0"	12 ft. 1"	10 ft. 10"	8 ft. 10"	12 ft. 1"	11 ft. 0"	9 ft. 2"
2 × 10	18 ft. 0"	16 ft. 1"	13 ft. 5"	15 ft. 4"	13 ft. 3"	10 ft. 10"	15 ft. 5"	13 ft. 9"	11 ft. 3"
2 × 12	21 ft. 9"	19 ft. 0"	15 ft. 4"	17 ft. 9"	15 ft. 5"	12 ft. 7"	18 ft. 5"	16 ft. 5"	13 ft. 0"

Understanding Loads

The supporting structural members of a deck—the posts, beams, and joists—must be sturdy enough to easily support the heaviest anticipated load on the deck. They must not only carry the substantial weight of the surface decking and railings, but also the weight of people, deck furnishings, and, in some climates, snow.

The charts and diagrams shown here will help you plan a deck so the size and spacing of the structural members are sufficient to support the load, assuming normal use. These recommendations are followed in most regions, but you should still check with your local building official for regulations that are unique to your area. In cases where the deck will support a hot tub or pool, you must consult your local building inspections office for load guidelines.

When choosing lumber for the structural members of your deck, select the diagram below that best matches your deck design, then follow the advice for applying the charts on the opposite page. Since different species of wood have different strengths, make sure to use the entries that match the type of lumber sold by your building center. When selecting the size for concrete footings, make sure to consider the composition of your soil; dense soils require footings with a larger diameter.

Post-and-beam or notched-post deck: Using Chart 1, determine the proper size for your joists, based on the on-center (OC) spacing between joists and the overall length, or span, of the joists (A). For example, if you will be using southern pine joists to span a 12-foot distance, you can use 2 × 8 lumber spaced no more than 16" apart, or 2 × 10 lumber spaced no more than 24" apart. Once you have determined allowable joist sizes, use Chart 2 to determine an appropriate beam size, post spacing, and footing size for your deck.

Cantilevered deck: Use the distance from the ledger to the beam (A) to determine minimum joist size, and use A + (2 × B) when choosing beam and footing sizes. For example, if your deck measures 9 ft. from ledger to beam, with an additional 3-ft. cantilevered overhang, use 9 ft. to choose a joist size from Chart 1 (2 × 6 southern pine joists spaced 16" apart, or 2 × 8 joists spaced 24" apart). Then, use A + (2 × B), or 15 ft., to find an appropriate beam size, post spacing, and footing size from Chart 2. NOTE: If your deck cantilevers more than 18" beyond the support beam, add 1" to the recommended diameter for footings.

Multiple-beam deck: Use distance A or B, whichever is larger, when determining joist size from Chart 1. For example, if your deck measures 8 ft. to beam #1 and another 4 ft. to beam #2, you can use 2 × 6 southern pine joists. Referring to Chart 2, use the total distance A + B to determine the size of beam #1, the spacing for the posts, and the size of the footings. Use joist length B to determine the size of beam #2, the post spacing, and footing size. For example, with an overall span of 12 ft. (8 ft. to the first beam, 4 ft. to the second), beam #1 could be made from two southern pine 2 × 8s; beam #2, from two 2 × 6s.

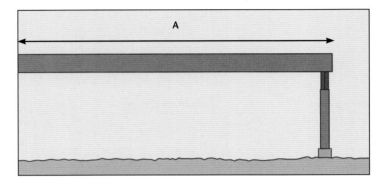

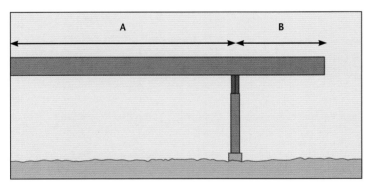

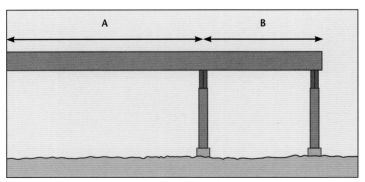

CHART 2: DIAMETERS FOR POST FOOTINGS (INCHES)

Joist Length		Post Spacing								
		4'	5'	6'	7'	8'	9'	10'	11'	12'
6'	Southern Pine Beam	1–2 × 6	1–2 × 6	1–2 × 6	2–2 × 6	2–2 × 6	2–2 × 6	2–2 × 8	2–2 × 8	2–2 × 10
	Ponderosa Pine Beam	1–2 × 6	1–2 × 6	1–2 × 8	2–2 × 8	2–2 × 8	2–2 × 8	2–2 × 10	2–2 × 10	2–2 × 12
	Corner Footing	6 5 4	7 6 5	7 6 5	8 7 6	9 7 6	9 7 6	10 8 7	10 8 7	10 9 7
	Intermediate Footing	9 8 7	10 8 7	10 9 7	11 9 8	12 10 9	13 10 9	14 11 10	14 12 10	15 12 10
7'	Southern Pine Beam	1–2 × 6	1–2 × 6	1–2 × 6	2–2 × 6	2–2 × 6	2–2 × 8	2–2 × 8	2–2 × 10	2–2 × 10
	Ponderosa Pine Beam	1–2 × 6	1–2 × 6	1–2 × 8	2–2 × 8	2–2 × 8	2–2 × 10	2–2 × 10	2–2 × 10	2–2 × 12
	Corner Footing	7 5 5	7 6 5	8 7 6	9 7 6	9 8 7	10 8 7	10 8 7	11 9 8	11 9 8
	Intermediate Footing	9 8 7	10 8 7	11 9 8	12 10 9	13 11 9	14 11 10	15 12 10	15 13 11	16 13 11
8'	Southern Pine Beam	1–2 × 6	1–2 × 6	2–2 × 6	2–2 × 6	2–2 × 8	2–2 × 8	2–2 × 8	2–2 × 10	2–2 × 10
	Ponderosa Pine Beam	1–2 × 6	2–2 × 6	2–2 × 8	2–2 × 8	2–2 × 8	2–2 × 10	2–2 × 10	2–2 × 10	3–2 × 10
	Corner Footing	7 6 5	8 6 6	9 7 6	9 8 7	10 8 7	10 8 7	11 9 8	11 9 8	12 10 9
	Intermediate Footing	10 8 7	11 9 8	12 10 9	13 11 9	14 11 10	15 12 10	16 13 11	16 13 12	17 14 12
9'	Southern Pine Beam	1–2 × 6	1–2 × 6	2–2 × 6	2–2 × 6	2–2 × 8	2–2 × 8	2–2 × 10	2–2 × 10	2–2 × 12
	Ponderosa Pine Beam	1–2 × 6	2–2 × 6	2–2 × 8	2–2 × 8	2–2 × 10	2–2 × 10	2–2 × 10	3–2 × 10	3–2 × 10
	Corner Footing	7 6 5	8 7 6	9 7 6	10 8 7	10 9 7	11 9 8	12 10 8	12 10 9	13 10 9
	Intermediate Footing	10 9 7	12 10 8	13 10 9	14 11 10	15 12 10	16 13 11	17 14 12	17 14 12	18 15 13
10'	Southern Pine Beam	1–2 × 6	1–2 × 6	2–2 × 6	2–2 × 6	2–2 × 8	2–2 × 8	2–2 × 10	2–2 × 10	2–2 × 12
	Ponderosa Pine Beam	1–2 × 6	1–2 × 6	2–2 × 8	2–2 × 8	2–2 × 10	2–2 × 10	2–2 × 12	3–2 × 10	3–2 × 12
	Corner Footing	8 6 6	9 7 6	10 8 7	10 8 7	11 9 8	12 10 8	12 10 9	13 11 9	14 11 10
	Intermediate Footing	11 9 8	12 10 9	14 11 10	15 12 10	16 13 11	17 14 12	17 14 12	18 15 13	19 16 14
11'	Southern Pine Beam	1–2 × 6	2–2 × 6	2–2 × 6	2–2 × 6	2–2 × 8	2–2 × 10	2–2 × 10	2–2 × 12	2–2 × 12
	Ponderosa Pine Beam	2–2 × 6	2–2 × 6	2–2 × 8	2–2 × 8	2–2 × 10	2–2 × 12	2–2 × 12	3–2 × 10	3–2 × 12
	Corner Footing	8 7 6	9 7 6	10 8 7	11 9 8	12 9 8	12 10 9	13 11 9	14 11 10	14 12 10
	Intermediate Footing	12 9 8	13 11 9	14 12 10	15 12 10	16 13 11	17 14 12	17 14 12	18 15 13	19 16 14
12'	Southern Pine Beam	1–2 × 6	2–2 × 6	2–2 × 6	2–2 × 8	2–2 × 8	2–2 × 10	2–2 × 10	2–2 × 12	3–2 × 10
	Ponderosa Pine Beam	2–2 × 6	2–2 × 6	2–2 × 8	2–2 × 10	2–2 × 10	2–2 × 12	2–2 × 12	3–2 × 12	3–2 × 12
	Corner Footing	9 7 6	10 8 7	10 9 7	11 9 8	12 10 9	13 10 9	14 11 10	14 12 10	15 12 10
	Intermediate Footing	12 10 9	14 11 10	15 12 10	16 13 11	17 14 12	18 15 13	19 16 14	20 16 14	21 17 15
13'	Southern Pine Beam	1–2 × 6	2–2 × 6	2–2 × 6	2–2 × 8	2–2 × 8	2–2 × 10	2–2 × 10	2–2 × 12	3–2 × 10
	Ponderosa Pine Beam	2–2 × 6	2–2 × 6	2–2 × 8	2–2 × 10	2–2 × 12	2–2 × 12	2–2 × 12	3–2 × 12	3–2 × 12
	Corner Footing	9 7 6	10 8 7	11 9 8	12 10 8	13 10 9	13 11 9	14 12 10	15 12 10	15 13 11
	Intermediate Footing	13 10 9	14 12 10	15 13 11	17 14 12	18 15 13	19 15 13	20 16 14	21 17 15	22 18 15
14'	Southern Pine Beam	1–2 × 6	2–2 × 6	2–2 × 6	2–2 × 8	2–2 × 10	2–2 × 10	2–2 × 12	3–2 × 10	3–2 × 12
	Ponderosa Pine Beam	2–2 × 6	2–2 × 8	2–2 × 8	2–2 × 10	2–2 × 12	3–2 × 10	3–2 × 12	3–2 × 12	Eng Bm
	Corner Footing	9 8 7	10 8 7	11 9 8	12 10 9	13 11 9	14 11 10	15 12 10	15 13 11	16 13 11
	Intermediate Footing	13 11 9	15 12 10	16 13 11	17 14 12	18 15 13	20 16 14	21 17 15	22 18 15	23 18 16
15'	Southern Pine Beam	2–2 × 6	2–2 × 6	2–2 × 8	2–2 × 8	2–2 × 10	2–2 × 12	2–2 × 12	3–2 × 10	3–2 × 12
	Ponderosa Pine Beam	2–2 × 6	2–2 × 8	2–2 × 8	2–2 × 10	3–2 × 10	3–2 × 10	3–2 × 12	3–2 × 12	Eng Bm
	Corner Footing	10 8 7	11 9 8	12 10 8	13 10 9	14 11 10	14 12 10	15 12 11	16 13 11	17 14 12
	Intermediate Footing	14 11 10	15 12 11	17 14 12	18 15 13	19 16 14	20 17 14	21 17 15	22 18 16	23 19 17

10	8	7
14	11	10

Soil composition: Clay Sand Gravel

Step-by-Step Overview

Deck-building is a project you'll tackle in stages, no matter what design you choose. Before you begin construction, review the photos on these two pages. They outline the basic procedure you'll want to follow when building your deck. The chapters to follow will explore each of these stages extensively.

Be sure to gather your tools and materials before you begin the project, and arrange to have a helper available for the more difficult stages. Check with local utilities for the location of underground electrical, telephone, or water lines before digging the footings. Apply for a building permit, where required, and make sure a building inspector has approved the deck design before beginning work.

The time it takes to build a deck depends on the size and complexity of the design as well as your building skills. If you're comfortable using tools and start with thorough, accurate plans, you should be able to complete a single-level deck in a few weekends.

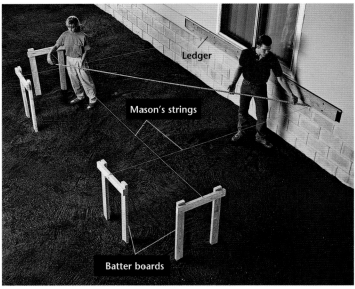

1. *Install a ledger to anchor the deck to the house and to serve as reference for laying out footings (page 173). Use batter boards and mason's strings to locate footings, and check for square by measuring diagonals.*

2. *Pour concrete post footings (page 190), and install metal post anchors. Set and brace the posts, attach them to the post anchors, and mark posts to show where beam will be attached.*

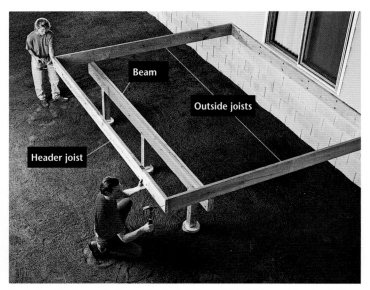

3. *Fasten the beam to the posts. Install the outside joists and header joist, using galvanized nails.*

4. Install metal joist hangers on the ledger and header joist, then hang the remaining joists (page 204). Most decking patterns require joists that are spaced 16" on center.

5. Lay decking boards, and trim them with a circular saw. If desired for appearance, cover pressure-treated header and outside joists with redwood or cedar facing boards (page 210).

6. Build deck stairs (page 222). Stairs provide access to the deck and establish traffic patterns.

7. Install a railing around the deck and stairway (page 230). A railing adds a decorative touch and may be required on any deck that is more than 30" above the ground. If desired, finish the underside of the deck.

Installing a Ledger

The first step in building an attached deck is to fasten the ledger to the house. The ledger anchors the deck and establishes a reference point for building the deck square and level. The ledger also supports one end of all the deck joists, so it must be attached securely to the framing members of the house.

If your deck's ledger is made from pressure-treated lumber, make sure to use hot-dipped, galvanized lag screws and washers to attach it to the house. Ordinary zinc-coated hardware will corrode and eventually fail if placed in contact with ACQ pressure-treating chemicals.

Install the ledger so that the surface of the decking boards will be 1 inch below the indoor floor level. This height difference prevents rainwater or melted snow from seeping into the house.

TOOLS & MATERIALS

- Pencil
- Level
- Circular saw with carbide blade or metal cutting blade
- Chisel
- Hammer
- Metal snips
- Caulk gun
- Ratchet wrench

- Awl
- Drill and bits (¼" twist, 1" spade, ⅜" and ⅝" masonry)
- Rubber mallet
- Pressure-treated lumber
- Galvanized flashing
- 8d galvanized common nails
- Silicone caulk

- ⅜ × 4" lag screws and 1" washers
- Lead masonry anchors for ⅜" lag screws (for brick walls)
- 2 × 4s for braces
- Chalk line
- Tin snips or utility knife
- Building felt

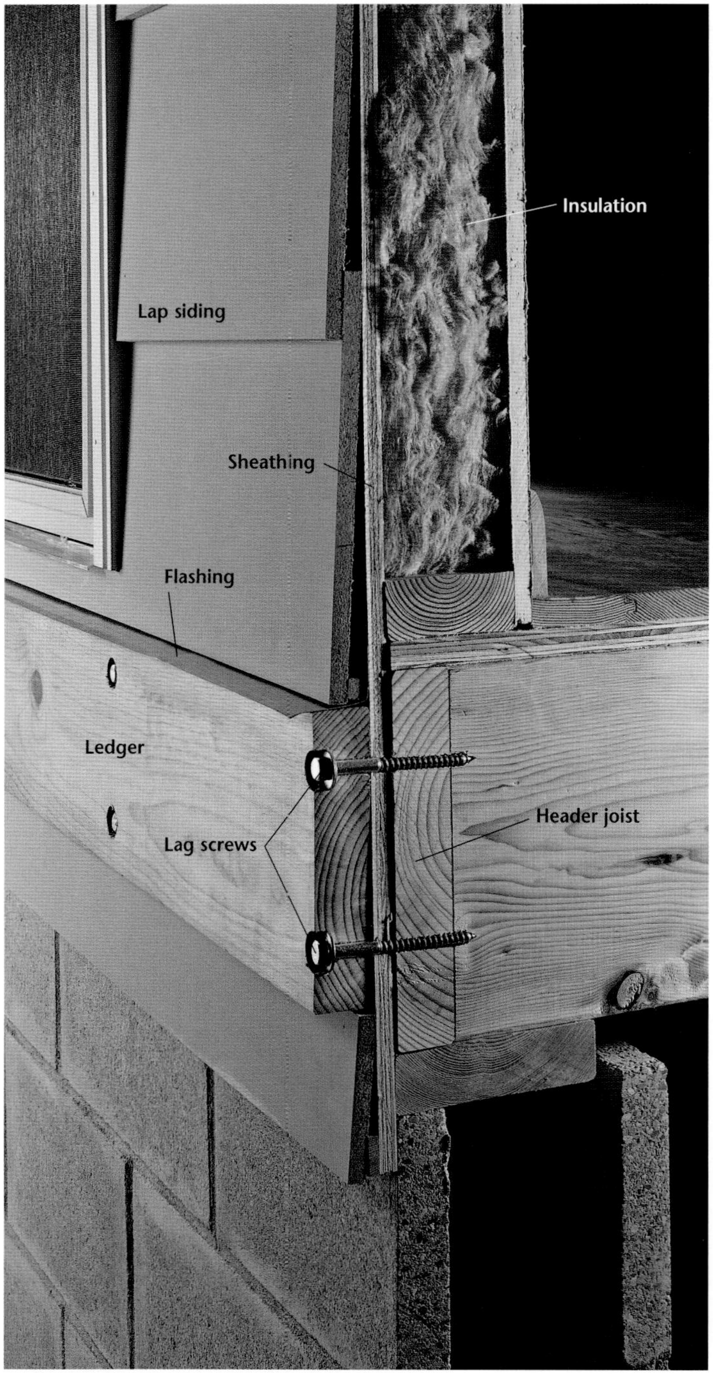

Labels: Insulation, Lap siding, Sheathing, Flashing, Ledger, Lag screws, Header joist

Ledger (shown in cross section) is made from pressure-treated lumber. Lap siding is cut away to expose sheathing and to provide a flat surface for attaching the ledger. Galvanized flashing tucked under siding prevents moisture damage to wood. Countersunk ⅜ × 4" lag screws hold ledger to header joist inside house. If there is access to the space behind the header joist, such as in an unfinished basement, attach the ledger with carriage bolts, washers, and nuts.

HOW TO ATTACH A LEDGER TO LAP SIDING

1. *Draw an outline showing where the deck will fit against the house, using a level as a guide. Include the thickness of the outside joists and any decorative facing boards that will be installed.*

2. *Cut out siding along outline using a circular saw. Set blade depth to same thickness as siding, so that blade does not cut into sheathing.*

3. *Use a chisel to finish the cutout where circular saw blade does not reach. Hold the chisel with the bevel-side in.*

4. *Measure and cut ledger from pressure-treated lumber. Remember that ledger will be shorter than overall length of cutout.*

5. Cut galvanized flashing to length of cutout using metal snips. Slide flashing up under siding. Do not nail the metal flashing in place.

6. Center the ledger in the cutout, underneath the flashing. Brace in position, and tack ledger into place with 8d galvanized nails. Apply a thick bead of silicone caulk to crack between siding and flashing.

7. Drill pairs of ¼" pilot holes spaced every 2 feet, through the ledger and sheathing and into the header joist.

8. Counterbore each pilot hole to ½" depth, using a 1" spade bit.

9. Attach ledger to wall with ⅜ × 4" lag screws and washers using a ratchet wrench or impact driver.

10. Seal lag screw heads with silicone caulk. Seal the crack between the wall and the sides and bottom of the ledger.

HOW TO ATTACH A LEDGER TO MASONRY

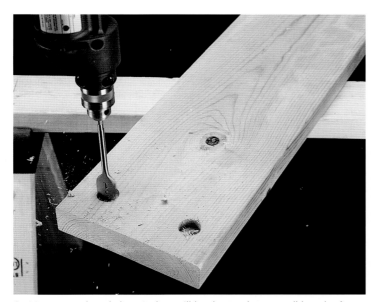

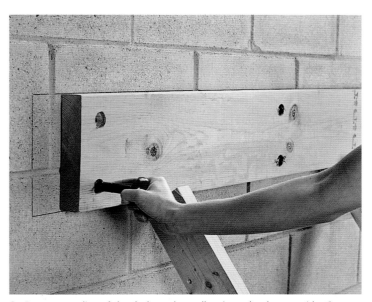

1. Measure and cut ledger. Ledger will be shorter than overall length of outline. Drill pairs of ¼" pilot holes every 2 feet in ledger. Counterbore each pilot hole to ½" depth using a 1" spade bit.

2. Draw an outline of the deck on the wall, using a level as a guide. Center ledger in outline on wall, and brace in position. Mark the pilot hole locations on wall using an awl or nail. Remove ledger.

179

3. *Drill anchor holes 3" deep into masonry, using a ⅝" masonry bit.*

4. *Drive lead masonry anchors for ⅜" lag screws into drilled holes using a rubber mallet.*

5. *Attach ledger to wall with ⅜ × 4" lag screws and washers using a ratchet wrench or impact driver. Tighten screws firmly, but do not overtighten.*

6. *Seal the cracks between the wall and ledger with silicone caulk. Also seal the lag screw heads.*

HOW TO ATTACH A LEDGER TO STUCCO

1. Draw outline of deck on wall, using a level as a guide. Measure and cut ledger, and drill pilot holes (page 178, Step 7). Brace ledger against wall, and mark hole locations using a nail or awl.

2. Remove ledger. Drill pilot holes through stucco layer of wall using a ⅜" masonry bit.

3. Extend each pilot hole through the sheathing and into the header joist, using a ¼" bit. Reposition ledger and brace in place.

4. Attach ledger to wall with ⅜ × 4" lag screws and washers, using a ratchet wrench. Seal the lag screw heads and the cracks between the wall and ledger with silicone caulk.

HOW TO ATTACH A LEDGER TO METAL OR VINYL SIDING

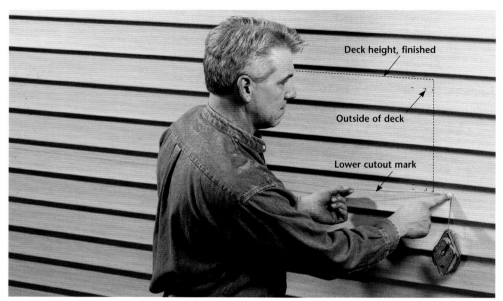

Deck height, finished

Outside of deck

Lower cutout mark

1. *Mark the length of the ledger location, adding 1½" at each end to allow for the rim joists that will be installed later. Also allow for fascia board thickness if it will be added and create space for metal rim-joist hangers. Then mark the top and bottom edges of the ledger at both ends of its location. Snap lines for the ledger position between the marks. Check the lines for level and adjust as necessary. You may be able to use the siding edges to help determine the ledger location, but only after checking to see if the edges are level. Don't assume siding is installed level.*

2. *Set the circular saw blade depth to cut through the siding. Use a metal cutting blade for metal siding; a 40-tooth carbide blade works well on vinyl siding. Cut on the outside of the lines along the top and sides of the ledger location, stopping the blade when it reaches a corner.*

3. *Snap a new level line ½" above the bottom line and make your final cut along this line. This leaves a small lip of siding that will fit under the ledger.*

4. Complete the cuts in the corners using tin snips on metal siding or a utility knife on vinyl siding. A hammer and sharp chisel also may be used.

5. Insert building felt underneath the siding and over the existing felt that has been damaged by the cuts. It is easiest to cut and install two long strips. Cut and insert the first strip so it is underneath the siding at the ends and bottom edge of the cutout and attach it with staples. Cut and insert the second strip so it is underneath the siding at the ends and top edge of the cutout, so that it overlaps the first strip by at least 3".

6. Cut and insert galvanized flashing (also called Z-flashing) underneath the full length of the top edge of the cutout. Do not use fasteners; pressure will hold the flashing in place until the ledger is installed.

7. Cut and install the ledger board (see pages 177 to 180).

Locating Post Footings

Establish the exact locations of all concrete footings by stretching mason's strings across the site. Use the ledger board as a starting point. These perpendicular layout strings will be used to locate holes for concrete footings and to position metal post anchors on the finished footings. Anchor the layout strings with temporary 2 × 4 supports, often called batter boards. You may want to leave the batter boards in place until after the footings are dug. That way, you can use the strings to accurately locate the J-bolts in the concrete.

TOOLS & MATERIALS

- Tape measure
- Felt-tipped pen
- Circular saw
- Framing square
- Masonry hammer
- Claw hammer
- Line level
- Plumb bob
- 2 × 4s
- Drill
- 10d nails
- 2½" wallboard screws
- Mason's strings
- Masking tape

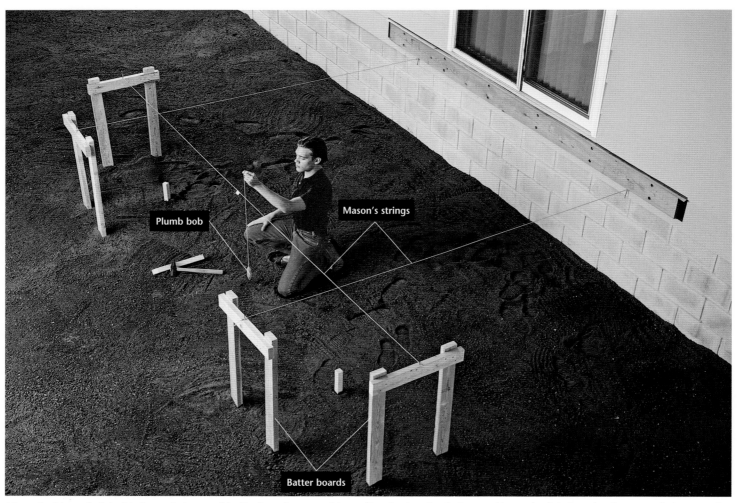

Plumb bob

Mason's strings

Batter boards

Mason's strings stretched between ledger and batter boards are used to position footings for deck posts. Use a plumb bob and stakes to mark the ground at the exact centerpoints of footings.

HOW TO LOCATE POST FOOTINGS

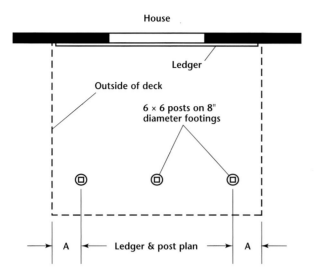

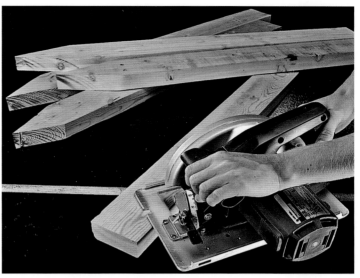

1. *Use your design plan to find distance (A). Measure from the side of the deck to the center of each outside post. Use your elevation drawings to find the height of each deck post.*

2. *Cut 2 × 4 stakes for batter boards, each about 8" longer than post height. Trim one end of each stake to a point using a circular saw. Cut 2 × 4 crosspieces, each about 2 feet long.*

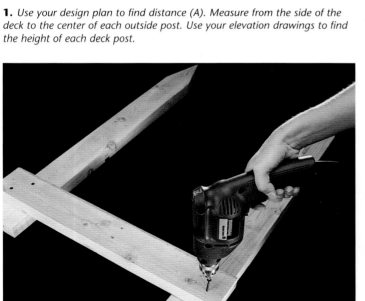

3. *Assemble batter boards by attaching crosspieces to stakes with 2½" wallboard screws. Crosspieces should be about 2" below tops of stakes.*

4. *Transfer measurement A (step 1) to ledger, and mark reference points at each end of ledger. String lines will be stretched from these points on ledger. When measuring, remember to allow for outside joists and facing that will be butted to the ends of the ledger.*

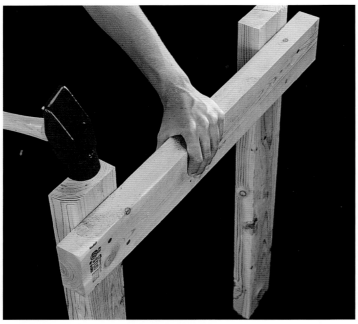

5. *Drive a batter board 6" into the ground, about 2 feet past the post location. Crosspiece of batter board should be parallel to the ledger.*

6. *Drive a 10d nail into bottom of ledger at reference point (step 4). Attach a mason's string to nail.*

7. *Extend the mason's string so that it is taut and perpendicular to the ledger. Use a framing square as a guide. Secure the string temporarily by wrapping it several times around the batter board.*

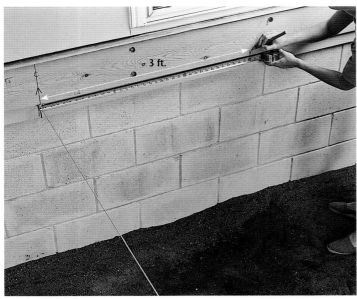

8. *Check the mason's string for square using "3-4-5 carpenter's triangle." First, measure along the ledger 3 feet from the mason's string and mark a point, using a felt-tipped pen.*

9. *Measure mason's string 4 feet from edge of ledger, and mark with masking tape.*

10. *Measure distance between marks. If string is perpendicular to ledger, the distance will be exactly 5 feet. If necessary, move string left or right on batter board until distance between marks is 5 feet.*

11. *Drive a 10d nail into top of batter board at string location. Leave about 2" of nail exposed. Tie string to nail.*

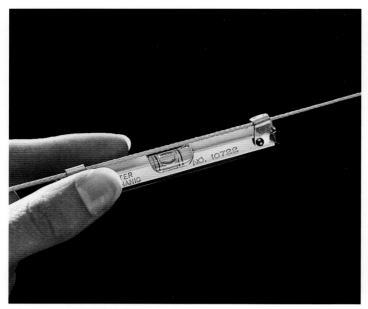

12. *Hang a line level on the mason's string. Raise or lower string until it is level. Locate other outside post footing, repeating steps 5 to 12.*

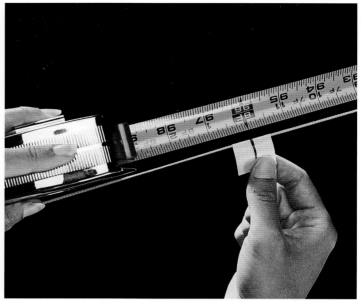

13. *Measure along mason's strings from ledger to find centerpoint of posts. Mark centerpoints on strings, using masking tape.*

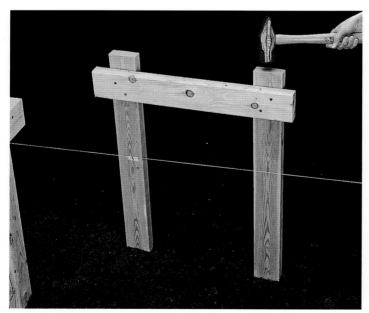

14. *Drive additional batter boards into ground, about 2 feet outside mason's strings and lined up with post centerpoint marks (step 13).*

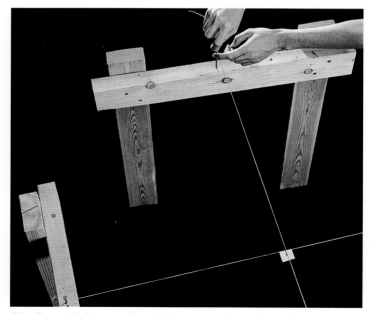

15. *Align a third cross string with the centerpoint marks on the first strings. Drive 10d nails in new batter boards, and tie off cross string on nails. Cross string should be close to, but not touching, the first strings.*

16. *Check strings for square by measuring distances A-B and C-D. Measure diagonals A-D and B-C from edge of ledger to opposite corners. If strings are square, measurement A-B will be same as C-D, and diagonal A-D will be same as B-C. If necessary, adjust strings on batter boards until square.*

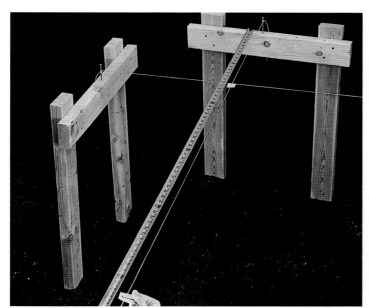

17. *Measure along the cross string and mark centerpoints of any posts that will be installed between the outside posts.*

18. *Use a plumb bob to mark post centerpoints on the ground, directly under the marks on the mason's strings. Drive a stake into ground at each point. Remove mason's strings before digging footings.*

Digging & Pouring Footings

Concrete footings hold deck posts in place and support the weight of the deck. Check local codes to determine the size and depth of footings required for your area. In cold climates, footings must be deeper than the soil frost line.

To help protect posts from water damage, each footing should be poured so that it is 2 inches above ground level. Tube-shaped forms let you extend the footings above ground level.

It is easy and inexpensive to mix your own concrete by combining Portland cement, sand, gravel, and water.

As an alternative to inserting J-bolts into wet concrete, you can use masonry anchors or install anchor bolts with an epoxy designed for deck footings and other masonry installations. The epoxy method provides you with more time to reset layout strings for locating bolt locations, and it eliminates the problem of J-bolts tilting or sinking into concrete that is too loose. Most building centers sell threaded rod, washers, nuts, and epoxy syringes, but you also can buy these items separately at most hardware centers.

Before digging, consult local utilities for location of any underground electrical, telephone, or water lines that might interfere with footings.

TOOLS & MATERIALS

- Power auger or clamshell posthole digger
- Tape measure
- Pruning saw
- Shovel
- Reciprocating saw or handsaw

- Torpedo level
- Hoe
- Trowel
- Shovel
- Old toothbrush
- Plumb bob
- Utility knife
- Concrete tube forms

- Portland cement
- Sand
- Gravel
- J-bolts
- Wheelbarrow
- Scrap 2 × 4
- Level

Power augers quickly dig holes for post footings. They are available at rental centers. Some models can be operated by one person, while others require two people.

HOW TO DIG & POUR POST FOOTINGS

1. Dig holes for post footings with a clamshell digger or power auger, centering the holes on the layout stakes. For holes deeper than 35", use a power auger.

2. Measure hole depth. Local building codes specify depth of footings. Cut away tree roots, if necessary, using a pruning saw.

3. Pour 2" to 3" of loose gravel in the bottom of each footing hole. Gravel will provide drainage under concrete footings.

4. Add 2" to hole depth so that footings will be above ground level. Cut concrete tube forms to length, using a reciprocating saw or handsaw. Make sure cuts are straight.

5. Insert tubes into footing holes, leaving about 2" of tube above ground level. Use a level to make sure tops of tubes are level. Pack soil around tubes to hold them in place.

6. *Mix dry ingredients for concrete in a wheelbarrow using a hoe.*

7. *Form a hollow in center of dry concrete mixture. Slowly pour a small amount of water into hollow, and blend in dry mixture with a hoe.*

8. *Add more water gradually, mixing thoroughly until concrete is firm enough to hold its shape when sliced with a trowel.*

9. *Pour concrete slowly into the tube form, guiding concrete from the wheelbarrow with a shovel. Fill about half of the form, using a long stick to tamp the concrete, filling any air gaps in the footing. Then finish pouring and tamping concrete into the form.*

10. *Level the concrete by pulling a 2 × 4 across the top of the tube form, using a sawing motion. Add concrete to any low spots. Retie the mason's strings on the batter boards and recheck measurements.*

11. *Insert a J-bolt at an angle into the wet concrete at center of the footing.*

12. *Lower the J-bolt slowly into the concrete, wiggling it slightly to eliminate any air gaps.*

13. *Set the J-bolt so ¾" to 1" is exposed above concrete. Brush away any wet concrete on bolt threads with an old toothbrush.*

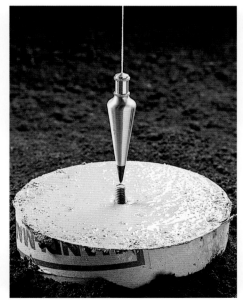

14. *Use a plumb bob to make sure the J-bolt is positioned exactly at center of post location.*

15. *Use a torpedo level to make sure the J-bolt is plumb. If necessary, adjust the bolt and repack concrete. Let concrete cure, then cut away exposed portion of tube with a utility knife.*

Footing Forms

Footing forms, which are also called piers, anchor a deck to the ground and create a stable foundation for the posts. They transfer the weight of the deck into the soil and prevent it from heaving upward in climates where the ground freezes. Generally, footings are made from long, hollow tubes of fiber-reinforced paper in several diameters. Once a tube footing is set into the ground below the frost line, you backfill around the outside with soil, tamp it down firmly, and fill with concrete. Metal connective hardware imbedded in the concrete will attach the footings permanently to the deck posts.

For soils that have a poor bearing capacity, or if you are building a particularly large deck, you can also buy plastic footing tubes with flared bases that bear heavier loads. Or, you can attach a flared footing to the bottom of a conventional tube. For low-profile decks that aren't attached to a house, you may be able to use precast concrete footings instead of buried piers. These precut footings simply rest on the surface of the soil.

Lumberyards and building centers will stock hollow footing forms in various diameters. The diameter you need will depend on the size and weight of your deck. Your building official will help you determine the correct size when you apply for a building permit.

Precast concrete footings are usually acceptable for building low-profile, freestanding decks. Notches on top of the pier are designed to hold joists without fasteners or other hardware.

When building heavy decks or placing footings in unstable, loose soil, you may need to use piers with flared footings. Some styles are molded in one piece, or you can attach a flared footing to a conventional footing form with screws.

Installing Flashing

Building codes require that a deck's ledger board be attached directly to wall sheathing and house framing. If your home is sided, you'll need to remove the siding in the ledger board area before attaching the ledger to the house. Be sure to install 15# or 30# building paper or self-sealing, adhesive backed membrane behind the ledger to prevent moisture damage. Rotting in the area behind the ledger is one of the leading causes of premature deck deterioration. Flashing is particularly important if there's no housewrap behind the siding. Once the ledger is in place, cap it with a piece of galvanized Z-flashing, tucked behind the siding, for added protection.

Although building code doesn't require it, you may also want to wrap the tops of beams and posts with self-sealing membrane to keep these areas dry and rot-free. Ledger flashing, self-sealing membrane, and building paper are available at most home centers and lumberyards. They're little details that can make a big difference to the longevity of your deck.

Building felt, also called building paper, is used behind house siding materials. Use it to replace felt damaged during a ledger installation. Ledger flashing, or Z-flashing, prevents moisture damage behind the deck ledger. Self-sealing membrane provides extra protection from moisture in damp climates or in areas where there is snow accumulation. It can be used over flashing or on top of beams and posts (see below), and it self-seals around nails or screws that pierce it.

To apply self-sealing membrane, cut a piece to size and position it over the application area. Starting at one end, begin removing the thin plastic backing that protects the adhesive. Firmly press the membrane in place as you remove the backing, working along the installation area. To install long pieces of membrane, enlist the aid of a helper.

Install self-sealing membrane behind the ledger as extra protection from moisture. Apply the membrane over the house wrap or building felt, using the same method shown at left.

Installing Posts

Posts support the deck beams and transfer the weight of the deck, as well as everything on it, to the concrete footings. They create the above-ground foundation of your deck. Your building inspector will verify that the posts you plan to use are sized correctly to suit your deck design.

Choose post lumber carefully so the posts will be able to carry these substantial loads for the life of your deck. Pressure-treated lumber is your best defense against rot or insect damage. Select posts that are straight and free of deep cracks, large knots, or other natural defects that could compromise their strength. Try not to cut off the factory-treated ends when trimming the posts to length; they contain more of the treatment chemicals and generally last longer than cut ends. Face the factory ends down against the post hardware where water is more likely to accumulate.

Use galvanized metal post anchors to attach the posts to concrete footings. If posts are set directly on concrete, the ends won't dry properly. You'll also have a harder time making the necessary mechanical connection to the footings. Post anchors have drainage holes and pedestals that raise the ends of the wood above the footings and improve drainage. Make sure the posts are installed plumb for maximum strength.

TOOLS & MATERIALS

- Pencil
- Framing square
- Ratchet wrench
- Tape measure
- Power miter saw or circular saw

- Hammer
- Level
- Combination square
- Metal post anchors
- Nuts for J-bolts
- Lumber for posts

- 6d galvanized common nails
- 2" wallboard screws
- Long, straight 2 × 4
- 1 × 4s
- Pointed 2 × 2 stakes

HOW TO ATTACH POST ANCHORS

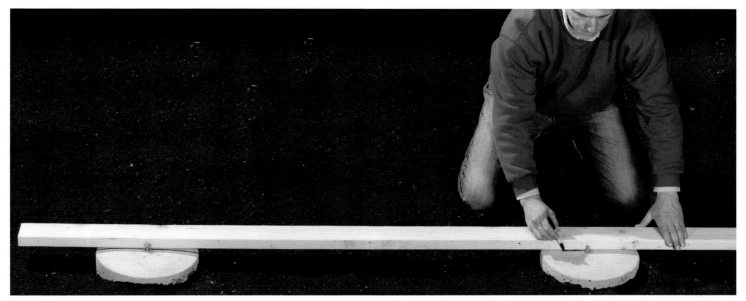

1. *Mark the top of each footing as a reference line for installing post anchors. Lay a long, straight 2 × 4 flat across two or three concrete footings, parallel to the ledger, with one edge tight against the J-bolts.*

2. *Draw a reference line across each concrete footing, using an edge of the 2 × 4 as a guide. Remove the 2 × 4.*

3. *Place a metal post anchor on each concrete footing, and center it over the J-bolt.*

4. *Use a framing square to make sure the post anchor is positioned square to the reference line drawn on the footing.*

5. *Thread a nut over each J-bolt, and tighten it securely with a ratchet wrench or impact driver.*

HOW TO SET POSTS

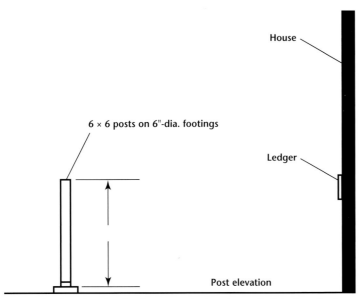

House

6 × 6 posts on 6"-dia. footings

Ledger

Post elevation

1. *Use the elevation drawing from your design plan to find the length of each post (A). Add 6" for a cutting margin.*

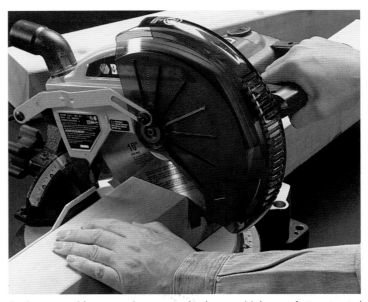

2. *Cut posts with power miter saw or circular saw. Make sure factory-treated ends of posts are square. If necessary, square them by trimming with a power miter saw or circular saw.*

3. *Place post in anchor, and tack into place with a single 6d galvanized common nail.*

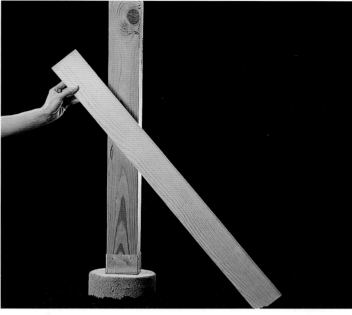

4. *Brace post with a 1 × 4. Place the 1 × 4 flat across post so that it crosses the post at a 45° angle about halfway up.*

5. *Attach the brace to the post temporarily with a single 2" wallboard screw.*

6. *Drive a pointed 2 × 2 stake into the ground next to the end of the brace.*

7. *Use a level to make sure the post is plumb. Adjust the post, if necessary.*

8. *Attach the brace to the stake with two 2" wallboard screws.*

9. *Plumb and brace the post on the side perpendicular to the first brace.*

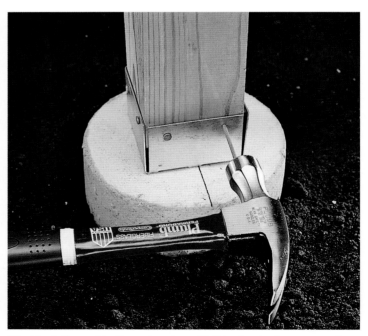

10. *Attach the post to the post anchor with 6d galvanized common nails.*

11. *Position a straight 2 × 4 with one end on the ledger and the other end across the face of the post. Level the 2 × 4, then lower its post end ¼" for every 3 ft. between the ledger and the post (for water runoff). Draw a line on the post along the bottom of the 2 × 4. This line indicates the top of the joists.*

12. *From the line shown in step 11, measure down and mark the posts a distance equal to the width of the joists.*

13. *Use a square to draw a line completely around the post. This line indicates the top of the beam. From this line, repeat steps 12 and 13 to determine the bottom of the beam.*

Installing Beams

Deck beams attach to the posts to help support the weight of the joists and decking. Installation methods depend on the deck design and local codes, so check with a building inspector to determine what is acceptable in your area.

In a saddle beam deck, the beam is attached directly on top of the posts. Metal fasteners, called post-saddles, are used to align and strengthen the beam-to-post connection. The advantage is that the post bears the weight of the deck.

A notched-post deck requires 6 × 6 posts notched at the post top to accommodate the full size of the beam. The deck's weight is transferred to the posts, as in a post-and-beam deck.

In years past, a third style of beam construction, called sandwiching, was also generally acceptable for deck construction. It consisted of two beams that straddled both sides of the post, connected by long through bolts. Because this method has less strength than the saddle or notched styles, it is no longer approved by most building codes.

TOOLS & MATERIALS

- Tape measure
- Pencil
- Circular saw
- Paintbrush
- Combination square
- Screwgun
- Drill
- ⅜" auger bit
- 1" spade bit

- Ratchet wrench
- Caulk gun
- Reciprocating saw or handsaw
- Pressure-treated lumber
- Clear sealer-preservative
- Joist hanger screws
- ⅜ × 8" carriage bolts with washers and nuts

- Silicone caulk
- Exterior-grade construction adhesive
- Hammer
- 10d galvanized common nails
- Spring clamps
- Saddle hardware
- Framing square

Deck beams, *resting in a notch on the tops of the posts and secured with through bolts and nuts, guarantee strong connections that will bear the weight of your deck.*

HOW TO FABRICATE A BEAM

1. *Select two straight boards of the same dimension (generally 2 × 8 or larger) and lay them face to face to see which alignment comes closest to flush on all sides. Apply exterior grade construction adhesive to one board and lay the mating board onto it. Drive a pair of 10d nails near the end of the assembly to pin the boards together.*

2. *Clamp the beam members together every two or three feet, forcing the boards into alignment as you go, if necessary. Drive 10d nails in a regular, staggered pattern every 12 to 16" or so. Flip the beam over and repeat the nailing pattern from the other side.*

HOW TO MARK POST LOCATIONS ON A BEAM

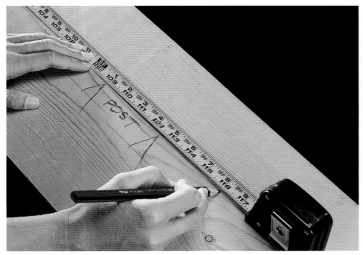

1. *Measure along the beam to the post locations, making sure the ends of the boards of a doubled beam are flush. Mark both the near and far edges of the post onto the beam.*

2. *Use a combination square or speed square to transfer the post marks onto the top and then the other face of the beam, allowing you to make sure the post and post hardware align with both faces.*

HOW TO INSTALL A BEAM WITH A POST SADDLE

1. Cut the post to final height after securing it in place. Make two passes with a circular saw or one pass with a reciprocating saw. For most DIYers, the circular saw option will yield a more even cut.

2. Attach the saddle hardware to the top of the post using joist hanger screws, 10d galvanized common nails, or joist hanger nails. You must drive a fastener at every predrilled hole in the saddle hardware.

3. Set the beam into the saddle, making sure the sides of the saddle align with the layout marks on the beam.

4. Secure the beam into the saddle by driving galvanized common nails or joist hanger screws through the predrilled holes in the top half of the saddle.

HOW TO INSTALL A BEAM FOR A NOTCHED-POST DECK

1. Remove 6 × 6 posts from post anchors and cut to finished height. Measure and mark a notch at the top of each post, sized to fit the thickness and width of the beam. Trace the lines on all sides using a framing square.

2. Use a circular saw to rough-cut the notches, then switch to a reciprocating saw or hand saw to finish. Reattach posts to the post anchors, with the notch-side facing away from the deck.

3. With someone's help, lift beam (crown side up) into the notches. Align beam and clamp to posts. Counterbore two ½"-deep holes, using a 1" spade bit, then drill ⅜" pilot holes through the beam and post, using a ⅜" auger bit.

4. Insert carriage bolts to each pilot hole. Add a washer and nut to the counterbore-side of each, and tighten using a ratchet. Seal both ends with silicone caulk. Apply self-sealing membrane to top surfaces of beam and posts if necessary.

Hanging Joists

Joists provide support for the decking boards. They are attached to the ledger and header joist with galvanized metal joist hangers and are nailed to the top of the beam.

For strength and durability, use pressure-treated lumber for all joists. The exposed outside joists and header joist can be faced with redwood or cedar boards for a more attractive appearance.

TOOLS & MATERIALS

- Tape measure
- Pencil
- Hammer
- Combination square
- Circular saw
- Paintbrush
- Drill

- Pressure-treated lumber
- 10d joist hanger nails
- Galvanized common nails (10d, 16d)
- Clear sealer-preservative
- Joist angle brackets

- Galvanized metal joist hangers
- Metal corner brackets (optional)

Metal joist hangers attached to rim joists or ledgers are practically foolproof for hanging intermediate deck joists. Look for hanger hardware that is triple-dipped galvanized metal.

HOW TO HANG JOISTS

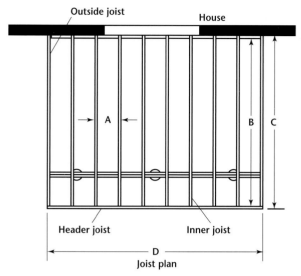

1. Use your deck plan to find the spacing (A) between joists, and the length of inner joists (B), outside joists (C), and header joist (D). Measure and mark lumber for outside joists using a combination square as a guide. Cut joists with a circular saw. Seal cut ends with clear sealer-preservative.

2. Attach joist hanger hardware near each end of the ledger board, according to your layout. Previous building codes allowed you to face nail the joists into the ends of the ledger, but this is no longer accepted practice. Attach only enough fasteners to hold the hanger in position while you square up the joist layout.

3. Attach the outside joists to the top of the beam by toenailing them with 10d galvanized common nails.

4. Trim off the ends of structural lumber to get a clean straight edge.

5. *Measure and cut header joist. Seal cut ends with clear sealer-preservative. Drill ¹⁄₁₆" pilot holes at each end of header joist. Attach header to ends of outside joists with 16d galvanized common nails. For extra reinforcement, you can add metal corner brackets to the inside corner joints.*

6. *Finish nailing the end joist hangers, making sure you have a joist hanger nail in every punched hole in the hanger.*

7. *Measure along ledger from edge of outside joist, and mark where joists will be attached to ledger.*

8. *Draw the outline of each joist on the ledger using a combination square as a guide.*

9. *Measure along the beam from outside joist, and mark where joists will cross the beam. Draw the outlines across top of both beam boards.*

10. *Measure along the header joist from the outside joist, and mark where joists will be attached to header joist. Draw the outlines on the inside of the header using a combination square as a guide.*

11. *Attach joist hangers to the ledger and to the header joist. Position each hanger so that one of the flanges is against the joist outline. Nail one flange to framing members with 10d galvanized common nails.*

12. Cut a scrap board to use as a spacer. Hold spacer inside each joist hanger, then close the hanger around the spacer.

13. Nail the remaining side flange to the framing member with 10d joist hanger nails. Remove spacer.

14. Measure and mark lumber for joists using a combination square as a guide. Cut joists with a circular saw or power miter saw.

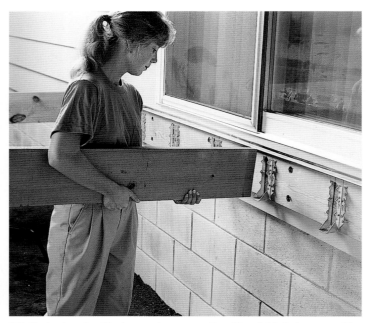

15. Seal cut ends with clear sealer-preservative. Place joists in hangers with crowned edge up.

16. Attach the ledger joist hangers to the joists with joist hanger nails. Drive nails into both sides of each joist.

17. Align the joists with the outlines drawn on the top of the beam. Anchor the joists to the beam by toenailing from both sides with 10d galvanized nails.

ALTERNATE METHOD

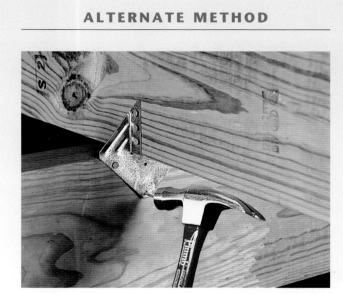

Fasten joists to beams using H-fit joist ties for strength and durability.

18. Attach the joists to the hangers on the joist with 10d joist hanger nails. Drive nails into both sides of each joist.

Laying Decking

Buy decking boards that are long enough to span the width of the deck, if possible. If boards must be butted end-to-end, make sure to stagger the joints so they do not overlap from row to row. Predrill the ends of boards to prevent screws or nails from splitting the wood.

Install decking so that there is a ⅛-inch gap between boards to provide drainage. Boards naturally "cup" as they age. Lay boards with the bark side facing down, so that the cupped surface cannot hold standing water.

General installation instructions for decking materials are shown here. Always follow the installation methods recommended by the manufacturer of the product you select.

TOOLS & MATERIALS

- Tape measure
- Circular saw
- Screwgun
- Hammer
- Drill
- ⅛" twist bit
- Pry bar
- Chalk line
- Jigsaw or handsaw
- Decking material

- Galvanized deck screws (2", 2½", 3")
- Galvanized common nails (8d, 10d)
- Redwood or cedar facing boards
- Spiral shank nails, hot-dipped galvanized ceramic coated screws, or stainless steel nails or deck screws

- T-clips
- Retaining clips
- Spiked clips
- Biscuit joiner
- Biscuit clips
- Constuction adhesive
- Caulk gun
- Undermount deck brackets
- Undermount clips

HOW TO LAY DECKING

1. *Position the first row of decking flush against the house. First decking board should be perfectly straight and should be precut to proper length. Attach the first decking board by driving a pair of 2½" galvanized deck screws into each joist.*

2. *Position remaining decking boards so that ends overhang outside joists. Space boards about ⅛" apart. Attach boards to each joist with a pair of 2½" deck screws driven into each joist.*

Aʟᴛᴇʀɴᴀᴛɪᴠᴇ: *Attach decking boards with 10d galvanized common nails. Angle the nails toward each other to improve holding power.*

3. *If boards are bowed, use a pry bar to maneuver them into position while fastening.*

4. *Drill ⅛" pilot holes in ends of boards before attaching them to outside joists. Pilot holes prevent screws from splitting decking boards at ends.*

5. *After every few rows of decking are installed, measure from edge of the decking board to edge of header joist. If measurements show that the last board will not fit flush against the edge of the deck, adjust board spacing.*

6. *Adjust board spacing by changing the gaps between boards by a small amount over three or four rows of boards. Very small spacing changes will not be obvious to the eye.*

213

7. Use a chalk line to mark the edge of decking flush with the outside of deck. Cut off decking using a circular saw. Set saw blade ⅛" deeper than thickness of decking so that saw will not cut side of deck. At areas where circular saw cannot reach, finish cutoff with a jigsaw or handsaw.

8. For a more attractive appearance, face the deck with redwood or cedar facing boards. Miter cut corners, and attach boards with deck screws or 8d galvanized nails.

ALTERNATIVE: Attach facing boards so that edges of decking overhang facing.

HOW TO INSTALL COMPOSITE DECKING

1. Lay composite decking as you would wood decking (pages 212 to 213). Position with the factory crown up so water will run off, and space rows ⅛ to ¼" apart for drainage.

2. Predrill pilot holes at ¾ the diameter of the fasteners, but do not countersink. Composite materials allow fasteners to set themselves. Use spiral shank nails, hot-dipped galvanized ceramic coated screws, or stainless steel nails or deck screws.

Cut away for clarity

ALTERNATIVE: Attach composite decking with self-tapping composite screws. These specially designed screws require no pilot holes. If the decking "mushrooms" over the screw head, use a hammer to tap back in place.

3. Lay remaining decking. For boards 16-ft. or shorter, leave a gap at deck ends and any butt joints, ¹⁄₁₆" for every 20°F difference between the temperature at the time of installation and the expected high temperature for the year.

HOW TO INSTALL TONGUE-AND-GROOVE DECKING

1. *Position starter strip at far end of deck. Make sure it is straight and properly aligned. Attach with 2½" galvanized deck screws driven into the lower runner found under the lip of the starter strip.*

2. *Fit tongue of a deck board into groove of starter strip. There will be approximately a ¼" gap between the deck board and the starter strip. Fasten the deck board to the joists with 2½" galvanized deck screws, working from the middle out to the sides of the deck.*

3. *Continue to add decking. To lay deck boards end-to-end, leave a ⅛" gap between them, and make sure any butt joints are centered over a joist.*

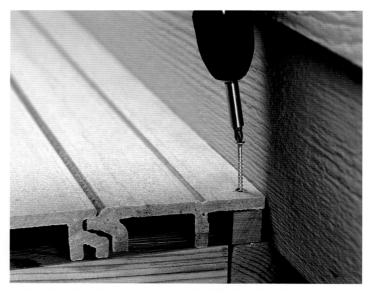

4. *Place final deck board and attach with 2½" galvanized deck screws driven through top of the deck board into the joist. If necessary, rip final board to size, then support the board with a length of 1 × 1, and attach both to the joist. Attach facing boards to conceal exposed ends (photo 4, next page).*

HOW TO INSTALL T-CLIP DECKING

1. *Insert 2" galvanized deck screws into T-clips. Loosely attach one T-clip to the ledger at each joist location.*

2. *Position a deck board tight against the T-clips. Loosely attach T-clips against bottom lip on front side of deck board, just tight enough to keep the board in place. Fully tighten T-clips at back of board, against the house.*

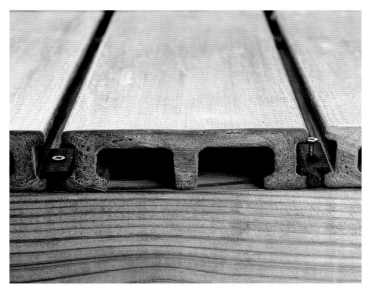

3. *Push another deck board tightly against the front T-clips, attach T-clips at front of the new board, then fully tighten the previous set of T-clips. Add another deck board and repeat the process, to the end of the deck.*

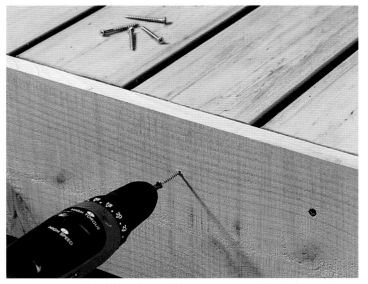

4. *Cover exposed deck board ends. Miter cut corners of the facing, and drill pilot holes ¾ the diameter of the screws. Attach with 3" galvanized deck screws.*

HOW TO INSTALL FIBERGLASS DECK SYSTEMS

1. *Place a length of retaining clips on top of the first joist. Center it on the joist and fasten with 2" galvanized deck screws. Attach lengths of retaining clips to the subsequent joists, so that the clips are perfectly aligned with the first length of clips, creating straight rows.*

2. *Place the open face of a decking board perpendicular to the joists, resting on top of a row of clips. Apply firm pressure to the top of the deck board until the decking snaps into place over the retaining clips. Work along the row, snapping the deck board in place. Attach the remaining deck boards in place, snapping each onto a row of retaining clips.*

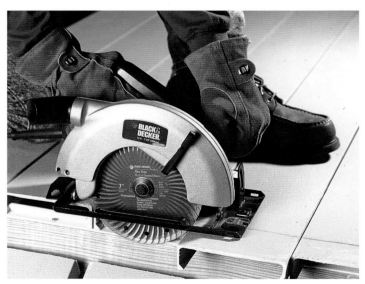

3. *Cut the overhanging ends of the decking boards flush with the outside joists using a circular saw with a fresh carbide-tipped blade or a masonry cut-off disc.*

4. *Use 2" galvanized deck screws to attach the pre-fabricated facing, covering the exposed hollow ends and creating a decorative trim. Cover the screw heads with the screw caps.*

HOW TO INSTALL DECKING WITH SPIKED CLIPS

1. *Drive a spiked clip into the edge of wood decking at joist locations. Use the included fastening block to prevent damage to the spikes.*

2. *Drive a deck screw through the hole in the clip and down at an angle through the deck board and into the joist. One screw secures two deck boards at each joist location.*

3. *Set the adjacent deck board into place. Tap it against the clips to seat the spikes using a scrap block and hand maul or sledge hammer.*

HOW TO INSTALL DECKING WITH BISCUIT-STYLE CLIPS

1. Cut a #20 biscuit slot into the edge of deck boards at each joist location using a biscuit joiner (plate joiner). Set the slot height so the bottom edge of the biscuit clip will touch the joist edge.

2. Insert the biscuit clip into the slot. Drive a deck screw through the hole in the clip and down at an angle through the deck board and into the joist. One screw secures two deck boards at this joist location.

3. Lay a bead of construction adhesive along the edge of the joist to keep it from squeaking later. Cut slots in the adjacent deck board and fit it over the clips of the previous board.

TIP

The hidden fastener options shown here are excellent alternatives to conventional face-nailing or screwing methods. The biggest advantage is probably aesthetic: You don't have to see row after row of fastener heads any longer with these new installation products. But there are other benefits to hidden fasteners as well. Face-screwed wood decking is more prone to rotting if water collects in the screw head pockets. If you nail the decking down, the nail heads can pop up as wood decking dries and contracts or moves. Hidden fasteners eliminate both of these problems.

If you use spike- or biscuit-style clip systems, be aware that you may need to remove large sections of deck boards in order to replace a damaged or defective board in the future because the fasteners lock adjacent boards together and hide access to the fasteners.

HOW TO INSTALL DECKING WITH UNDERMOUNT DECK BRACKETS

1. Install the deck brackets along the top edge of each joist, alternating brackets from one side of the joist to the other in a continuous series. Secure the brackets with screws driven into the side of the joist.

2. Secure the deck boards by driving screws up through the bracket holes and into the joists. Depending on space constraints, these screws can be driven from above if necessary.

3. Continue installing all of the deck boards from below. When you reach the last board, you may need to install it from above for access reasons. Drive deck screws through the deck board and into the joists below. To maintain the hidden fastener appearance, counterbore the pilot holes for the screws and fill the counterbore with a plug cut from a piece of scrap decking.

Building Stairs

Designing deck stairs requires four calculations:

The number of steps depends on the vertical drop of the deck. The vertical drop is the distance from the surface of the deck to the ground.

Rise is the vertical space between treads. Building codes require that the rise measurement be about 8".

Run is the depth of the treads. A convenient way to build deck stairs is to use a pair of 2 × 6s for each tread.

Span is figured by multiplying the run by the number of treads. The span lets you locate the end of the stairway and position support posts.

TOOLS & MATERIALS

- Tape measure
- Pencil
- Framing square
- Level
- Plumb bob
- Circular saw
- Hammer
- Drill
- 1/8" twist bit
- 1" spade bit
- Ratchet wrench

- Shovel
- Caulk gun
- Metal post anchors
- Lumber (2 × 4, 2 × 6, 2 × 12, 6 × 6)
- Metal cleats
- 1/4 × 1 1/4" lag screws
- Joist angle brackets
- 10d joist hanger nails
- 3/8" × 4" lag screws & 1" washers

- 16d galvanized common nails
- Silicone caulk
- Masking tape
- Deck screws
- Hand tamp
- Compactable gravel
- Reciprocating saw
- Chisel
- Materials for pouring concrete footings (see page 190)

Building deck stairs *both increases the safety of your deck and adds to its architectural aesthetics.*

MATERIALS FOR DECK STAIRS

Most local building codes require that you use pressure-treated lumber for stairway posts and stringers. Install stair treads and risers cut from material that matches the surface decking. If possible, create treads that use the same board pattern as the decking. You may cover visible pressure-treated portions of the stairway with material matching the decking, too, or stain them to match the decking as closely as possible. Local codes may require handrails on stairways with three or more treads.

Platform steps feature wide treads. Each step is built on a framework of posts and joists.

Stairway Styles

Open steps have metal cleats that hold the treads between the stringers. The treads on this stairway are built with 2 × 6s to match the surface decking.

Boxed steps, built with notched stringers and solid risers, give a finished look to a deck stairway. Predrill ends of treads to prevent splitting.

Long stairways sometimes require landings. A landing is a small platform to which both flights of stairs are attached.

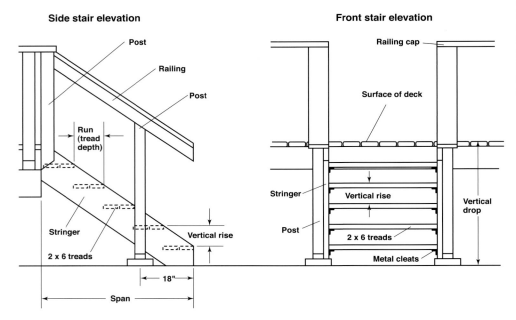

Side stair elevation

Post

Railing

Post

Run (tread depth)

Stringer

2 x 6 treads

Vertical rise

18"

Span

Front stair elevation

Railing cap

Surface of deck

Stringer

Vertical rise

Post

2 x 6 treads

Metal cleats

Vertical drop

*A **common deck stairway** is made from two 2 × 12 stringers and pairs of 2 × 6 treads attached with metal cleats. Posts set 18" back from the end of the stairway help to anchor the stringers and the railings. Calculations needed to build stairs include the number of steps, the rise of each step, the run of each step, and the stairway span.*

HOW TO FIND MEASUREMENTS FOR STAIRWAY LAYOUT

			SAMPLE MEASUREMENTS (39" High Deck)
1. Find the number of steps: Measure vertical drop from deck surface to ground. Divide by 7. Round off to nearest whole number.	Vertical drop:		39"
	÷ 7 =		÷ 5.57"
	Number of steps: =		= 6
2. Find step rise: Divide the vertical drop by the number of steps.	Vertical drop: =		39"
	Number of steps: ÷		÷ 6
	Rise: =		= 6.5"
3. Find step run: Typical treads made from two 2 × 6s have a run of 11¼". If your design is different, find run by measuring depth of tread, including any space between boards.	Run:		11¼"
4. Find stairway span: Multiply the run by the number of treads. (Number of treads is always one less than number of steps.)	Run:		11¼"
	Number of treads:		× 5
	Span: =		= 56¼"

HOW TO BUILD A BOX-FRAME STEP

1. *Construct a rectangular frame for the step using dimension lumber (2 × 6 lumber is standard). Join the pieces with deck screws. The step must be at least 36" wide and 10" deep. Cut cross blocks and install them inside the frame, spaced every 16".*

2. *Dig a flat-bottomed trench, about 4" deep, where the step will rest. Fill the trench with compactable gravel, and pack with a tamper. Set the step in position, then measure and attach deck boards to form the tread of the step.*

HOW TO BUILD A SUSPENDED STEP

1. *Screw 2 × 4 furring strips against one side of the deck joists where the step joists will be installed. These strips provide an offset so the step joists will not conflict with the joist hangers attached to the beam. Use a reciprocating saw and chisel to make 1½"-wide notches in the rim joist adjacent to the furring strips.* Note: *To maintain adequate structural strength, notches in the joists should be no more than 1½" deep.*

2. *Measure and cut step joists, allowing about 3 ft. of nailing surface inside the deck frame and 10" or more of exposed tread. Make sure the step joists are level with one another, then attach them to the deck joists, using deck screws. Cut and attach deck boards to the tread area of the step.*

225

HOW TO BUILD BASIC DECK STAIRS

1. *Use the stairway elevation drawings to find measurements for stair stringers and posts. Use a pencil and framing square to outline where stair stringers will be attached to the side of the deck.*

2. *Locate the post footings so they are 18" back from the end of stairway span. Lay a straight 2 × 4 on the deck so that it is level and square to side of deck. Use a plumb bob to mark the ground at centerpoints of footings.*

3. *Dig holes and pour footings for posts. Attach metal post anchors to footings and install posts. Check with your building department to find out if 6 × 6 posts are required.*

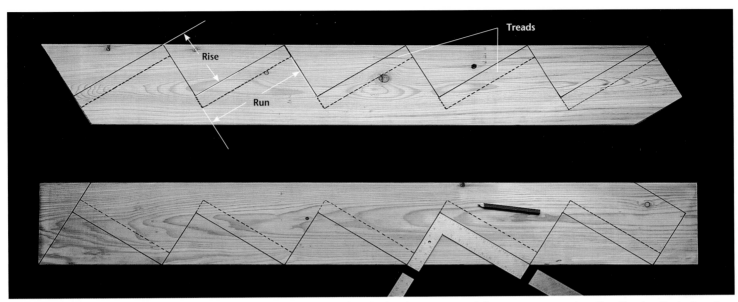

4. *Lay out stair stringers. Use tape to mark the rise measurement on one leg of a framing square, and the run measurement on the other leg. Beginning at one end of stringer, position the square with tape marks flush to edge of board, and outline the rise and run for each step. Then draw in the tread outline against the bottom of each run line. Use a circular saw to trim ends of stringers as shown.*

5. *Attach metal tread cleats flush with bottom of each tread outline using ¼ × 1¼" lag screws. Drill ⅛" pilot holes to prevent the screws from splitting the wood.*

6. *Attach angle brackets to upper ends of stringers using 10d joist hanger nails. Brackets should be flush with cut ends of stringers.*

227

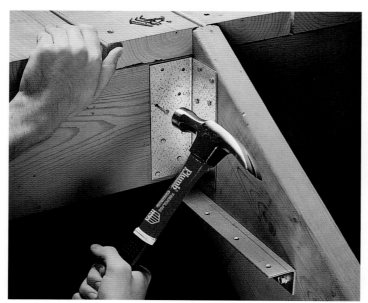

7. *Position the stair stringers against side of deck, over the stringer outlines. Align top point of stringer flush with the surface of the deck. Attach stringers by nailing the angle brackets to the deck with 10d joist hanger nails.*

8. *Drill two ¼" pilot holes through each stringer and into each adjacent post. Counterbore each hole to depth of ½" using a 1" spade bit. Attach stringers to posts with ⅜ × 4" lag screws and washers using a ratchet wrench or impact driver. Seal screw heads with silicone caulk.*

9. *Measure width of stair treads. Cut two 2 × 6s for each tread using a circular saw.*

10. *For each step, position the front 2 × 6 on the tread cleat, so that the front edge is flush with the tread outline on the stringers.*

11. *Drill ⅛" pilot holes, then attach the front 2 × 6 to the cleats with ¼ × 1¼" lag screws.*

12. *Position the rear 2 × 6 on the cleats, allowing a small space between boards. Use a 16d nail as a spacing guide. Drill ⅛" pilot holes, and attach 2 × 6 to cleats with ¼ × 1¼" lag screws. Repeat for remaining steps.*

Stair Variation

Notched stringers precut from pressure-treated wood are available at building centers. Edges of cutout areas should be coated with sealer-preservative to prevent rot.

Installing Railings

Railings must be sturdy and firmly attached to the framing members of the deck. Never attach railing posts to the surface decking. Check local building codes for guidelines regarding railing construction. Most codes require that railings be at least 36 inches above decking. Vertical balusters should be spaced no more than 4 inches apart. In some areas, a grippable handrail may be required for any stairway over four treads. Check with your local building inspector for the building codes in your area.

TOOLS & MATERIALS

- Tape measure
- Pencil
- Power miter saw
- Drill
- Twist bits (1/16", 1/8", 1/4")
- 1" spade bit
- Combination square
- Awl
- Ratchet wrench
- Level

- Reciprocating saw or circular saw
- Jigsaw with wood-cutting blade
- Railing lumber (4 × 4s, 2 × 6s, 2 × 4s, 2 × 2s)
- Clear sealer-preservative
- 3/8 × 4" lag screws and 1" washers
- Deck screws (2", 2½", 3")
- Screwdriver or nail

- 10d galvanized common nails
- Hammer
- Galvanized casing nails
- Silicone caulk
- Caulking gun
- 10d splitless cedar siding nails
- Galvanized metal L-brackets
- Paintbrush

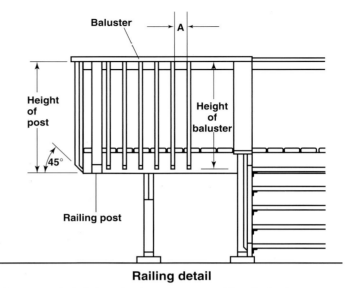

Railing detail

Refer to your deck design plan for spacing (A) and length of railing posts and balusters. Posts should be spaced no more than 6 ft. apart.

Railings are mandatory safety features for any deck that's more than 30" above grade. There are numerous code issues and stipulations that will dictate how you build your deck railings. Consult with your local building inspector for any code clarification you may need.

Types of Railings

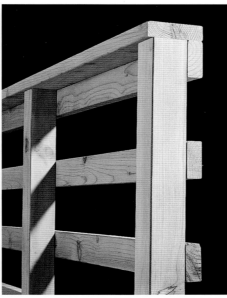

Vertical balusters with posts and rails are a good choice for houses with strong vertical lines. A vertical baluster railing like the one shown above is a good choice where children will be present.

Horizontal railings are often used on low, ranch-style homes. Horizontal railings are made of vertical posts, two or more wide horizontal rails, and a railing cap.

Lattice panels add a decorative touch to a deck. They also provide extra privacy.

RAILING CODES

Railings usually are required by building code on any deck that is more than 30" high. Select a railing design that fits the style of your home.

For example, on a low, ranch-style house, choose a deck railing with wide, horizontal rails. On a Tudor-style home with a steep roof, choose a railing with closely spaced, vertical balusters. See pages 246 to 255 for information on how to build other railing styles, including a curved railing.

Some codes may require easily gripped hand rails for stairways (page 244). Check with your local building inspector.

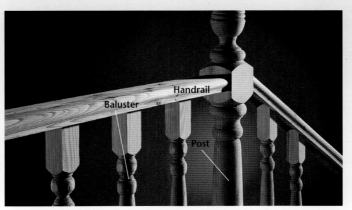

Preshaped products let you easily build decorative deck railings. Railing products include shaped handrails, balusters, and posts.

HOW TO INSTALL A BASIC DECK RAILING

1. *Measure and cut 4 × 4 posts using a power miter saw or circular saw. Cut off tops of the posts square and cut the bottoms at 45° angle. Seal cut ends of lumber with clear sealer-preservative.*

2. *Measure and cut balusters for main deck using a power miter saw or circular saw. Cut off tops of the balusters square and cut bottoms at 45° angle. Seal cut ends of lumber with clear sealer-preservative.*

3. *Drill two ¼" pilot holes spaced 2" apart through bottom end of each post. Counterbore each pilot hole to ½" depth using a 1" spade bit.*

4. *Drill two ⅛" pilot holes spaced 4" apart near bottom end of each baluster. Drill two ⅛" pilot holes at top of each baluster, spaced 1½" apart.*

5. Measure and mark position of posts around the outside of the deck using a combination square as a guide. Plan to install a post on outside edge of each stair stringer.

6. Position each post with beveled end flush with bottom of deck. Plumb post with a level. Insert a screwdriver or nail into pilot holes and mark side of deck.

7. Remove post and drill ¼" pilot holes into side of deck.

8. Attach railing posts to side of deck with ⅜ × 4" lag screws and washers using a ratchet wrench or impact driver. Seal screw heads with silicone caulk.

9. Measure and cut 2 × 4 side rails. Position rails with edges flush to tops of posts and attach to posts with 2½" corrosion-resistant deck screws.

10. Join 2 × 4s for long rails by cutting ends at 45° angles. Drill 1/16" pilot holes to prevent nails from splitting end grain and attach rails with 10d galvanized nails. (Screws may split mitered ends.)

11. Attach ends of rails to stairway posts, flush with edges of posts, as shown. Drill 1/8" pilot holes and attach rails with 2½" deck screws.

12. At stairway, measure from surface of decking to the top of the upper stairway post (A).

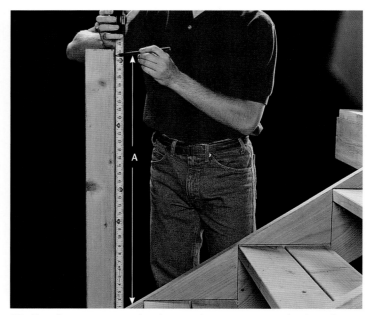

13. Transfer measurement A to lower stairway post, measuring from the edge of the stair stringer.

14. Position 2 × 4 rail against inside of stairway posts. Align rail with top rear corner of top post and with the pencil mark on the lower post. Have a helper attach rail temporarily with 2½" deck screws.

15. Mark the outline of the post and the deck rail on the back side of the stairway rail.

16. Mark the outline of the stairway rail on the lower stairway post.

17. Use a level to mark a plumb cutoff line at the bottom end of the stairway rail. Remove the rail.

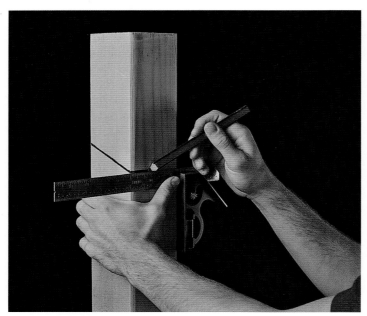

18. *Extend the pencil lines across both sides of the stairway post using a combination square as a guide.*

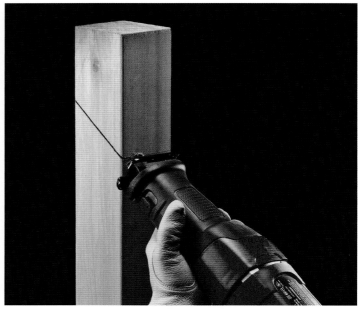

19. *Cut off lower stairway post along diagonal cutoff line using a reciprocating saw or circular saw.*

20. *Use a jigsaw to cut the stairway rail along the marked outlines.*

21. *Position the stairway rail flush against top edge of posts. Drill ⅛" pilot holes, then attach rail to posts with 2½" deck screws.*

22. Use a spacer block to ensure equal spacing between balusters. Beginning next to a plumb railing post, position each baluster tight against spacer block, with top of baluster flush to top of rail. Attach each baluster with 2½" deck screws.

23. For stairway, position baluster against stringer and rail, and adjust for plumb. Draw diagonal cutoff line on top of baluster using top of stair rail as a guide. Cut baluster on marked line using power miter saw. Seal ends with clear sealer-preservative.

24. Beginning next to upper stairway post, position each baluster tight against spacer block, with top flush to top of stair rail. Attach baluster with 2½" deck screws.

25. Position 2 × 6 cap so edge is flush with inside edge of rail. Drill ⅛" pilot holes and attach cap to rail with 2½" deck screws driven every 12". Also drive screws into each post and into every third baluster. For long caps, bevel ends at 45°. Drill 1/16" pilot holes and attach at post using 10d nails.

26. At corners, miter ends of railing cap at 45°. Drill ⅛" pilot holes and attach cap to post with 2½" deck screws.

27. At top of stairs, cut cap so that it is flush with stairway rail. Drill ⅛" pilot holes and attach cap with 2½" deck screws.

28. Measure and cut cap for stairway rail. Mark outline of post on side of cap and bevel cut the ends of the cap.

29. Position cap over the stairway rail and balusters so that edge of cap is flush with inside edge of rail. Drill ⅛" pilot holes and attach cap to rail with 2½" deck screws driven every 12". Also drive screws through cap into stair post and into every third baluster.

Wood Railing Style Variations

Vertical baluster railing is a popular style because it complements most house styles. To improve the strength and appearance of the railing, the advanced variation shown here uses a "false mortise" design. The 2 × 2 balusters are mounted on 2 × 2 horizontal rails that slide into mortises notched into the posts (see page 242).

Horizontal railing visually complements modern ranch-style houses with predominantly horizontal lines. For improved strength and a more attractive appearance, the style shown here features 1 × 4 rails set on edge into dadoes cut in the faces of the posts. A cap rail running over all posts and top rails helps unify and strengthen the railing (see page 242).

Wall-style railing is framed with short 2 × 4 stud walls attached flush with the edges of the deck. The stud walls and rim joists are then covered with siding materials, usually chosen to match the siding on the house. A wall-style railing creates a more private space and visually draws the deck into the home, providing a unified appearance.

Stairway railings are required for any stairway with more than three steps. They are usually designed to match the style used on the deck railing.

Even if you are committed to using wood posts and railings for your deck, there are numerous ways to customize your railing system to make it look fresh and different from other decks. One dramatic step you can take is to choose an unusual material option for the balusters. Balusters are available in various metals, including aluminum, stainless or powder-coated steel, copper, and iron. Metal balusters are fabricated in straight or contoured styles as well as turned and architectural profiles. They install into holes in wooden top and bottom rails or attach with screws. Strips of tempered glass are another baluster option, and they fasten in place with screws or slip into grooves in the rails. Or, fill the spaces between posts and rails with brightly colored outdoor fabric. It can be ordered with metal grommets installed so you tie it in place with weather-resistant rope.

If you use metal balusters, consider adding a centerpiece railing between them. These unique railings are made in various fleur de lis, classic, and nouveau patterns. They'll add shape and distinctiveness to your baluster pattern.

Wooden posts need not be drab, either. One option is to cover them with composite or vinyl sleeves in various colors or outfit them with a sleeve that looks like stacked stone. Instead of running hand rails over the top of your deck posts, let them extend above the railings and install post caps or decorative wood finials. Caps and finials simply fit over the tops of posts and nail or screw in place. Caps are widely available from home centers in copper or stainless steel. You can also order them made from stained glass or as low-voltage solar lights. Then, add a little flair to the bottoms of your posts with one-piece, composite trim skirts in decorative profiles.

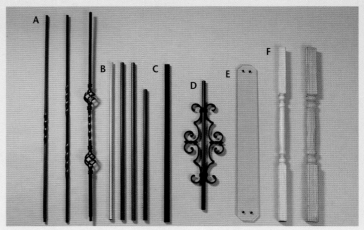

Balusters are available in a variety of styles and material options. Metal balusters are fabricated into many contoured profiles (A). You can also buy tubular styles (B) made of aluminum, stainless steel, and copper, or with a painted finish. Flat-bar balusters (C) or decorative centerpiece railings (D) are other options, as well as strips of tempered glass (E). Wood balusters (F) are more economical than other styles, but they still lend a nicely crafted touch.

Dress up your deck railing posts with decorative top caps. You'll find them in various ball (A) and finial (B) shapes. Consider topping off your posts with paint (C) or copper (D), or maybe low-voltage or solar powered cap lights (E). Top caps will also help your wooden posts last longer by preventing water from wicking down into the end grain, leading to rot.

IG OPTIONS

Post caps are available in a variety of styles made of metal, composites, or wood. Aside from adding a decorative touch, they also extend the life of the posts by preventing water from wicking down into the end grain.

If you'd prefer not to build your railing from scratch, you can buy PVC or other composite railing systems that are simple to install and long lasting (see page 242). Another advantage is you'll never need to stain or paint them.

Tempered glass railings are an excellent choice if your deck offers an impressive view (see page 244). There are no balusters or handrails to peek through or over—just clear "windows" to the world beyond.

Contoured metal balusters will give your deck a fresh, contemporary twist. They attach with screws, just like wooden balusters.

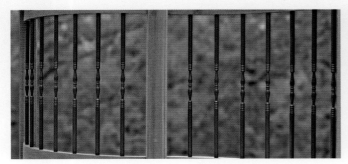

Spindle-style, turned balusters are available in various metal tones and colors. They can lend a tailored effect to wooden railings.

Tempered glass railing systems offer the same safety as wood balusters, but with the added advantage of a virtually unobstructed view.

Composite Railing

Several manufacturers of composite decking now offer composite railing kits that are easy to install by do-it-yourselfers. Aside from the advantages of using reclaimed and recycled materials for your railings, composites are also virtually maintenance-free and come in a variety of styles and colors. Some railing systems are packaged in kits with all the components necessary to build six-foot sections of railing. Other companies sell the pieces individually. You may need to cut the components to size to fit your railing application.

TOOLS & MATERIALS

- Level
- Ratchet and sockets or impact driver
- Drill/driver
- Railing support bracket
- 16-gauge pneumatic nailer and nails
- Posts
- Balusters
- Rail cap
- ½"-diameter bolts, washers and nuts
- Corrosion-resistant deck screws

Composite deck railing systems are very durable and require only minimal maintenance.

HOW TO INSTALL A COMPOSITE RAILING

1. *Fasten composite railing posts to the deck rim joists with pairs of ½"-dia., countersunk bolts, washers, and nuts. Position the posts 72" on center. Do not notch the posts.*

2. *Install railing support brackets, if applicable, to the posts using corrosion-resistant deck screws. For the railing system shown here, an assembly bracket tool sets the placement of the brackets on the posts without measuring.*

3. *Assemble the balusters, top, and bottom rails into the correct configuration on a flat work surface. Again, the assembly tool shown here sets the spacing of the balusters. Fasten the bottom rails to the balusters with 16-gauge pneumatic nails or deck screws, according the manufacturer's recommendations.*

4. *Fasten the top rails to the balusters with 16-gauge pneumatic nails.*

5. *Place the assembled railing section onto the railing support brackets and check it for level. Drive pairs of deck screws up though the support bracket holes and into the handrail. Toenail the bottom rail to the post with 16-gauge pneumatic nails.*

243

Glass-panel Railing

For the ultimate in unobstructed viewing, you can install a glass-panel railing system on your deck and avoid balusters altogether. The system shown here is quite manageable to install without special tools. It consists of a framework of aluminum posts and top and bottom rails that fasten together with screws. Extruded vinyl liner inserts that fit inside the top and bottom rails hold the glass without fasteners. Tempered glass panels that are at least ¼" thick will meet building codes, provided the railing posts are spaced five feet on center. It is recommended that you assemble the railing framework first, then measure and order the glass panels to fit the rail openings.

TOOLS & MATERIALS

- Tape measure
- Level
- Ratchet and sockets or impact driver
- Drill/driver
- Posts
- Post brackets
- Tempered glass panels
- Fasteners
- Railings
- Lag screws
- Attachment screws
- Rubber setting blocks

Tempered glass panels are both DIY friendly and code approved, provided you install them according to the manufacturer's guidelines.

HOW TO INSTALL A GLASS-PANEL RAILING

1. Once you've determined the layout of the deck posts, fasten the post brackets to the deck with lag screws. Install all the posts and bottom rails.

2. Insert the top post sleeves into the post ends, then measure and cut the top rails to length. Assemble the rails and sleeves, fastening the parts with screws. Check each post for plumb with a level before driving the attachment screws and adjust if necessary.

3. Measure the length of the top rail inner channels and cut glass insert strips to fit. Fasten the glass rail brackets to the posts with screws.

4. Measure the distance between the glass inserts and add ¾" to determine the height of the glass panels. Measure the distance between posts and subtract 3 to 6" to find the glass panel width, less air gaps. Order glass. Install the bottom rails on the brackets.

5. Slip each glass panel into the top insert, swing it into place over the bottom insert, and lower it into the bottom channel to rest on the rubber setting blocks. No further attachment is required.

Steel Cable Railing

Another railing option that can improve the view from your deck is to use braided steel cables between the railing posts. Here, lengths of cable pass continuously through holes in the posts and tension is created with a special threaded fitting on the cable end. Cables must be spaced no more than 3" apart, with railing posts located 3 ft. on center. You can buy prefabricated metal posts as we show here or make them from wood. The endmost posts should be made of 4 × 6 lumber to handle the cable tension, although the intermediate posts can be conventionally sized. You'll also need to install a 2 × 6 cap rail securely to all posts and add 1 × 4 blocking under the cap rail to provide additional lateral reinforcement.

TOOLS & MATERIALS

- Measuring tape
- Level
- Drill/driver
- Hack saw
- Cable cutters
- Self-locking pliers
- Wrenches
- Electric grinder
- Cable-lacing needle
- Cap rails
- Steel lag screws & washers
- Self-locking fitting
- Cable
- Flanged metal posts

TIP

Cut off the excess threaded bolt at the nut with a hack saw. Grind or file away any sharp edges.

A series of braided steel cables can replace ordinary wood balusters and give your deck a clean, contemporary look. Posts must be spaced closely together to handle the cable tension and ensure safety.

HOW TO INSTALL CABLE RAILINGS

1. If you install flanged metal posts, secure them to the deck's framing with stainless steel lag screws and washers.

2. Drill holes through the railing posts to fit the cables, threaded end fittings, and quick connect locking fittings. Pass the terminal threaded ends of the cables through one railing end post and install washer nuts about ¼" onto the threads.

3. Feed the cables through the intermediate posts and the opposite end post. Work systematically to prevent tangling the cables. A cable-lacing needle will make it easier to pass cables through each post without snagging it. Attach cap rails (*Inset*).

4. Slip a self-locking fitting over the end of each cable and seat the fitting in the cable hole in the post. You may need to counterbore this hole first to accommodate the fitting. Pull the cable tight. Jaws inside the fitting will prevent the cable from becoming slack again.

5. Tighten each cable nut with a wrench, starting from the center cable and working outward. A locking pliers will keep the cable from twisting as you tighten the nut. Tighten the nut until you cannot flex the cables more than 4" apart.

6. Cut off the excess cable at the quick-connect fitting end with a cable cutter or hack saw. Grind the end of the cable flush with the fitting, and cover it with a snap-on end cap.

Fasteners & Hardware

Certain structural connections of your deck will require the use of lag screws, through bolts, and concrete anchors to withstand the heavy loads and sheer forces applied to a deck. Attaching ledger boards to your home's band joist, fastening beams to posts, or anchoring posts to concrete footings are all areas where you'll need to step up to larger fasteners and anchors. Be sure to use hot-dipped galvanized or stainless steel hardware to prevent rusting or corrosion from pressure-treating chemicals. Building codes require that you install a washer beneath the heads of lag screws or bolts and another washer before attaching nuts. Washers prevent fasteners from tearing through wood and secure hardware under stress.

Another fastening option to consider is high-strength epoxy, applied from a syringe. If you are fastening deck posts or ledger boards to cured concrete, the epoxy will bond threaded rod permanently in place without needing an additional metal anchor.

Here is an overview of the anchoring fasteners you may need for your project.

Galvanized or stainless steel lag bolts and washers are the correct fasteners for installing ledgers to the band joist of a house. You can also use them for making other wood-to-wood connections.

Anchoring Fasteners

Use ½"-dia. or larger through bolts, washers, and nuts for fastening beams to posts or railing posts to joists. They should be galvanized or made of stainless steel for corrosion resistance.

J-bolts, embedded in the wet concrete of deck footings, provide a secure connection for attaching concrete footings to metal connecting hardware.

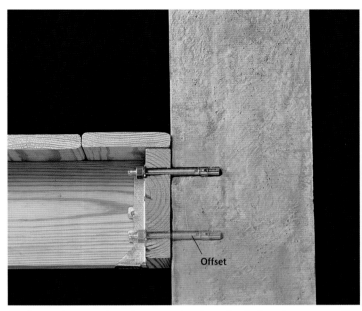

Wedge or sleeve anchors draw a wedge through a hollow sleeve, expanding it to form a tight fit in solid concrete. A nut and threaded end hold the ledger boards in place.

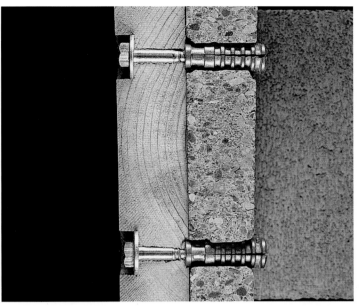

Soft metal shield anchors expand when lag screws are driven into them. They make suitable connections in either solid concrete or hollow block foundations.

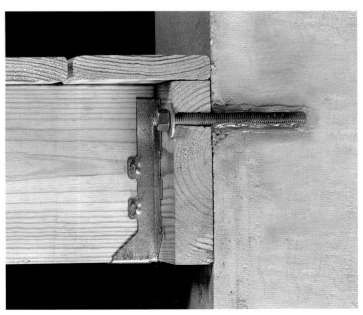

A bolt driven through the foundation from the inside can be fitted with a washer and bolt to secure the ledger.

High strength epoxy and threaded rod are good options for attaching metal connecting hardware to concrete footings.

Metal Connecting Hardware

Sheet-metal connecting hardware comes in assorted shapes and styles. It is used to create strong wood-to-wood or wood-to-concrete joints quickly and easily. For instance, metal post anchors not only provide a simple way to attach posts and footings, but they also create space between the two surfaces so post ends stay dry. Joist hangers are a fast way to hang long, heavy joists accurately. Post beam caps, T-straps, and angled joist hangers are ideal solutions for building stacked joints or when space doesn't allow you access to drive screws or nails from behind the joint.

Make sure to buy hot-dipped galvanized or stainless steel connecting hardware. Some styles are designed for interior use only and do not have adequate corrosion protection. The product label should identify whether or not the hardware is suitable for pressure-treated wood and outdoor use. Use joist hanger nails made from the same material as the hardware.

Deck post ties *fasten stair or railing posts to stringers or joists without through bolts. Hardware is manufactured in 2 × 4 and 4 × 4 size options.*

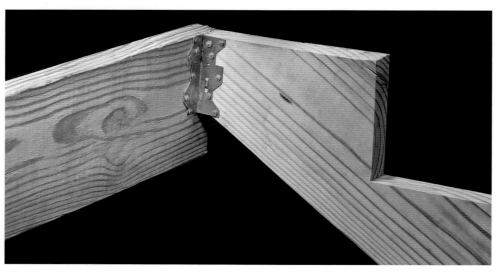

Framing anchors *can be used to fasten rim joists together at corners or make other right-angle attachments, such as stair stringers to rim joists.*

Hanger Hardware for Decks

Post anchors hold deck posts in place, and raise the base of the posts to help prevent water from entering end grain of wood.

Angle brackets help reinforce header and outside joists. Angle brackets are also used to attach stair stringers to the deck.

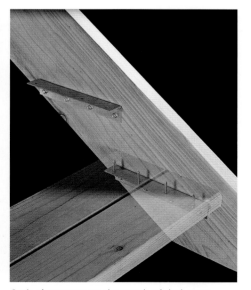

Joist hangers are used to attach joists to the ledger and header joist. Double hangers are used when decking patterns require a double-width joist.

Angled joist hangers are used to frame decks that have unusual angles or decking patterns.

Stair cleats support the treads of deck steps. Cleats are attached to stair stringers with ¼ × 1¼" galvanized lag screws.

Post-beam caps *secure beams on top of posts and are available in one-piece or adjustable styles.*

H-fit rafter ties *attach 2× joists or rafters to the top of a beam between beam ends.*

Seismic ties *attach 2× joists or rafters to the top of a beam at its ends.*

Skewable joist hangers *attach 2× lumber, such as stair stringers, to the face of framing at an adjustable angle.*

Skewable angle brackets reinforce framing connections at angles other than 90° or at beam ends where 45° joist hangers won't fit.

Direct bearing footing connectors attach beams directly to footings on low-profile decks.

T-straps reinforce the connection between beam and post, particularly on long beams requiring spliced construction. Local building codes may also allow their use in place of post caps.

Strapping plates, also known as nailing plates or mending plates, are useful for a variety of reinforcement applications.

Screws & Nails

When you attach the beams and joists of your deck, and probably the decking as well, you'll need a collection of screws and/or nails to get these jobs done. It may not seem like screw and nail technology would change all that much, but in fact there are many new products available for making these essential connections. If you build your deck from pressure-treated lumber, be sure to use stainless, hot-dipped galvanized, or specially coated fasteners that are approved for use with the more corrosive ACQ and CBA wood preservatives. Spiral or ring-shank nails will offer better holding power than smooth nails. Use screws with auger tips and self-drilling heads to avoid drilling pilot holes. Some screws are specially designed for installing composite decking. They have a variable thread pattern that keeps the heads from mushrooming the surrounding material when driven flush.

If you are building a large deck, consider using a pneumatic nailer with collated nails instead of hand nailing. Collated screws are a faster way to lay deck boards than driving each screw individually. Here's an overview of your fastener options.

Whether you are fastening framing together or installing deck boards, your screw options include stainless steel or galvanized. You can also buy screws with colored coatings formulated to resist corrosion from pressure-treated wood. Stainless or coated screws will prevent black staining that can occur on cedar.

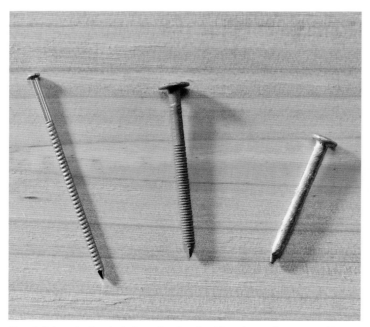

Use stainless steel or hot-dipped galvanized framing nails to assemble beams and joists. Install metal connector hardware with 8d or 10d hot-dipped galvanized metal connector nails.

For large deck projects, galvanized pneumatic nails or coated, collated screws are a faster way to fasten framing and decking than driving each nail or screw by hand.

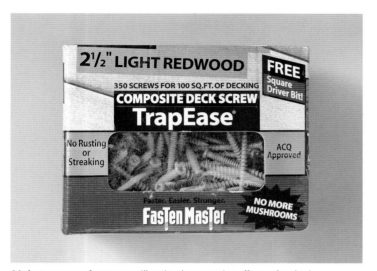

Make sure your fasteners will resist the corrosive effects of today's pressure-treating chemicals. Fastener manufacturers will usually provide this information on the product label.

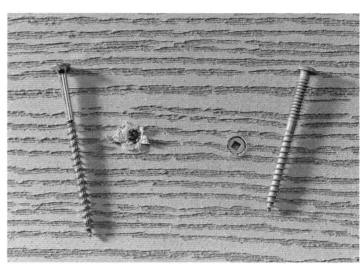

One drawback to composite decking is that it tends to "mushroom" around screwheads unless the screws are driven into pilot holes. Some screws are designed with undercut heads and a variable pitch pattern to avoid this problem.

If you'd prefer not to see screwheads in your decking but still want to drive them from the surface, you can buy screws with snap-off heads. A special tool breaks the head off after the screw is driven. The resulting hole is much smaller than a screwhead.

Choose your nails and screws carefully. Screws with "bright" or black-oxide coatings and uncoated nails will not stand up to exterior use or pressure-treating chemicals. Fasteners are as crucial to your deck's long-term durability as the quality of the framing lumber or decking.

Second-story Walkout Deck

This simple rectangular deck provides a secure, convenient outdoor living space. The absence of a stairway prevents children from wandering away or unexpected visitors from wandering in. It also makes the deck easier to build.

Imagine how handy it will be to have this additional living area only a step away from your dining or living room, with no more need to walk downstairs for outdoor entertaining, dining, or relaxing.

And if you'd like to add a stairway, just refer to the discussion on building stairs (see page 222).

Simplicity, security, and convenience are the hallmarks of this elevated deck.

Cutaway View

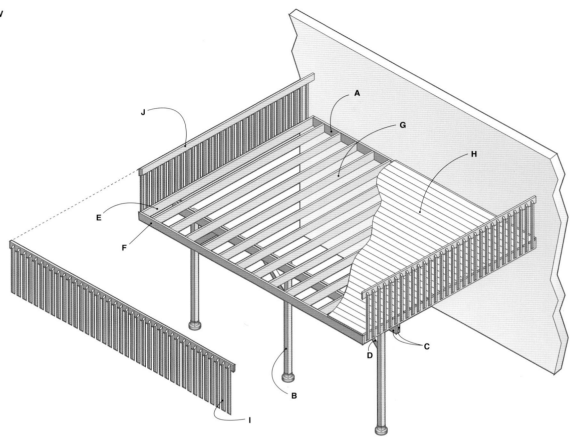

TOOLS & MATERIALS

- 12"-diameter footing forms (3)
- J-bolts (3)
- 6 × 6 metal post anchors (3)
- 2 × 10 joist hangers (26)
- Galvanized deck screws (3", 2½")
- Joist hanger nails
- ⅜ × 4" lag screws and washers (28)
- ¼ × 5" lag screws and washers (16)
- ⁵⁄₁₆ × 7" carriage bolts, washers, and nuts (6)

- 16d galvanized nails
- Metal flashing (18 ft.)
- Silicone caulk (3 tubes)
- Concrete, as required
- Angle brackets
- Gravel, as required
- Pencil
- Circular saw
- Pressure-treated lumber
- Reciprocating saw or handsaw
- Level
- Metal snips
- Drill

- 1" spade bit
- Ratchet wrench
- Chalk line
- Tape measure
- Caulk gun
- Plumb bob
- Stakes
- Clamshell digger or power auger
- Power miter saw
- Combination square
- Joist nails
- Router
- ½" round-over bit

Lumber List

Qty.	Size	Material	Part
2	2 × 12" × 20'	Trtd. lumber	Beam boards (C)
2	2 × 10" × 18'	Trtd. lumber	Ledger (A), Rim joist (F)
15	2 × 10" × 14'	Trtd. lumber	Joists (G), End joists (E)
3	6 × 6" × 10'	Trtd. lumber	Deck posts (B)
2	4 × 4" × 8'	Trtd. lumber	Braces (D)
32	2 × 6" × 18'	Cedar	Decking (H), Top rail (J)
2	2 × 6" × 16'	Cedar	Top rail (J)
50	2 × 2" × 8'	Cedar	Balusters (I)
*	2 × 4	Trtd. lumber	Scrap pieces for braces

Framing Plan

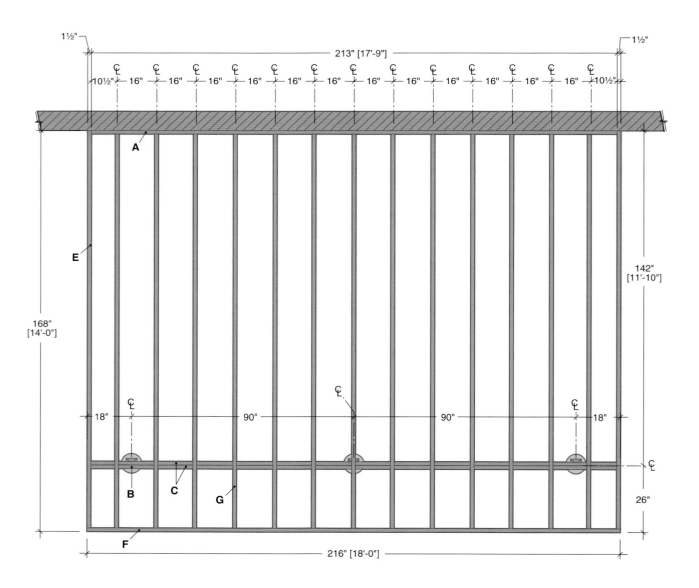

Elevation

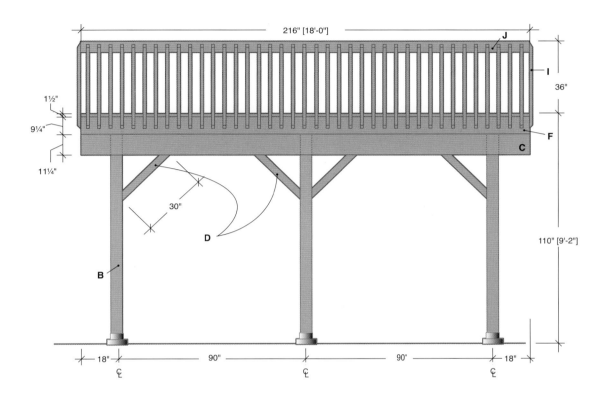

Railing Detail

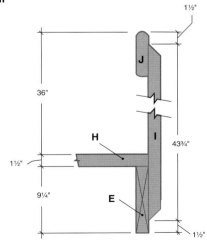

Face Board Detail

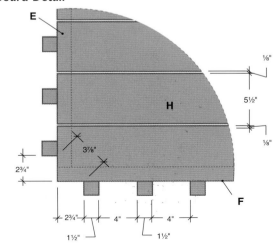

HOW TO BUILD A SECOND-STORY WALKOUT DECK

Step A: Attach the Ledger

1. Draw a level outline on the siding to show where the ledger and the end joists will fit against the house. Install the ledger so that the surface of the decking boards will be 1" below the indoor floor level. This height difference prevents rainwater or melted snow from seeping into the house.

2. Cut out the siding along the outline with a circular saw. To avoid cutting the sheathing that lies underneath the siding, set the blade depth to the same thickness as the siding. Finish the cutout with a chisel, holding the beveled side in to ensure a straight cut.

Use a template made from 2 × 4s to locate the post footings on the ground, then mark the footings with stakes.

3. Cut galvanized flashing to the length of the cutout using metal snips. Slide the flashing up under the siding at the top of the cutout.

4. Measure and cut the ledger (A) from pressure-treated lumber. Center the ledger end to end in the cutout, with space at each end for the end joist.

5. Brace the ledger into position under the flashing. Tack the ledger into place with galvanized nails.

6. Drill pairs of ¼" pilot holes at 16" intervals through the ledger and into the house header joist. Counterbore each pilot hole ½" using a 1" spade bit. Attach the ledger with 4" lag screws and washers using a ratchet wrench.

7. Apply silicone caulk between the siding and flashing. Also seal the lag screw heads and the cracks at the ends of the ledger.

Step B: Pour the Footings

1. To establish a reference point for locating the footings, drop a plumb bob from the ends of the ledger down to the ground.

2. Position a straight 14 ft.-long 2 × 4 perpendicular to the house at the point where the plumb bob meets the ground. NOTE: If you are building on a steep slope or uneven ground, the mason's string method of locating footing positions will work better.

3. Check for square using the 3-4-5 triangle method. From the 2 × 4, measure 3 ft. along the wall and make a mark. Next, measure 4 ft. out from the house and make a mark on the 2 × 4. The diagonal line between the marks will measure 5 ft. when the board is accurately square to the house. Adjust the board as needed using stakes to hold it in place.

4. Extend another reference board from the house at the other end of the ledger, following the same procedure.

5. Measure out along both boards, and mark the centerline of the footings (see Framing Plan, page 258).

6. Lay a straight 2 × 4 between the centerline marks, and drive stakes to mark the footing locations.

7. Remove the boards and dig the post footings using a clamshell digger or power auger. Pour 2 to 3" of loose gravel into each hole for drainage. NOTE: When measuring the footing size and depth, make sure you comply with local building codes, which may require flaring the base to 18".

8. Cut the footing forms to length using a reciprocating saw or handsaw, and insert them into the footing holes, leaving 2" above ground level. Pack soil around the forms for support, and fill the forms with concrete, tamping with a long stick or rod to eliminate any air gaps.

9. Screed the tops flush with a straight 2 × 4. Insert a J-bolt into the center of each footing and set with ¾ to 1" of thread exposed. Clean the bolt threads before the concrete sets.

Plumb each post with a level, then use braces and stakes to hold in place until the beam and joists are installed.

Step C: Set the Posts

1. Lay a long, straight 2 × 4 flat across the footings, parallel to the house. With one edge tight against the J-bolts, draw a reference line across the top of each footing to help orient the post anchors.

2. Place a metal post anchor on each footing, centering it over the J-bolt and squaring it with the reference line. Attach the post anchors by threading a nut over each bolt and tightening with a ratchet wrench.

3. The tops of the posts (B) will eventually be level with the bottom edge of the ledger, but initially cut the posts several inches longer to allow for final trimming. Position the posts in the anchors and tack into place with one nail each.

4. With a level as a guide, use braces and stakes to ensure that the posts are plumb.

5. Determine the height of the beam by using a chalk line and a line level. Extend the chalk line out from the bottom edge of the ledger, make sure that the line is level, and snap a mark across the face of a post. Use the line and level to transfer the mark to the remaining posts.

Step D: Notch the Posts

1. Remove the posts from the post anchors and cut to the finished height.

2. Measure and mark a 3 × 11¼" notch at the top of each post, on the outside face. Use a framing square to trace lines on all sides. Rough-cut the notches with a circular saw, then finish with a reciprocating saw or handsaw.

3. Reattach the posts to the post anchors, with the notch-side facing away from the deck.

Step E: Install the Beam

1. Cut the beam boards (C) to length, adding several inches to each end for final trimming after the deck frame is squared up.

2. Join the beam boards together with 2½" galvanized deck screws. Mark the post locations on the top edges and sides using a combination square as a guide.

3. Lift the beam, one end at a time, into the notches with the crown up. Align and clamp the beam to the posts. NOTE: Installing boards of this size and length, at this height, requires caution. You should have at least two helpers.

4. Counterbore two ½"-deep holes using a 1" spade bit, then drill ⁵⁄₁₆" pilot holes through the beam and post.

5. Thread a carriage bolt into each pilot hole. Add a washer and nut to the counterbore-side of each bolt and tighten with a ratchet wrench. Seal both ends of the bolts with silicone caulk.

6. Cut the tops of the posts flush with the top edge of the beam, using a reciprocating saw or handsaw.

Step F: Install the Frame

1. Measure and cut the end joists (E) to length using a circular saw.

2. Attach the end joists to the ends of the ledger with 16d galvanized nails, or angle brackets and 10d joist hanger nails.

3. Measure and cut the rim joist (F) to length with a circular saw. Fasten to the ends of end joists with 16d nails.

4. Square up the frame by measuring corner to corner and adjusting until the measurements are equal. When the frame is square, toenail the end joists in place on top of the beam.

5. Trim the ends of the beam flush with the faces of the end joists using a reciprocating saw or a handsaw.

Step G: Install the Braces

1. Cut the braces (D) to length (see Elevation, page 259) with a circular saw or power miter saw. Miter both ends at 45°.

2. Install the braces by positioning them against the beam boards and against the posts. Make sure the outside faces of the braces are flush with the outside faces of the beam and the posts. Temporarily fasten with deck screws.

3. Secure the braces to the posts with 5" lag screws. Drill two ¼" pilot holes through the upper end of each brace into the beam. Counterbore to a ½"-depth using a 1" spade bit, and drive lag screws with a ratchet wrench. Repeat for the lower end of the braces into the posts.

Step H: Install the Joists

1. Measure and mark the joist locations (see Framing Plan, page 258) on the ledger, rim joist, and beam. Draw the outline of each joist on the ledger and rim joist using a combination square.

2. Install a joist hanger at each joist location. Attach one flange of the hanger to one side of the outline using joist nails. Use a spacer cut from scrap 2 × 8 lumber to achieve the correct spread for each hanger, then fasten the remaining side flange with joist

Snap a chalk line flush with the outside edge of the deck, and cut off overhanging deck boards with a circular saw.

After cutting balusters to length, gang them up and drill ⅛" pilot holes through the top and bottom.

To make a joint in the top rail, cut the ends at 45° and drill a pair of pilot holes. Then fasten the ends together with deck screws.

nails. Remove the spacer and repeat the same procedure for the remaining joist hangers.

3. Measure, mark, and cut lumber for joists (G), using a circular saw. Place joists in hangers with crown side up and attach with joist hanger nails. Align joists with the outlines on the top of the beam, and toenail in place.

Step I: Lay the Decking

1. Measure, mark, and cut the decking boards (H) to length as needed.

2. Position the first row of decking flush against the house, and attach by driving a pair of galvanized deck screws into each joist.

3. Position the remaining decking boards, leaving a ⅛" gap between boards to provide for drainage, and attach to each joist with deck screws.

4. Every few rows of decking, measure from the edge of the decking to the outside edge of the deck. If the measurement can be divided evenly by 5⅝", the last board will fit flush with the outside edge of the deck as intended. If the measurement shows that the last board will not fit flush, adjust the spacing as you install the remaining rows of boards.

5. If your decking overhangs the end joists, snap a chalk line to mark the outside edge of the deck and cut flush with a circular saw set to a 1½" depth. If needed, finish the cut with a jigsaw or handsaw where a circular saw can't reach.

Step J: Build the Railing

1. Measure, mark, and cut the balusters (I) to length, with 45° miters at both ends.

2. Gang the balusters together and drill two ⅛" pilot holes at both ends.

3. Clamp a 1½" guide strip flush with the bottom edge of the deck platform to establish the baluster height (see Railing Detail, page 259).

4. To ensure that the balusters are installed at equal intervals, create a spacing jig, less than 4" wide, from two pieces of scrap material.

5. Attach the corner balusters first (see Face Board Detail, page 259) using a level to ensure that they are plumb. Then use the spacing jig for positioning, and attach the remaining balusters to the deck platform with 3" deck screws.

6. Measure, mark, and cut the top rail sections (J) to length. Round over three edges (see Railing Detail, page 259) using a router with a ½" round-over bit. Cut 45° miters on the ends that meet at the corners.

7. Hold or clamp the top rail in position, and attach with 2½" deck screws driven through the balusters.

8. If you need to make straight joints in the top rail, cut the ends of the adjoining boards at 45°. Drill angled ⅛" pilot holes and join with deck screws.

263

Ground-level Walkout Deck

This deck is classic in its simplicity. Moderately sized and easy to build, this rectangular deck won't cost you an arm and a leg—in either time or money. The framing and decking plans are quite straightforward, and you can likely build the entire deck in just two or three weekends, even with limited carpentry and building experience. Within just a few weeks time, you can transform your yard into a congenial gathering place for cooking, entertaining, and relaxing; a place where you, your family, and your friends can enjoy the fresh air in convenience and comfort.

Extend your living space and increase your home's value.

Cutaway View

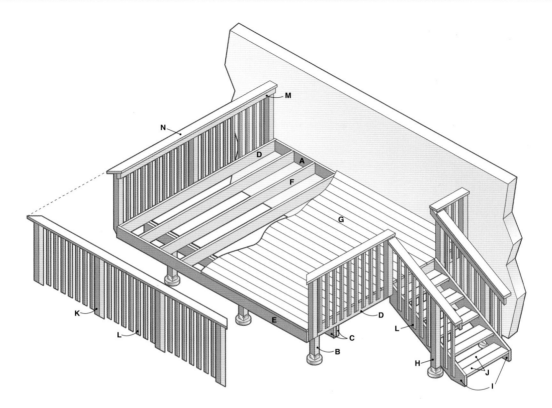

TOOLS & MATERIALS

- 10"-dia. footing forms (3)
- 8"-dia. footing forms (2)
- J-bolts (5)
- 6 × 6" metal post anchors (3)
- 4 × 4" metal post anchors (2)
- 6 × 6" metal post-beam caps (3)
- 2 × 8" joist hangers (16)
- 1½ × 6" angle brackets (6)
- 1½ × 10" angle brackets (10)
- 10d joist hanger nails
- 16d galvanized nails
- Common nails
- Galvanized deck screws (2½", 3")
- ⅜ × 4" lag screws & washers (20)

- ⅜ × 5" lag screws & washers (22)
- ¼ × 1¼" lag screws & washers (80)
- Flashing (12 ft.)
- Exterior silicone caulk (3 tubes)
- Concrete as needed
- Pencil
- Level
- Circular saw
- Chisel
- Hammer
- Drill
- 1" spade bit
- Metal snips
- Pressure-treated lumber

- Ratchet wrench
- Caulking gun
- Mason's string
- Masking tape
- Plumb bob
- Clamshell digger and power auger
- Reciprocating saw or handsaw
- Combination square
- Clamps
- Awl
- Power miter saw
- Gravel for footings as needed

Lumber List

Qty.	Size	Material	Part
4	2 × 8" × 12'	Trtd. lumber	Ledger (A), Beam bds (C), Rim joist (E)
1	6 × 6" × 8'	Trtd. lumber	Deck posts (B)
10	2 × 8" × 10'	Trtd. lumber	End joists (D), Joists (F)
25	2 × 6" × 12'	Cedar	Decking (G), Rail cap (N)
7	4 × 4" × 8'	Cedar	Stair posts (H), Rail post (K)
2	2 × 12" × 8'	Cedar	Stringers (I)
5	2 × 6" × 6'	Cedar	Treads (J)
32	2 × 2" × 8'	Cedar	Balusters (L)
2	2 × 4" × 12'	Cedar	Top rail (M)
2	2 × 4" × 10'	Cedar	Top rail (M)
*	2 × 4	Trtd. lumber	Batterboards, braces

Framing Plan

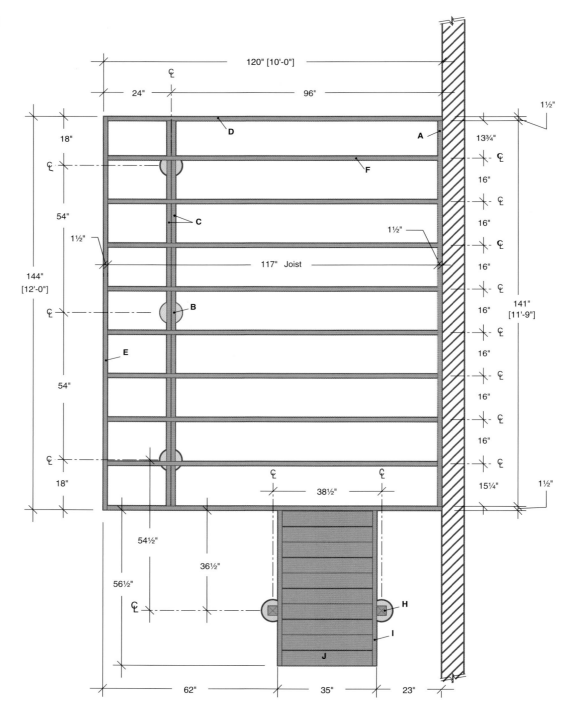

Elevation

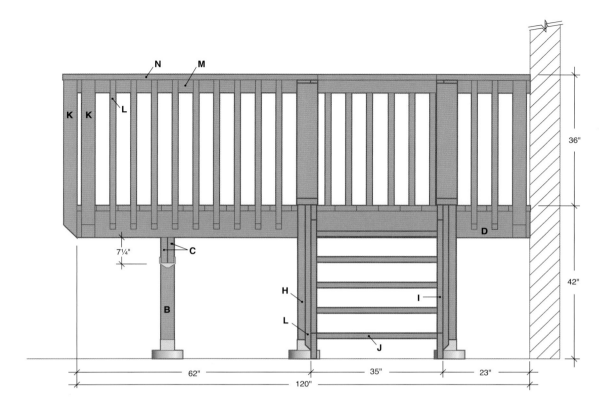

Stairway Detail

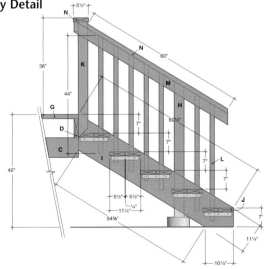

Railing Detail

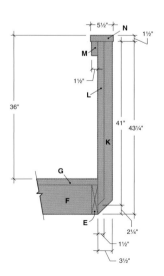

HOW TO BUILD A GROUND LEVEL WALKOUT DECK

Step A: Attach the Ledger

1. Draw a level outline on the siding to show where the ledger and the end joists will fit against the house. Install the ledger so that the surface of the decking boards will be 1" below the indoor floor level. This height difference prevents rainwater or melted snow from seeping into the house.

2. Cut out the siding along the outline with a circular saw. To prevent the blade from cutting the sheathing that lies underneath the siding, set the blade depth to the same thickness as the siding. Finish the cutout with a chisel, holding the beveled side in to ensure a straight cut.

3. Cut galvanized flashing to the length of the cutout using metal snips. Slide the flashing up under the siding at the top of the cutout.

4. Measure and cut the ledger (A) from pressure-treated lumber. Center the ledger end to end in the cutout, with space at each end for the end joist.

5. Brace the ledger in position under the flashing. Tack the ledger into place with galvanized deck screws.

6. Drill pairs of ¼" pilot holes at 16" intervals through the ledger and into the house header joist. Counterbore each pilot hole ½" using a 1" spade bit. Attach the ledger to the wall with ⅜ × 4" lag screws and washers using a ratchet wrench.

7. Apply a thick bead of silicone caulk between siding and flashing. Also seal the lag screw heads and the cracks at the ends of the ledger.

Step B: Pour the Footings

1. Referring to the measurements shown in the Framing Plan, page 266, mark the centerlines of the two outer footings on the ledger and drive nails at these locations.

2. Set up temporary batter boards and stretch a mason's string out from the ledger at each location. Make sure the strings are perpendicular to the ledger, and measure along the strings to find the centerpoints of the posts.

3. Set up additional batter boards and stretch another string parallel to the ledger across the post centerpoints.

4. Check the mason's strings for square by measuring diagonally from corner to corner and adjusting the strings so that the measurements are equal.

5. Measure along the cross string and mark the center post location with a piece of tape.

6. Use a plumb bob to transfer the footing centerpoints to the ground and drive a stake to mark each point.

7. Remove the mason's strings and dig the post footings using a clamshell digger or power auger. Pour 2 to 3" of loose gravel into each hole for drainage. NOTE: When measuring the footing size and depth, make sure you comply with your local building code, which may require flaring the base.

8. Cut the footing forms to length using a reciprocating saw or handsaw, and insert them into the footing holes, leaving 2" above ground level. Pack soil around the forms for support and fill the forms with concrete, tamping with a long stick or rod to eliminate any air pockets.

9. Screed the tops flush with a straight 2 × 4. Insert a J-bolt into each footing, set so ¾ to 1" of thread is exposed. Retie the mason's strings and position the J-bolts at the exact center of the posts using a plumb bob as a guide. Clean the bolt threads before concrete sets.

Step C: Set the Posts

1. Lay a long, straight 2 × 4 flat across the footings, parallel to the ledger. With one edge tight against the J-bolts, draw a reference line across each footing.

2. Place a metal post anchor on each footing, centering it over the J-bolt and squaring it with the reference line. Attach the post anchors by threading a nut over each bolt and tightening with a ratchet wrench.

3. Cut the posts to length, adding approximately 6" for final trimming. Place the posts in the anchors and tack into place with one nail.

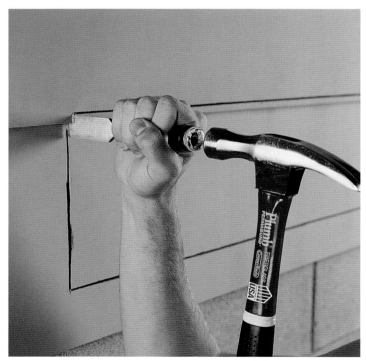

A. *After outlining the position of the ledger and cutting the siding with a circular saw, use a chisel to finish the corners of the cutout.*

C. *After the posts have been set in place and braced plumb, use a straight 2 × 4 and a level to mark the top of the beam on each post.*

4. With a level as a guide, use braces and stakes to plumb the posts. Finish nailing the posts to the anchors.

5. Determine the height of the beam by extending a straight 2 × 4 from the bottom edge of the ledger across the face of a post. Level the 2 × 4, and draw a line on the post.

6. From that line, measure 7¼" down the post and mark the bottom of the beam. Using a level, transfer this line to the remaining posts.

7. Use a combination square to extend the level line completely around each post. Cut the posts to this finished height using a reciprocating saw or handsaw.

Step D: Install the Beam

1. Cut the beam boards (C) several inches longer than necessary, to allow for final trimming.

2. Join the beam boards together with 2½" galvanized deck screws. Mark the post locations on the top edges and sides using a combination square as a guide.

3. Attach the post-beam caps to the tops of the posts. Position the caps on the post tops, and attach using 10d joist hanger nails.

4. Lift the beam into the post-beam caps, with the crown up. Align the post reference lines on the beam with the post-beam caps. NOTE: You should have at least two helpers when installing boards of this size and length, at this height.

5. Fasten the post-beam caps to the beam on both sides using 10d joist hanger nails.

Step E: Install the Frame

1. Measure and cut the end joists to length using a circular saw.

2. Attach end joists to the ends of the ledger with 10d common nails.

3. Measure and cut the rim joist (E) to length with a circular saw. Fasten to end joists with 16d galvanized nails.

4. Square up the frame by measuring corner to corner and adjusting until measurements are equal. Toenail the end joists in place on top of the beam, and trim the beam to length.

5. Reinforce each inside corner of the frame with an angle bracket fastened with 10d joist hanger nails.

Step F: Install the Joists

1. Mark the outlines of the inner joists (F) on the ledger, beam, and rim joist (see Framing Plan, page 268), using a tape measure and a combination square.

F. *Install joists in hangers with crown side up.*

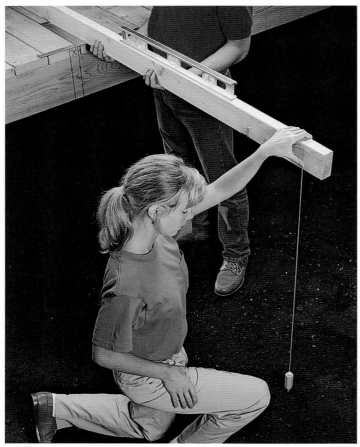

H. To locate the stairway footings, refer to the measurements in the Framing Plan, and extend a straight 2 × 4 perpendicularly from the deck. Use a plumb bob to transfer centerpoints to the ground.

2. Attach joist hangers to the ledger and rim joist with 10d joist hanger nails using a scrap 2 × 8 as a spacer to achieve the correct spread for each hanger.

3. Measure, mark and cut lumber for inner joists using a circular saw. Place the joists in the hangers with crown side up, and attach at both ends with 10d joist hanger nails. Be sure to use all the holes in the hangers.

4. Align the joists with the marks on top of the beam, and toenail in place.

Step G: Lay the Decking

1. Cut the first decking board (G) to length, position it against the house, and attach by driving a pair of 2½" galvanized deck screws into each joist.

2. Position the remaining decking boards with the ends overhanging the end joists. Leave a ⅛" gap between boards to provide for drainage, and attach the boards to each joist with a pair of deck screws.

3. Every few rows of decking, measure from the edge of the decking to the outside edge of the deck. If the measurement can be divided evenly by 5⅝, the last board will fit flush with the outside edge of the deck as intended. If the measurement shows that the last board will not fit flush, adjust the spacing as you install the remaining rows of boards.

4. If your decking overhangs the end joists, snap a chalk line to mark the outside edge of the deck and cut flush with a circular saw. If needed, finish the cut with a jigsaw or handsaw where a circular saw can't reach.

Step H: Build the Stairway

1. Refer to the Framing Plan, page 266, for the position of the stairway footings.

2. Locate the footings by extending a 2 × 4 from the deck, dropping a plumb bob, and marking the centerpoints with stakes.

3. Dig post holes with a clamshell digger or an auger, and pour the stairway footings using the same method as for the deck footings.

I. After attaching the stringers to the deck, fasten them to the posts. Drill and counterbore two pilot holes through the stringers into the posts, and attach with lag screws.

4. Attach metal post anchors to the footings, and install posts (H), leaving them long for final trimming.

5. Cut the stair stringers (I) to length and use a framing square to mark the rise and run for each step (see Stairway Detail, page 267). Draw the tread outline on each run. Cut the angles at the end of the stringers with a circular saw. (For more information on building stairways, see page 222.)

6. Position a 1½ × 10" angle bracket flush with the bottom of each tread line. Attach the brackets with 1¼" lag screws.

7. Fasten angle brackets to the upper ends of the stringers, using 1¼" lag screws; keep the brackets flush with cut ends on stringers. Position the top ends of the stringers on the side of the deck, making sure the top point of the stringer and the surface of the deck are flush.

8. Attach the stringers by driving 10d joist hanger nails through the angle brackets into the end joist and by drilling ¼" pilot holes from inside the rim joist into the stringers and fastening with ⅜ × 4" lag screws.

9. To connect the stringers to the stair posts, drill two ¼" pilot holes and counterbore the pilot holes ½" deep with a 1" spade bit. Use a ratchet wrench to fasten the stringers to the posts with 4" lag screws and washers.

10. Measure the length of the stair treads (J) and cut two 2 × 6 boards for each tread. For each tread, position the front board on the angle bracket so the front edge is flush with the tread outline on the stringers. Attach the tread to the brackets with ¼ × 1¼" lag screws.

11. Place the rear 2 × 6 on each tread bracket, keeping a ⅛" space between the boards. Attach with 1¼" lag screws.

12. Attach the treads for the lowest step by driving deck screws through the stringers.

Step I: Install the Railing

1. Cut posts (K) and balusters (L) to length (see Railing Detail, page 267) with a power miter saw or circular saw. Cut the top ends square and the bottom ends at a 45° angle.

2. Mark and drill two ¼" pilot holes at the bottom end of each post. Holes should be spaced 4" apart and counterbored ½" with a 1" spade bit.

3. Drill two ⅛" pilot holes, 4" apart, near the bottom of each baluster. At the top of each baluster, drill a pair of ⅛" pilot holes spaced 1½" apart.

4. Using a combination square, mark the locations of the posts on the outside of the deck. NOTE: Position corner posts so there is no more than 4" clearance between them.

5. Clamp each post in place. Keep the beveled end flush with the bottom of the deck, and make sure the post is plumb. Use an awl to mark pilot hole locations on the side of the deck. Remove posts and drill ¼" pilot holes at marks. Attach the railing posts to the side of the deck with ⅜ × 5" lag screws and washers.

I. *Position the rail cap over the posts and balusters. Make sure mitered corners are tight, and attach with deck screws.*

6. Cut top rails (M) to length, with 45° miters on the ends that meet at the corners. Attach to posts with 2½" deck screws, keeping the top edge of the rail flush with the top of the posts. Join rails by cutting 45° bevels at ends.

7. Temporarily attach stairway top rails with 3" galvanized screws. Mark the outline of the deck railing post and top rail on the back side of the stairway top rail. Mark the position of the top rail on the stairway post. Use a level to mark a plumb cutoff line at the lower end of the rail. Remove the rail.

8. Cut the stairway post to finished height along the diagonal mark, and cut the stairway rail along outlines. Reposition the stairway rail and attach with deck screws.

9. Attach the balusters between the railing posts at equal intervals of 4" or less. Use deck screws, and keep the top ends of balusters flush with the top rail. On the stairway, position the balusters against the stringer and top rail, and check for plumb. Draw a diagonal cut line at top of baluster and trim to final height with a power miter saw.

10. Confirm measurements and cut rail cap sections (N) to length. Position sections so that the inside edge overhangs the inside edge of the rail by ¼". Attach cap to rail with deck screws. At corners, miter the ends 45° and attach caps to posts.

11. Cut the cap for stairway rail to length. Mark angle of deck railing post on side of cap and bevel-cut the ends of the cap. Attach cap to top rail and post with deck screws. NOTE: Local building codes may require a grippable handrail. Check with your building inspector.

Casual Curve Deck

Gentle, sweeping curves define this delightful design. Easily adapted to other dimensions, this plan offers a great deal of functional appeal without a large outlay of time or money.

If your local building code requires a concrete pad at the base of the large stair area, consider hiring a professional to install it, unless you have a high degree of skill at installing large concrete areas. Stair railings shouldn't be necessary with the height and step design of this plan, but check with your local building inspector. A simple metal railing could be installed without affecting the visual appeal of this design.

Simple in design but stylish in appearance.

Cutaway View

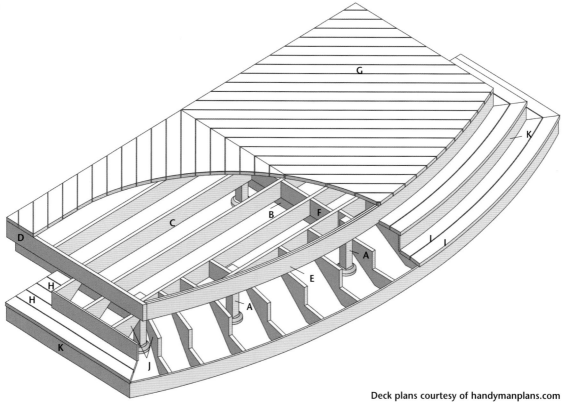

Deck plans courtesy of handymanplans.com

TOOLS & MATERIALS

- 10"-dia. footing forms (9)
- 3" direct bearing hardware (6)
- 2 × 8" double joist hangers (4)
- 2 × 8" joist hangers (72)
- 2½", 3" composite decking screws
- Joist hanger nails
- 16d galvanized box nails
- 12d galvanized casing nails

- ⅜ × 4" carriage bolts, washers, and nuts (12)
- ⅜ × 4" lag screws (22)
- Lead masonry anchors (22)
- Ledger flashing (20 ft.)
- Concrete, as required
- Pencil
- Mason's string
- Masking tape
- Plumb bob

- Speed square
- Jigsaw
- Clambshell digger or power auger
- Gravel, as required
- J-bolts (11)
- Reciprocating saw or power auger
- Pressure-treated lumber
- Level

Lumber List

Qty.	Size	Material	Part
3	6 × 6" × 8'	Trtd. lumber	Posts (A)
6	2 × 8" × 8'	Trtd. lumber	Beam (B), rim joists (D)
3	2 × 8" × 8'	Trtd. lumber	Beam (B), blocking (F)
1	2 × 8" × 12'	Trtd. lumber	Joists (C)
6	2 × 8" × 16'	Trtd. lumber	Joists (C), rim joist (D)
7	1 × 8" × 10'	Trtd. lumber	Curved rim joist (E), stair risers (K)
2	1 × 8" × 12'	Trtd. lumber	Stair risers (K)
32	¼ × 6" × 8'	Trtd. lumber	Decking (G)
4	⁵⁄₄ × 6" × 10'	Trtd. lumber	Decking (G)
8	⁵⁄₄ × 6" × 12'	Trtd. lumber	Decking (G)
3	2 × 6" × 10'	Trtd. lumber	Stair treads (H)
9	2 × 12" × 8'	Trtd. lumber	Stair stringers (J)
8	2 × 12" × 10'	Trtd. lumber	Curved stair tread (I)

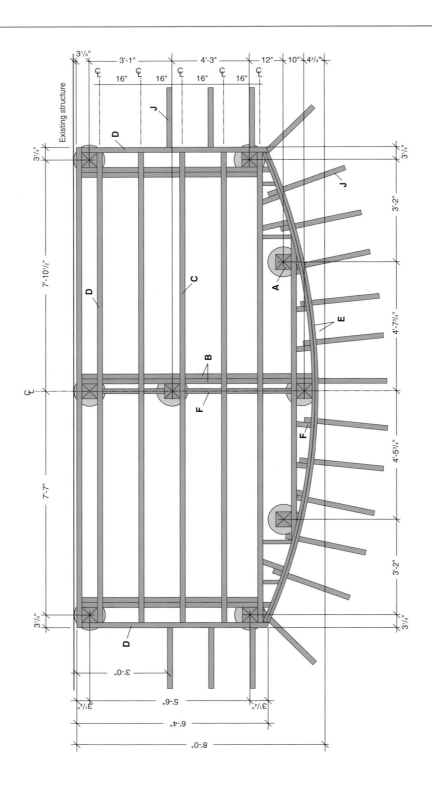

Framing Plan

HOW TO BUILD A CASUAL CURVE DECK

Step A: Pour the Footings

NOTE: A ledger isn't used for this deck plan. If you alter these plans to include a ledger board, see pages 176 to 183 for ledger installation methods.

1. Mark the deck location on the wall of the house (see Framing Plan, page 266), then stretch mason's strings across the site using 2 × 4 batterboards. Temporarily attach batterboards to the wall with deck screws. Check the mason's strings for square using the 3-4-5 triangle method. Adjust as necessary until they are square. Measure along the strings to locate the centerpoints of the footings and mark each with tape. NOTE: Allow yourself room to dig the footings at the house wall; the centerpoint of the posts can be up to 16" from the end of the beam.

2. Drop a plumb bob at the tape locations and drive stakes into the ground to mark the centerpoints of the footings.

3. Remove the mason's strings and dig holes for the footings using a clamshell digger or power auger. Make certain the hole sizes and depths comply with your local building code, which may require flaring the footings at their base.

4. Pour 2" to 3" of loose gravel into each hole for drainage.

5. Cut the footing tube forms to length, so they extend 2" above grade using a reciprocating saw or handsaw. Insert the forms into the holes and backfill with soil.

6. Fill the tube forms with concrete in stages, tamping the concrete at each stage with a long stick to eliminate any air pockets. Screed the tops flush with a flat 2 × 4.

7. Retie the mason's strings and drop a plumb bob to establish centerpoint of the footing. Insert a J-bolt into each footing, leaving ¾ to 1" of thread exposed. Clean the bolt threads before the concrete sets. NOTE: Another option is to install threaded rods with epoxy after the concrete has cured (see page 193).

Step B: Set the Posts

1. Start by laying a long straight 2 × 4 flat across pairs of footings. With one edge tight against the J-bolts, draw a reference line across each footing. Do this in both directions for pairs of footings where necessary.

2. Place a metal post anchor on each footing, center it over the J-bolt, and square it with the reference line. Thread a nut over each J-bolt and tighten each of the post anchors in place.

3. Cut 30"-long posts from pressure-treated 4 × 4 lumber. Place each post in a post anchor and tack it in place with one nail. With a level as a guide, plumb the posts using braces and stakes to hold them in place. Finish nailing the posts to the anchor.

4. At the centermost post along the wall, measure down from the door, allowing 7¼" for the joists, 1¼" for the decking, and 1" between the decking surface and the interior floor, then mark the post at this measurement.

5. Use a string, water, or laser level to transfer this mark to the other posts. Each mark will be level with the top edge of the beams.

Step C: Install the Beams

1. Measure and cut two pressure-treated 2 × 8s to length for each of the three beams (see Framing Plan, page 274). Place their faces together so that their crown sides are aligned and attach them together with pairs of galvanized nails or deck screws driven every 12".

2. Position the crown (top) edge of each beam against the level marks on the appropriate posts and clamp it in place. Drill pairs of holes for ⅜ × 8" carriage bolts through the beam and post at each location. Attach each beam to the posts with the carriage bolts, washers, and nuts, inserting the bolts through the beam.

Step D: Install the Rim Joists

1. Measure and cut the two outer rim joists. Provide a 1 × 2" space between one end of each joist and the wall and a 2" extension beyond the outer corner post at the other end. Position their bottom edges so they are level with the top edges of the beams and attach them to the posts with 3" deck screws.

2. Measure, cut, and attach the wall-side rim joist between the ends of the outer rim joists. Align the wall-side rim joist face that is nearest the wall so it is flush with the ends of the outer joists. Drill pilot holes through the outer rim joist and drive deck screws through into the wall-side rim joist ends.

3. Cut and install the inner joist between the outer rim joists on the front faces of the outer corner posts. Attach it to the posts with deck screws and to the beams with rafter ties.

Step E: Install the Curved Rim Joist

1. Measure and cut a pressure-treated 1 × 8 a few inches longer than needed to span from the outer rim joist to the centerpoint of the middle post at the front of the deck. This will be the first piece of the curved rim joist. Cut numerous ¼"-deep kerfs along the back width of this board.

2. Place one end of the board in the intersection of an outer rim joist and inner joist at an outer corner post, with the kerfed face against the inner joist and its top edge flush with the top edges of the joists. Drill pilot holes and drive 3" deck screws through the end of the board into the joist and post.

3. Bend the other end of the board until it meets the face of the center post and attach it to the post with deck screws driven 1" from the centerpoint. Make sure the bottom edge of the curved joist is level with the top edge of the beam. Mark a straight cut line at the centerpoint of the post on the curved joist using a speed square. Cut the board with a circular saw with its blade set ⅛" deeper than the thickness of the board.

Cut ¼"-deep kerfs along the back width of the first 1 × 8 for the curved rim joist. Bend and attach it to the posts using clamps to hold it in position.

Install the next layer of kerfed 1 × 8s, driving pairs of screws every 12" and at each post location.

4. Measure, cut, and kerf another 1 × 8 a few inches longer than needed to complete the span. Attach one end in the intersection of the other outer rim joist and corner post. Bend and clamp the board into position. Mark a cutting line for the board to meet the other curved joist at the center post. Cut it with the circular saw, drill pilot holes, and drive deck screws to attach it to the post before removing the clamps.

5. Measure, cut, and kerf another pair of 1 × 8s. Clamp them to the first layer, staggering the joints so they do not fall on the center post and aligning the ends so they protrude rim joists. Drill pilot holes and fasten with deck screws every 12" and at post locations, then trim the ends of the rim joists flush with the outer face of the curved rim joist using a reciprocating saw.

Step F: Install the Joists

1. Measure, cut, and install the remaining inner joists with 16" on-center spacing beginning at the wall side of the deck.

2. Select a 2 × 8 for the inner joist closest to the curved rim joist that is about 12" longer than necessary. Position it so its ends overlap the curved rim joist with its inner face aligned with the adjacent posts. Mark the profile of the inner face of the curved rim joist each end of the inner joist. Cut the inner joist at these marks with a reciprocating saw, then install it with deck screws driven through it and into the curved rim joist.

3. Cut and install 2 × 8 blocking at the midpoints of the joist spans to provide support for the diagonal decking. Also install blocking between the curved rim joist and adjacent joists as necessary to help support the curved profile. Cut the tops of the posts flush with the top edges of the joists. Remove all braces and stakes supporting posts.

Step G: Build the Stairs

If the height and grade level for your deck won't accommodate these stairs:

1. Cut the stair stringers to length from pressure-treated 2 × 12 lumber and use a framing square to mark the rise and run for each step. Cut the notches and the angles at the end of the stringers with a circular saw, then use a jigsaw to complete the corners.

2. Attach the side stair stringers to the joist ends. Attatch the stringers for the curved stair to the blocking between the inner joists and the curved rim joist. Install additional blocking as necessary. Rip ¼"-thick plywood sheets into 2 × 8-ft.-long pieces and trace the profile of the curved rim joist onto them. Cut out this profile, using a jigsaw, and use the plywood templates to mark the inside curve for the inner tread of the top step onto 10-ft.-long pieces of 2 × 12 lumber. Cut a 2"-wide piece of 2 × 6 lumber and use it as a spacer to mark the outside curve for the inner tread. Guide one end of the spacer along the inside curve line while holding a pencil point at the other end.

3. Cut the curved inner tread pieces using a jigsaw. Use the outside curved edge of the inner tread to mark the inside curve of the outer tread for the top step. Use the spacer to mark the outside edge, then cut the treads using a jigsaw.

4. Use the outside curved edge of the outer tread for the top step to mark the inside curved edge on the inner tread of the bottom step. Repeat the process used to mark and cut the top step treads to complete the bottom step treads.

5. Install the curved treads, drilling pilot holes and using deck screws. Make sure joints between tread pieces are supported by stringers.

6. Measure and cut treads from 2 × 6 lumber, and attach them to the side stair stringers.

Step H: Install the Decking

1. Cut a 45° angle at the end of a deck board and position it with the long point ¼" from the wall and centered on the midpoint blocking. The other end should overhang the rim joists at the opposite corner. Attach the board by driving two deck screws into each joist.

2. Cut and attach the rest of the deck boards on this side of the deck.

3. Cut and attach the deck boards for the other side of the deck, again letting ends overhang the rim joists wherever possible. Trim the ends of the deck boards.

4. Mark and snap chalk lines across the overhanging board. Set the depth of the circular saw blade ⅛" deeper than the

thickness of the decking and cut along the lines. Complete the cuts at the wall with a jigsaw and a hammer and sharp chisel.

5. Use the plywood templates you cut for the stair installation to mark the curve on the ends of the decking boards overhanging the curved rim joist and trim using a jigsaw.

Cut a 2"-wide piece of 2 × 6 lumber and use it as a spacer to mark the outside curve for the inner tread.

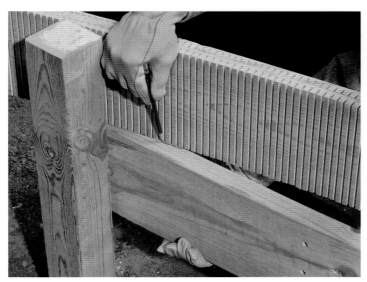

Mark the profile of the inner face of the curved rim joist on each end of the 2 × 8 for the inner joist at the curve. Cut the joist at the marks, then fasten to the posts with carriage bolts and to the curved rim joist with deck screws.

Use a jigsaw to trim the decking boards overhanging the curved rim joist.

277

Wraparound Deck

By wrapping around an outside corner of your house, this versatile deck increases your living space and lets you take advantage of views in several directions. The plan also creates two symmetrical areas for sitting or relaxing, providing space for two distinct activities. Our plan also calls for a front stairway for easy access to your yard or garden. The horizontal rails and notched posts provide striking visual elements that enhance the deck's overall design and add to its intimate nature.

Combine multiple seating possibilities with an expansive view.

Cutaway View

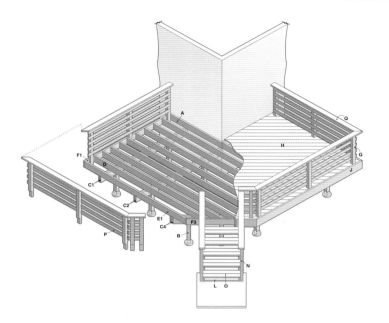

TOOLS & MATERIALS

- 10"-dia. footing forms (8)
- J-bolts (8)
- 6 × 6" metal post anchors (8)
- Post-beam caps (8)
- 90° 2 × 8" joist hangers (26)
- 45° 2 × 8" joist hangers (3)
- 1½ × 1½" galvanized metal angle brackets (26)
- Joist hanger nails
- ⅜ × 4" lag screws & washers (20)
- ⅜ × 3" lag screws & washers (32)
- 6 × 30" mending plate (1)

- Silicone caulk (3 tubes)
- 3" masonry screws
- Galvanized deck screws (1½", 2½", 3")
- ⅝" galvanized screws
- Concrete, as required
- Gravel, as required
- Pencil
- Level
- Circular saw
- Chisel
- Hammer
- Galvanized flashing (12 ft.)
- Metal snips
- Caulking gun

- Pressure-treated lumber
- Circular Saw
- 1" spade bit
- Ratchet wrench
- Mason's strings
- Masking tape
- Plumb bob
- Clamshell digger or power auger
- Reciprocating saw or handsaw
- 8d galvanized nails
- 10d galvanized nails
- 16d galvanized nails
- Chalkline
- Clamps

Lumber List

Qty.	Size	Material	Part
9	2 × 8" × 16'	Trtd. Lumber	Joists (D)
6	2 × 8" × 12'	Trtd. Lumber	Ledgers (A), Beam boards (C), End joist (E), Rim joist (F)
13	2 × 8" × 10'	Trtd. Lumber	Beam boards (C), Joists (D), End joist (E), Rim joists (F), Lower gusset (L)
1	2 × 6" × 4'	Trtd. lumber	Stairway nailer (I)
1	2 × 4" × 4'	Trtd. lumber	Upper gusset (L)
3	4 × 4" × 8'	Trtd. lumber	Deck posts (B)
9	4 × 4" × 8'	Cedar	Deck railing posts (G), Stairway railing posts (N)
28	¾ × 6" × 16'	Cedar	Decking (H)
2	2 × 10" × 12'	Cedar	Face boards (J)
2	2 × 10" × 10'	Cedar	Face boards (J)
1	2 × 10" × 6'	Cedar	Face boards (J)
1	2 × 12" × 12'	Cedar	Stringers (K)
5	2 × 6" × 12'	Cedar	Railing cap (Q)
5	2 × 6" × 8'	Cedar	Treads (O)
10	1 × 4" × 12'	Cedar	Rails (P)
11	1 × 4" × 10'	Cedar	Rails (P)
8	1 × 4" × 6'	Cedar	Rails (P)
*	2 × 4	Trtd. lumber	Batterboards, braces (scraps, as needed)

Framing Plan

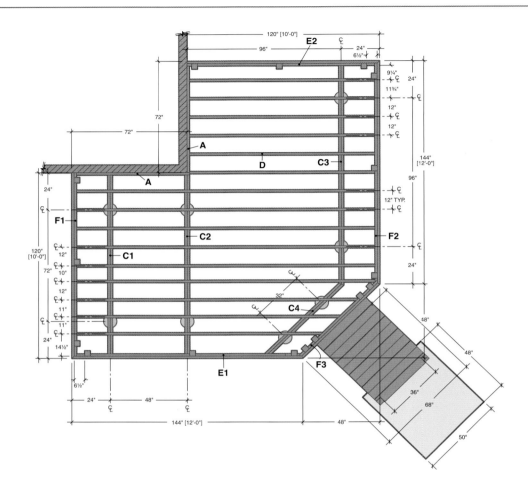

Elevation

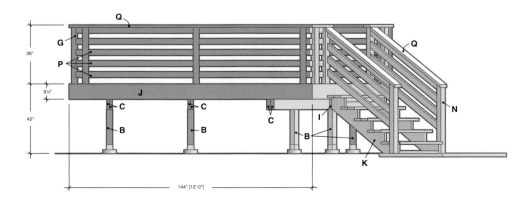

Railing Detail

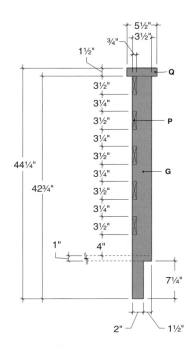

Stairway Detail

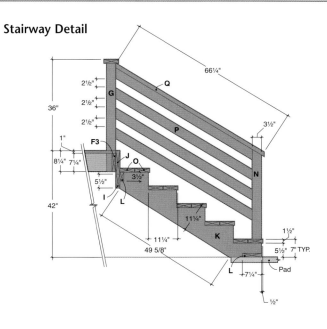

Footing Location Diagram

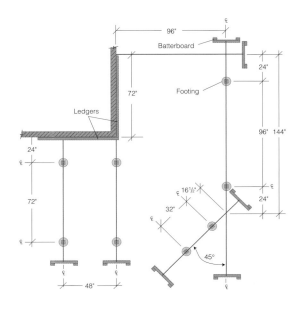

Corner Post Detail

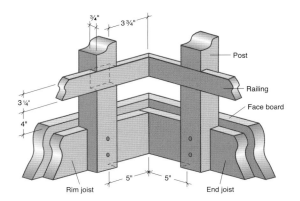

HOW TO BUILD A WRAPAROUND DECK

Step A: Attach the Ledgers

1. Draw a level outline on the siding to show where the ledgers and the adjacent end joist and rim joist will fit against the house.

2. Position the top edge of the ledgers so that the surface of the decking boards will be 1" below the indoor floor level. This height difference prevents rainwater or melted snow from seeping into the house. Draw the outline long enough to accommodate the thickness of rim joist F-1 and end joist E-2.

3. Cut out the siding along the outline with a circular saw. To keep the blade from cutting the sheathing underneath the siding, set the blade depth to the same thickness as the siding. Finish the corners of the cutout with a chisel, holding the beveled side in to ensure a straight cut. Cut galvanized flashing to the length of the cutout using metal snips, and slide the flashing up under the siding.

4. Measure and cut the ledgers (A) to length from pressure-treated lumber using a circular saw. Remember, the ledger boards should be shorter than the overall length of the cutouts. Position the ledgers in the cutout, underneath the flashing, and brace them in place. Fasten them temporarily with deck screws.

5. Drill pairs of ¼" pilot holes through the ledger and sheathing and into the house header joist at 2' intervals. Counterbore each pilot hole ½" deep using a 1" spade bit. Attach the ledgers to the wall with ⅜ × 4" lag screws and washers using a ratchet wrench.

6. Apply a thick bead of silicone caulk between the siding and the flashing. Also seal the lag screw heads and any gaps between the wall and the ledger.

Step B: Pour the Footings

1. Referring to the Footing Location Diagram (page 281), stretch mason's strings across the site using 2 × 4 batter boards. Check the mason's strings for square, using the 3-4-5 triangle method. From the point where each string meets the ledger, measure 3' along the ledger and make a mark. Next, measure 4' out along the mason's string and mark with tape. The distance between the points on the ledger and the string should be 5'. If not, adjust the mason's strings accordingly. Measure along the strings to locate the centerpoints of the footings. Mark the locations with tape.

2. Drop a plumb bob at the tape locations and drive stakes into the ground to mark the centerpoints of the footings. Remove the mason's strings and dig holes for the footings using a clamshell digger or power auger. Pour 2 to 3" of loose gravel into each hole for drainage. Make certain the hole dimensions comply with your local building code, which may require flaring the footings at the base. Cut the footing forms to length using a reciprocating saw or handsaw. Insert the forms into the holes, leaving 2" of each form above grade. Pack soil around the forms.

3. Fill the forms with concrete and tamp the concrete with a long stick to eliminate any air pockets. Screed the tops flush

Use a speed square to mark a 22½° miter cut where the ends of beams C-3 and C-4 fit together.

with a flat 2 × 4. Insert a J-bolt into each footing, leaving ¾ to 1" of thread exposed.

4. Retie the mason's strings and drop a plumb bob to position each J-bolt at the exact center of the footing. Clean the bolt threads before the concrete sets.

Step C: Set the Deck Posts

1. Start by laying a long, straight 2 × 4 flat across each pair of footings. With one edge tight against the J-bolts, draw a reference line across each footing.

2. Place a metal post anchor on each footing, center it over the J-bolt, and square it with the reference line. Thread a nut over each J-bolt and tighten each of the post anchors in place.

3. Cut the posts (C) to their approximate length, adding several inches for final trimming. Place the posts in the anchors and tack them into place with one nail each.

4. With a level as a guide, use braces and stakes to plumb the posts. Once the posts are plumb, finish nailing them to the anchors. To determine the height of the posts, make a mark on the house, 7¼" down from the bottom edge of the ledger. Use a straight 2 × 4 and a level to extend this line across a post. Transfer this line to the remaining posts. Cut the posts off with a reciprocating saw or a handsaw and attach post-beam caps to the tops using 8d nails.

Step D: Install the Beams

1. Cut the beams from 2 × 10" lumber, adding several inches to each beam for final trimming. Position the beam boards (C) so the crowns face the same direction, and fasten them together with 10d galvanized nails spaced every 16".

2. Position beams C-1 and C-2 in their post-beam caps and attach them with nails. Mark and cut the angled end of beam C-3 by mitering it at 22½°. Position the beam in the post caps.

3. Make a 22½° miter cut at one end of beam C-4 to form a 45° corner with beam C-3. Leave the other end long for final trimming. Place beam C-4 in the post-beam caps. Fit the beams tightly together, fasten them with 3" deck screws, and attach them to the post caps with 8d nails.

Step E: Install the Joists

1. Referring to the Framing Plan on page 280, cut rim joist F-1 to final length, and cut end joist E-1 generously long, to allow for final trimming.

2. Fasten one end of rim joist F-1 to the ledger with 16d galvanized nails. Rest end joist E-1 in place on beams C-1 and C-2. Fasten F-1 and E-1 together with deck screws. Use a framing square to finalize the location of E-1 on the beams. Mark the beams and trim them to length. Toenail E-1 in place on the beams.

3. Cut end joist E-2 to length. Install it by nailing it to the end of the ledger, checking for square, and toenailing it to the top of beam C-3. Trim the beam to length. Mark the outlines of the inner joists (D) on the ledger, beams, and rim joist F-1 (see Framing Plan, page 280) using a tape measure and a combination square.

4. Attach joist hangers to the ledger and rim joist F-1 with 1¼" joist hanger nails using a scrap 2 × 8 as a spacer to achieve the correct spread for each hanger. NOTE: Spacing between the joists is irregular to accommodate the installation of railing posts.

Fit beam C-4 tightly against beam C-3 and attach the two beams to each other with deck screws.

Mark the three remaining inside joists for cutting by snapping a chalk line. Brace and miter-cut the three inside joists.

5. Place the inside joists in the hangers on the ledger and on rim joist F-1, crown up, and attach them with 1¼" joist hanger nails. Be sure to use all the nail holes in the hangers. Toenail the joists to the beams and leave the joists long for final trimming.

6. Mark the final length of the inside joists by making a line across the tops of the joists from the end of end joist E-2. Check for square. Brace the inside joists by tacking a board across their edges for stability. Cut them to length with a circular saw.

7. Cut rim joist F-2 long to allow for final trimming, and nail into position with 16d galvanized nails.

8. To mark the remaining joists for trimming at a 45° angle, make a mark 139" from the 90° corner on end joist E-1. Make a second mark 139" from the other 90° corner along rim joist F-2. The distance between these two points should be at least 70". If necessary, move the line back until it measures 70". Regardless of the overall dimensions of your deck, this length will ensure adequate space for mounting the railing posts at the top of the stairway.

9. Mark the last three joists for cutting by snapping a chalk line between the marked points on end joist E-1 and rim joist F-2. Transfer the cut marks to the faces of the joists with a combination square, and cut the miters with a circular saw.

10. Measure, cut, and attach rim joist F-3 across the angle with deck screws.

Step F: Install the Railing Posts

1. Cut the railing posts (G) to size and notch the lower ends to fit around the rim joists (see Railing Detail, page 281).

2. Clamp all but two of the posts together to lay out and cut ¾" × 3½" notches, or dadoes, for the horizontal rails. NOTE: The posts at the stairway are not notched for rails.

Drill pilot holes through the posts and into the rim joists, and attach the posts with lag screws. Note the unnotched stairway post.

3. Cut the dadoes by making a series of parallel ¾"-deep cuts within each 3½" space, about ¼" apart, with a circular saw. Knock out the waste wood between the cuts using a hammer. Then, chisel smooth the bottom of each dado.

4. To locate the railing posts on the diagonal corner, find the centerline of rim joist F-3 and measure 18" in both directions. These points are the inner faces of the railing posts and the outer faces of the stringers. Drill ¼" pilot holes through the railing posts into the rim joist, and secure the posts with lag screws.

5. To position the corner railing posts, measure 3" both ways from the outside corners of rim joist F-3. Predrill the posts, and use a ratchet wrench to attach them to the rim joists with lag screws.

6. Use the Framing Plan, page 280, and the Corner Post Detail, page 283, to locate the remaining railing posts.

Step G: Install the Decking

1. If possible, buy decking boards that are long enough to span the deck.

2. Measure, mark, and cut the decking (H) to size, making notches to fit around the railing posts. Position the first board above the stairway, and attach it by driving a pair of deck screws into each joist.

3. Position the remaining decking boards so that the ends overhang the deck, leaving a ⅛" gap between the boards to allow for drainage.

4. Where more than one board is required to span the deck, cut the ends at 45° angles and make the joint at the center of a joist.

5. Snap a chalk line flush with the edge of the deck, and cut off the overhanging ends of the deck boards with a circular saw set for a 1½"-deep cut.

Step H: Install the Nailer & Face Boards

1. Measure, mark, and cut the stairway nailer (I) to size and attach it to the rim joist with a mending plate and deck screws (see Stairway Detail, page 289).

2. Measure, mark, and cut the face boards (J) to length, making 45° miter cuts at the right angle corners and 22½° miter cuts at the stairway corners. Attach the face boards to the rim and end joists with pairs of deck screws at 2' intervals.

Step I: Build the Stairway

1. Lay out and cut the stringers (K) to size, according to the Stairway Detail, page 289. The center stringer is notched at the top and bottom to fit around the gussets. Mark the rises and runs with a framing square. Cut the notches with a circular saw using a reciprocating saw or handsaw to finish the corners.

2. Measure, mark, and cut the gussets (L) to length. Assemble the stairway framework by nailing the gussets in place between the outer stringers with 16d nails. Turn the framework upside down and attach the center stringer by nailing through the gussets.

3. Position the framework against the deck, and attach with deck screws driven through the upper gusset into the face board and nailer. Drill pilot holes through the lower gusset into the concrete pad; attach with masonry screws.

4. Cut the stairway railing posts (N) to length. To install the railing posts, clamp them in place against the stringers, drill pilot

Cut the notches for the first decking board and position it above the stairway.

Clamp the long rails, mark the ends, and transfer the lines across the face of the board with a combination square to ensure a tight-fitting 22½° miter with the short rail.

Drill ⅛" pilot holes through the treads to prevent splitting. Then, attach the treads to the stringers with deck screws, using a power driver.

holes through the stringers into the posts, and attach the posts with ⅜ × 4" lag screws.

5. Measure, mark and cut the treads (O) to length. For the bottom treads, use a piece of railing post scrap to trace a line for the notch. Then, cut the notch with a circular saw. Attach the treads to the stringers with deck screws.

Step J: Build the Railing

1. Measure and cut to length the 10' rails, each with one end mitered at 45°. Install the rails using 1½" deck screws. Miter one end of the long rails at 45°. Leave the other end long for final trimming. Clamp each long rail in place and use a straightedge to mark cut lines at the angled corner). Transfer this line to the face of each rail using a combination square. Remove the rails and miter-cut the ends for the angled corners at 22½°. Reposition the rails and attach them to the railing posts with 1½" deck screws. Measure, mark, and cut the short rails to length with one end mitered at 22½° and the other end cut square.

2. Fasten the ends of the short rails to the railing posts above the stairway with angle brackets. Use ⅝" galvanized screws to attach the brackets to the rails and 1½" deck screws to attach them to the posts. Attach them to the notched post as well using 1½" deck screws.

3. Measure, mark, and cut the deck railing cap (Q), and install it with 3" deck screws.

Step K: Build the Stairway Railing

1. Mark and cut the stairway posts to length. Measure, mark, and cut the stairway railing caps (see Stairway Detail, page 289).

Use angle brackets to attach the stairway railing pieces and angled rails. To attach the brackets to the rails, use ⅝" galvanized screws.

Place a cedar 2 × 6 on top of the stairway posts, mark the angles for the ends, and cut to length, allowing for a 1" overhang at the end of the stairway.

2. Install the stairway railing caps with 3" deck screws. To cut the stairway rails, hold each one tight against the bottom of the cap and mark the ends.

3. Cut the rails to length so that they fit tight between the posts. To install the rails, mark the positions of the rails on the posts and attach them with angle brackets using ⅝" screws and 1½" deck screws.

Low-profile Deck

This low-profile deck creates a distinctive focal point for homes with ground-level entries. The composite decking complements the rich tones of the cedar, and the V-pattern directs your view to the centerpoint of the deck. This deck is ideal for flat, level lots or for covering up an old cement patio, and it requires no posts, so construction is easier than building a higher deck. Since this deck is less than 24" high, there's also no requirement for a railing. This deck can hold a BBQ, table, chairs, and lots of other accessories. Our plan also calls for a suspended step that's perfect for areas with snow and frost.

Cutaway View

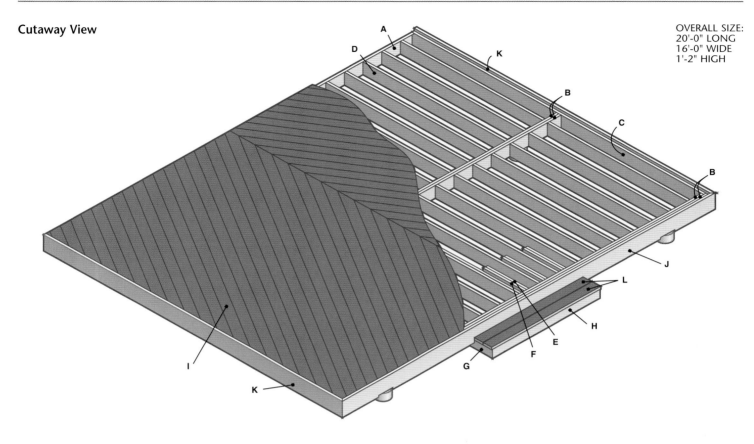

TOOLS & MATERIALS

- 8"-diameter concrete footing forms (6)
- 3" direct-bearing hardware (6)
- 2 × 8" double joist hangers (4)
- 2½" composite decking screws
- 2 × 8" joist hangers (72)
- 10d joist hanger nails
- 16d galvanized box nails
- 12d galvanized casing nails
- ⅜ × 4" carriage bolts, washers, and nuts (12)

- ⅜ × 4" lag screws (22)
- Lead masonry anchors (22)
- Ledger flashing (20 ft.)
- Exterior silicone caulk (3 tubes)
- Concrete, as required
- Tape measure
- Circular saw
- Pencil
- Drill
- 1" spade bit
- Awl
- ⅜" masonry bit
- Rubber mallet

- Ratchet wrench
- Mason's string
- Masking tape
- Plumb bob
- Clamshell digger or auger
- Gravel, as required
- Reciprocating saw or handsaw
- Pressure-treated lumber
- Caulk gun
- Chisel
- Hammer
- Chalkline
- Clamps

Lumber List

Qty.	Size	Material	Part
5	2 × 8" × 20'	Trtd. lumber	Ledger (A) & Beam bds (B)
2	2 × 8" × 16'	Trtd. lumber	End joists (C)
40	2 × 8" × 8'	Trtd. lumber	Joists (D)
3	2 × 4" × 8'	Trtd. lumber	Step support spacers (E)
2	2 × 6" × 8'	Trtd. lumber	Interior step supports (F)
1	2 × 6" × 6'	Cedar	End step supports (G)
2	2 × 6" × 6'	Cedar	Step riser (H)
74	2 × 6" × 10'	Composite	Decking (I)
2	2 × 6" × 6'	Composite	Tread (L)
1	2 × 10" × 20'	Cedar	Front face bd (J)
2	2 × 10" × 16'	Cedar	Side face bds (K)

Framing Plan

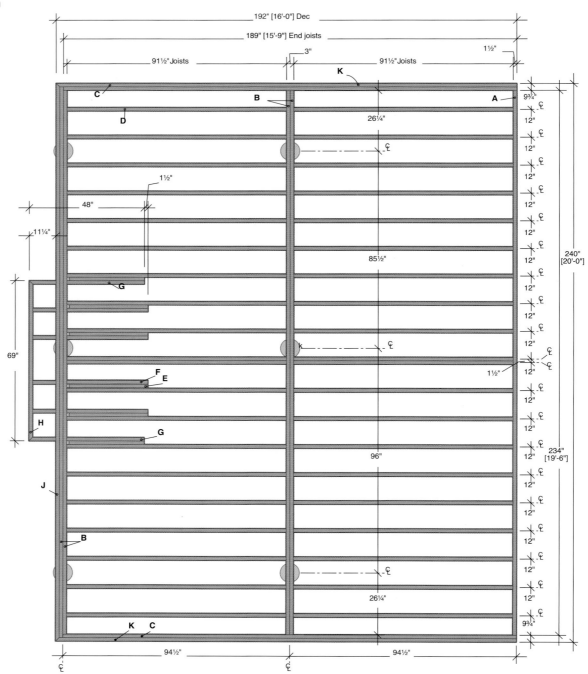

Elevation and Details

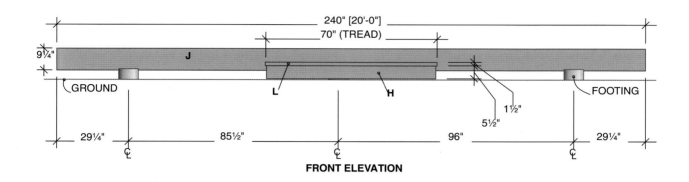

FRONT ELEVATION

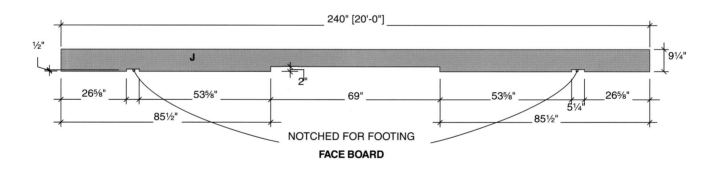

NOTCHED FOR FOOTING
FACE BOARD

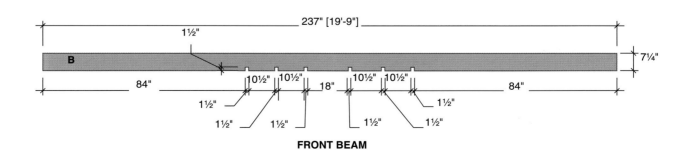

FRONT BEAM

Step A: Attach the Ledger

1. Measure and cut the ledger (A) to length. Drill pairs of ¼" pilot holes at 2-ft. intervals. Counterbore each hole ½" using a 1" spade bit.

2. Determine ledger location and draw its outline on the wall. Make sure you include a 3" space at each end of the ledger for the end joists and side face boards. Temporarily brace the ledger in position using 2 × 4s. Make sure the ledger is level and mark the hole locations on the wall with an awl or nail.

3. Remove the ledger and drill anchor holes 3" deep using a ⅜" masonry bit. Drive lead anchors into the drilled holes using a rubber mallet, and attach the ledger to the wall with lag screws and washers using a ratchet wrench.

4. Seal the screw heads, and the joint between the wall and ledger, with silicone caulk.

Step B: Pour the Footings

1. To locate the footings, refer to the measurements in the Framing Plan (page 280) and mark the centerline for each pair of footings on the ledger.

2. Construct three temporary 2 × 4 batter boards. Position the batter boards out from the footing marks, approximately 19 ft. from the ledger. Stretch mason's string from the bottom of the ledger at each mark to the corresponding batter board, making sure that the strings are level and perpendicular to the ledger.

3. Check for square using the "3-4-5 carpenter's triangle" method. From the point where each string meets the ledger, measure 3 ft. along the ledger and make a mark. Next, measure 4 ft. out along the string and mark with tape. The distance between the points on the ledger and the string should be 5 ft. If it's not, adjust the string position on the batter board accordingly.

4. To locate the centers of the six footings, build four more batter boards and stretch two additional mason's strings parallel to the house (refer to the Framing Plan, page 280 for measurements). Use a plumb bob to transfer the footing centerpoints to the ground, and drive a stake to mark each point.

5. Remove the mason's strings and dig the footings using a clamshell digger or power auger. Pour 2 to 3" of loose gravel

A. *Attach the ledger to the wall with lag screws and washers using a ratchet wrench.*

B. *Level the footing forms against the mason's strings, pour the concrete, and set the direct-bearing hardware into the wet concrete using the layout strings to ensure accurate alignment (INSET).*

into each footing hole for drainage. NOTE: When measuring the footing size and depth, make sure you comply with your local building code, which may require flaring the base to 12".

6. Cut the footing forms to length using a reciprocating saw or handsaw, and insert them into the footing holes.

7. Retie the mason's strings, making sure they are level.

8. Level the tops of the forms by setting them flush with the mason's strings and packing soil around them to hold them securely in place.

9. Remove the mason's strings and fill the footing forms with concrete, tamping with a long stick or rod to eliminate any air gaps.

10. Screed the concrete flush using a straight 2 × 4, then insert direct-bearing hardware into each footing while the concrete is still wet. Reattach the layout strings to ensure that the hardware is aligned correctly.

Step C: Install the Beams

1. Measure, mark, and cut the beam boards (B) to length using a circular saw. NOTE: Three of the beam boards are the same length as the ledger. The fourth board is 3" longer to accommodate the 1½" end joist on each end.

2. Make each beam by fastening two beam boards together with pairs of box nails driven at 16" intervals. At both ends of the outer beam, the long beam board overhangs 1½", creating a notch for attaching the end joist.

3. Position the beams crown-side-up on the direct-bearing hardware. Double-check that both beams are correctly aligned with the ledger, and attach to the hardware with carriage bolts.

Step D: Install the Joists

1. Measure, mark, and cut the end joists (C) to length. The end joists extend from the house to the notch in the end of the outer beam. In our plan the end joists are 189" long, but verify this measurement before cutting. Attach the end joists to the ledger and beams with box nails.

2. Measure, mark, and cut double center joists (D). Mark the centerline of the deck on the ledger and beams, install double joist hangers at each mark, and nail the joists in place. Seal the seam between the beam boards in the double joists with silicone caulk to protect against moisture.

3. Locate the remaining joists by measuring along the ledger and beams from the center joists and marking centerlines at 12" intervals (see Framing Plan, page 280). Install a joist hanger at each centerline.

4. Measure, mark, and cut the inner joists (D), verifying the actual lengths, and install in joist hangers with joist hanger nails.

C. Set the beams in the direct-bearing hardware on the footings. Note the "notch" for the end joist at the end of the outer beam.

D. Measure, cut, and install the joists with joist hangers, verifying the length of each one as you go.

E. *Cut notches for the step supports in the outer beam with a reciprocating saw or handsaw. Finish the notches with a hammer and chisel.*

F. *Lay composite decking boards with a ⅛ to ¼" gap to allow for drainage, expansion, and contraction.*

Step E: Build the Step

1. Measure, mark, and cut the step support spacers (E). Set the spacers back approximately 1" from the front beam, and attach to the deck joists with deck screws (see Step Detail, right).

2. Cut 1½ × 1½" notches in the bottom edge of the front beam, adjacent to the step support spacers. Use a reciprocating saw or handsaw to make the vertical cuts, and finish each notch with a chisel and hammer.

3. Measure, mark, and cut the step supports (F) and end step supports (G) to length. Make a 45° miter cut at the front of the end step supports where they meet the step riser. Attach the step supports to the spacers with deck screws. The interior step supports extend 11¼" beyond the beam, while the end step supports extend 12¾" to allow for the miter joints at the riser.

4. Measure, mark, and cut the step riser (H) to length, with 45° mitered ends. Attach the riser to the step supports with 12d galvanized casing nails.

Step F: Lay the Decking

1. To create reference lines, mark a point in the center of the front of the deck. Measure equal distances along the double center joist, and along the outer beam, then snap a chalk line between these points. As you progress with rows of decking, periodically measure between the ends of the decking boards and the reference line to help you maintain a consistent angle.

2. Begin laying the composite decking at the front center of the deck. Cut one end of the first decking board at a 45° angle and leave the other end slightly long. Position it above the step, aligning the 45° cut with the centerline of the double joist, and fasten with 2½" composite screws.

3. Cut and attach the next deck board in similar fashion, leaving ⅛ to ¼" spaces between the boards.

4. Cut and attach the remaining deck boards, periodically checking the angle of the decking against the reference lines and making any necessary adjustments.

5. After installing the decking, trim the excess that overhangs the deck ends. For boards 16 ft. or smaller, leave a gap at the deck ends and at any butt joints—¹⁄₁₆" for every 20°F difference between the temperature at the time of installation and the expected high for the year—as composite decking will expand

Step Detail

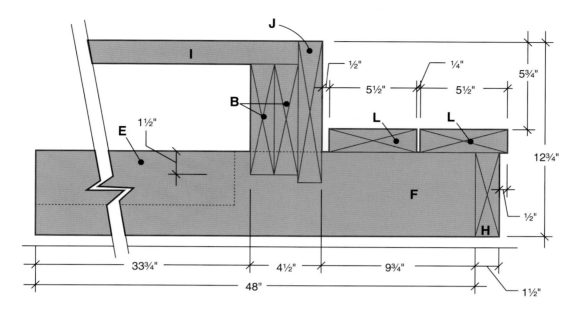

and contract. Set the blade depth on your circular saw at slightly more than 1½", and trim the decking to size.

Step G: Install the Face Boards

1. Measure, mark, and cut the front face board (J) to size (see Detail, above), and notch it to fit around the step supports. Cut 45° miters on both ends.

2. Temporarily clamp the face board in place and mark for notching around the footings. Also mark the points where the carriage bolts in the direct-bearing hardware contact the back of the board.

3. Remove the board, cut the footing notches, and chisel out the back of the board to accommodate the carriage bolts. Attach the face board with 12d galvanized casing nails.

4. Measure, mark, and cut the side face boards (K) to length, making 45° miter cuts at the front ends. Attach the face boards to the end joists with deck screws.

5. Complete the suspended step by cutting the composite treads (L) to length and attaching them to the step supports using 2½" composite screws. Leave a ½" gap at the front face board and a ¼" gap between the treads.

G. Cut the composite step treads to length and attach with composite screws, leaving a ½" gap between the first tread and the face board.

Platform Deck

A freestanding platform deck is a low-maintenance option for creating an outdoor floor. Because it can be constructed virtually anywhere, in almost any size, a platform deck works in nearly any landscape. The wood can be left natural, stained, or painted to blend with your house and other landscape elements.

You'll be able to build this deck over a single weekend. It uses lumber in standard lengths, so you won't need to do a lot of cutting. In addition, this deck uses precast concrete footings, rather than poured footings. These precast footings are available at home improvement centers and lumberyards.

This 12 × 12-ft. deck rests on a 10 × 10-ft. base formed by 18 concrete footings arranged in three rows of six footings each. Joists are secured in slots in the tops of the footings, simplifying the building process.

Framing Plan

12' × 12' decking

12' 2"

10'

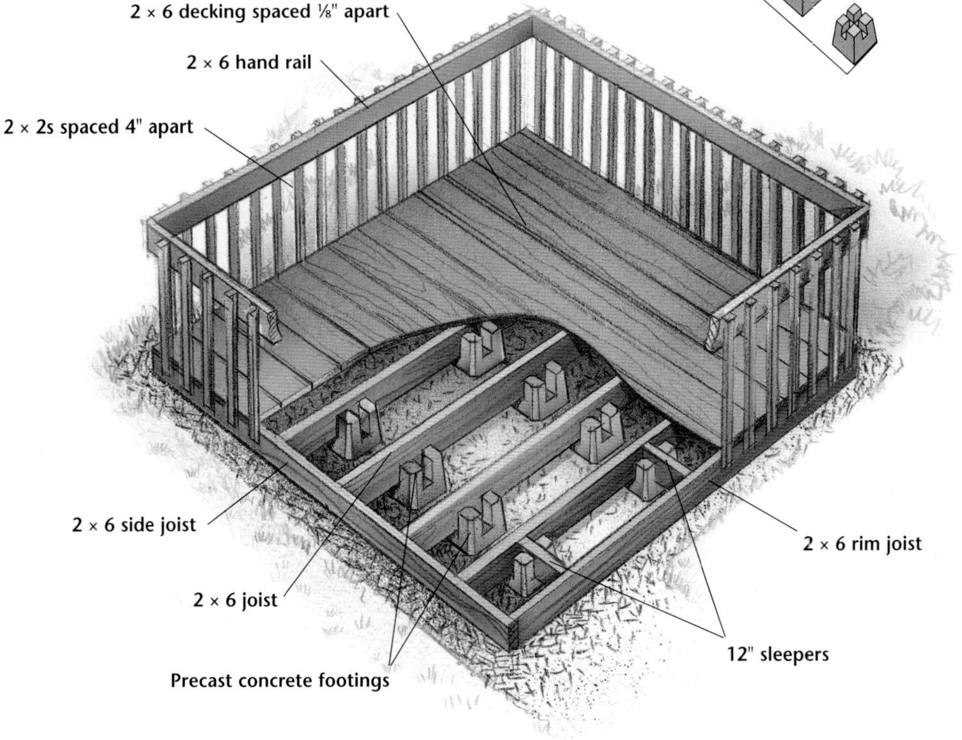

TOOLS & MATERIALS

- Stakes
- Level
- Wood sealer/protectant
- Paintbrush
- Precast concrete footings (18)

- 2 × 6" × 12' lumber
- 3" galvanized deck screws (2 lbs.)

- For optional railing: 42" 2 × 2s (75) 12" 2 × 6s (4)

2 × 6 decking spaced ⅛" apart

2 × 6 hand rail

2 × 2s spaced 4" apart

2 × 6 side joist

2 × 6 joist

Precast concrete footings

2 × 6 rim joist

12" sleepers

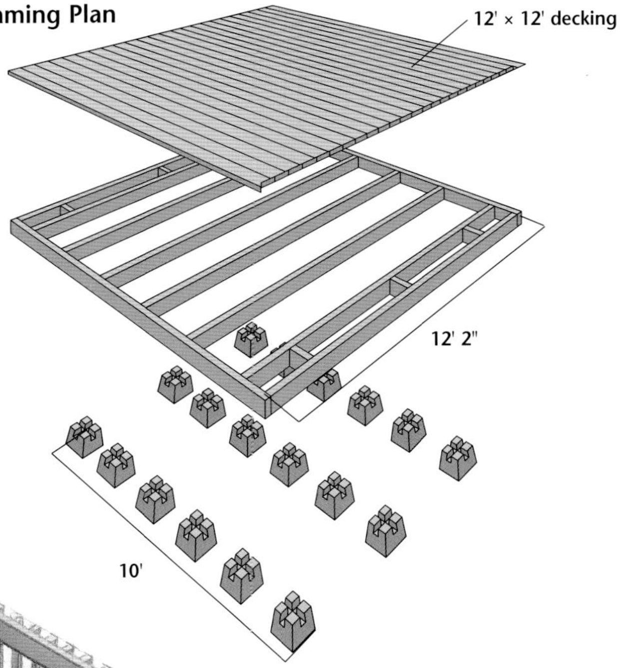

HOW TO BUILD A PLATFORM DECK

Step A: Install & Level the Footings

1. Measure a 10 × 10-ft. area for the deck foundation, and mark the corners with stakes.

2. Position a footing at each corner, then measure from corner to corner, from the center of each footing. Adjust until the diagonal measurements are equal, which means the footings are square.

3. Place a 2 × 6 across the corner footings for the back row, setting it in the center slots. Check this joist with a level, then add or remove soil beneath footings as necessary to level it.

4. Center a footing between these corner footings. Use a level to recheck the joist, then add or remove soil beneath the center footing, if necessary. Remove the joist.

5. Repeat the process described in #3, #4, and #5 to set and level the footings for the front row.

6. Position the remaining 12 footings at equal intervals, aligned in three rows. Position a 2 × 6 from the front row of footings to the back, and adjust soil as necessary to bring the interior footings into alignment with the front and back rows.

Step B: Install the Joists

1. Seal the ends of each 2 × 6 with wood sealer/protectant and let them dry completely.

2. Center a 12-ft. joist across each row of footings. Using a level, check the joists once again and carefully adjust the footings if necessary.

Step C: Add the Side Joists & Rim Joists

1. Line up a 2 × 6 flush against the ends of the joists along the left side of the deck, with the ends extending equally past the front and back joists.

2. Attach the side joist by driving a pair of deck screws into each joist.

3. Repeat this process to install the right side joist.

4. At the front of the deck, position a 2 × 6 rim joist flush between the ends of the side joists, forming a butt joint on each end.

5. Attach the rim joist to the side joists by driving a pair of deck screws through the faces of the side joists, into the ends of the rim joist.

6. Repeat #4 and #5 to install the other rim joist.

Position the corner footings and the center footing for the back joist. Remove or add soil beneath the footings to level them.

Position the remaining footings and insert the joists. Check to make sure the framework is level, and adjust as needed.

Step D: Position the Sleepers

1. Measure and cut six 2 × 6 sleepers to fit between the front and back joists and the rim joists. Seal the cut ends with wood sealer/protectant and let them dry completely.

2. Position one sleeper in each row of footings, between the first joist and the rim joist. Attach each sleeper by driving a pair of galvanized deck screws through each of the joists and into the sleeper.

Step E: Square Up the Frame

1. Once the framing is complete, measure the diagonals from corner to corner. Compare the measurements to see if they are equal.

2. Adjust the framing as necessary by pushing it into alignment. Have someone help you hold one side of the framework while you push against the other.

Step F: Lay the Decking

1. Seal the 2 × 6 decking boards with wood sealer/protectant and let them dry. Seal all exposed framing members as well.

2. Lay a 2 × 6 over the surface of the deck, perpendicular to the joists and flush with the rim joist. Secure this board with deck screws.

3. Repeat # 2 to install the rest of the decking. Use a framing square to set a ⅛" space between boards. Rip cut the last decking board if needed.

Install the front and back rim joists between the ends of the side joists, securing them with pairs of deck screws.

Position the sleepers in the slots of the footings, then attach them to both joists with pairs of deck screws.

After the framing is completed, measure the diagonals and adjust the frame until it's square.

Install the decking by driving a pair of screws into each joist. Use a framing square to leave a ⅛" space between boards.

Although this platform deck rests low to the ground, you may want to add a hand rail around two or three sides of the deck, especially if the deck will be used by young children or an elderly person. For each side of the deck to which you're adding railings, you'll need twenty-five 2 × 2s, 42" long.

The wooden railing shown here is just one of many different railing styles to consider. For more railing options and material choices, see the Deck Railings section, pages 254 to 255. Or, you could install fixed benches with backrests, which would add functionality to the deck and double as railings.

Step A: Prepare the Balusters

1. Place the 2 × 2s flush together, adjust them so the ends are even, and draw a pair of straight lines, 3" apart, across each board, 1½" above the beveled end. Repeat the process and draw a single line 2¾" from the top of the other end. Using the lines as guides, drill pilot holes into the 2 × 2s.

2. Apply wood sealer/protectant to the ends of the 2 × 2s.

Step B: Attach the Balusters

1. Position a 2 × 2 flush with the bottom of the joist, then clamp it in place to use as a placement guide.

2. Position the corner 2 × 2s against the side joists, beveled end down, 4" in from the corner. Check for plumb, then drive deck screws through the pilot holes.

3. Attach the remaining 2 × 2s for each side, spacing them 4" apart.

Step C: Attach the Hand Railing

1. Hold a 12-ft. 2 × 6 that forms the top of the railing in place, behind the installed 2 × 2s.

2. Attach the 2 × 2s to the 2 × 6 top rails by driving deck screws through the pilot holes.

3. Connect the top rails at the corners using pairs of deck screws.

4. Finish the railing by applying a coat of wood sealer, according to the manufacturer's directions.

Gang together all the 2 × 2s, then drill a pair of pilot holes into the beveled ends and a single pilot hole in the opposite ends.

Attach the 2 × 2s to the side joists, leaving a 4" gap between them.

Level the 2 × 6 railing behind the 2 × 2s, then attach it by driving screws through the pilot holes.

Multi-level Deck

This multi-level deck is ideal where you need access from different areas and levels of your home. The size and shape also provide many functional spaces for entertaining, privacy, or relaxation, as well as unobtrusive storage areas for recreational accessories.

The lower deck in this plan has been built around a patio. If you want this as a deck area instead, simply extend the lower ledger board across the house and run joists between the ledger and the center beam. You can remove the spa area from the plans and adjust the shape of the lower deck if you wish, too.

With some modification, this design also can help you make use of an otherwise unusable steep slope. However, you may need to eliminate or reduce the storage and small deck area underneath the landing. Some excavation of the existing slope area might also be required.

Create a multitude of possibilities with this multi-level design.

Cutaway View: Lower Deck & Tub

OVERALL SIZE:
27'-2" LONG
20'-6½" WIDE
8'-9" HIGH

Deck plans courtesy of handymanplans.com

TOOLS & MATERIALS

- 2 × 6" metal joist hangers (138)
- 2 × 6" double metal joist hangers (2)
- 6 × 6" metal post anchors (28)
- 16d galvanized nails (3½", 25 lbs.)
- 10d galvanized nails (3", 30 lbs.)
- 3" galvanized deck screws (15 lbs.)
- 60-lb. dry concrete in bags (62)
- ⅜ × 6" galvanized carriage bolts, washers, and nuts (26)
- ⅜ × 4" galvanized lag screws (26)
- ⅜ × 6" galvanized lag screws (12)

- ⅜ × 4" galvanized expansion bolts (8)
- Weather-resistant hinges* (4)
- Weather-resistant door latch* (2)
- Metal ledger flashing (34')
- Decorative post cap* (19)
- Pencil
- Level
- Circular saw
- Hammer & chisel
- Building felt
- Metal snips
- Drill
- 1" spade bit
- Impact driver or ratchet

- Silicone caulk & caulk gun
- Mason's string
- Pressure-treated lumber
- Masking tape
- Plumb bob
- Stakes
- Clamshell digger or auger
- Gravel, as needed
- Footing forms
- Reciprocating saw or handsaw
- J-bolts
- 3½" deck screws
- Jigsaw

*optional

Lumber List

Qty.	Size	Material	Part
18	6 × 6" × 8'	Trtd. lumber	Post (A, B, C, D, F, G)
5	6 × 6" × 10'	Trtd. lumber	Post (E)
40	2 × 6" × 4'	Trtd. lumber	Rim joist (J), joist (K)
52	2 × 6" × 6'	Trtd. lumber	Beam (I), rim joist (J), joist (K), tread (O), kick plate (T)
27	2 × 6" × 8'	Trtd. lumber	Ledger (H), beam (I), rim joist (J), joist (K), cross bracing (N)
12	2 × 6" × 10'	Trtd. lumber	Ledger (H), rim joist (J), joist (K)
2	2 × 6" × 12'	Trtd. lumber	Beam (I)
76	2 × 6" × 16'	Trtd. lumber	Decking (M)
1	2 × 6" × 18'	Trtd. lumber	Rim joist (J)
6	2 × 8" × 4'	Trtd. lumber	Face board (L)
5	2 × 8" × 8'	Trtd. lumber	Face board (L)
3	2 × 8" × 10'	Trtd. lumber	Face board (L)
1	2 × 10" × 6'	Trtd. lumber	Stair hanger (U)
2	2 × 12" × 8'	Trtd. lumber	Stair face board (S)
1	2 × 12" × 10'	Trtd. lumber	Stair face board (S)
3		Trtd. lumber	7-tread precut Stair stringer (Q)
4		Trtd. lumber	5-tread precut Stair stringer (R)
16	2 × 4" × 4'	Trtd. lumber	Top & bottom rails (V)
8	2 × 4" × 6'	Trtd. lumber	Top & bottom rails (V)
2	2 × 4" × 8'	Trtd. lumber	Top & bottom stair rails (W)
2	2 × 4" × 10'	Trtd. lumber	Top & bottom stair rails (W)
12	1 × 8" × 6'	Trtd. lumber	Riser (P)
68	2 × 12" × 10'	Trtd. lumber	Balusters (X)

Cutaway View: Upper Deck & Landing

Lower Deck Framing Plan

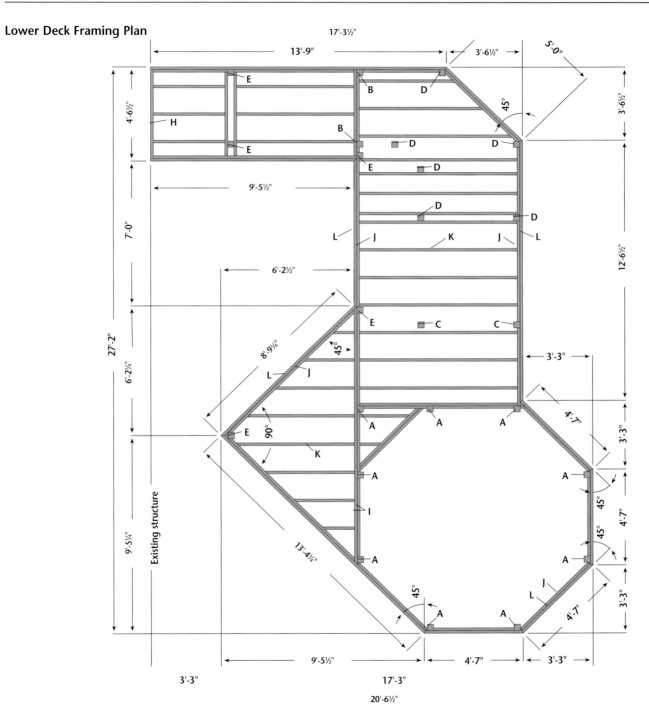

Upper Deck Framing Plan

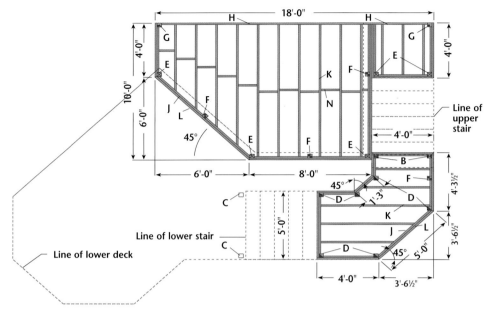

Front Elevation

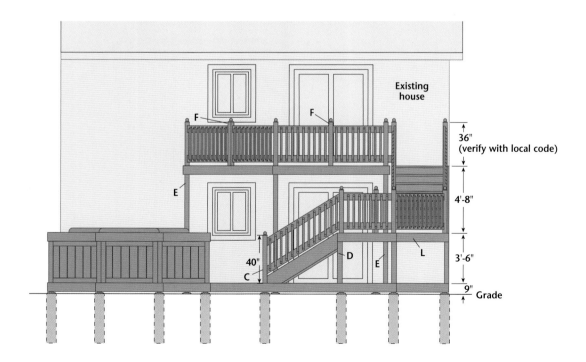

Post Location Plan

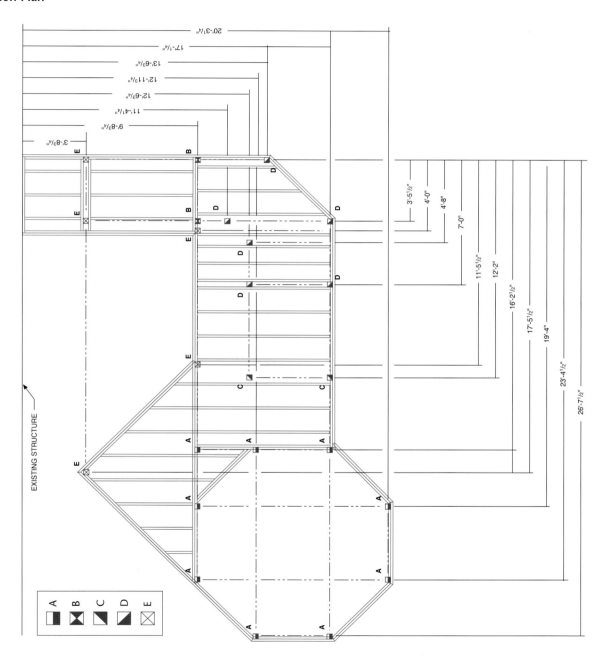

Lower Stair Details

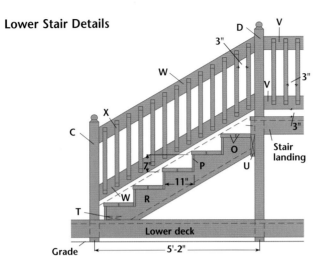

Upper Stair Detail

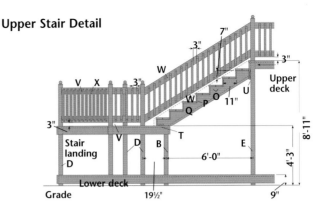

HOW TO BUILD A MULTI-LEVEL DECK

Step A: Attach the Ledgers

1. Draw a level outline on the siding in both locations to show where the ledgers and the end joists will fit against the house (See the Lower Deck Framing Plan and Upper Deck Framing Plan, pages 300 and 301). Position the top edge of each ledger so that the surface of the decking boards will be 1" below the indoor floor level. This height difference prevents rainwater or melted snow from seeping into the house.

2. Cut out the siding along the outline with a circular saw. To keep the blade from cutting too deeply into the sheathing underneath the siding, set the blade depth the same thickness as the siding. Finish the corners of the cutouts with a hammer and chisel, holding the beveled side in to ensure a straight cut.

3. Install new building felt over the existing felt exposed by siding removal. Cut galvanized flashing to the length of each cutout using metal snips, and slide it up under the siding.

4. Measure and cut the ledgers to length from pressure-treated 2 × 6 lumber. Center the ledgers in the cutouts, underneath the flashing, with space at the ends for the end joists. Brace ledgers in place, fastening them temporarily to the house with 3" deck screws.

5. Drill pairs of ¼" pilot holes through the ledger and sheathing and into the house header joist at 16" intervals. Counterbore each pilot hole ½" deep using a 1" spade bit. Attach the ledgers to the wall with ⅜ × 4" lag screws and washers using an impact driver or a ratchet wrench.

6. Apply a thick bead of silicone caulk between the siding and the flashing. Also seal the lag screw heads and any gaps between the wall and the ledgers.

Step B: Pour the Footings

1. Referring to the Post Location Plan on page 304, stretch mason's strings across the site using 2 × 4 batterboards. Check the mason's strings for square using the 3-4-5 triangle method. Adjust as necessary until they are square. Measure along the strings to locate the centerpoints of the footings. Mark the locations with tape.

2. Drop a plumb bob at the tape locations and drive stakes into the ground to mark the centerpoints of the footings. Remove the mason's strings and dig holes for the footings using a clamshell digger or power auger. Make certain the hole sizes and depths comply with your local building code, which may require flaring the footings at their base.

3. Pour 2" to 3" of loose gravel into each hole for drainage. Cut the footing tube forms to length, long enough so they will extend 2" above grade using a reciprocating saw or handsaw. Insert the forms into the holes and backfill with soil. Lay out and mark the location for a concrete pad within the hexagonal spa area (see Lower Deck Framing Plan, page 301). Excavate and build forms for the pad.

4. Fill the tube forms with concrete in stages, tamping the concrete at each stage with a long stick to eliminate any air pockets. Screed the tops flush with a flat 2 × 4. Retie the mason's strings and drop a plumb bob to establish centerpoint of the footing. Insert a J-bolt into each footing, leaving ¾ to 1" of thread exposed. Clean the bolt threads before the concrete sets.

5. Pour concrete into the spa pad form and tamp to remove air pockets. Screed the top flush with the form (no other finishing techniques are necessary for this pad) and allow the pad to cure.

Step C: Set the Posts

1. Lay a long, straight 2 × 4 flat across pairs of footings. With one edge tight against the J-bolts, draw a reference line across each footing. Do this in both directions for pairs of footings where necessary.

2. Place a metal post anchor on each footing, center it over the J-bolt, and square it with the reference line. Thread a nut over each J-bolt and tighten each of the post anchors in place.

3. Cut deck support posts A through E to their approximate length, adding several inches for final trimming (see Front Elevation, page 303, and Upper Stair Detail, page 305). Place the posts in the anchors and tack them into place with one nail each.

4. With a level as a guide, plumb the posts, using braces and stakes to hold posts B through E plumb. Once the posts are plumb, finish nailing them to the anchors.

Step D: Install the Beam, Rim Joists & Face Boards for the Lower & Upper Decks

1. Using a string, water, or laser level, mark the top edge of the lower deck rim joists and center beam locations on posts A and at the footing ends of appropriate posts B through E (see Lower Deck Framing Plan, page 301). Make mark level with the top edge of the lower ledger.

2. Mark posts E for the upper deck rim joists using the top edge of the upper ledger as the reference.

3. Measure, cut, and install rim joists for the upper deck from pressure-treated 2 × 6 lumber. Do this one piece at a time to ensure accurate measuring. Cut 45° miters at the ends of the pieces that meet posts at the 45° corners. Attach rim joists by toenailing them to the post faces using 3½" deck screws.

4. Measure, cut, and install face boards from pressure-treated 2 × 8 lumber. Do this one piece at a time as with the rim joists. Cut 22½° miters at the ends of the pieces that meet at the 45° corners. Attach face board pieces that fit flush with the post faces using ⅜ × 6" carriage bolts, washers, and nuts. Attach pieces that don't fit flush with the post faces at the 45° corners with ⅜ × 4" lag screws and washers. Make sure to stagger the bolt and/or screw locations on posts where two pieces attach. Attach the face boards to the rim joists with pairs of 3" deck screws driven at 24" intervals.

5. Build the center beam from doubled 2 × 8 pressure-treated lumber. Measure, cut, and attach it to the posts with ⅜ × 8" carriage bolts, washers, and nuts. Cut 45° miters in the ends of the pieces that will meet the rim joist face at a nonperpendicular junction.

6. Measure, cut, and install the rim joists and face boards for the lower deck in the same manner you followed for the upper deck. However, cut 45° miters in the ends of the pieces that will meet the center beam face at a nonperpendicular junction. Cut the tops of posts A flush with the top edges of the rim joists and center beam using a reciprocating saw.

Step E: Install the Rim Joists & Face Boards for the Landing

1. Measure 42" up from the top of the lower deck rim joists attached to posts B and D and mark the posts (see Upper Stair Detail, page 305).

2. Measure, cut, and attach the landing rim joists, aligning their top edges with the 42" marks and the face boards in the same manner you followed for the lower and upper decks. Cut the tops of posts B flush with the top edges of the rim joists.

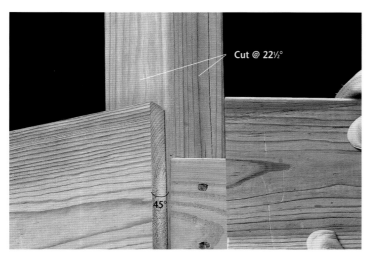

Cut 45°-miters at the ends of rim joists that meet posts at a 45° corner. Cut 22½°-miters at the ends of face boards that meet at a 45° corner.

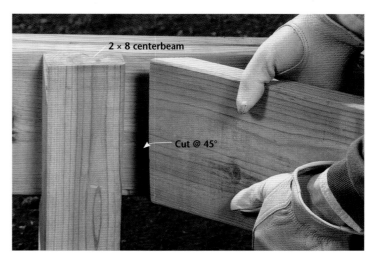

Cut a 45°-miter at the ends of rim joists and face boards that meet the center beam of the lower deck at a 45° corner.

Step F: Install the Joists

1. Measure and mark the outlines for joist locations spaced 16" on center on the ledger and rim joists of the upper deck (see Upper Deck Framing Plan, page 303). The spacing of the joists measured along the 45° angled rim joist will be 22⅝" on center. Measure and mark the outlines for joist locations for the stair landing.

2. Measure and mark the outlines for joist locations spaced 16" on center on the ledger, rim joists, and center beam of the lower deck (see Lower Deck Framing Plan, page 304). The joist spacing will be 22⅝" on center measured on the 45°-angled rim joist.

3. Attach the joist hangers to the ledgers, rim joists, and center beam with 10d joist hanger nails using a scrap 2 × 6 as a spacer to maintain the correct spread for each hanger. Use 45° joist hangers of the proper direction where joists meet the angled rim joists.

4. Measure, mark, and cut 2 × 6 pressure-treated lumber for the joists. Make certain to cut a 45° miter in the joist ends that will fit the 45° joist hangers.

5. Insert the joists into the hangers with crown side up, and attach at both ends with 10d joist hanger nails. Be sure to drive a nail in every hole in the hangers. Add cross bracing for the joists in the upper deck as necessary.

Step G: Install the Railing Posts

1. Cut railing posts F and G to their approximate length, adding several inches for final trimming.

2. Clamp each post in place to the inner face of the rim joist. Drill pilot holes for two ⅜ × 6" carriage bolts through the rim joist and the post. Counterbore the holes in the rim joist ½"-deep using a 1" spade bit. Attach the posts to the rim joists with the carriage bolts, washers, and nuts.

Step H: Install the Decking

1. Position a deck board along the outer 45° rim joist on the upper deck, overhanging the rim joists at both ends. Mark the railing post locations.

2. Cut notches for the railing posts using a jigsaw. Test fit the board: Its leading edge should be flush with the front face of the 45° rim joist. Adjust as necessary. Attach the board by driving two deck screws into each joist.

3. Cut and attach the remaining deck boards, again letting ends overhang the rim joists. Leave a ⅛" gap between the boards for drainage. Cut notches for railing posts.

4. Mark and snap lines across the overhanging board ends that are aligned with the outer faces of the rim joists. Set the depth of the circular saw blade ⅛" deeper than the thickness of the decking and cut along the line, and complete cuts at corners or walls with a jigsaw, and a hammer and sharp chisel. Remove all braces and stakes supporting posts. Install the decking on the stair landing and lower deck following the same methods.

Step I: Building the Stairs

1. Cut the stair stringers for the upper stairs to length and use a framing square to mark the rise and run for each step. (See Upper Stair Detail, page 305.) Cut the notches and the angles at the ends of the stringers with a circular saw, then complete the cuts at corners with a jigsaw.

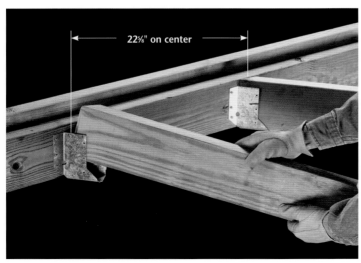

Use 45°-angled joist hangers where joists meet the angled rim joists. Space joists 22⅝" on center.

Attach the railing posts to the upper deck rim joists with carriage bolts, washers, and nuts.

2. Measure and cut a stair hanger and attach it to the posts E at the stair location with deck screws. Its top edge should butt against the bottom edge of the rim joist.

3. Position the middle stringer so the bottom end is flat against the middle of the stair landing and the upper end is against the stair hanger. Mark where the front edge of the stringer meets the landing. Measure and cut a 2×6 kick plate to fit between the outer stringers. Align the front edge of the kick plate with the mark so the board is parallel to the near edge of the landing. Fasten with deck screws. Cut a notch for the 2×6 kick plate in the middle stringer.

4. Position each outer stringer against one end of the kick plate and against the stair hanger. Drive a screw through each stringer into the kick plate. Square each stringer to the hanger using a framing square, and mark its position. Attach the upper ends of the stringers to the hanger with angle brackets. Position the middle stringer evenly between the outer stringers. Attach it to the stair hanger with a skewable joist hanger and to the kick plate using deck screws driven at an angle.

5. Measure and cut riser boards from pressure-treated 1×8 lumber. Attach the riser boards to the stringers with two deck screws per each stringer. Drill pilot holes for the screws at the ends of the boards.

6. Measure and cut two 2×6 stair treads for each step. Their ends should be flush with the outer faces of the stringers. Attach the treads with two deck screws per tread at each stringer, leaving a ¼" gap between treads. The back tread should touch the riser on each step.

7. Measure, layout, cut, and install the lower stairs following the same methods.

Step J: Install the Railing

1. For railing installation, refer to the Upper Stair Detail on page 305.

Step K: Enclose the Spa

1. Install the spa on the pad and connect it to the utilities following the manufacturer's instructions. Have a professional do the installation if you are not comfortable working on plumbing, wiring, or gas systems.

Attach the center stair stringer to the kick plate using deck screws driven at an angle.

Cut notches in the decking boards that meet the railing posts. Test fit the board: The leading edge should be flush with the face boards.

Cut and install railings into notches cut into the inner faces of the railing posts.

Porches

Few elements of your home will conjure up sweeter memories than a breezy front porch on a perfect summer evening. Linking your home to your landscape, a porch creates an inviting threshold to your home.

Porch designs and styles are endless, limited only by your imagination. For instance, a porch can wrap around your home to allow you to take advantage of a spectacular view. If insects are a problem where you live, a screened-in porch can be beneficial. Or if you simply want to dress up a bare entry, a portico can not only provide decoration, but also keep rain and snow from falling directly over the entrance.

This section will help you plan, design, and build your porch from the ground up. Tips are offered on evaluating your property, working with building codes and authorities, and drawing working plans. And because every porch project is unique, step-by-step instructions are provided to assist you in understanding the parts and techniques needed to build a standard porch, from attaching ledgers to installing railings.

Whether you're looking to create a comfortable spot to contemplate your flower garden or to simply make your home's entrance more pleasant, a porch will not only increase your home's value, but it will create a new outdoor living space you'll enjoy for years to come.

IN THIS CHAPTER:

- Planning & Designing Porches
  - *Anatomy of a Porch*
  - *Step-by-Step Overview*
- Basic Techniques
  - *Attaching Ledgers & Installing Posts*
  - *Installing Joists*
  - *Installing Porch Floors*
  - *Installing Beams & Trusses*
- *Installing Sheathing & Fascia*
- *Installing Step Flashing*
- *Wrapping Posts & Beams*
- *Finishing the Cornice & Gable*
- *Installing Soffits & Ceilings*
- *Building Railings*
- Porch Screen Kit
  - *Installing a Porch Screen Kit*

Planning & Designing Porches

As with any addition you make to your home, a porch requires some forethought. There will be the fun of dreaming up ideas and designs, but you will also have to do research and planning. An evaluation of your property will help you determine if, in fact, you have the space available to build the porch you envision. Your local zoning ordinances and building codes will specify where and how you can build. Finally, you will have to create detailed plans that comply with those building codes in order to obtain a building permit.

Because porches and entries come in many shapes and forms, choosing the best design for your home is an important decision, worthy of careful consideration. The choices you make will affect your property's value, so make sure your porch design not only meets your needs, but makes sense when viewed with the rest of your home. Browse through magazines, walk through neighborhoods, and visit libraries to gather as much information as you can, then jot down ideas that can be incorporated into your design. A professional designer or architect can also help you plan a project to meet your specific needs and budget, while satisfying local building codes.

Review your list of porch ideas and uses, and compare it to your site. Take stock of your property. Determine whether there is room to build in the proposed location, or if it is possible to build around existing landscape elements without running afoul of your local building and zoning restrictions. Also:

- Note the location of windows, electrical service lines, and any other obstructions that might affect the position or design of your porch.

A porch can transform your home's entrances, providing both a pleasing frame for your doorway and a convenient outdoor sitting space for warm afternoons.

Anatomy of a Porch

This illustration shows each part of a typical porch. Though the structural components are standard, the decorative details may differ, based on your specific porch details and design.

Ledgers anchor the porch deck to the house, supporting one side of the joists.

Concrete footings with post anchors support the weight of the porch and hold it in place.

Posts transfer the weight of the porch roof and porch deck to the footings.

Joists are horizontal members that support the porch floor.

Porch flooring commonly consists of tongue-and-groove porch boards installed over a plywood subfloor. The subfloor is attached to the joists. Trim, called the **apron**, is added to conceal the joist frame.

Beams distribute bearing loads of the roof to the posts.

Trusses and rafters bear on the beams, and give shape and stability to the roof. The angle of the rafter chords creates the roof pitch, allowing water to shed.

Sheathing ties the framing members together, creating rigidity and strength in the structure.

Fascia boards are the trim at the gable ends and eaves of a roof. **Frieze boards** are blocking between the sheathing and fascia boards.

Roofing materials (such as building paper, drip-edge, and asphalt shingles) shed water to protect the structural members of the roof from rot.

Post collars, cornices, soffits, and ceilings all help to conceal the framing members and decorate the structure.

Railings create a security barrier between the edge of the porch and the ground, while steps allow access to and from the porch and yard.

311

A floor plan shows overall project dimensions, the size and spacing of floor joists, the size and location of posts, and the types of hardware to be used for connecting and anchoring structural members.

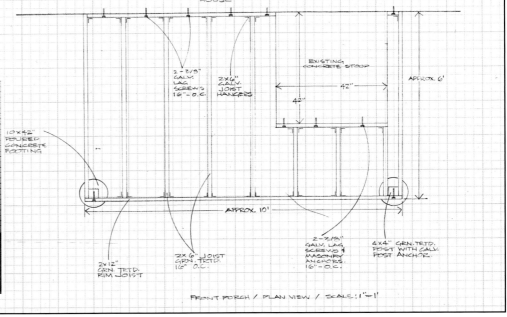

- Note whether the proposed porch area is exposed to direct sun or wind, which can be determining factors in the porch design.
- Consider the style and construction of your house and what porch roof style would blend best with your home.
- Mark your property lines and measure distances from the planned project area to municipal sidewalks or streets. (To avoid future disputes, mark property lines 1 ft. in from your actual property boundaries.)
- Measure the slope of the proposed building site to determine whether you must regrade. If the slope is greater than 1" per foot, you may have to consult a landscape architect.

It is also important to assess the building materials used in and around the planned project area. If you have stucco siding, for example, allow extra time for siding removal.

Contact your local building departments early in the planning process. The types of projects that require building permits vary among localities, but it is safe to say that a major project—such as a porch—will require a permit. Inspections may be required before, during, and even after porch construction.

The building department can also be a helpful resource. The staff inspectors can grant building permits, answer questions, and provide information. For example, if your porch will occupy space near property borders or municipal streets or sidewalks, an inspector can tell you whether you will need a variance from the local zoning commission.

Building codes often prescribe minimum sizes for structural members of your project, like deck joists, beams, posts, and ledgers. The height, width, and estimated weight of the project must be suitable for the support methods used and comply with any neighborhood covenants. Screw sizes and spacing are usually indicated for most parts of the project, from structural elements to roof covering. Depending upon where you live, there may be special requirements for your project. For example, in cold climates, concrete frost footings of 48" or deeper sometimes are required. You will also be required to pay a permit fee, based on your project's estimated cost.

Before issuing a building permit for your porch project, the building department will require a detailed plan that includes both an elevation drawing and a floor plan. There are some very specific conventions you must follow to create these drawings, so get assistance if you have not done this kind of work before. Refer to pages 28 to 29 for more information and techniques on drawing plans.

Begin by drawing a site map on which you can sketch your final ideas and plans. Your site map should include relevant features, such as shade patterns, trees, and other landscaping details. Also measure the height of door thresholds and the length and height of any walls or buildings adjacent to the proposed project area. Use tracing paper to try out a few different design ideas before drawing up your final plans. Remember, your local building department may require changes to your plans based on codes and zoning restrictions.

If you have a larger-scale or elaborate porch project in mind, you may need to enlist the aid of an architect or designer to help you develop your ideas into detailed drawings.

Once you have your permit, you can begin construction, but take some commonsense precautions to work safely outdoors:

- Always follow basic safety rules for working with ladders and scaffolding, and provide level, stable footing for extension ladders.
- Set up your work site for quick disposal of waste materials, and create a storage surface to keep tools safely off the ground.
- Wear sensible clothing and use protective equipment, including a cap, eye protection, a particle mask, work gloves, full-length pants, and a long-sleeved shirt.
- Plan your work days to avoid extreme heat, take frequent breaks, and drink plenty of fluids.

Because of the size of the structure and the amount of work involved, make sure to enlist some help during the building of your porch.

Try to use the same roof slope as your house. *To measure, hold a carpenter's square against the roofline with the long arm perfectly horizontal. Position the square so the long arm intersects the roof at the 12" mark. On the short arm, measure down to the point of intersection: The number of inches gives you the roof slope in a 12" span. For example, if the top of the square is 4" from the roofline, then your roof slope is 4-in-12.*

Learn about house construction. *The model above shows the basic construction of a platform-framed house—by far the most common type of framing today. Pay special attention to locations of rim joists and framing members, since you likely will need to anchor any large porch or patio project to one or both of these elements.*

Step-by-Step Overview

Every porch project is different because each home offers special challenges and every owner has specific design considerations in mind. However, there are some elements of a porch that are constant. From the ground up, the bare bones of porches are the same.

This overview provides the basic techniques you will need in order to build a porch. As with a deck, it is a good idea to build a porch in several stages, gathering tools and materials for each stage before beginning. And because of the size and complexity of most porch designs, have at least one helper for the more difficult stages.

Have the electrical, telephone, and water lines marked, and refer to your building plans often. Use the techniques illustrated in this project as a guide to help you convert your own porch plan into a reality.

A. *Install a ledger to anchor the porch deck to the house, then use it as reference to lay out the footings and posts (pages 316 to 319). If building over old steps, attach a step ledger to the riser of the top step (page 321).*

B. *Build the porch deck frame, then install metal joist hangers on the ledger and rim joist, and install the remaining joists (pages 320 to 321).*

C. *Install a plywood subfloor over the joists, then tongue-and-groove porch boards (pages 322 to 323). The porch boards, usually made of fir, are nailed to the subfloor with a floor nailer tool (shown).*

D. *Install a roof ledger and beams, then hoist the trusses up onto the beams, and fasten into place (pages 324 to 327).*

E. *Lay plywood sheathing across the trusses, then install the gable sheathing, frieze boards, and fascia boards (pages 328 to 329). Finish the roof with asphalt shingles (pages 380 to 381) using step flashing when tying into the house (page 330 to 331).*

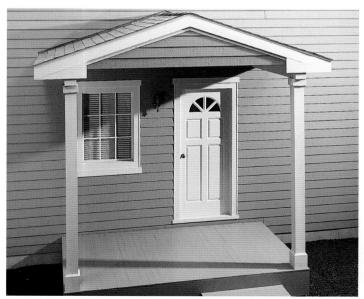

F. *Wrap the posts and beams with finish-grade lumber to give them a more solid, proportional look (pages 332 to 333). Install cornices and finish the gable siding (pages 334 to 335). Install soffits and ceilings to hide the remaining construction details (pages 336 to 337).*

G. *With the porch completed, you will need to add railings (pages 338 to 339) if your porch deck is higher than 20". Build concrete steps to provide access to the porch.*

Basic Techniques

Attaching Ledgers & Installing Posts

You want your porch to be permanent, and permanence requires a sturdy foundation and a strong roof. After all, you don't want to discover that your porch has drifted away from your home or that your roof sags as time goes by.

Ledger boards and posts will support the roof and the deck of a porch for its entire life. A ledger board is a sturdy piece of lumber, anywhere from a 2 × 6 to a 2 × 12, that is secured to a house wall to support joists or rafters for the porch. The techniques for installing a porch ledger are the same as for a deck. Refer to pages 176 to 183 for more information on installing ledgers to different types of siding materials.

Ledgers must be attached to the wall at framing member locations or attached directly to the house rim joist, if the rim joist is at the correct height. Before starting ledger installation, you must locate and mark framing members.

Posts used in most porch projects are 4 × 4 or 6 × 6 lumber that is attached to concrete footings with post-anchor hardware.

In most cases, porches are built with posts at the front only. A ledger is installed at deck level to support the floor, and another is usually installed at ceiling level to anchor the roof beams and the rafters or trusses.

The project shown here incorporates a set of old concrete steps for the foundation by making a cutout in the deck-level ledger board that is the same width and position as the steps and attaching the cut section to the face of the top riser with masonry anchors. If this is not the case for your project, install a standard ledger board.

A. *Mark the center and endpoint of the ledger location, then mark the ledger height. Use a straight, scrap 2 × 4 and a level to ensure the ledger is at the same height as the steps.*

Drip-edge flashing

B. *Apply exterior panel adhesive to the flashing, and slip the flashing behind the siding at the top of the cutout.*

HOW TO INSTALL THE LEDGER & POSTS

Step A: Mark the Ledger Outline

1. Mark the center of the project area onto the wall of your house to use as a reference point for establishing the layout.

2. Measure out from the center and mark the endpoints of the ledger location, then mark the ledger height at the centerline. The top of the ledger should be even with the back edge of the steps. Use a straightedge and a level to extend the height mark to the endpoints of the ledger location.

3. Mark cutting lines for the ledger board cutout on the siding, ½" around the ledger layout. Extend the marks across the project area with the level and straightedge.

Step B: Remove the Siding & Install the Flashing

1. Remove the siding at the cutting lines (pages 173 to 174). For wood siding, set the blade of your circular saw so it cuts through the thickness of the siding. Cut along the cutting lines, and finish the cuts at the corners with a wood chisel.

2. Cut a piece of metal or vinyl drip-edge flashing to fit the length of the cutout area. Apply caulk or exterior panel adhesive to the back face of the flashing, and slip the flashing between the siding at the top of the cutout.

TOOLS & MATERIALS

- Pencil
- Tape measure
- Hammer
- Circular saw or handsaw
- Chisel
- Drill and bits (¼" twist & 1" spade, or ⅜" & ⅝" masonry)
- Caulk gun
- Carpenter's level
- Framing square
- Stakes

- Mason's string
- Straightedge
- Plumb bob
- Line level
- Shovel
- Wheelbarrow
- Combination square
- Construction plans
- Framing lumber
- Metal or vinyl drip-edge flashing
- Exterior panel adhesive or caulk

- Concrete
- Concrete footing tube forms
- Post anchors
- 10d joist hanger nails
- 8d galvanized nails
- ⅜ × 4" lag screws
- 2½" deck screws
- J-bolts
- Stakes
- Masking tape

Step C: Mark Joist Locations on the Ledger & Rim Joist

1. Cut a 2 × 8 ledger board to size, which should be 4" shorter than the full length of the porch. Also cut the rim joist from 2 × 12 lumber, according to your project plans.

C. *Align the ledger and the rim joist. Mark on center joist locations on both boards every 16", using a straightedge.*

2. Lay the ledger board next to the rim joist to gang-mark deck joist locations onto the ledger and the rim joist. Set a 2 × 6 spacer at each end of the ledger to make up for the difference in length between the two, then mark the joist locations onto the ledger and the rim joist. Start 15¼" from one end of the rim joist, and mark deck joist locations 16" apart on center.

Step D: Mark, Cut & Install the Ledger

1. Position the ledger on the back steps, and mark cutting lines onto the full-length ledger board at the edges of the steps. Cut the ledger into sections.

2. Position the ledger board sections in the cutout areas, up against the drip-edge flashing. Tack in place with 8d galvanized common nails.

3. Drill two counterbored pilot holes into the ledger at framing member locations or at 16" intervals if attaching at the rim joist. Drive ⅜ × 4" galvanized lag screws, with washers, into the pilot holes to secure the ledger.

Step E: Locate the Footings

1. Build two batter boards and drive one into the ground at each side of the porch, 12" past the front of the project area, aligned with the project edge.

2. Drive a nail at each end of the ledger, and tie a mason's string to each nail. Tie the other end of each string to a batter board.

3. Square the string with the ledger, using the 3-4-5 method: Mark the ledger board 3 ft. from the end, then mark the mason's string 4 ft. out from the same point. Adjust the mason's string until the endpoints from the 3-ft. and 4-ft. marks are exactly 5 ft. apart, then retie. Make sure the mason's string is taut.

4. Measure out from the ledger board and mark the post centers on the mason's string with a piece of tape.

5. Hang a plumb bob from each piece of tape, then drive a stake into the ground at the post-center location.

Step F: Pour the Footings

1. Set an 8"-dia. concrete tube form onto the ground, centered around the stake. Mark the edges of the form onto the ground. Remove the form and the stake, and dig a hole past the frost-line depth. Avoid moving the mason's string.

2. Set the concrete tube form into the hole so the top is about 2" above the ground. Use a level to make sure the top of the form is level. Repeat for the other post footing.

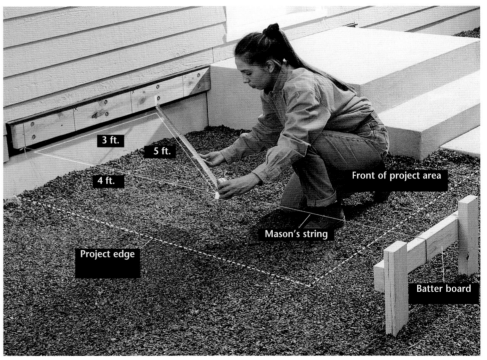

D. Cut the ledger to size using a circular saw or handsaw.

E. Establish square lines for the sides of the porch by using the 3-4-5 carpenter's triangle, then measure for the location of the posts and drop a plumb bob to transfer the center point of the post to the ground.

3. Mix concrete and fill the forms. Screed the surface of the concrete with a scrap of 2 × 4.

4. Drop a plumb bob from the tape marks on the mason's string to find the post centers on the surface of the concrete. Insert a J-bolt into the concrete at that point. The threaded end of the J-bolt should extend up at least 2". Let the concrete cure for three days.

Step G: Install the Posts

1. Set a metal post anchor over the J-bolt, and secure with a washer and nut.

2. Cut a post that is at least 6" longer than the planned post height.

3. With a helper, set the post into the post anchor and secure with 8d galvanized nails driven through the pilot holes in the post anchor. Install both posts.

4. Brace each post with a pair of 2 × 4s attached to stakes driven in line with the edges of the posts, but outside of the project area. Secure the braces to the stakes with 2½" deck screws, then use a level to make sure the posts are plumb. Attach the braces to the posts with 2½" deck screws.

F. *Drop a plumb bob to determine the exact center of the footing, and then install a J-bolt at the point to attach the post anchor.*

G. *Having someone help you, install the post in the post anchor and brace on adjacent sides with 2 × 4s staked to the ground.*

319

Installing Joists

To build the porch floor, a framework of joists is needed to transfer weight loads to the posts and then to the footings. A rim joist—2 × 12 used here—is secured between the posts at the front end of the porch, with joists installed at the edges of the project and usually every 16" on center in between, perpendicular to the house.

Porch joists usually can be made from 2 × 6 or 2 × 8 lumber, but check your local code requirements before building. Also, joists should slope away from the house at a rate of ⅛" per foot for drainage.

Joists for a porch floor are installed using the same techniques as in basic deck construction. For further details, refer to pages 166 to 229 in the Decks section of this book.

HOW TO INSTALL THE JOIST FRAME AND JOISTS
Step A: Establish the Slope Line

1. With the post braces still in place, run a mason's string between the edge of the ledger and a post. Use a line level to make sure the string is level.

2. Measure down ⅛" for every foot of distance between the ledger and the post to establish the slope line. Mark a slope line on each post.

Step B: Install the Outer Joists

1. Cut the outer joists to fit between the back of the ledger and the front of each post. Use the angle created by the slope line and the post as a guide for cutting the ends of the joists.

2. Attach the outer joists to the ends of the ledger and the posts with deck screws. You may need to bend up the drip-edge flashing above the ledger.

TOOLS & MATERIALS

- Tape measure
- Drill
- ⅜" masonry bit
- Carpenter's level
- Hammer & maul

- Ratchet & socket set
- Framing lumber
- ⅜ × 4" lag screws with washers
- Joist hangers
- Corner brackets

- Masonry-anchor sleeves
- 10d joist hanger nails
- 3" galvanized deck screws
- Mason's string
- Line level

A. To create a slope, measure down from a level mason's string ⅛" for every foot of distance between the ledger and the post and mark.

B. Cut the outer joists to size, drill pilot holes, and fasten to the post with 3" galvanized deck screws.

C. Attach joist hangers to the ledger and rim joist at each marked location using 10d joist hanger nails.

Step C: Attach Joist Hangers

1. Measure and mark the joist locations on the ledger and rim joist according to your plans. On-center spacing for joists is typically 16".

2. Attach joist hangers to the ledger and to the rim joist at the joist locations with 10d joist hanger nails. Place a 2 × 8 scrap into each hanger before nailing, so the hanger will hold its shape during installation.

Step D: Install the Rim Joist

1. Tack the porch rim joist on position. The top of the rim joist should be flush with the tops of the outer joists.

2. Drill four counterbored pilot holes through the rim joist and into each post, then drive ⅜ × 4" lag screws with washers at each pilot hole to secure the rim joist to the post.

3. Install metal corner brackets with joist-hanger nails at each of the four inside corners, to stabilize the frame.

Step E: Install the Step Ledger & Remaining Joists

NOTE: If you are building your porch over old steps, as shown here, attach the step ledger to the riser of the top step using masonry-anchor sleeves. Otherwise, proceed with steps 4 and 6 below.

1. Drill pairs of counterbored ⅜"-dia. through holes at 16" intervals into the step ledger. Adjust the hole locations as necessary so they do not interrupt the joist hanger locations.

2. Lay a straightedge across the joists next to the steps as a reference for ledger board alignment. Shim under the ledger to hold it in position, then mark the through-hole locations on the riser. Remove the ledger.

3. Drill holes for ⅜"-dia. masonry-anchor sleeves into the riser at the marks using a hammer drill and ⅜" masonry bit. Drive the masonry sleeves into the holes with a maul or hammer.

4. Attach a joist hanger at each joist location on the ledger using 10d joist hanger nails.

5. Reposition the step ledger, aligning the holes of the ledger with the holes in the riser. Attach the ledger with ⅜ × 4" lag screws driven into the masonry sleeves.

6. Cut the remaining joists with the same end angles as the outer joists, and install them in the joist hangers with joist hanger nails. (Refer to pages 206 to 211 for further detail on installing joists.)

D. *Tack the rim joist in position, drill four counterbored pilot holes, and fasten to the post with ⅜ × 4" lag screws with washers.*

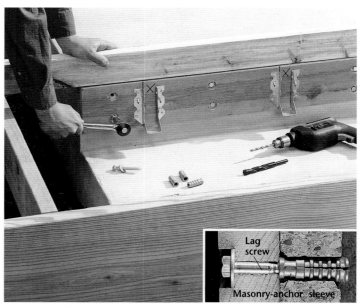

Lag screw

Masonry-anchor sleeve

E. *To install the step ledger, drill ⅜"-dia. holes into the top riser of the steps and install masonry-anchor sleeves (INSET). Fasten the ledger to the riser with ⅜ × 4" lag screws.*

Installing Porch Floors

Like most of the floors inside your home, the floor of your porch is built in layers to increase its strength and durability. The joists provide the bottom layer, giving the floor form and size. The subfloor—usually plywood—provides a stable base. And the porch boards, the layer you see, provide the finished outer layer. "Trim" is achieved with side skirt boards and a front apron that can be cut from exterior-grade plywood to conceal the outer joists and the rim joist, creating a cleaner appearance.

For maximum strength, the joists are usually installed parallel to the house, then the subfloor is laid perpendicular to the joists. Note that this project shows joists perpendicular to the house.

Before laying the porch boards, it is helpful to make a cleat and spacer from two pieces of scrap lumber that are similar in thickness to the skirt board—usually ¾" (see Step E). The cleat provides a secure, straight edge for aligning the first porch board, and the spacer creates an overhang for the skirt board.

To save time and simplify installation, use a floor nailer to attach porch boards directly to the subfloor. Check your local rental center for availability of this specialty tool.

HOW TO INSTALL PORCH FLOORS
Step A: Install the Subfloor
1. Measure and cut ¾" exterior-grade plywood to length, so that any seams fall over joists. Keep a slight (⅛") expansion gap between the pieces. Notch any pieces to fit around posts.
2. Nail a 2 × 4 cleat to any posts that are not fitted against joists. Make sure the cleat is flush with the tops of the joists.
3. Fasten the plywood pieces with 1½" deck screws. If you are installing the floor over old steps, apply exterior-grade construction adhesive to the steps to bond with the plywood.
Step B: Cut the Starter Board
1. To create a starter board, ripcut the grooved edge off a tongue-and-groove porch board with a circular saw.

TOOLS & MATERIALS

- Tape measure
- Circular saw & handsaw
- Caulk gun
- Speed square
- Jigsaw
- Drill
- Hammer
- Floor nailer

- Mallet
- Nail set
- ¾" exterior-grade plywood
- Exterior-grade construction adhesive
- Tongue-and-groove flooring

- Finish flooring
- Floor nailer nails
- Galvanized deck screws (1¼", 1½", 2")
- 8d siding nails
- Chalk line
- Galvanized finish nails
- Straightedge

A. Cut pieces of plywood subfloor to size and install with deck screws. INSET: Notch plywood pieces to fit around posts, and fasten to nailing cleats attached to posts.

B. Mark the location of the post on the starter board, then notch-out with a jigsaw.

2. Measure, mark, and cut the starter board 1" longer than the finished length, including a ¾" overhang for the porch apron.

3. Position the starter board so the tongue edge is pressed against the post. Mark the location of the post onto the board.

4. Measure and mark the cutting depth to fit around the post. Notch the board with a jigsaw.

Step C: Install the Cleat & Spacer

1. Sandwich together two pieces of scrap lumber that are the same thickness as the skirt board—usually ¾" (see Step E). Align the top edge of the outer piece (the cleat) at least 2" above the top edge of the inner piece (the spacer). Fasten the cleat to the spacer with 1¼" deck screws.

2. Attach the cleat and spacer to the outer joist, with the top of the spacer just below the top of the outer joist. Tack in place with 2" deck screws.

Step D: Install the Porch Boards

1. Draw reference lines on the subfloor, perpendicular to the house, to be used to check the alignment of the porch boards.

2. Butt the notched porch board against the cleat so it fits around the post. Nail it in place, spacing the nails every 6 to 8". If you are using a tongue-and-groove floor nailer, load a nail strip, then position the nailer over the exposed tongue and rap the striking head with a mallet to discharge and set the nails.

3. Cut and position the next porch board (notch for the post, if needed) so the groove fits around the tongue of the first board, and nail it in place.

4. Continue installing porch boards. Occasionally check the alignment by measuring from a porch board to the nearest reference line, making sure the distance is equal at all points. Adjust the position of the boards, as needed.

5. Notch and install porch boards to fit around the other post.

6. Ripcut the last board to size, leaving an overhang equal to the starter board overhang (typically ¾"). Position the board, and drive galvanized finish nails through the face of the board and into the subfloor. Set the nail heads with a nail set, then remove the cleat and spacer.

Step E: Install the Skirt Boards & Apron

1. Mark several porch boards ¾" out from the front edge of the rim joist to create an overhang to cover the top of the apron. Snap a chalk line to connect the marks, creating a cutting line.

2. Use a straightedge as a guide and trim off the boards at the cutting line using a circular saw. Use a handsaw to finish the cuts around the posts.

3. Cut skirt boards for the sides of the porch from exterior-grade plywood so they are flush with the front edge of the rim joist. Install them beneath the porch board overhangs and nail them in place with 8d siding nails.

4. Cut the front apron long enough to cover the edge grain of the skirt boards. Fasten it to the rim joist with 8d siding nails.

C. *Sandwich a cleat and spacer together that are the same thickness as the apron, and fasten so the cleat is 2" above the top of the outer joist.*

D. *Cut porch flooring to size, notching pieces to fit around posts where necessary. Install using a tongue-and-groove floor nailer and mallet.*

E. *Cut exterior-grade plywood to size for side skirt boards and the front apron. Secure with 8d siding nails.*

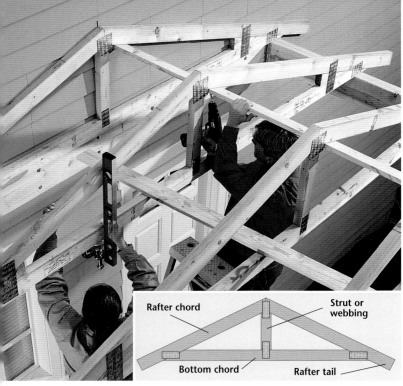

Use prebuilt roof trusses for porch construction. They are easier to work with than site-built rafters. When ordering trusses, you must know the roof pitch, the distance to be spanned, and the rafter tail overhang past the beams. Trusses can be purchased in stock sizes or custom-ordered at most building centers—consult with the salesperson to make sure you get the right trusses for your project.

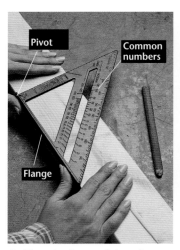

A. *Place the flange of the rafter square against the edge of the board at the endpoint of the angle.*

B. *Hold the flange securely at the endpoint and pivot the rafter square to the proper slope dimension, then mark along the marking edge.*

Installing Beams & Trusses

Beams and trusses or rafters support the porch roof. These pieces are large and awkward to handle, so install them with patience and care. It's a good idea to always have at least one helper on hand when installing these structural members.

Beams transfer the weight of the roof—trusses and roofing materials—to the posts. Beams can be built out of two pieces of framing lumber sandwiched together (2 × 6s shown here), or prefabricated laminate beams can be purchased. Before installing beams, though, a roof ledger needs to be installed, which is accomplished in roughly the same fashion as the deck ledger. (Refer to pages 316 to 319 for installing ledgers.)

Prebuilt trusses can simplify your porch project. When ordering trusses, you must know the roof pitch, the distance to be spanned, and the amount of overhang past the beams. Trusses can be purchased in stock sizes, or custom-ordered at most building centers—consult with the salesperson to make sure you get the right trusses for your project.

If building your own trusses or installing rafters (pages 373 to 376), the rafter square is a traditional roofer's tool that is very helpful for any projects that involve angle cutting.

HOW TO USE A RAFTER SQUARE
Step A: Align the Rafter Square
Once you have the slope information, begin marking a cutting line onto a board by holding the flange of the rafter square against the edge of the board.
Step B: Pivot to Slope Angle & Mark
1. Look for the word COMMON and the row of numbers aligned with it.

2. Holding the end of the flange securely against the edge of the board, pivot the square so the COMMON numbers equaling the rise of slope in inches-per-foot aligns with the same edge where the pivot point rests.

3. Mark the cutting line along the marking edge.

TOOLS & MATERIALS

- Tape measure
- Carpenter's level
- Drill with ¼" twist bit, 1" spade bit
- Hammer
- Framing square
- Rafter square
- Stud finder (optional)
- Torpedo level
- Circular saw or handsaw

- Clamps
- Ladders
- Chalk line
- Framing lumber, according to your construction plans
- Prebuilt roof trusses
- Double-joist hangers
- 10d joist hanger nails
- Metal post caps

- Galvanized common nails (6d, 8d, 10d & 20d)
- ⅜ × 4" galvanized lag screws
- 2" galvanized deck screws
- Pencil
- Straightedge
- Torpedo level
- Carpenter level

HOW TO INSTALL BEAMS & TRUSSES

Step A: Create the Roof Layout

1. Measure to find the midpoint of the porch deck, and mark it on the house.

2. Refer to your construction plan to determine the peak area of the planned roof. Transfer the centerline to the peak using a straight 2 × 4 and a carpenter's level.

3. Measure up from the porch deck and mark the top and bottom of the roof ledger onto the siding, near the center mark.

Also mark the ledger height at the ends of the project area, then connect the height marks with a chalk line.

Step B: Attach the Roof Ledger

1. For the roof ledger, set the ledger board (a 2 × 8 is used here) on the deck, so it extends past the edges of both front posts. Mark the outside edges of the posts onto the ledger, then make another mark directly above each edge of the deck.

2. Cut the roof ledger at the deck length marks using a circular saw or handsaw.

3. Make a reference mark at the midpoint on the board, then measure from the midpoint to one end.

4. At the roof ledger outline on the house, measure out in each direction from the center point the measurement found in #3 (above), and mark. Use a straightedge to draw the ends of the roof ledger outline.

5. Enlarge the outline by ½" on all sides, then remove the siding in that area. Locate and mark the framing members, looking for rows of nails every 16". If necessary, use an electronic stud finder to locate the framing members.

6. Position the ledger in the outline, and tack in place with 8d common nails. Drill pairs of ¼" pilot holes at each framing member, then counterbore each ½"-deep, using a 1" spade bit. Fasten the ledger to the framing members with ⅜ × 4" lag screws.

A. *Transfer the midpoint of the deck onto the house at the porch's roofline. Use it as a reference to create the roof ledger outline.*

B. *Place the roof ledger on the deck, flush against the posts. Mark the edges of the deck and the posts, then cut the ledger to size.*

Step C: Mark the Beam Locations

1. Lay out the locations for the beams onto the ledger, according to your construction plan.

2. Insert a pair of lumber scraps with the same dimensions as the beam members (2 × 8s used here) into the double-joist hanger. Position the hanger against the ledger using a torpedo level to make sure it is plumb. Fasten the double-joist hangers to the ledger with 10d common nails.

3. Set a straight board in each joist hanger, and hold the free end against the post. Use a carpenter's level to adjust the height of the board until it is level. Mark the post where it meets the bottom of the straight board. Draw cutting lines on all sides of the post at the height mark using a combination square.

4. Steady the post, having a helper brace the post from below, and trim off the top at the cutting line.

Step D: Create the Beams

1. Refer to your construction plan to determine the dimensions of the beam members (2 × 8s are used here). Measure the distance from the ledger at the double-joist hangers to 1½" past the fronts of the posts. Cut the beam members to size.

2. Nail pairs of beam members together, using 10d common nails, to create the beams. Drive the nails at slight angles, in rows of three, spaced every 12 to 16".

3. Lay out truss locations onto the tops of the beams, starting at the beam-ends that will fit into the double-joist hangers. Mark both edges of each truss, drawing an "X" between the lines for reference. Generally, trusses should be spaced at 24" intervals. Check your construction plan for exact placement.

Step E: Attach the Beams

1. Set a metal post cap onto the top of each post, and nail it in place with 10d joist hanger nails.

2. With a helper, raise the beams, and set them into the post caps and double-joist hangers. Secure the beams with 10d joist hanger nails.

3. For beams that are thinner than the posts, cut plywood spacers and install them between the inside edges of the beams and the inner flange of the post cap. The spacers should fit snugly and be trimmed to roughly the size of the post cap flanges. Drive 10d joist hanger nails through the post cap flanges, into the spacers and beams.

C. *Hold a straight 2 × 4 in the double-joist hanger and against the post, level, and mark a cutting line on the post.*

D. *Nail the beam members together in pairs, then lay out the truss locations 24" on center across the tops using a framing square.*

E. *Set the beam in the double-joist hanger at the ledger and in the saddle fastener at the post. Fasten with 10d joist hanger nails.*

F. *Install the first truss flush against the house, with the peak aligned with the project centerline and the rafter tails overhanging the beams equally on both sides. Make sure it is plumb and fasten to the framing members with 20d common nails.*

Step F: Attach the First Truss

1. With help, turn the first truss upside down (to make it easier to handle), and hoist it into position. Rest one end of the truss on a beam, then slide the other end up and onto the opposite beam.

2. Invert the truss so the peak points upward, and position it against the house, with the peak aligned on the project centerline.

3. Make sure that the first truss is flush against the siding, with the peak aligned on the project centerline and that the rafter tails overhang the beams evenly on each side. Nail the rafter chords and bottom chord of the truss to the house at framing member locations, using 20d common nails.

Step G: Attach the Subsequent Trusses

1. Lift the remaining trusses onto the beams.

2. Install the trusses at the locations marked on the beams, working away from the house, by toenailing through the bottom chords and into the beams with 8d common nails. Install the remaining trusses so the rafter tails overhang the beams equally.

3. Nail the last truss flush with the ends of the beams.

4. Use a level to plumb each truss, then attach 1 × 4 braces to the underside of each row of rafter chords using 2" deck screws.

G. *With all the trusses in place, check each for plumb, then fasten 1 × 4 bracing to the undersides of the rafter chords.*

Installing Sheathing & Fascia

Plywood sheathing ties the structural elements of the roof together and provides a work and nailing surface for installing roofing.

When installing sheathing, make sure seams between sheets of plywood fall on framing members, such as rafter chords or studs. Leave a ⅛" gap between sheets of plywood and a ¼" gap at the peak. Fasten sheathing with 8d galvanized box nails driven every 6" around the edges and every 12" in the field. If necessary, install nailers to create a nailing surface for the roof sheathing overhang at the gable end.

Fascia adds a finished look to your roof and helps prevent moisture and pests from damaging the structural elements of the roof. Fascia is usually fashioned from 1× lumber and fastened to the rafter chord tails, lookouts, or face, using finish nails.

Often, frieze boards are installed in conjunction with the fascia to create a nailer for the fascia and to bridge the seam from the siding. A ⅜ to ¼" plowed groove can be routed into the side fascia to accommodate soffit panels (pages 336 to 337).

TOOLS & MATERIALS

- Tape measure
- Hammer
- Drill
- Circular saw and handsaw
- Rafter square
- Framing square
- T-square
- Router with ⅜ to ½" straight bit
- 4d box nails
- 8d galvanized box nails
- 8d galvanized finish nails
- 2½" deck screws
- 1× lumber
- ¾" exterior-grade plywood sheathing
- Deck screws (1½", 2½")
- Speed square

HOW TO INSTALL ROOF SHEATHING & FASCIA BOARDS

Step A: Attach the Roof Sheathing

1. Cut 2 × 4 nailing strips to match the dimensions of the front-truss rafter chords. Attach the nailing strips to the rafter chords using 2½" deck screws.

2. Cut ¾" exterior-grade plywood sheathing to cover the trusses and nailing strips. The sheathing should be flush with the ends of the rafter tails, and seams should fall over rafter locations. Leave ⅛" gaps between pieces, and fasten sheathing with 8d galvanized box nails, nailing every 6" at the edges, and every 12" in the field.

3. Fill in the rest of the sheathing, saving the pieces that butt together at the peak for last. Leave a ¼" gap at the peak.

Step B: Attach the Gable Sheathing

1. Measure the triangular shape of the gable end, from the bottom of the truss to the bottoms of the nailing strips. Divide

Sheathing *ties the roof's structural elements together, whereas fascia adds to the finished look of your roof.*

Frieze board

Gable sheathing

Gable fascia

Side fascia board

Plowed groove

A. *Install plywood roof sheathing, working from the rafter tails to the peak. Leave a ⅛" gap between sheets and a ¼" at the peak.*

the area into two equal-sized triangular areas, and cut ¾"
exterior-grade plywood to fit.

2. Butt the pieces together directly under the peak, and attach
them to the front truss with 1½" deck screws.

Step C: Attach the Frieze Boards & Fascia

1. Cut 1 × 4 frieze boards to fit against the plywood gable
sheathing, beneath the nailing strips. Use a rafter square to cut
the ends at the angle of the roof pitch (page 317). Attach the
frieze boards to the gable sheathing with 4d box nails.

2. Cut 1 × 6 fascia boards long enough to extend several inches
past the ends of the rafter tails. Use a speed square to cut the
ends at the angle of the roof pitch. Nail the fascia boards to
the nailing strips, aligning the tops flush with the tops of the
roof sheathing.

Step D: Attach the Side Fascia Boards

1. Calculate the length of the side fascia boards by measuring
from the house to the back faces of the gable-end fascia boards.

2. Cut the side fascia boards to fit and rout a plowed groove
for the soffit panels, if necessary. Attach fascia boards with 8d
galvanized finish nails driven into the ends of the rafter tails.
Make sure the tops of the side fascia boards do not protrude
above the plane of the roof sheathing.

3. Trim off the ends of the gable-end fascia boards, so they are
flush with the side fascia boards using a handsaw.

4. Drive two or three 8d galvanized finish nails through
the gable-end fascia boards and into the ends of the side
fascia boards.

B. *Measure the triangular shape of the gable, divide into two pieces, and cut
¾" exterior-grade plywood to size.*

C. *Cut fascia boards long enough to extend several inches past the ends of
the rafter tails and attach using 8d galvanized finish nails.*

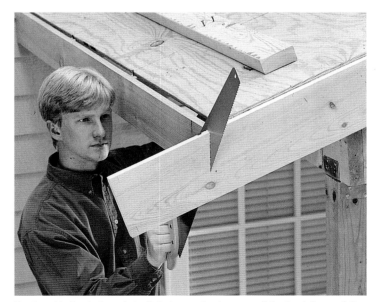

D. *Cut side fascia boards to fit between the house and the back faces of the
gable-end fascia, then trim off the gable-end fascia boards with a handsaw.*

329

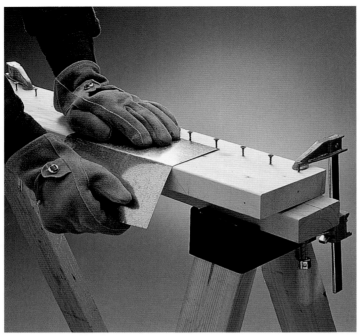

Make a flashing-bending jig *with screws lined up along a piece of scrap wood.*

Installing Step Flashing

Step flashing is used to tie a gable roofline into an existing wall. The galvanized metal or rubber barrier protects seams and makes water flow over shingled surfaces, away from gaps around roofing elements or at the tie-in points in the siding. It is installed during the shingling process. For techniques on installing building paper, drip-edge, and asphalt shingles, refer to pages 380 to 385 in the Sheds & Outbuildings section of this book.

Step flashing is typically available in 5 × 7" and 5 × 10" aluminum or metal blanks. These blanks are then bent into "ells" (and trimmed to size with aviation snips, if necessary), and installed with one leg of the ell behind the siding and the other underneath the shingles. To ensure water won't seep between pieces, each subsequent blank of flashing overlaps the next; one blank for each row of shingles.

To bend your own flashing, make a bending jig by driving screws into a piece of scrap wood, creating a line one-half the width of the flashing when measured from the edge of the board. Clamp the bending jig to a worksurface, press a step flashing blank flat on the board, then bend it over the edge.

Step flashing is installed at the same time as the roofing material. Roofing material comes in many different styles and materials—from asphalt shingles to cedar shakes. It protects your roof and home from water seepage and the elements.

A. *Cut away 2" of siding above the roof sheathing.*

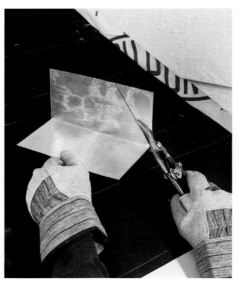

B. *Trim the flashing to follow the vertical edge of the roof with aviation snips.*

C. *Apply roofing cement to the base of the flashing, then tuck the flashing under the siding and secure it to the roof.*

TOOLS & MATERIALS

- Tape measure
- Circular saw
- Reciprocating saw
- Aviation snips
- Caulk gun
- Hammer
- Trowel

- Galvanized metal step flashing blanks
- Roofing cement
- Roofing nails
- Rubber-gasket nails
- Scrap wood

- Screws
- 15# building paper
- Asphalt shingles
- Drip-edge flashing
- Chisel
- Spacers

HOW TO INSTALL STEP FLASHING

Step A: Remove the Siding

1. Remove siding about 2" above the roof sheathing using a circular saw with the cutting depth set to the siding thickness.

2. Use a reciprocating saw held at a very low angle to cut the siding flush with the top of the roof.

3. Connect the cuts at the ends with a wood chisel, and remove the siding.

Step B: Begin Roofing & Cut the Flashing

1. Install building paper, drip-edge flashing (pages 380 to 381). Carefully pry up the siding and tuck at least 2" of paper under the siding. Leave the siding unfastened until after you install the step flashing.

2. Shingle up to the siding, trimming the last shingle if necessary. Bend a piece of step flashing in half and set it next to the lowest corner of the roofline. Mark a trim line on the flashing, following the vertical edge of the roof.

3. Cut and remove the waste portion of the flashing using aviation snips.

Step C: Install the Flashing

1. Pry out the lower courses of siding and any trim that's in the way. Insert spacers to prop the siding or trim away from the work area.

2. Apply roofing cement to the base of the flashing in the area where the overlap with the step flashing will be formed. Tuck the trimmed piece of step flashing under the siding and secure the flashing. Fasten the flashing with one rubber-gasket nail driven near the top and into the roof deck.

Step D: Add the Shingles

1. Apply roofing cement to the top side of the first piece of step flashing, where it will be covered by the next shingle course.

2. Install the shingle by pressing it firmly into the roofing cement. Don't nail through the flashing underneath.

Step E: Continue Shingling

1. Tuck another piece of flashing under the trim or siding, overlapping the first piece of flashing by at least 2". Set the flashing into roofing cement applied on the top of the shingle.

2. Nail the shingle in place, taking care not to drive nails through the flashing.

3. Continue shingling and flashing the roof. Make sure shingle tabs are staggered in regular patterns, with a consistent exposed area on shingle tabs.

4. Cut off shingle tabs and use them to create the roof ridge.

D. *Apply roofing cement to the flashing, then press the shingle into it. Do not nail through the flashing when attaching the shingle.*

E. *Continue to shingle and flash the roof, maintaining a regular shingle pattern with a consistent exposed area on the shingle tabs.*

Wrapping Posts & Beams

Even in the simplest front porch, standard posts and beams can look spindly and plain. Rather than spending the money for large timbers, it is a common practice to wrap the posts and beams with finish-grade 1× lumber to give them a more proportional look. Sanded ¾" exterior-grade plywood could also be used as wrap material.

To wrap the structural members of a porch, cut dimensions of 1× lumber to size, so that it will conceal any exposed hardware, framing lumber, and as many end grains as possible. Finish-grade pine is used here, giving the appearance of solid 6 × 6 stock, and hiding the fact that the beams were actually made from doubled 2 × 8s.

Pieces of finish lumber can also be cut to fit around the bases of the posts (called "post collars"), giving the posts a more solid appearance. 1 × 6s are used here to create the bottom post collars, and 1 × 4s for the top collars where the posts meet the beams. Make sure to cut pieces so the front collar piece covers the end grain of the side pieces.

Roof ledgers often are still visible after the porch ceiling is installed, so cover the ledger with finish lumber. If the ledger

TOOLS & MATERIALS

- Tape measure
- Circular saw or handsaw
- Hammer
- Level
- 1× finish-grade lumber
- ½" exterior-grade plywood (for spacers)
- Furring strips
- 8d box nails
- Galvanized finish nails (4d, 8d)

protrudes past the siding, cut a furring strip to cover the gap between the inside face of the ledger cover and the siding. If the ledger extends past the outer face of the beam, the easiest solution is to paint it to match the siding.

HOW TO WRAP POSTS & BEAMS

Step A: Cover the Inner Beams

1. Cut wrap boards for the inner sides of the beams to the same length as the beams using 1 × 10 finish-grade lumber, wide enough to cover the beams and any metal fasteners or hardware.

2. If necessary, add ½" plywood strips at the top and bottom of the beam with 8d box nails, to compensate for the ½" spacers

A. Cut a 1 × 10 to the same length as the inner-side of the beam, and attach with 8d finish nails.

B. Measure and cut 1× lumber to create an end cap for the post. Fasten with 8d finish nails.

C. Cut 1 × 4s and 1 × 6s to length, preassemble with 4d finish nails, then fasten to the posts with 8d finish nails.

in the metal post caps. Attach the inner sideboards to the beams with 8d galvanized finish nails.

Step B: Finish the Beams

1. Cut strips of wood from 1× finish-grade lumber to cover the bottoms of the beams from the house siding to the post, ripping to the proper width.

2. Pre-assemble the bottom board and side board by driving 8d galvanized finish nails at the butt joint, making sure to keep the joint square.

3. Attach the assembly to the beam so the free end of the bottom board forms a butt joint with the inner beam wrap board.

4. Cut boards to create an end cap for each beam, covering the ends of the beam and beam wrap pieces. Attach another piece to cover the gap beneath the beam overhang. Nail the end caps over the end of each beam with 8d galvanized finish nails.

Step C: Wrap the Posts

1. Cut boards for wrapping the posts, so they span from the floor to the bottoms of the wrapped beams. For a 4 × 4 post, two 1 × 4s and two 1 × 6s per post can be used.

2. Nail a 1 × 6 to the front of the post, overhanging ¾" on the outside edge. Nail a 1 × 4 to the outer face of the post, butted against the 1 × 6.

3. Pre-assemble the other two wrap boards, nailing through the face of the 1 × 6 and into the edge of the 1 × 4.

4. Set the assembly around the post, nailing the 1 × 6 to the post and nailing through the other 1 × 6 and into the edge of the 1 × 4. (There will be a slight gap between the second 1 × 4 and the post.) Repeat steps 1-4 for the other post.

Step D: Install the Post Collars

Cut pieces of 1 × 6 finish lumber to create the bottom post collars. Cut 1 × 4 finish lumber to create the top collars where the posts meet the beams. Nail the collars together with 4d galvanized finish nails.

Step E: Cover the Ledger

1. Measure the exposed ledger and cut a 1 × 10 to size. If the ledger protrudes past the siding, cut a furring strip to cover the gap between the inside face of the ledger cover and the siding.

2. Install the ledger cover and the furring strips with 8d galvanized finish nails.

D. *Build post collars from 1 × 4s for the tops of the posts, and 1 × 6s for the bases.*

Furring strip

E. *Cover the ledger with a 1 × 10 using furring strips to fill the gap between the bottom of the ledger and the wrapped beam.*

Finishing the Cornice & Gable

The cornice and gable are prominent features on the front of any porch. The cornice, sometimes called the "cornice return" or the "fascia return," is usually fitted with trim that squares off the corner where it meets the soffit. The gable is the area just below the peak, which is usually covered with trim and siding material.

The cornice and gable are finished to match the siding and the trim on your house. Make sure to caulk all seams at the peak of the gable and between the fascia boards and the cornice (photo at left). Use ¾" sanded plywood or 1× finish-grade lumber to make the cornice, and use siding that matches your house for the gable trim. To make installation easier, paint the siding materials before installation.

A framing square or speed square can be used to find the slope for the ends of the siding pieces, but an optional technique also exists. First, position a scrap board on the horizontal chalk line on the gable sheathing and mark the points where the edges of the board intersect with the frieze board. Connect the points to establish the slope line, then cut the scrap board on the line. Use the board as a template to mark your siding for cutting.

Caulk all seams between the fascia boards and cornice and at the peak of the gable (INSET).

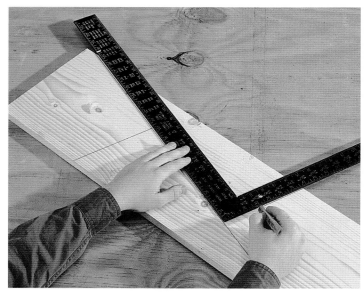

A. Lay out the dimensions of the cornice pieces on 1× finish-grade lumber using a framing square.

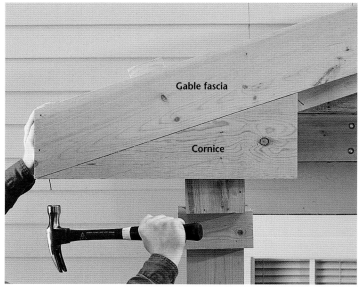

Gable fascia

Cornice

B. Attach the cornice pieces to the ends of the wrapped beams with 8d finish nails and to the bottom edge of the fascia with 4d finish nails.

TOOLS & MATERIALS

- Tape measure
- Caulk gun
- Framing square
- Hammer
- Circular saw

- Nail set
- Chalk line
- Rafter square
- Caulk
- Finish-grade lumber

- Galvanized finish nails (4d, 8d)
- Siding
- 4d siding nails
- Straightedge

HOW TO INSTALL A CORNICE

Step A: Cut the Cornice Pieces

1. At each end of the front porch, measure the area from the end of the gable fascia to a spot about 6" inside the porch beam.

2. Lay out a triangular piece of plywood or finish-grade lumber to fit the area using a framing square to create right angles.

3. Cut out the cornice pieces using a circular saw and straightedge guide.

Step B: Attach the Cornice Pieces

1. Test-fit the cornice pieces over the ends of the porch gable, then install with 8d finish nails driven into the ends of the beams and 4d nails driven up through the ends of the cornice pieces and into the underside of the gable fascia.

2. Use a nail set to embed the heads of the nails below the surface of the wood, being careful not to split the cornice pieces.

3. Caulk the seams between the fascia boards and the cornice.

HOW TO INSTALL GABLE SIDING

Step A: Cut the Siding to Size

1. Caulk the seam at the peak of the gable.

2. Measure the dimensions of the area covered by the gable sheathing on the house. If you have installed fascia and frieze boards, measure from the bottom of the frieze boards. Add 2" of depth to the area to make sure that the siding will cover the edges of the ceiling once the ceiling and soffits are installed.

3. Snap a horizontal chalk line near the bottom of the gable sheathing as a reference line for installing the siding.

4. Mark a cutting line that matches the slope of the roof onto the end of one piece of siding. Use a framing square or a rafter square (page 328) to mark the slope line.

5. Cut the bottom siding board to length, cutting the ends along the slope reference line.

Step B: Install the Siding

1. Use 4d siding nails to install the bottom siding board so it is flush with the bottom edge of the frieze boards. The bottom edge of the siding board should be 2" lower than the bottom of the gable sheathing.

2. Cut the next siding board so it overlaps the first board from above, creating the same amount of exposed siding as on the rest of the house. Be careful to keep the siding level.

3. Continue cutting and installing siding pieces until you reach the peak of the gable.

A. Mark cutting lines on the pieces of siding to match the slope of the roof using a framing square or a rafter square and a straightedge.

B. Measure from the bottom edge of the frieze boards to find the size of the subsequent pieces of siding. Overlap the siding so the reveal matches the siding on your house.

335

Installing Soffits & Ceilings

Soffits are panels that close off the area between rafter ends and the side of the porch. They can be nailed directly to the rafters or attached horizontally to nailers on the porch beams, boxing off the eaves.

To attach soffits directly to the rafters, measure from the back of the plowed groove of the fascia to the beam—following the bottom of the rafter tail—to establish the required width for the soffit panel. Measure the length from the house to the cornice or gable, then cut a piece of ⅜"-thick plywood to those dimensions. Insert one edge of the plywood panel into the plowed groove, and press the soffit panel up against the rafter tail. Nail the panel in place with 4d galvanized box nails.

A porch ceiling can be made from plywood or tongue-and-groove boards to give the porch a finished appearance. If you plan to install ceiling lights, have them wired before finishing off the ceiling.

With installation complete, paint the soffits and ceiling to match the rest of the porch trim. Add quarter-round molding at the joints between the soffit and the beam and the ceiling and the beam, or fill the gaps with tinted exterior-grade caulk.

TOOLS & MATERIALS

- Tape measure
- Hammer
- Torpedo level
- Chalk line
- Caulk gun
- Miter box
- Nail set
- Putty knife
- ⅜" sanded plywood
- 4d galvanized box nails
- 2 × 2 nailers
- 2 × 4 blocking
- Pencil
- 8d galvanized common nails
- ¾" cove molding
- 4d galvanized finish nails
- Wood putty
- Paint

HOW TO INSTALL HORIZONTAL SOFFIT PANELS

Step A: Attach the Nailers

1. Use a torpedo level to transfer the top height of the plowed groove of the fascia board to the beam, near one end.

2. Mark the groove height at the other end of the beam, then connect with a chalk line.

3. Align the bottom edge of a 2 × 2 nailer with the chalk line. Check for level, then secure to the nailer with 8d common nails.

Side fascia board

Plowed groove

2 × 2 nailer

Soffit panel

A. *Transfer the top height of the plowed groove in the side fascia to the beam and mark a reference for the nailer using a torpedo level. INSET: Plowed groove in side fascia.*

B. *Insert one edge of the soffit panel in the plowed groove and place the other end against the nailer. Fasten with 4d galvanized box nails.*

Step B: Install the Soffit Panels

1. Measure from the back of the plowed groove to the beam, just below the nailer, to find the required width of the soffit panel. Measure the length—from the house to the back face of the cornice—then cut a piece of ⅜"-thick plywood to fit.

2. Insert one edge of the soffit panel into the plowed groove and nail the other edge to the nailer with 4d galvanized box nails.

HOW TO INSTALL A PORCH CEILING

Step A: Attach the Blocking

Measure the distance between the trusses and cut 2 × 4s to size for blocking. Space the blocking 24" on center, flush with the bottom chords of the trusses. Fasten with 8d common nails.

Step B: Install the Ceiling

1. Measure the ceiling space and cut material to fit. Cut pieces so the seams fall on the centers of the bottom chords and blocking.

2. Attach the plywood to the bottom chords and blocking with 4d galvanized box nails, spacing them at 8 to 12" intervals.

3. Install ¾" cove molding around the edges of the ceiling to cover the gaps and create a more decorative look. Miter the corners and attach the molding with 4d galvanized finish nails.

4. Set the nail heads slightly, then cover them with wood putty before painting.

TIP: FINISHING

Paint the soffits and ceiling, along with the rest of the porch trim, to match the trim of the house. Add quarter-round molding at the joints between soffits and the beam, or fill gaps with tinted exterior-grade caulk.

A. *Install 2 × 4 blocking between the bottom chords of the trusses to use as nailing surfaces for installing the ceiling panels.*

B. *Measure the ceiling space and cut ceiling material to fit. Fasten using 4d galvanized box nails.*

Building Railings

A porch railing not only provides security from falls, but can also make an important contribution to the visual appeal of a porch. Basic railing components include the posts, the bottom and top rails, the balusters sometimes called *spindles*, and cap rails. These parts can be purchased in a wide variety of styles and sizes, ranging from plain framing lumber to ornately milled balusters, grooved cap rails, or decorative post tops (see page 250).

It is usually easiest to assemble the railing before you install it. Check local building codes before designing a railing. In most cases, railings should be at least 36" high, and the spaces between balusters and between the porch floor and bottom rail should be no more than 4".

TOOLS & MATERIALS

- Tape measure
- Drill & bits (⅛" twist, 1" spade bit)
- Ratchet wrench
- Caulk gun
- Circular saw
- Rafter square

- Framing square
- Handsaw
- Framing lumber
- ¾" plywood
- Finish lumber
- Milled cap rail
- Deck screws (1¼", 2½")

- Construction adhesive
- ⅜ × 4" galvanized lag screws
- 4d galvanized finish nails
- 8d casing nails
- Pencil

HOW TO BUILD & INSTALL A PORCH RAILING

Step A: Build the Railing Post

1. Cut two pieces of ¾" plywood to match the finished size of the posts, including any post wrap boards, to make a base plate.

2. Stack the pieces together and fasten with 1¼" screws and construction adhesive. Do not put screws in corners.

3. Cut the post to finished height (usually 38 to 40"), allowing for the thickness of the base plate.

4. If you plan to wrap the post, use scrap lumber the same thickness as the wrap boards to center the post on the base plate. Attach the base plate to the bottom of the post with three counterbored ⅜ × 4" galvanized lag screws.

Step B: Install the Railing Post

1. Set the post in position on the porch floor. Drive ⅜ × 4" galvanized lag screws through pilot holes at each corner of the base plate and into the porch floor.

2. Cut and install wrap boards to match the other porch posts. Also cut and install collar boards to cover the edges of the base plate and the bottom of the post using 4d galvanized finish nails.

Step C: Cut & Mark the Top, Bottom & Cap Rails

1. Cut the rails to length. If you have installed post collars at the post base, the bottom rail will have to be cut shorter than the top and cap rails.

2. Mark baluster layout onto top and bottom rails, no more than 4" apart. Drill ⅛" pilot holes through the rails at the marks.

A. *Use wood scraps to center the base plate on the bottom of the post. Drill counterbored pilot holes and fasten with ⅜ × 4" galvanized lag screws.*

B. *Position the post on the porch floor, drill pilot holes at each corner of the base plate, and secure with ⅜ × 4" galvanized lag screws.*

Step D: Assemble the Railing

1. Clamp, measure, and gang-cut the balusters to finished length using a circular saw.

2. Lay the top and bottom rails on a worksurface. Use shims to support the balusters and top rail so they align with the center of the bottom rail.

3. Attach the balusters to the rails by driving 2½" deck screws through the pilot holes in the rails and into the baluster ends. Use a spacing block to keep balusters from shifting.

Step E: Install the Railing Assembly & Post Caps

1. Insert the railing assembly between posts using blocks to support it at the desired height.

2. Drill ⅛" angled holes through the ends of the top and bottom rails and into the posts. Toenail railings to posts with 8d casing nails.

3. Slip the cap rail over the top rail. Attach the cap rail by driving 2½" deck screws at 18" intervals, up through the top rail and into the cap rail.

4. Add preformed post caps to post tops by driving finish nails through the top of the caps into the posts, or use post caps with preinstalled screws.

VARIATION: ROUND POSTS

To install railings between round posts, position the railing assembly between the posts, and mark the position of each railing onto the posts. Cut along the lines with a handsaw, then use a chisel to remove wood between the cuts. Insert the rail ends of the assembly into the post notches, then toenail the rail ends to the posts.

C. *Drill ⅛" pilot holes through the top and bottom rails, centered side-to-side at each baluster layout mark.*

Spacing block

Shims

D. *Support the balusters and top rail with shims. Use a spacer block to align the balusters with the pilot holes, and fasten with 2½" deck screws.*

E. *Position the cap rail on the top rail, and attach with 2½" deck screws every 18". NOTE: Attach post caps to posts using finish nails.*

Porch Screen

If you have ever built a stud wall and repaired a window screen, you already have most of the skills needed for a screen-in project. A screen-in can be accomplished on many areas of a house or yard, including decks, patios, and gazebos. But by far the most popular is the front porch. The quick and simple front porch screen-in demonstrated here is a good example of how to make outdoor living spaces, such as your porch, more livable.

There are many strategies you can take to accomplish a front porch screen-in. Porches and entryways covered by the main roof of the house often can be screened-in simply by attaching the screen materials directly to the existing structure of the porch using retaining strips to fasten the screens. Or, check with your local building center to learn more about manufactured screen-in systems. Generally, these systems use rubber spline cords and tracks to secure the screens, allowing the installer to create greater screen tension and reduce the need for screen frames.

Another easy way, demonstrated here, is to build a self-contained frame inside the railings, posts, and beams to support the screening. The self-contained frame is a versatile option that can be used in almost any outdoor structure.

If your floor is constructed of deck boards, cover the gaps between the boards from below using retaining strips and brads to tack fiberglass insect mesh to the bottom edges of the floor joists. If you cannot reach from below, the best solution is to remove the deck boards, attach a layer of insect mesh to the tops of the joists, and then reinstall the boards.

If you plan to paint the frames a different color than the surrounding porch surfaces, paint all of the wood parts for the screen-in before you install them.

TOOLS & MATERIALS

- Tape measure
- Chalk line
- Framing square
- Circular saw or handsaw
- Carpenter's level

- Hammer
- Wood chisel
- Screwdrivers
- Staple gun
- Utility knife
- Framing lumber

- 3" deck screws
- 16d casing nails
- Screen door
- 2½" door hinges (3)
- Wood screws (¾", 1")
- Fiberglass insect

- mesh screening
- Screen retaining strips
- 1¼" brass brads
- Straightedge
- Spacers

HOW TO SCREEN-IN A PORCH

Step A: Outline the Screen Walls

1. Outline the project area on the porch floor using a chalk line. Create the largest possible space not obstructed by beams, posts, railings, trim, or the ceiling.

2. Check the corners of the outline with a framing square to make sure the chalk lines are square.

3. Mark the door rough opening—the door width plus 3" for the doorframe and ½" for clearance.

Step B: Install the Sole Plates

1. Measure and cut 2 × 4s to length for sole plates using a circular saw. Attach to the porch floor outside the chalk line using 3" deck screws driven at 12" intervals. Do not install sole plates in the door rough opening.

2. Mark 2 × 4 doorframes at the sides of the door rough opening using a straightedge. The doorframes should rest on the floor, butted against the sole plates.

3. Mark doubled 2 × 4 posts at the front corners of the project outline, and mark 2 × 4 end posts on the sole plate next to the wall of the house.

4. Mark 2 × 4 studs for screen supports, spaced at even intervals of 24 to 36", depending on the total distance spanned.

Step C: Install the Top Plates

1. Cut 2 × 4 top plates to match the sole plates using a circular saw. Lay the top plates next to the sole plates, and copy the post and stud marks onto the top plates. The top plate over the door opening is not cut out.

2. Using a straight 2 × 4 and a level, mark the locations for the top plates on the ceilings directly above the sole plates.

3. Attach the top plates to the ceiling with 3" deck screws driven into joists or beams, if possible. Make sure the top plates are aligned directly above the sole plates, with the framing member marks also in alignment.

A. *Outline the project area on the floor using a chalk line. Check the corners with a framing square to make sure the outline is square.*

B. *Cut 2 × 4s for sole plates to length, align with the reference lines, and fasten to the porch floor with 3" deck screws.*

C. *Mark the locations for the top plates on the ceiling directly above the sole plates using a straight 2 × 4 and a level.*

D. *Install studs and posts at reference marks on the top and sole plates. Toenail in place with 16d casing nails.*

E. *Measure and cut 2 × 4 spreaders to size, and fasten between studs at the height of the railings.*

Step D: Install the Studs

1. Measure the distance between the bottom plate and top plate at each stud location, then cut studs and posts to length using a circular saw.

2. Position and install the studs and posts at the marks on the top plates and the sole plates. Toenail them in place with 16d casing nails.

3. Install the 2 × 4 doorframes by nailing through the frames and into the ends of the sole plates.

NOTE: If the ledger board sticks out past the siding, work around it when installing the 2 × 4 end posts. Butt two 2 × 4s together so one fits between the floor and the ledger, with the edge against the wall. Toenail the other 2 × 4 into the top plate and sole plate, and nail it to the edge of the first 2 × 4.

Step E: Install the Spreaders

Cut 2 × 4 spreaders to fit between the studs and posts using a circular saw. Position the spreaders at the same height as the porch railing, then toenail them with 16d casing nails. The spreaders prevent framing members from warping and provide a nailing surface for screen retaining strips.

Step F: Install the Door Header & Stop Molding

1. Install a 2 × 4 door header to create a rough opening that is ¾" higher than the height of the screen door.

2. Nail door-stop molding to the inside faces of the doorframes and header. Recess the molding back from the outside edges of the doorframe to match the thickness of the door, so when the door closes, it is flush with the outside edges of the doorframe.

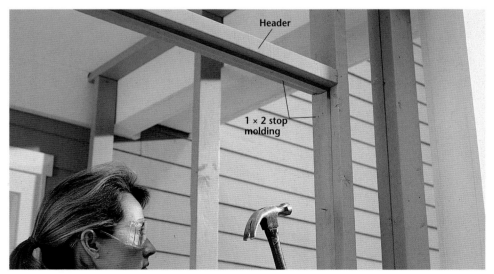

Header

1 × 2 stop molding

F. *Install the door header ¾" higher than the actual height of the door. Attach 1 × 2 stop molding along the inside face of the doorframe so it creates a recess the same thickness as the door.*

Step G: Install the Door

1. Measure and mark the locations for the door hinges on the edge of the door. Mark at 12" from the top of the door and 12" from the bottom, then space the third hinge evenly between the two.

2. Cut a mortise to the depth matching the thickness of the hinges into the edge of the door at each location using a wood chisel. Attach the hinges with ¾" wood screws.

3. Set the door in the opening, using ½"-thick spacers to hold it up off the floor. Outline the hinge plates onto the front edge of the doorframe.

4. Remove the door and cut mortises into the doorframe at the hinge locations using a wood chisel. The mortises should be deep enough so the hinge plate will be flush with the surface of the wood.

5. Set the door in the opening, and screw the hinges to the frame with 1" wood screws.

6. Install desired door hardware, including a door pull, a closer or spring, a wind chain, a latch or lock, and a rubber door sweep for the bottom of the door, if desired. Follow the manufacturer's directions for each piece of hardware.

Step H: Attach the Screen

1. Measure and mark centerlines along the inside faces of all studs and posts for reference lines when installing the screens.

2. Use a scissors to cut strips of screening so they are at least 4" wider and 4" longer than the opening in the framework where each screen will be installed.

3. Cut wooden retaining strips—for fastening the screens—to the width of the framework openings.

4. Begin attaching screens at the tops of the framework openings by securing them with the retaining strips. Attach the retaining strips with 1¼" brass brads at 6 to 12" intervals.

Step I: Finish Securing the Screen

1. With a helper, pull the screen down until taut. Use a retaining strip (cut to the width of the opening) to press the screen against the reference line, then attach near the ends of the strip with 1¼" brass brads.

2. Staple the screen at the sides, flush against the reference lines, then attach retaining strips over the staples at the reference lines with 1¼" brass brads.

3. Install screens in all remaining openings, then use a utility knife to trim the excess screening at the edges of the retaining strips.

G. Mark the hinge locations onto the doorframe, then chisel mortises deep enough so the hinge plate will be flush with the surface of the frame.

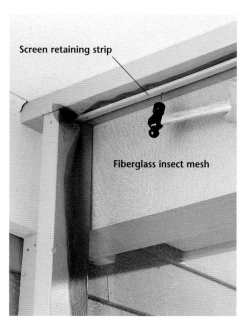

Screen retaining strip

Fiberglass insect mesh

H. Mark center reference lines on the inside faces of all studs and posts. Align mesh and retaining strips with the lines, then fasten with brass brads.

I. Secure the screen at the stretcher with retaining strips and brads. At the sides, pull the screen taut and staple in place, then cover with retaining strips and fasten with brads.

Porch Screen Kit

A screening system is an ingeniously simple and effective way to enclose a porch with minimal time and effort. A basic system includes three main components: a base channel that mounts directly to the porch posts, railings, and other framing members; the screening (and spline, if applicable); and a trim cap that snaps in place over the base channel to cover the screen edges and add a finished look to the installation. The base and cap pieces are made to go together, but the screen and spline are purchased separately. Be sure to follow the system manufacturer's specifications for screen type and spline size. Screen systems typically are compatible with fiberglass and aluminum screen materials.

With the system shown in this project, each piece of screen is secured into the base channels using standard vinyl or rubber spline and a spline roller. The screen goes up quickly and easily after a little practice, and it doesn't have to be perfectly tight right away; when the cap pieces are snapped on, they add tension to the screening, pulling it tight from all sides of the opening. This does a good job of eliminating the unsightly sag that occurs all too quickly with standard stapled-up screening. Replacing screen sections also is much easier with a screen system: Just remove the surrounding cap pieces, pull out the spline, and install a new piece of screen.

TOOLS & MATERIALS

- Hammer
- Pruning sheers or aviation snips
- Drill
- Spline roller
- Utility knife
- Rubber mallet
- Screen system components
- 1" corrosion-resistant screws
- Screening
- Spline cord
- 2 × 4 lumber or composite equivalent
- Clamps
- Circular saw
- Tape measure
- Pencil
- Straightedge
- Power hand planer
- Sandpaper
- Galvanized finish nails
- Exterior construction adhesive
- 3½" deck screws

Screen systems are quick, easy products for screening in porches and other areas, such as the under-deck space seen here. They are commonly available at home centers and hardware stores and through Internet sites.

CLADDING POSTS

With their textures and grain, plain wood posts are right at home in many parts of many homes. But when you combine them with gleaming new white vinyl-based products, they can look a little rough. One way to make your porch posts blend better when you're installing under-deck or screening systems is to clad them and paint them to match. Traditionally, clear dimensional lumber is used for the cladding. But to get seamless results, this often means you need to cut complicated dado-rabbet joints that run all the way from top to bottom at each corner. Then, you need to sand thoroughly and apply several coats of paint. An easier option for making all of your screen porch parts match is to clad posts with one-piece PVC post cladding (see Resources, page 523). The product shown here is designed to fit around a 6 × 6" post. On the interior surface it is kerfed, but the exterior vinyl surface is solid. This way, it can be bent around corners crisply and seamlessly.

Vinyl cladding can be wrapped around wood posts seamlessly.

Spline-based screening systems are available at home centers and hardware stores and through many websites. Screen Tight, the system shown here (see Resources, page 523), is made with UV-resistant PVC and is available with trim colors of white, gray, beige, and brown. Parts of the system include: stretchable spline cord (A); spline roller (B); adhesive for bonding rigid vinyl (C); storm door handles (D); storm door hinges (E); 1" corrosion-resistant screws (F); screw-eye door latch (G); deck screws (H); decorative white-cap screws (I); track cap (J); track base (K); composite 2 × 4 (L); fiberglass screening (M).

HOW TO CREATE SCREENED ROOMS WITH A SPLINE KIT

1. *Begin installing the track backers that frame the openings you will be screening. You may use pressure-treated 2 × 4s or 2 × 2s. For a long-lasting and low-maintenance framework, we used composite 2 × 4-sized backers that came with the screen system materials. These products are quite new and are not rated for structural use. Attach the backers to the inside faces of the posts, centered, using exterior construction adhesive and 3½" deck screws.*

2. *Secure sole plates to the patio or porch floor using construction adhesive and appropriate mechanical fasteners (use concrete anchors for concrete, stone, or paver patios, and use deck screws for wood and nonwood decking).*

3. *Attach cap plates to the beam or joist at the top of installation area, leaving 1½" between plates to create recesses for the vertical backers.*

4. *Install the vertical track backer members with the top ends fitted in the gaps you left in the cap plate. Make sure the vertical members are plumb and then drive deck screws toenail style through the members and into the sole plate. Also drive screws up at angles through the vertical members and into the beam or joist at the top of the area. Drill pilot holes.*

5. *Install the door header and the horizontal track backers using adhesive and deck screws. Locate the horizontal members 36 to 42" above the ground.*

6. *Cut a base channel to length for each vertical member in the porch frame. At the tops of the posts, hold the base channel back to allow room for the horizontal channels, if applicable (see step 14 photo). This results in less cutting of the cap trim later. Cut the channels using pruning shears, aviation snips, or a power miter saw.*

7. *Fasten the vertical channel pieces to the framing with 1" corrosion-resistant screws. Drive a screw into each predrilled hole in the channel, then add a screw 2" from each end. Drive each screw in snugly but not so far that it warps the channel.*

8. *Cut the horizontal base channels to length and install them with screws. The butted joints where the horizontal channels meet the verticals don't have to be precise or tight-fitting.*

8. *Begin installing the screen by positioning a full piece of screening over an opening so it overlaps several inches on all sides. Secure the screen into the horizontal base channel at one of the top corners using spline. You can plan to run the spline around the corners or cut it off at the ends as needed.*

9. *Embed the spline at the starting point, where it should fit fully into the groove of the base channel. Use a spline roller. Then, using one hand to pull the screen taut, press the spline into place to secure the screen along the top of the opening.*

10. *Secure the screen along both sides, then along the bottom using the same technique as for the top. When you're finished, the screen should be flat and reasonably tight, with no sagging or wrinkling. If you make a mistake or the screen won't cooperate, simply remove the spline and start over.*

11. *Trim off the excess screening with a sharp utility knife. Fiberglass screen cuts very easily, so control the knife carefully at all times. Repeat steps as needed to screen-in the remaining openings.*

12. *Install the trim caps over the base channels, starting with the vertical pieces. Working from the bottom up, center the cap over the base, then tap it into place using a rubber mallet.* Tip: *If you have a continuous horizontal band along the top of the screening, install those trim pieces before capping the verticals.*

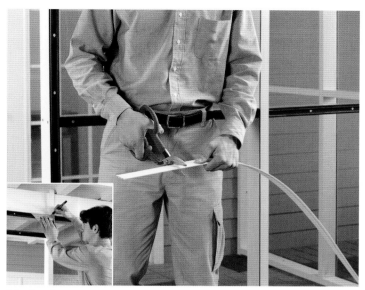

13. Cut the cap pieces to length as you install them. Mark cutting lines with a pencil, and make the cuts with pruning shears or snips. If desired, use a square to mark a straight cutting line across the face or backside of the trim cap (INSET).

14. Install the horizontal pieces once the vertical cap pieces are in place using the same techniques. Butt the horizontals tight against the verticals to start each piece, and then trim it to length as you approach the opposite end.

15. Complete the screening project by installing a screen door. A low-maintenance vinyl door provides a good match with the finish of the vinyl trim cap, but a traditional painted wood door is also appropriate.

OPTION: To protect the screening from being damaged by pets, kids, or other causes, make lattice frames and install them in the framed areas.

HOW TO INSTALL A PORCH SCREEN DOOR

1. *Measure the door opening. The new screen door should be ¼" to ⅜" narrower and ¼" to ½" shorter than the opening. Plan to trim the door, if necessary, for proper clearance. Some vinyl doors should not be cut, while others may be cut only a limited amount. If the door is vinyl, check with the manufacturer:*

2. *To trim the height of a door, mark the cutting line, then clamp a straightedge to the door to guide your circular saw for a straight cut. For wood doors, score deeply along the cutting line with a utility knife before setting up the straightedge; this prevents splintering on the top side when cutting across the grain.*

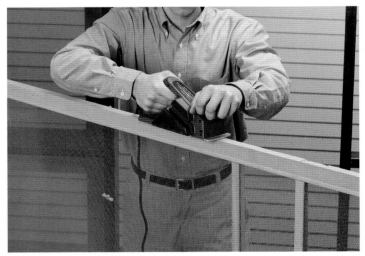

3. *To trim the width of a door, it's usually best to remove material from the hinge side, which is less visible. Mark a full-length cutting line, and make the cut with a circular saw. Or, you can use a power hand planer to trim off material from the edge. Use sandpaper or a file to round-over the cut side (and bottom, if applicable) edges to match the uncut edges and to prevent splinters.*

4. *Test-fit the door in the opening using wood shims along the bottom to raise the door to the right heights. Center the door from side to side; the reveal here should be about ⅛" on each side.*

5. Mount the hinges to the door using screws driven into pilot holes (three hinges is preferable, but two will work for most doors). Position the top hinge about 7" from the top of the door, the bottom hinge about 10" from the bottom, and the middle hinge halfway between the other two.

6. Install the door. Set the door into the opening using shims at the sides to establish equal reveals. For surface-mount hinges, mark and drill pilot holes, then screw the hinges to the side jamb or post to hang the door. For mortised hinges, transfer the hinge locations to the jamb, cut mortises for the hinges, then hang the door.

7. Install doorstop molding around the sides and top of the door opening using galvanized finish nails if your screen door is not prehung. Position the stops so the outer door face is flush with the outer jamb edges, trim, or doorposts, as applicable. Install the stop along the top of the opening first, then along the sides.

8. Add door handles, latches, and closer hardware as desired, following the manufacturer's instructions. A closer is a good idea to prevent the door from being left open and admitting insects. Closers come in a range of types, including spring-loaded hinges, hydraulic pistons, and old-fashioned extension springs. Most also have a stop chain that prevents the door from blowing all the way open.

Sheds & Outbuildings

Constructing your own outbuilding is a satisfying process—from hand-picking the lumber to nailing off the final piece of trim. In the end, you'll have a well-built, custom structure that will far outlast any typical wood or sheet-metal kit building. And if you're a beginner, you'll enjoy the added reward of learning the fundamentals of carpentry and building design.

Each of the five building projects in this section includes a complete set of architectural plans and step-by-step instructions for completing the construction. If you need more detail on any of the procedures, look for it in the Basic Construction Techniques section, starting on page 354.

The Techniques section gives you general information on the most popular types of finishes, as well as how-to projects for installing the finishes used in the projects. You'll also learn the basic construction methods for building foundations, framing floors, walls, and roofs, and completing the finish carpentry.

In addition to basic techniques, this chapter includes detailed projects that describe how to build multiple sheds and outbuildings, including greenhouses. Look for ideas about how to build these structures from scratch or by using pre-fabricated kits.

IN THIS CHAPTER:

Basic Construction Techniques

Architectural plan drawings are two-dimensional representations of what a building looks like from five different perspectives, or *views*: front, rear, right side, left side, and plan view. The first four are called ELEVATIONS, and they show you what you would see with a direct, exterior view of the building. There are elevation drawings for the framing and for the exterior finishes. PLAN views have an overhead perspective, looking straight down from above the building. FLOOR PLANS show the wall layout, with the top half of the building sliced off. There are also roof framing plans and other drawings with plan views.

To show close-up views of specific constructions or relationships between materials, there are various DETAILS. And all plans include a comprehensive building SECTION—a side view of the building sliced in half down the middle, showing both the framing and finish elements.

Because plan drawings are two-dimensional, it's up to you to visualize the building in its actual, three-dimensional form. This can be done by cross-referencing the different drawings and confirming the quantities and sizes of materials using the materials list. It helps to spend some time just looking over the drawings. Chances are, you'll find yourself absorbed in solving the puzzle of how it all fits together.

NOTE: the plan drawings in this section are not sized to a specific scale, but all of the elements within each drawing are sized proportionately. And although the plan dimensions are given in feet and inches (6'-8", for example), the instructions provide dimensions in inches, so you don't have to make the conversion.

Here are some of the common terms and conventions used in the drawings in this section:

• **Wall height** is measured from the top of the finished floor to the top of the wall framing.

• **Rough openings** for doors and windows are measured between the framing members inside the opening. An opening's width and height often are given on separate drawings.

• **Grade** represents the solid, level ground directly beneath the building.

• **Door & window details** typically show a gap between the 1 × frame and the framing of the rough opening—this represents the shim space needed for installing the frames using shims.

• **Framing layout** is noted with a dimension (usually 16 or 24"), followed by "on center" or "O. C." This describes the spacing between the center of one framing member to the center of the next member. Use the spacing for the general layout, adding extra members, such as for corners and door or window frames, where noted. The last space in a layout is often smaller than the given on-center dimension.

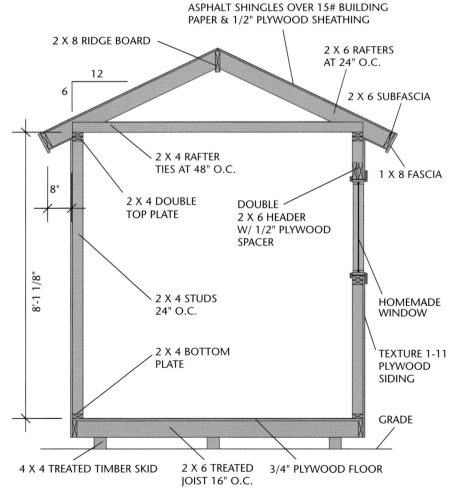

ASPHALT SHINGLES OVER 15# BUILDING PAPER & 1/2" PLYWOOD SHEATHING

2 X 8 RIDGE BOARD

2 X 6 RAFTERS AT 24" O.C.

2 X 6 SUBFASCIA

12

6

2 X 4 RAFTER TIES AT 48" O.C.

1 X 8 FASCIA

8"

2 X 4 DOUBLE TOP PLATE

DOUBLE 2 X 6 HEADER W/ 1/2" PLYWOOD SPACER

8'-1 1/8"

2 X 4 STUDS 24" O.C.

HOMEMADE WINDOW

2 X 4 BOTTOM PLATE

TEXTURE 1-11 PLYWOOD SIDING

GRADE

4 X 4 TREATED TIMBER SKID

2 X 6 TREATED JOIST 16" O.C.

3/4" PLYWOOD FLOOR

Anatomy of a Shed

Shown as a cutaway, this shed illustrates many of the standard building components and how they fit together. It can also help you understand the major construction stages—each project in this section includes a specific construction sequence, but most follow the standard stages in some form:

1. Foundation—including preparing the site and adding a drainage bed;

2. Framing—the floor is first, followed by the walls, then the roof;

3. Roofing—adding sheathing, building paper, and roofing material;

4. Exterior finishes—including siding, trim, and doors and windows.

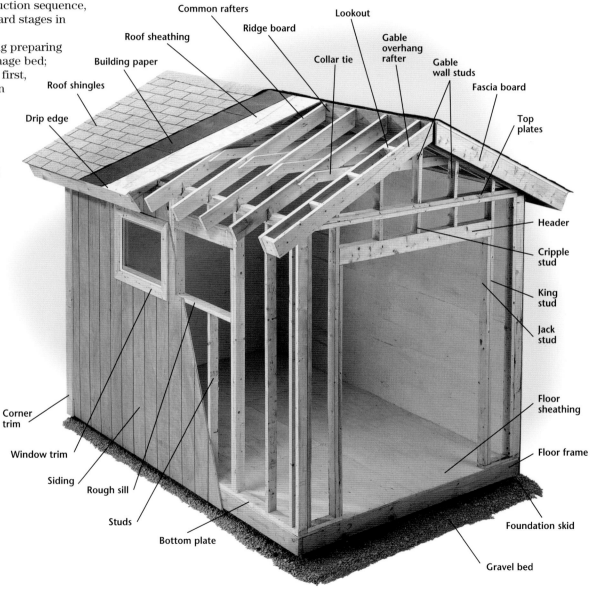

Common rafters

Ridge board

Lookout

Roof sheathing

Gable overhang rafter

Collar tie

Gable wall studs

Building paper

Fascia board

Roof shingles

Top plates

Drip edge

Header

Cripple stud

King stud

Jack stud

Floor sheathing

Corner trim

Floor frame

Window trim

Siding

Foundation skid

Rough sill

Studs

Bottom plate

Gravel bed

Building Foundations

Like a house, a shed or outbuilding needs a foundation to provide a sturdy base to build upon and to protect the structure from the damaging effects of moisture and soil. In some cases the foundation ties the building to the earth or keeps the building from shifting during seasonal freeze-thaw cycles.

You can build a shed with a variety of foundations; the most commonly used types are the wooden skid and the concrete slab. In addition to being far easier and cheaper to construct, a skid foundation allows you to move the shed if you need to. It also ensures—in most areas—that the building is classified as a temporary structure. A concrete slab, by contrast, gives

you a nice, hard-wearing floor as well as an extremely durable foundation. But a concrete foundation means the building is considered "permanent," which could affect the tax assessment of your property; you'll also most likely need a permit for the project.

A concrete block or concrete pier foundation is an excellent option between these extremes. Neither in danger of blowing away, or permanently embedded in the ground, one of these foundation options may be perfect for your structure. As always, check with your local building inspector for permits and regulations.

Wooden Skid Foundation

A skid foundation couldn't be simpler: two or more treated wood beams or landscape timbers (typically 4×4, 4×6, or 6×6) set on a bed of gravel. The gravel provides a flat, stable surface that drains well to help keep the timbers dry. Once the skids are set, the floor frame is built on top of them and is nailed to the skids to keep everything in place.

Building a skid foundation is merely a matter of preparing the gravel base, then cutting, setting, and leveling the timbers. The timbers you use must be rated for ground contact. It is customary, but purely optional, to make angled cuts on the ends of the skids—these add a minor decorative touch and make it easier to *skid* the shed to a new location, if necessary.

Because a skid foundation sits on the ground, it is subject to slight shifting due to frost in cold-weather climates. Often a shed that has risen out of level will correct itself with the spring thaw, but if it doesn't, you can lift the shed with jacks on the low side and add gravel beneath the skids to level it.

A. *Excavate the building site and add a 4" layer of compactable gravel. Level, then tamp the gravel with a hand tamper or rented plate compactor (INSET).*

TOOLS & MATERIALS

- Basic tools
- Shovel
- Rake
- 4-ft. level

- Straight $2 \times 4 \times 8$-ft.
- Hand tamper
- Circular saw
- Square

- Treated wood timbers
- Compactable gravel
- Wood sealer-preservative

HOW TO BUILD A WOOD SKID FOUNDATION
Step A: Prepare the Gravel Base

1. Remove 4" of soil in an area about 12" wider and longer than the dimensions of the building.

2. Fill the excavated area with a 4" layer of compactable gravel. Rake the gravel smooth, then check it for level using a 4-ft. level and a straight, 8-ft.-long 2 × 4. Rake the gravel until it is fairly level.

3. Tamp the gravel thoroughly using a hand tamper or a rented plate compactor. As you work, check the surface with the board and level, and add or remove gravel until the surface is level.

Step B: Cut & Set the Skids

1. Cut the skids to length using a circular saw or reciprocating saw. (Skids typically run parallel to the length of the building and are cut to the same dimension as the floor frame.)

2. To angle-cut the ends, measure down 1½ to 2" from the top edge of each skid. Use a square to mark a 45° cutting line down to the bottom edge, then make the cuts.

3. Coat the cut ends of the skids with a wood sealer-preservative and let them dry.

4. Set the skids on the gravel so they are parallel and their ends are even. Make sure the outer skids are spaced according to the width of the building.

Step C: Level the Skids

1. Level one of the outside skids, adding or removing gravel from underneath. Set the level parallel and level the skid along its length, then set the level perpendicular and level the skid along its width.

2. Place the straight 2 × 4 and level across the first and second skids, then adjust the second skid until it's level with the first. Make sure the second skid is level along its width.

3. Level the remaining skids in the same fashion, then set the board and level across all of the skids to make sure they are level with one another.

B. *If desired, mark and clip the bottom corners of the skid ends. Use a square to mark a 45° angle cut.*

C. *Using a board and a level, make sure each skid is level along its length and width and is level with the other skids.*

357

Concrete Slab Foundation

The slab foundation commonly used for sheds is called a slab-on-grade foundation. This combines a 3½- to 4"-thick floor slab with an 8- to 12"-thick perimeter footing that provides extra support for the walls of the building. The whole foundation can be poured at one time using a simple wood form.

Because they sit above ground, slab-on-grade foundations are susceptible to frost heave and in cold-weather climates are suitable only for detached buildings. Specific design requirements also vary by locality, so check with the local building department regarding the depth of the slab, the metal reinforcement required, the type and amount of gravel required for the subbase, and whether a plastic or other type of moisture barrier is needed under the slab.

The slab shown in this project has a 3½"-thick interior with an 8"-wide × 8"-deep footing along the perimeter. The top of the slab sits 4" above ground level, or *grade*. There is a 4"-thick layer of compacted gravel underneath the slab, and the concrete is reinforced internally with a layer of 6 × 6" 10/10 welded wire mesh (WWM). (In some areas, you may be required to add rebar in the foundation perimeter—check the local code.) After the concrete is poured and finished,

8"-long J-bolts are set into the slab along the edges. These are used later to anchor the wall framing to the slab.

A slab for a shed requires a lot of concrete (see TIP, right). Considering the amount involved, you'll probably want to order ready-mix concrete delivered by truck to the site (most companies have a one-yard minimum). Order *air-entrained* concrete, which will hold up best, and tell the mixing company that you're using it for an exterior slab. An alternative for smaller slabs is to rent a concrete trailer from a rental center or landscaping company. They fill the trailer with one yard of mixed concrete and you tow it home.

If you've never worked with concrete, finishing a large slab can be a challenging introduction, and you might want some experienced help with the pour.

TOOLS & MATERIALS

- Basic tools
- Circular saw
- Drill
- Mason's line
- Hammer
- Line level
- Framing square
- Shovel
- Wheelbarrow
- Rented plate compactor
- Bolt cutters
- Bull float
- Hand-held concrete float

- Concrete edger
- Compactable gravel
- Lumber (2 × 3, 2 × 4)
- Deck screws (1¼", 2½")
- ¾" A-C plywood
- 8d nails
- 6 x 6" 10/10 welded wire mesh
- 1½" brick pavers
- 8" J-bolts
- Tie wire
- Concrete
- Rake

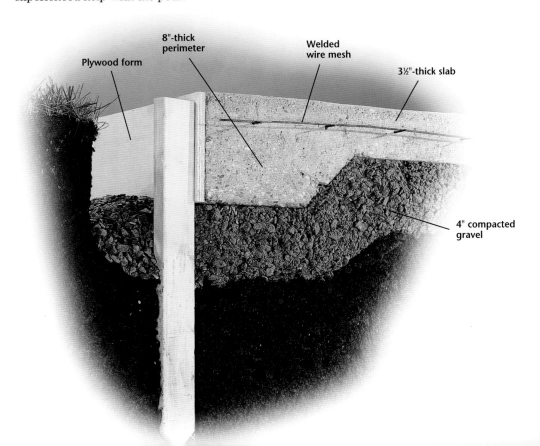

Plywood form • 8"-thick perimeter • Welded wire mesh • 3½"-thick slab • 4" compacted gravel

HOW TO BUILD A CONCRETE SLAB FOUNDATION
Step A: Excavate the Site

1. Set up batter boards (see pages 180 to 183) and run level mason's lines to represent the outer dimensions of the slab. Use the 3-4-5 method (see "Right Angles" on page 182) to make sure your lines are perpendicular, and check your final layout for squareness by measuring the diagonals.

2. Excavate the area 4" wider and longer than the string layout—this provides some room to work. For the footing portion along the perimeter, dig a trench that is 8" wide × 8" deep.

3. Remove 3½" of soil over the interior portion of the slab, then slope the inner sides of the trench at 45°. Set up temporary cross strings to check the depth as you work.

4. Add a 4" layer of compactable gravel over the entire excavation and rake it level. Compact the gravel thoroughly using a rented plate compactor.

Step B: Build the Form

1. Cut sheets of ¾" A-C plywood into six strips of equal width—about 7⅞", allowing for the saw cuts. To make sure the cuts are straight, use a table saw or a circular saw with a straightedge.

2. Cut the plywood strips to length to create the sides of the form. Cut two sides 1½" long so they can overlap the remaining two sides. For sides that are longer than 8 ft., join two strips with a mending plate made of scrap plywood; fasten the plate to the back sides of the strips with 1¼" screws.

3. Assemble the form by fastening the corners together with screws. The form's inner dimensions must equal the outer dimensions of the slab.

Step C: Set the Form

1. Cut 18"-long stakes from 2 × 3 lumber—you'll need one stake for every linear foot of form, plus one extra stake for each corner. Taper one end of each stake to a point.

2. Place the form in the trench and align it with the mason's lines. Drive a stake near the end of each side of the form, setting the stake edge against the form and driving down to 3" above grade.

3. Measuring down from the mason's lines, position the form 4" above grade. Tack the form to the stakes with partially driven 8d nails (drive through the form into the stakes). Measure the diagonals to make sure the form is square and check that the top of the form is level. Drive the nails completely.

4. Add a stake every 12" and drive them down below the top edge of the form. Secure the form with two 8d nails driven into each stake. As you work, check with a string line to make sure the form sides are straight and measure the diagonals to check for square.

Step D: Add the Metal Reinforcement

1. Lay out rows of 6 × 6" 10/10 welded wire mesh so their ends are 1 to 2" from the insides of the forms. Cut the mesh with bolt cutters or heavy pliers, and stand on the unrolled mesh as you cut, to prevent it from springing back. Overlap the rows of mesh by 6" and tie them together with tie wire.

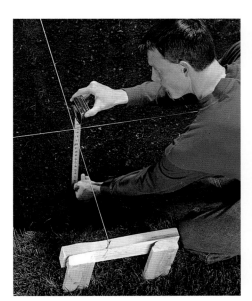

A. *Measure down from the temporary cross strings to check the depth of the excavation.*

B. *Assemble the form pieces with 2½" deck screws, then check the inner dimensions of the form. For long runs, join pieces with plywood mending plates.*

C. *Drive stakes every 12" to support the form, using the mason's lines to make sure the form remains straight.*

2. Prop up the mesh with pieces of 1½"-thick brick pavers or metal bolsters.

3. Mark the layout of the J-bolts onto the top edges of the form, following your plan. (J-bolts typically are placed 4 to 6" from each corner and every 4 ft. in between.)

Step E: Pour the Slab

1. Starting at one end, fill in the form with concrete using a shovel to distribute it. Use the shovel blade or a 2 × 4 to stab into the concrete to eliminate air pockets and settle it around the wire mesh and along the forms. Fill with concrete to the top of the form.

2. As the form fills, have two helpers screed the concrete using a straight 2 × 4 or 2 × 6 that spans the form. Drag the screed board along the top of the form, working it back and forth in a sawing motion. Throw shovelfuls of concrete ahead of the screed board to fill low spots. The goal of screeding is to make the surface of the concrete perfectly flat and level, if not smooth.

3. Rap the outsides of the form with a hammer to settle the concrete along the inside faces of the form. This helps smooth the sides of the slab.

Step F: Finish the Concrete & Set the J-bolts

1. Immediately after screeding the concrete, make one pass with a bull float to smooth the surface. Add small amounts of concrete to fill low spots created by the floating, then smooth those areas with the float. Floating forces the aggregate down and draws the water and sand to the surface.

2. Set the J-bolts into the concrete 1¾" from the outside edges of the slab. Work the bolts into the concrete by wiggling them slightly to eliminate air pockets. The bolts should be plumb and protrude 2½" from the slab surface. After setting each bolt, smooth the concrete around the bolt using a magnesium or wood concrete float.

3. Watch the concrete carefully as it dries. The bull-floating will cause water (called *bleed water*) to rise, casting a sheen on the surface. Wait for the bleed water to disappear and the surface to become dull. Pressure-test the concrete for firmness by stepping on it with one foot: If your foot sinks ¼" or less, the concrete is ready to be finished. NOTE: Air-entrained concrete may have very little bleed water, so it's best to rely on the pressure test.

4. Float the concrete with a hand-held magnesium or wood float, working the float back and forth until the surface is smooth. If you can't reach the entire slab from the sides, lay pieces of 2"-thick rigid foam insulation over the concrete and kneel on the insulation. Work backward to cover up any impressions.

5. Use a concrete edging tool to round over the slab edge, running the edger between the slab and the form. If you want a very smooth finish, work the concrete with a trowel.

6. Let the concrete cure for 24 hours, then strip the forms. Wait an additional 24 hours before building on the slab.

D. *Lay out rows of wire mesh, tie the rows together, then prop up the mesh with brick pavers or metal bolsters.*

E. *Screed the concrete after filling the form, using two people to screed, while a third fills low spots with a shovel.*

F. *Float the slab with a bull float, then set the J-bolts at the marked locations (INSET).*

Concrete Block Foundation

Concrete block foundations are easy and inexpensive to build. In terms of simplicity, a block foundation is second only to the wooden skid. But the real beauty of this design is its ability to accommodate a sloping site: All you have to do is add blocks as needed to make the foundation level.

Blocks suitable for foundations are commonly available at home centers and masonry suppliers. Standard blocks measure 8 × 16" and come in 2 and 4" thicknesses. Be sure to use only solid concrete blocks, not regular building block—the kind with large voids for filling with concrete. Also avoid the various types of decorative block, which may have holes or odd shapes and probably won't be strong enough for this application.

On a level site, you can use a single 4"-thick block for each support point. On a slope, a combination of 4 and 2" blocks should get you close enough to shim the foundation up to level (with lumber or asphalt shingles). Setting the blocks on small beds of gravel helps prevent erosion or excess water from undermining the foundation. Avoid excavating and refilling beneath the blocks other than to create a base for compactable gravel, as that may lead to settling.

TOOLS & MATERIALS

- Mason's lines & stakes
- Excavation tools
- Hand tamper
- Level (2-ft., 4-ft.)
- Long, straight 2 × 4
- Caulking gun
- Compactable gravel
- Solid concrete blocks
- Asphalt shingles or 1 × 8 pressure-treated lumber, as needed
- Construction adhesive

A 2 × 8 mud sill adds strength to a standard 2 × 6 floor frame. First, you fasten the side rim joists to the sill, then you set the assembly on top of the foundation blocks and install the remaining floor joists.

A foundation created with solid concrete blocks on a prepared base is simple to build and an easy solution to dealing with low slopes.

HOW TO BUILD A CONCRETE BLOCK FOUNDATION
Step A: Prepare the Site

1. Using four mason's lines tied to stakes, plot the foundation layout. The foundation exterior should equal the outer dimensions of the floor frame. Use the 3-4-5 method to ensure perfectly square layout lines.

2. Mark the block locations onto the strings, and then onto the ground. Locate the corner blocks at the string intersections, and locate the intermediate blocks at equal intervals between the corner blocks. For an 8 × 10-ft. or 8 × 12-ft. shed, one row of four blocks (or block stacks) running down each side of the shed is sufficient.

3. Remove the mason's lines, but leave the stakes in place. At each block location dig a 16 × 20" hole that is 4" deep. Tamp the soil.

4. Add a layer of compactable gravel in each hole and tamp well, adding gravel if necessary to bring the top of the gravel up to grade. Tamp all added gravel.

Step B: Set the Blocks

1. For the first block, retie the mason's lines. At the highest point on the gravel bed, square up a 4"-thick block to the layout lines.

2. Level the block in both directions, adding or removing gravel as needed.

3. Tape a 4-ft. level to the center of a long, straight 2 × 4.

4. Set up each of the remaining blocks or block stacks using the level and 2 × 4 spanning from the first block to gauge the proper height. Start each stack with a 4"-thick block, and make sure the block itself is level before adding more blocks. Use 2" blocks as needed to add height, or shim stacks with trimmed pieces of asphalt shingles or 1 × 8 pressure-treated lumber.

5. Use the level and 2 × 4 to make sure all of the blocks and stacks are level with one another.

Step C: Glue the Block Stacks

1. Glue stacked blocks together with construction adhesive. Also glue any shim material to the tops of the blocks.

2. After gluing, check to make sure all blocks and stacks are level with one another and that they are on the layout lines, then remove the strings and stakes.

A. *Create a bed of compacted gravel centered at each block location in your layout.*

B. *Set a block at the highest point on the site, check it with a level, and adjust as needed. (INSET) Use a level and board spanning across the blocks to establish the height of each stack so all the tops are level.*

C. *Bind stacked blocks together with exterior-rated construction adhesive to prevent shifting.*

Concrete Pier Foundation

Foundation piers are poured concrete cylinders that you form using cardboard tubes. The tubes come in several diameters and are commonly available from building materials suppliers. For a standard 8 × 10-ft. shed, a suitable foundation consists of one row of three 8"-diameter piers running down the long sides of the shed.

You can anchor the shed's floor frame to the piers using a variety of methods. The simplest method (shown here) is to bolt a wood block to the top of each pier, then fasten the floor frame to the blocks. Other anchoring options involve metal post bases and various framing connectors either set into the wet concrete or fastened to the piers after the concrete has cured. Be sure to consult your local building department for the recommended or required anchoring specifications.

Piers that extend below the frost line—the ground depth to which the earth freezes each winter—will keep your shed from shifting during annual freeze-thaw cycles. This is a standard requirement for major structures, like houses, but not typically for freestanding sheds (check with your building department). Another advantage of the pier foundation is that you can extend the piers well above the ground to accommodate a sloping site. NOTE: All concrete should have compacted gravel underneath and against back walls as backfill. All reinforcing steel should have a minimum of 1½" concrete cover.

A concrete pier foundation is a stable structure base that combines the permanence of post footings with the potential mobility of a wood-framed floor.

HOW TO BUILD A CONCRETE PIER FOUNDATION

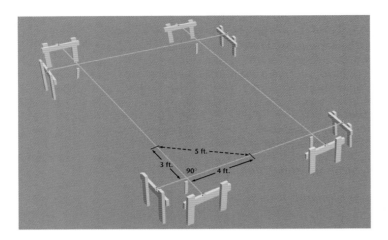

TOOLS & MATERIALS

- Circular saw
- Drill
- Mason's line
- Line level
- Framing square
- Plumb bob
- Shovel
- Posthole digger
- Utility knife
- Ratchet wrench

- Reciprocating saw or handsaw
- 2 × 4 lumber
- 2½" screws
- Stakes
- Nails
- Masking tape
- Cardboard concrete forms
- Paper

- Concrete mix
- J-bolts with washers and nuts
- 2 × 10 pressure-treated lumber (rated for ground contact)
- Tape meaure
- Gravel, as needed

Step A: Construct the Batter Boards

1. Cut two 24"- long 2 × 4 legs for each batter board (for most projects you'll need eight batter boards total). Cut one end square and cut the other end to a sharp point using a circular saw. Cut one 2 × 4 crosspiece for each batter board at about 18".

2. Assemble each batter board using 2½" screws. Fasten the crosspiece about 2" from the square ends of the legs. Make sure the legs are parallel and the crosspiece is perpendicular to the legs.

Step B: Set the Batter Boards & Establish Perpendicular Mason's Lines

1. Measure and mark the locations of the four corner piers with stakes, following your project plan.

2. Set two batter boards to form a corner about 18" behind each stake. Drive the batter boards into the ground until they are secure, keeping the crosspieces roughly level with one another.

3. Stretch a mason's line between two batter boards at opposing corners (not diagonally) and tie the ends to nails driven

A. *Cut the batter board pieces from 2 × 4 lumber and assemble them with screws.*

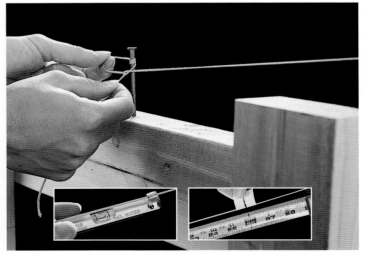

B. *Tie the mason's lines securely to the nails, and level the lines with a line level (INSET, left). Use tape to mark points on the lines (INSET, right).*

into the top edge of the crosspieces; align the nails and line with the stakes. Attach a line level to the line, and pull the line very taut, making sure it's level before tying it.

4. Run a second level line perpendicular to the first. Tie off the end that's closest to the first string, then stretch the line to the opposing batter board while a helper holds a framing square at the intersection of the lines. When the lines are perpendicular, drive a nail and tie off the far end.

5. Confirm that the lines are exactly perpendicular using the 3-4-5 method: Starting at the intersection, measure 3 ft. along one string and make a mark onto a piece of masking tape. Mark the other string 4 ft. from the intersection. Measure diagonally between the two marks; the distance should equal 5 ft. Reposition the second string, if necessary, until the diagonal measurement is 5 ft.

Step C: Mark the Footing Locations

1. Following your plan, measure from the existing lines and use the 3-4-5 method to add two more perpendicular lines to form a layout with four 90° corners. Use the line level to make sure the mason's lines are level. The intersections of the lines should mark the centers of the corner piers, not necessarily the outside edge of floor framing.

2. Check the squareness of your line layout by measuring diagonally from corner to corner: When the measurements are equal, the frame is square. Make any necessary adjustments.

3. Plumb down with a plumb bob and place a stake directly under each line intersection. Mark the locations of intermediate piers onto the layout strings, then plumb down and drive stakes at those locations.

4. Untie each line at one end only, then coil the line and place it out of the way. Leaving one end tied will make it easier to restring the lines later.

Step D: Set the Forms

1. Dig holes for the forms, centering them around the stakes. The holes should be a few inches larger in diameter than the cardboard forms. The hole depth must meet the local building code requirements—add 4" to the depth to allow for a layer of gravel. For deep holes, use a posthole digger or a rented power auger. Add 4" of gravel to the bottom of each hole.

2. Cut each cardboard form so it will extend at least 3" above the ground. The tops of all piers/forms should be level with each other. Also, the top ends of the forms must be straight, so place the factory-cut end up whenever possible. Otherwise, mark a straight cutting line using a large piece of paper with at least one straight edge. Wrap the paper completely around the form so that it overlaps itself a few inches. Position the straight edge of the paper on the cutting mark, and align the overlapping edges of the paper with each other. Mark around the tube along the edge of the paper. Cut the tube with a reciprocating saw or handsaw.

3. Set the tubes in the holes and fill in around them with dirt. Set a level across the top of each tube to make sure the top is level as you secure the tube with dirt. Pack the dirt firmly using a shovel handle or a stick.

C. Use a plumb bob to mark the pier locations. Drive a stake into the ground directly below the plumb bob pointer.

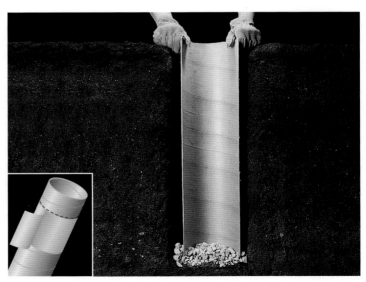

D. Wrap paper around the form to mark a straight cutting line (INSET). Set the forms in the holes on top of a 4" gravel layer.

Step E: Pour the Concrete

1. Restring the mason's lines and confirm that the forms are positioned accurately.

2. Mix the concrete following the manufacturer's directions; prepare only as much as you can easily work with before the concrete sets. Fill each form with concrete using a long stick to tamp it down and eliminate air pockets in the concrete. Overfill the form slightly.

3. Level the concrete by pulling a 2 × 4 on edge across the top of the form, using a side-to-side sawing motion. Fill low spots with concrete so that the top is perfectly flat.

4. Set a J-bolt into the wet concrete in the center of the form. Lower the bolt slowly, wiggling it slightly to eliminate air pockets. Use a plumb bob to make sure the bolt is aligned exactly with the mark on the mason's line. NOTE: You can set the bolt at 1½" above the concrete so it will be flush with the top of the block or extend it about 2½" so the washer and nut will sit on top of the block; doing the latter means you won't have to countersink the washer and nut. Make sure the bolt is plumb, then smooth the concrete around the bolt and let the concrete cure.

Step F: Install the Wood Blocks

1. Cut 8 × 8" square blocks from 2 × 10 pressure-treated lumber that's rated for ground contact.

2. Drill a hole for the J-bolt through the exact center of each block; if you're countersinking the hardware, first drill a counterbore for the washer and nut.

3. Position each block on a pier, then add a galvanized washer and nut. Use the layout strings to align the blocks, then tighten the nuts to secure the blocks.

E. *Fill the forms with concrete, then set the J-bolts. Check with a plumb bob to make sure the bolts are centered.*

F. *Anchor a block to each pier with a washer and nut. If desired, countersink the hardware (INSET).*

Framing

Framing is one of the most satisfying phases of a building project. Using basic tools and materials, you'll assemble the skeleton of the structure, piece-by-piece, and in the process learn the fundamentals of carpentry. The style of framing shown here is standard 2 × 4 framing, also called *stick framing*.

The tools you'll use for most framing are the circular saw (and power miter saw, if you have one), framing square, level, chalk line, and, of course, a framing hammer. Nails used for most framing are called common nails. These have a larger diameter than box nails, making them stronger, but also more likely to split thinner stock. Box nails are better for siding, trim, and other nonstructural materials. The three most commonly used nailing techniques are shown in the TIP to the right. Some framing connections, such as where rafters meet wall plates, require metal anchors for increased strength.

TIP: NAILING TECHNIQUES

Endnailing **Facenailing** **Toenailing**

Floor Framing

Floor frames for sheds are simple versions of house floor frames. They have outside, or *rim*, joists that are set on edge and nailed to the ends of the common joists. Gazebos have floor frames similar to decks, with angled joists that are connected to support beams with joist hangers (see TIP, page 368). On top of floor frames, a layer of tongue-and-groove plywood (or decking boards) provides the floor surface and adds strength to the frame. To prevent rot, always use pressure-treated lumber and galvanized nails and hardware for floor frames.

TOOLS & MATERIALS

- Basic tools
- Circular saw
- Square

- Pressure-treated 2 × lumber
- Galvanized common nails (8d, 16d)

- ¾" tongue-and-groove exterior-grade plywood

HOW TO BUILD A SHED FLOOR FRAME
Step A: Cut the Joists & Mark the Layout

1. Cut the two rim joists and the common joists to length, making sure all ends are square. Note that rim joists run the full length of the floor, while common joists are 3" shorter than the floor width.

2. Check the rim joists for crowning—arching along the narrow edges. Pick up one end of the board and hold it flat. With one eye closed, sight down the narrow edges. If the board arches, even slightly, mark the edge on the top (convex) side of the arch. This is the crowned edge and should always be installed facing up. If the board is crowned in both directions, mark the edge with the most significant crowning.

3. Lay one rim joist flat on top of the other so the edges and ends are flush and the crowned edges are on the same side. Tack the joists together with a few 8d nails. Turn the joists on-edge and mark the common joist layout on the top edges: Mark 1½" and 15¼" from the end of one joist. Then, measuring from the 15¼" mark, make a mark every 16"—at 32", 48", 64" and so on, to the end of the board (if the plan calls for 24" spacing, make a mark at 1½" and 23¼", then every 24" from there). Don't worry if

A. *Tack together the rim joists, then mark the joist layout. Use a square to transfer the marks to the second rim joist.*

the last space before the opposite end joist isn't as wide as the others. Make a mark 1½" in from the remaining end. After each mark, draw a small X designating to which side of the line the joist goes—this is a handy framers' trick to prevent confusion. This layout ensures that the edges of a 4-ft. or 8-ft. board or sheet will fall, or *break*, on the center of a joist.

4. Using a square, draw lines through each of the layout marks, carrying them over to the other rim joist. Draw Xs on the other joist, as well. Separate the joists and remove the nails.

Step B: Assemble & Square the Frame

1. Check the two end joists for crowning, then nail them between the rim joists so their outside faces are flush with the rim joist ends and the top edges are flush. Drive two 16d galvanized common nails through the rim joists and into the ends of the end joists, positioning the nails about ¾" from the top and bottom edges.

2. Install the remaining joists, making sure the crowned edges are facing up.

3. Check the frame for squareness by measuring diagonally from corner to corner. When the measurements are equal, the frame is square. To adjust the frame, apply inward pressure to the corners with the longer measurement.

4. If you're building the floor over skids, secure each joist to the outside skids with a metal anchor and toenail the joists to the internal skid(s) with 16d galvanized nails.

Step C: Install the Plywood Floor

1. Lay a full sheet of ¾" tongue-and-groove exterior-grade plywood over the frame so the groove side is flush with a rim joist and one end is flush with an end joist. Fasten the plywood to the joists with 8d galvanized nails driven every 6" along the edges and every 8" in the field of the sheet. Do not nail along the tongue edge until the next row of plywood is in place.

2. Cut the second piece to fit next to the first, allowing for a ⅛" gap between the sheets. Install the second sheet with its outside edges flush with the frame.

3. Start the next row with a full sheet (ripped to width, if necessary). Install the sheet starting from the corner opposite the first sheet, so the joints between rows are offset. Make sure the tongue-and-groove joint is tight; if necessary, use a wood block and a sledgehammer to close the joint.

4. Cut and install the remaining piece of plywood.

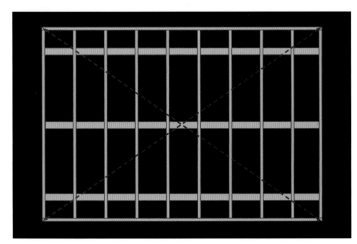

B. *Measure diagonally from corner to corner: If the measurements are equal, the frame is square.*

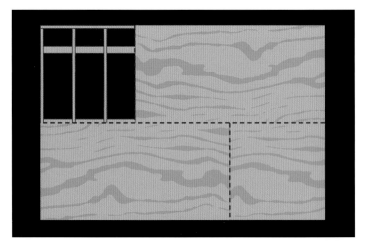

C. *Install the plywood perpendicular to the joists. Start each row with a full sheet and stagger the end joints between rows.*

Wall Framing

Standard framed walls have vertical 2 × 4 *studs* nailed between horizontal top and bottom *plates*. The top plates are doubled to provide additional support for the roof frame and to strengthen the wall connections. Door and window frames are made up of *king* studs; a *header*, which supports *cripple* studs above the opening; and *jack* studs, which support the header. A window frame also has a *rough sill* and cripple studs below the opening. The opening defined by the frame is called the *rough opening*. Wall frames gain rigidity from plywood sheathing or siding.

Building walls involves three major phases: 1. laying out and framing the wall, 2. raising the wall, and 3. tying the walls together and adding the double top plates. NOTE: If your building has a concrete slab floor, use pressure-treated lumber for the bottom plates and anchor the plates to the J-bolts set in the slab (see page 370).

TOOLS & MATERIALS

- Basic tools
- Broom
- Circular saw or power miter saw
- Square

- 4-ft. level
- Handsaw
- 2 × lumber
- 8d, 10d, and 16d common nails

- ½" plywood
- Construction adhesive
- Pencil
- Chalk lines
- Caulk gun

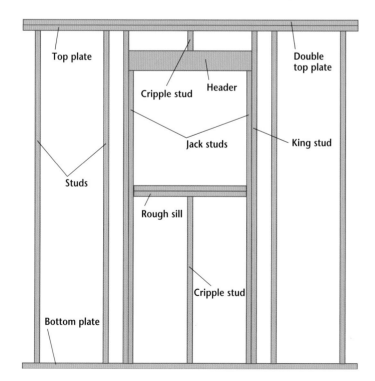

HOW TO FRAME WALLS

Step A: Mark the Bottom-plate Layout Lines

1. Sweep off the floor and make sure it's dry. Cut a short (about 4 to 6") piece of plate material to use as a spacer. Position the spacer at one corner of the floor, with its outside edge flush with the outside of the floor frame. Mark a pencil line along the inside edge of the spacer.

2. Use the spacer to mark the wall ends at each corner of the floor (eight marks total). Snap chalk lines through the marks. These lines represent the inside edges of the bottom plates.

Step B: Lay Out the Plates

1. Measure along the plate layout lines to find the lengths of the plates. Follow your project plans to determine which walls run to the edges of the building (called *through* walls) and which butt into the other walls (called *butt* walls).

2. Select straight lumber for the plates. Cut a top and bottom plate for the first wall, making sure their dimensions are the same. Use a circular saw or a power miter saw, but make sure both ends are square. Lay the bottom plate flat on the floor and set the top plate on top of it. Make sure their edges and ends are flush, then tack the plates together with a few 8d nails.

A. *Use a block cut from plate material to lay out the bottom plates. Mark at the ends of each wall then snap a chalk line.*

3. Turn the plates on-edge and mark the stud layout onto the front edges. If the wall is a through wall, make a mark at 1½ and 2¾" to mark the end stud and extra corner stud. Then, mark at 15¼ (for 16" on-center spacing) or 23¼" (for 24" on-center spacing)—measuring from this mark, make a mark every 16" (or 24") to the end of the plates. Make a mark 1½" in from the opposite end. Following your plan, draw an X next to each mark, designating to which side of the line the stud goes.

Mark the king and jack studs with a K and J respectively, and mark the cripple studs with a C.

If the wall is a butt wall, mark the plate at 1½", then move the tape so the 3½" tape mark is aligned with the end of the plate. Keeping the tape at that position, mark at 15¼ (for 16" spacing) or 23¼" (for 24" spacing). Then mark every 16" (or 24") from there. The 3½" that are "buried" account for the width of the through wall.

4. Using a square, draw lines through each of the layout marks, carrying them over to the other plate. Draw Xs on the other plate as well.

Step C: Cut the Studs & Build the Headers

1. Cut the studs to length, following the framing plan; make sure both ends are square. (Before cutting, give each stud a quick inspection to check for excessive bowing or crowning; reserve any bad studs for scrap or blocking.)

SECURING PLATES TO CONCRETE SLABS

When building walls over a concrete slab, drill holes in the bottom plates for the anchor bolts before marking the stud layouts. Position each plate on its layout line with the ends flush with the edges of the slab. Use a square to mark the edges of the bolt onto the plate (top photo). Measure from the layout line to the bolt center and transfer that dimension to the plate. Drill holes through

the plates slightly larger in diameter than the bolts. After raising the walls, anchor the plates to the bolts with washers and nuts (bottom photo).

B. Mark the stud layout onto the wall plates, designating the stud locations with Xs. On the plates of the through wall, also mark the location of the extra corner stud (INSET).

C. Construct the headers from 2× lumber and a ½" plywood spacer. Assemble the pieces with adhesive and nails.

2. Select straight lumber for the door-frame studs. Cut the jack studs to equal the height of the rough opening minus 1½" (this accounts for the thickness of the bottom plate); cut the jack studs for the window frame to equal the height of the top of the rough opening minus 1½". Cut the king studs the same length as the common studs.

3. To build the headers, cut two pieces of 2× lumber (using the size prescribed by the plans) to equal the width of the rough opening plus 3". Check the boards for crowning, and mark the top edges (see Step A, page 367). Cut a piece of ½" plywood to the same dimensions as the lumber pieces.

4. Apply two wavy beads of construction adhesive to each side of the plywood and sandwich the lumber pieces around the plywood, keeping all edges flush. Nail the header together with pairs of 16d common nails spaced about 12" apart. Drive the nails at a slight angle so they won't protrude from the other side. Nail from both sides of the header.

Step D: Assemble the Wall

1. Separate the marked plates and remove the nails. Position the plates on-edge, about 8 ft. apart, with the marked edges facing up.

2. Set the studs on-edge between the plates, following the layout marks. Before setting the door- or window-frame studs, facenail the jack studs to the inside faces of the king studs with 10d common nails staggered and spaced every 12"; make sure the bottom ends and side edges are flush.

3. Nail all of the studs to the bottom plate, then to the top plate. Position each stud on its layout mark so its front edge is flush with the plate edge, and nail through the plate and into the stud end with two 16d common nails (use galvanized nails on the bottom plate if your floor is concrete). Drive the nails about ¾" in from the plate edges.

4. Set the header in place above the jack studs and nail through the king studs and into the header ends with 16d nails—use four nails on each end for a 2 × 6 header and six for a 2 × 8 header.

For a window frame, measure up from the bottom of the bottom plate and mark the top of the sill on the inside faces of the jack studs—this defines the bottom of the rough opening. Cut two sill pieces to fit between the jack studs and nail them together with 10d nails. Toenail the sill to the jack studs with 16d nails.

5. Cut the cripple studs to fit between the header and the top plate (and the sill and bottom plate, for window frames). Toenail the cripple studs to the plates and headers (and sill) with two 8d nails on one side and one more through the center on the other side.

Step E: Square the Wall Frame

1. Check the wall frame for squareness by measuring diagonally from corner to corner. When the measurements are equal, the frame is square. To adjust the frame, apply inward pressure to the corners with the longer measurement.

D. *Frame the walls with 16d nails endnailed through the plates into the studs. Toenail cripples to headers with 8d nails.*

E. *Install a diagonal brace to keep the wall square. Make sure the brace ends won't interfere with the construction.*

371

2. When the frame is perfectly square, install a temporary 1 × 4 or 2 × 4 brace diagonally across the studs and plates. Nail the brace to the frame with 8d nails. Use two nails on the plates and on every other stud. To stabilize the structure, leave the wall braces in place until the walls are sheathed or sided.

3. At each end of the wall, attach a board to brace the wall upright after it is raised; nail it to the end stud with one 16d nail. NOTE: Install only one end brace for the second and third walls; no end brace is needed for the final wall.

Step F: Raise the Wall

1. With a helper, lift the top end of the wall and set the bottom plate on the layout lines you snapped in Step A. Swing out the free ends of the end braces and tack them to the floor frame to keep the wall upright. If you have a slab floor, nail the braces to stakes in the ground.

2. Fine-tune the wall position so the bottom plate is flush with the chalk line, then nail the plate to the floor with 16d nails. Drive a nail every 16" and stagger them so that half go into the rim joist and half go into the common joists. Do not nail the plate inside the door opening.

3. Pull the nails at the bottom ends of the end braces, and adjust the wall until it is perfectly plumb, using a 4-ft. level; set the level against a few different studs to get an accurate reading. Reattach the end braces with 16d nails.

Step G: Complete the Wall Frames & Install the Double Top Plates

1. Build and raise the remaining walls, following the same procedure used for the first wall. After each wall is plumbed and braced in position, nail together the end studs of the adjacent walls with 16d nails, driven every 12". Make sure the wall ends are flush.

2. Cut the double top plates from 2 × 4 lumber. The double top plates must overlap the top plate joints, so that on through walls, the double plate is 3½" shorter on each end than the top plate; on butt walls, the double plate is 3½" longer on each end. Nail the double top plates to the top plates with 10d nails. Drive two nails at the ends of the plates that overlap intersecting walls and one nail every 16" in between.

3. Use a handsaw or reciprocating saw to cut out the bottom plate in the door opening.

F. *Nail the bottom plate to the floor frame, then plumb the wall and secure it with end braces.*

G. *Nail together the corner studs of intersecting walls (INSET). Add the double top plates, overlapping the wall corners.*

Roof Framing

A roof frame is an important structure not only because it supports the roofing and helps keep the building dry, but because its style and shape have a great impact on the character of the building, the feel of the interior space, and the amount of storage space available.

There are four common roof types shown in this book. A *gable* roof is the classic, triangular design, with two sloped sides meeting at the peak, and flat ends (called *gable ends*). *Gambrel* roofs are like gable roofs with an extra joint on each side, resulting in two different slopes. A *hip* roof is structurally similar to a gable, but has no gable ends. *Shed* roofs are the simplest style, with only one sloped plane. They can be built with frames or, for small structures, a sheet of plywood.

All of these roof styles have a designated slope, which is the degree of angle of each side. The slope is expressed in a ratio that states the number of inches of vertical rise per 12" of horizontal run. For example, a roof that rises 6" for every 12" of run is said to have a slope of 6-in-12. Roof slope is indicated in plan drawings by a triangular symbol known as the *roof-slope indicator*. You'll use the roof slope to lay out rafters and fascia.

In standard roof framing, rafters are the principal structural members, rising from the walls to the ridge board (or *hub*, in gazebos) at the peak of the roof. Rafters in outbuildings typically are made from 2 × 4s or 2 × 6s, are spaced 16 or 24" on center, and are installed perpendicular to the length of the building. To keep the roof planes from spreading apart, *rafter ties*, or *collar ties*, are nailed between opposing rafters to form a structural triangle. With shed-style roofs, the rafters span from wall-to-wall and no ridge board or ties are needed.

The key to successful roof framing is making accurate cuts on the rafters. Take your time to cut the first two rafters, making any necessary adjustments, then use one as a pattern for marking the rest. The project on pages 374 through 375 shows you how to cut and install rafters in a gable roof frame, but the basic procedures are the same for gambrel and hip roofs.

As an alternative to rafter framing, you can take your plans to a truss manufacturer and have custom trusses built for your project. However, this will cost you more and probably will limit your storage space: The internal supports in truss frames leave little room for storage.

Ridge board · **Roof sheathing** · **Collar tie** · **Rafters**

TOOLS & MATERIALS

- Basic tools
- Circular saw
- Framing square
- 4-ft. level
- 2 × lumber
- Rafter square
- Common nails (8d, 10d, 16d)
- Joist ties
- Pencil
- Tape measure

TIP: MARKING ANGLES WITH A RAFTER SQUARE

A rafter square is a handy tool for marking angled cuts—using the degree of the cut or the roof slope. Set the square flange against the board edge and align the Pivot point with the top of the cut. Pivot the square until the board edge is aligned with the desired Degree marking or the rise of the roof slope, indicated in the row of Common numbers. Mark along the right-angle edge of the square.

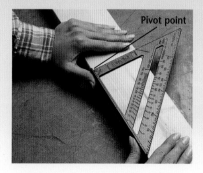

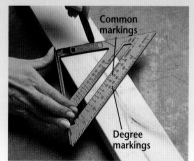

HOW TO BUILD A ROOF FRAME

NOTE: The following instructions are based on the sample rafter template shown here, which is designed for a 6-in-12 roof slope.

Step A: Mark the Plumb Cuts

1. Select a straight board to use for the pattern rafter. Mark the top plumb cut near one end of the board: Position a framing square with the 6" mark of the tongue (short part) and the 12" mark of the blade (wide part) on the top edge of the board. Draw a pencil line along the outside edge of the tongue.

2. Starting from the top of the plumb-cut mark, measure along the top edge of the board and mark the overall length of the rafter, then use the square to transfer this mark to the bottom edge of the board. Position the square so the tongue points down, and align the 6" mark of the tongue and the 12" mark of the blade with the bottom board edge, while aligning the tongue with the overall length mark. Draw a line along the tongue. If the bottom end cut of the rafter is square (perpendicular to the edges) rather than parallel to the top end, mark a square cut at the overall length mark.

Step B: Mark the Bird's Mouth Cuts

1. Measure from the bottom of the lower plumb cut and mark the plumb cut of the bird's mouth. Position the square as you did for the lower plumb cut and draw a line across the board face at the new mark.

2. Measure along the bird's mouth plumb cut and mark the bird's mouth level cut. Use the square to draw the level cut—it must be perpendicular to the bird's mouth plumb cut.

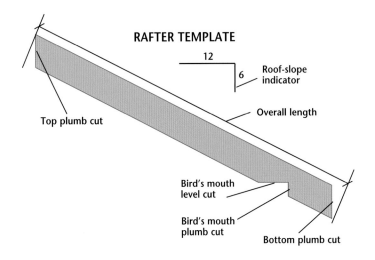

RAFTER TEMPLATE

12

6

Roof-slope indicator

Top plumb cut

Overall length

Bird's mouth level cut

Bird's mouth plumb cut

Bottom plumb cut

Step C: Make the Cuts

1. Cut the rafter ends at the plumb-cut lines using a circular saw or power miter saw.

2. Set the base of a circular saw to cut at the maximum depth. Make the bird's mouth cuts, overcutting slightly to complete the cut through the board. As an alternative to overcutting (for aesthetic reasons), you can stop the circular saw at the line intersections, then finish the cuts with a handsaw.

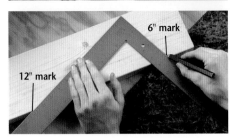

A. *Position the framing square at the 6 and 12" marks to draw the top and bottom plumb-cut lines.*

B. *Mark the bird's mouth level cut by squaring off of the bird's mouth plumb cut.*

C. *Cut the bird's mouth by overcutting the lines just until the blade cuts entirely through the thickness of the board.*

D. *Test-fit the pattern and duplicate rafters using a 2× spacer to represent the ridge board.*

E. *Mark the rafter layout onto the wall plates and the ridge board, starting from the same end of the building for each.*

F. *Endnail the first rafter to the ridge, then toenail the second. Reinforce the bottom connection with a metal anchor (INSET).*

3. Select another straight board to use as the duplicate rafter. Use the pattern rafter to trace the cutting lines onto the duplicate, then make the cuts on the duplicate rafter.

Step D: Test-fit the Rafters

1. Cut a 12"-long spacer block from 2 × 6 or 2 × 8 material.

2. With a helper or two, set the two rafters in place on top of the walls, holding the spacer block between the top rafter ends. Make sure the rafters are in line with each other (perpendicular to the walls) and are plumb.

3. Check the cuts for fit: The top-end plumb cuts should meet flush with the spacer block, and the bird's mouths should sit flush against the wall plates. Make sure the top ends are at the same elevation. Recut any angles that don't fit and test-fit the rafters again.

4. Write "PAT" on the pattern rafter, then use it to trace the cutting lines onto the remaining rafters. Before marking, check each rafter for crowning and mark the crowned edge (see Step A on page 367); always install the crowned edge up. If your building has overhangs at the gable ends, mark the end cuts for the overhang rafters but not the bird's mouth cuts—overhang rafters don't have them. Also, if you have the fascia material on-hand, use the pattern rafter to mark the angle for the top ends of the fascia boards.

5. Cut the remaining rafters.

Step E: Lay Out the Wall Plates & Ridge Board

NOTE: Start the rafter layouts at the same ends of the walls from where you started the wall stud layouts. This ensures the rafters will fall above the studs. Install rafters aligned with the end studs but not the extra corner studs.

1. Make a mark on the top wall plate, 1½" in from the end. Then, mark at 15¼" (for 16" on-center spacing) or 23¼" (for 24" on-center spacing)—measuring from this mark, make a mark every 16" (or 24") to the end of the wall. Make a mark 1½" in from the remaining end. Following your plan, draw an X next to each mark, designating to which side of the line the rafter goes.

2. Mark the wall on the other side of the building, starting from the same end.

3. Cut the ridge board to length using the plan dimensions. Check the board for crowning, then lay it on top of the walls next to one of the marked plates, making sure it overhangs the end walls equally at both ends. Use a square to transfer the rafter layout onto both faces of the ridge board.

Step F: Install the Rafters

1. You'll need a couple of helpers and a long, straight 2 × 4 to get the rafters started. Lay the first two rafters on top of the wall, then nail the 2 × 4 to the far end of the ridge board to serve as a temporary support. Set up the rafters at the end of the walls and hold the free end of the ridge board in place between them. Have a helper tack the rafters to the wall plates. Hold a level on the ridge board and make sure it's level, then have a helper tack the support to the far wall to keep the ridge level.

2. Slide one rafter a few inches to the side and endnail the other rafter through the ridge board with three 16d common nails (use two nails for 2 × 4 rafters). Slide the other rafter onto its layout mark and toenail it to the ridge with four 16d nails (three for 2 × 4s). Toenail the lower end of each rafter to the wall plate with two 16d nails, then reinforce the joint with a metal anchor, using the nails specified by the manufacturer.

3. Make sure the rafters are plumb and the ridge is level. Install the remaining rafters, checking for plumb and level periodically as you work.

Step G: Install the Collar Ties

1. Cut the collar ties (or rafter ties) to span between opposing rafters at the prescribed elevation, angle-cutting the ends to match the roof slope.

2. Position the collar tie ends against the rafter faces so the ends are about ½" from the top rafter edges. Make sure the ties are level, then facenail them to the rafters with three 10d common nails at each end.

Step H: Frame the Gable Wall

NOTE: Gable walls consist of top plates that attach to the undersides of the end rafters, and short studs set on top of the wall plates (see page 355). They appear only on gable and gambrel roofs.

1. Cut the top plates to extend from the side of the ridge board to the wall plates. Angle-cut the ends so they meet flush with the ridge and wall plate. The top-end angle matches the rafter plumb cut; the bottom angle matches the level cut of the bird's mouth.

2. Fasten the plates to the rafters so the front plate edges are flush with the outside faces of the rafters; use 16d nails.

3. Mark the gable stud layout onto the wall plate, then use a level to transfer the layout to the gable plates. Cut the gable studs to fit, angle-cutting the ends to match the roof slope. Install the gable studs with 8d toenails. Also install a square-cut stud directly under the ridge board.

Step I: Build the Gable Overhang (Gable & Gambrel Roofs)

NOTE: Gable overhangs are built with additional rafters installed at the gable ends (see page 355). They are supported by the ridge board and blocks—called *lookouts*—attached to the end rafters.

1. Mark the layouts for the lookouts onto the end rafters, following the project plan. Cut the lookouts and toenail them to the rafters with 8d nails (or endnail them with 16d nails) so that the top edges of the blocks are flush with, and parallel to, the tops of the rafters.

2. Install the overhang rafters over the ends of the lookouts with 16d endnails.

G. *Angle-cut the ends of the collar ties to match the roof slope and facenail the ties to the rafters.*

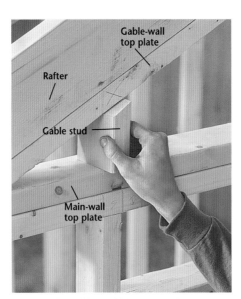

H. *Mark the gable stud layout onto the main-wall top plate and gable-wall top plate, then install the gable studs.*

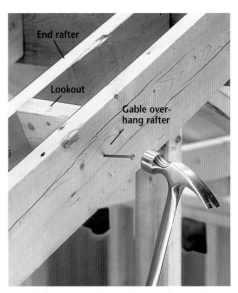

I. *Nail the outer gable overhang rafters to the lookouts, making sure the top edges of the rafters are flush.*

Roofing

The roofing phase typically follows the framing for most building projects. As it's presented here, roofing includes installing the fascia board, the roof sheathing, and, of course, the shingles. You'll also see how to install roof vents.

Fascia board is 1× trim material, typically made of cedar, that covers the ends of the rafters. On gable and gambrel roofs, fascia also covers the end (or gable overhang) rafters. Sheathing is the structural deck of the roof. Depending on the type of roofing used, the sheathing may be plywood, tongue-and-groove decking boards, or spaced 1× or 2× lumber.

As for the roofing, deciding on a material is a matter of personal taste and practicality. The most common type used for outbuildings is asphalt shingles, while cedar shingles and metal roofing are also popular options.

For the money, asphalt shingles are the most durable and low-maintenance material available, and they come in a wide range of colors and styles.

Cedar shingles are a big step up in price from asphalt, but their visual appeal is undeniable. The easiest type to install is the factory-sawn shingle with flat, tapered sides. Contact a roofing professional if you decide to go with cedar shingles.

Metal roofing has gained popularity in recent years for residential construction. Modern forms of metal roofing are extremely durable and easy to install.

Fascia & Sheathing

Fascia board and roof sheathing are always installed before the roofing, but which one you install first is up to you. Some buildings also have a 1× or 2× board installed behind the fascia, called *subfascia* or *frieze board*. Made of rough lumber, the subfascia helps compensate for inconsistency in rafter length, ensuring the fascia will be straight. It also provides a continuous nailing surface for the fascia.

The type of sheathing you use depends on the roof covering. Use CDX plywood (exterior-grade) for asphalt and cedar shingles. Depending on the building design, the fascia may be installed flush with the top of the sheathing, or the plywood may overlap the fascia. If you install the fascia first, cut spacers from the sheathing stock and use them when measuring and installing the fascia. Both shingle types must be installed over a layer of #15 building paper (also called *tar paper* or *roofing felt*), which goes on after the sheathing and fascia. The paper protects the sheathing from moisture and prevents the shingles from bonding to it.

As an alternative to plywood sheathing, you can use decking boards as a shingle underlayment. Typically sold in ⁵⁄₄ dimension (1¹⁄₁₆" thick), board sheathing creates an attractive "ceiling" for

INSTALLING ROOF VENTS

Roof vents, used in conjunction with soffit vents, can help keep the air in your shed cooler and cleaner. Vents are rated by square inches of ventilation area; most sheds need only two 68" roof vents and two to four 50" soffit vents.

Install roof vents centered between two rafters, about 16 to 24" from the ridge board. Cut a hole through the roof sheathing, following the manufacturer's instructions (below, left). Apply building paper (page 379), then center the vent over the hole and trace around its base flange.

Install shingles to a point at least 2" inside the bottom of the outline—don't cover the hole. Apply roofing cement to the underside of the base flange, then install the vent over the shingles using rubber-gasket roofing nails driven into all of the flange sides.

Shingle over the side and top vent flanges, leaving the bottom flange exposed; do not nail through the flanges with the shingle nails (below, right).

TOOLS & MATERIALS

- Basic tools
- Framing square
- Circular saw
- Stapler
- Fascia & trim material

- Galvanized finish nails (6d, 8d)
- 8d box nails
- CDX plywood roof sheathing

- 15# building paper
- Pencil
- Drill
- Hammer

the inside of a building, and nails won't show through as they do with plywood sheathing.

For metal roofing, install *purlins*—evenly spaced, parallel rows of 1× or 2× boards nailed perpendicularly to the rafters. Install the fascia over the ends of the purlins, flush with the tops.

HOW TO INSTALL FASCIA BOARD

NOTE: This procedure includes the steps for installing fascia on a gable roof. The basic steps are the same for a gambrel roof. For a hip roof, which has no gable ends, skip Step A and start your installation by tacking the first fascia board to the rafter ends, then working from there.

To install subfascia, follow the same procedure used for fascia, but don't worry about mitering the ends—just overlap the boards at the corners.

Step A: Cut & Fit the Gable-end Fascia

1. Mark a plumb cut on the top end of the first fascia board. If you didn't mark the fascia boards with the pattern rafter (page 375), use a framing square to mark the plumb cut, following the same method used for marking rafters (see page 374). Make the cut with a circular saw or power miter saw.

2. Hold the cut end of the fascia against the end rafter. If the fascia will be flush with the top of the sheathing, use spacers set on the rafter and position the top edge of the fascia flush with the spacers.

3. Have a helper mark the lower end for length by tracing along the rafter end onto the back side of the fascia. Make the cut with a 45° bevel. If you're using a circular saw, tilt the blade to 45° and follow the traced line; if you have a compound miter saw, rotate the blade to match the cutting line and tilt the blade to 45°.

4. Temporarily tack the fascia in place against the rafter with a couple of 8d galvanized finish nails. Repeat this process to mark, cut, and tack-up the opposing fascia piece, then do the same at the other gable end.

Step B: Install the Fascia Along the Eaves

1. Cut a 45° bevel on the end of another fascia piece and fit it against one of the pieces on the gable end. If the board is long enough to span the building, mark the opposite end to length. If you'll need two pieces to complete the eave, mark the board about ¼" from the far edge of a rafter; cut that end with a 45° bevel angled so the longer side of the board will be against the rafter. Cut the remaining piece with a 45° bevel angled in the other direction. This is known as a *scarf* joint—drill pilot holes to prevent splitting and nail these with 8d galvanized finish nails.

2. Make sure the corner joints fit well, then tack the fascia to the rafters.

3. Cut and tack-up the fascia along the other eave. Make sure all of the joints fit well, then fasten the fascia permanently with 8d galvanized finish nails: drive three nails into each rafter end and a pair of nails every 16" along the gable ends.

4. Lock-nail each corner joint with three 6d galvanized finish nails. If necessary, drill pilot holes to prevent splitting.

5. Install any additional trim, such as 1 × 2, called for by the plan. Miter the ends for best appearance.

A. *Mark the bottom end of the gable fascia by tracing along the end of the rafter (or the subfascia). If the fascia will be installed flush with the sheathing, use a spacer for positioning.*

B. *Fasten the fascia to the rafters (or subfascia) with 8d finish nails, then lock-nail the corner joints with 6d nails. Use scarf joints to join boards in long runs (INSET).*

HOW TO INSTALL PLYWOOD SHEATHING & BUILDING PAPER

Step A: Install the Sheathing

1. Lay a full sheet of CDX plywood on top of the rafters at one of the lower corners of the roof. Position the edges of the sheet ⅛" from the fascia (or the outside edges of the rafters) and make sure the inside end of the sheet falls over the center of a rafter; trim the sheet, if necessary.

2. Fasten the sheet to the rafters with 8d box nails spaced every 6" along the edges and every 12" in the field of the sheet.

3. Cut and install the next sheet to complete the first row, leaving a ⅛" gap between the sheet ends.

4. Start the second row with a half-length sheet so the vertical joints will be staggered between rows. Measure from the top of the first row to the center of the ridge board, and rip the sheet to that dimension.

5. Install the first sheet of the second row, then cut and install the remaining sheet to complete the row.

6. Sheath the opposite side of the roof following the same process.

Step B: Install the Building Paper

NOTE: If you are installing asphalt shingles, add the metal drip edge along the eaves before laying the building paper (see page 380).

1. Roll out 15# building paper across the roof along the eave edge. If you've installed drip edge, hold the paper flush with the drip edge; if there's no drip edge, overhang the fascia on the eave by ⅜". Overhang the gable ends by 1 to 2". (On hip roofs, overhang the hip ridges by 6".)

2. Secure the paper with staples driven about every 12".

3. Apply the remaining rows, overlapping the preceding row by at least 2". Overhang the ridge by 6". Overlap any vertical joints by at least 4".

4. Install the paper on the other roof side(s), again overlapping the ridge by 6".

5. Trim the paper flush with the fascia on the gable ends.

A. *Install the plywood sheathing so the vertical joints are staggered between rows. Leave an ⅛" gap between sheets.*

B. *Apply building paper from the bottom up, so the lower paper is overlapped by the paper above it.*

Asphalt Shingles

Asphalt shingles come in a variety of styles, but most are based on the standard three-tab system, in which each shingle strip has notches creating three equally sized tabs on the lower half of the strip. When installed, the tabs cover the solid portion of the shingle below it, giving the appearance of individual shingles.

For durability, use fiberglass-based shingles rather than organic-based. Also check the packaging to make sure the shingles comply with the ASTM D3462 standard for durability. If you choose a specialty style, such as a decorative shingle or a type that is made to appear natural (like wood or slate), check with the manufacturer for specific installation instructions.

Prepare the roof for shingles by installing building paper and metal drip edge along the roof perimeter. Drip edge covers the edges of the fascia and supports the shingle edges.

TOOLS & MATERIALS

- Basic tools
- Metal snips
- Chalk line
- Utility knife
- Straightedge
- Metal drip edge
- Asphalt shingles
- 2d roofing nails
- Roofing cement
- Building paper

HOW TO INSTALL ASPHALT SHINGLES

Step A: Install the Drip Edge

NOTE: Install drip edge along the eaves before applying building paper; install drip edge along the gable ends on top of the paper.

1. Cut a 45° miter on the end of a piece of drip edge using metal snips. Hold the end flush with the corner of the fascia, and fasten the flange of the drip edge to the sheathing with roofing nails driven every 12". To prevent corrosion, use galvanized nails with galvanized drip edge and aluminum nails with aluminum drip edge. Overlap vertical joints by 2".

2. Apply building paper over the entire roof (see page 379). Install drip edge along the gable ends, over the paper, cutting 45° miters to meet the ends of the eave drip edge. Overlap horizontal joints by 2", overlapping the higher piece on top of the lower. At the roof peak, trim the front flanges so the opposing edge pieces meet at a vertical joint.

Step B: Install the Starter Course of Shingles

1. Snap a chalk line 11½" up from the front edge of the drip edge (this will result in a ½" overlap for standard 12" shingles).

2. Trim off one-half (6") of the end tab of a shingle using a utility knife and straightedge.

A. *Install drip edge along the eaves over the sheathing. Add the building paper, then install drip edge along the gable ends.*

B. *Trim 6" from the end tab to begin the starter row. Position the starter row shingles upside-down so the tabs point up.*

3. Position the shingle upside-down, so the tabs are on the chalk line and the half-tab overhangs the gable drip edge by ⅜". Fasten the shingle with four 2d roofing nails, about 3½" up from the bottom edge: Drive one underneath each tab, one 2" in from the gable edge, and one 1" from the inside edge. Drive the nails straight and set the heads just flush to avoid tearing the shingle.

4. Use full shingles for the remainder of the row, butting their edges together. Trim the last shingle so it overhangs the gable edge by ⅜".

Step C: Install the Remaining Courses

1. Install the first course of shingles, starting with a full shingle. Position the tabs down and align the shingle edges with those in the starter course. Drive four nails into each shingle: one ⅝" above each tab, and one 1" in from each end, at the same level. Trim the last shingle to match the starter course.

2. Snap a chalk line on the building paper, 17" up from the bottom edge of the first course; this will result in a 5" exposure for each course.

3. Begin the second course with a full shingle, but overhang the end of the first course by half of a tab. Begin the third course by overhanging a full tab, then one and one half tabs for the fourth course. Start the fifth course with a full shingle aligned with the first course, to repeat the staggered pattern. Snap a chalk line for each course, maintaining a 5" exposure. After every few courses, measure from the ridge to the shingle edges to make sure the shingles are running parallel to the ridge. If

necessary, make slight adjustments with each course until the shingles are parallel to the ridge.

4. Trim the top course of shingles at the ridge. If you are working on a hip roof, trim the shingles at each hip ridge.

5. Repeat the procedure to shingle the remaining side(s) of the roof. Overlap the ridge with the top course of shingles and nail them to the other roof side; do not overlap more than 5". On a hip roof, trim the shingles along the hip ridge.

Step D: Install the Ridge Caps

1. Cut ridge caps from standard shingle tabs. Taper each tab along the side edges, starting from the top of the slots and cutting up to the top edge. Cut three caps from each shingle—you'll need one cap for every 5" of ridge.

2. Snap a chalk line across the shingles, 6" from the ridge. Starting at the gable ends (for a gable roof) or the bottom edge (for a hip roof), install the caps by bending them over the ridge and aligning one side edge with the chalk line. Fasten each cap with one nail on each roof side, 5½" from the finished (exposed) edge and 1" from the side edge. Maintain a 5" exposure for each shingle. Fasten the last shingle with a nail at each corner, then cover the nail heads with roofing cement.

3. Trim the overhanging shingles along the gable ends: Snap chalk lines along the gable ends, ⅜" from the drip edges. (These should line up with the first, fifth, etc., courses.) Trim the shingles at the lines. Cover any exposed nails with roofing cement.

C. *Stagger each course of shingles by ½ tab, repeating the pattern after overhanging the edge by 1½ tabs.*

D. *Divide the shingles into thirds, then trim the corners to create the shingle caps (INSET). Install the caps at the ridge.*

Metal Roofing

Metal roofing panels typically are available in 3-foot-wide panels, with most styles using some form of standing seam design, which adds strength and provides means for joining sheets. You can buy the roofing through metal roofing suppliers and at home centers, but the former typically offer more color options, and they'll custom-cut the panels to fit your project. Most manufacturers supply rubber-washered nails or screws for a watertight seal—use the recommended fasteners to prevent premature rusting due to galvanic action (caused by contact between dissimilar metals).

Install metal roofing over 1 × 4 or 2 × 4 purlins nailed perpendicular to the rafters at 12 to 24" on center—check with the manufacturer for purlin spacing and load requirements. Some roof panels require purlins with matching profiles. At the gable ends, add blocking between the purlins to provide a nailing surface for the end panels and the drip edge.

TOOLS & MATERIALS

- Chalk line
- Circular saw
- Drill
- 1 × 4 or 2 × 4 lumber
- 16d common nails
- Metal roofing panels and preformed ridge cap, with fasteners

HOW TO INSTALL METAL ROOFING
Step A: Install the Purlins

1. Mark the purlin layout on the top edges of the the rafters, and snap a chalk line for each row. Fasten 2 × 4 purlins to the rafters with 16d common nails; use 8d nails for 1 × 4s. Make sure the upper-most purlins will support the roofing ridge cap.

2. On the gable ends, cut blocking to fit between the purlins, and install it so the outside edges are flush with the outer faces of the outer rafters.

Step B: Install the Roof Panels

1. Set the first roof panel across the purlins so the finished side edge overhangs the gable-end fascia by 2" and the bottom end overhangs the eave by 2". Fasten the panel with self-tapping screws or roofing nails with rubber washers, following the manufacturer's directions for spacing.

2. Install the subsequent panels, overlapping each panel according to the manufacturer's directions.

3. Rotate the final panel 180° from the others, so the finished side edge is at the gable end. Overlap the preceding panel by as much as necessary so the finished edge overhangs the gable edge by 2". Fasten the final panel.

A. *Install the purlins across the rafters, then add blocking at the gable ends.*

Step C: Install the Ridge Cap

1. Center the preformed ridge cap over the peak so it overlaps the roofing panels. Make sure the cap overhangs the gable ends equally on both sides. NOTE: Some products include ridge-cap sealing strips.

2. Fasten the ridge cap to the top purlins.

B. *Install the panels to the purlins using pole barn screws or other rubber-washer, self-tapping screws.*

C. *Add the ridge cap at the roof peak, covering the panels on both roof sides.*

Cedar Shingles

Cedar shingles come in 16", 18", and 24" lengths and in random widths, generally between 3 and 10" wide. The exposure of the shingles depends on the slope of the roof and the length and quality of the shingles (check with the manufacturer). Because they're sold in a few different grades, make sure the shingles you get are high-enough quality to be used as roofing. Also, be aware that galvanized nails may cause some staining or streaking on the shingles; to avoid this, use aluminum or stainless steel nails.

The project shown here uses 18" shingles with a 5½" exposure installed on a gable roof. At the ridge, the shingles are covered with a 1× cedar ridge cap, which is easier to install than cap shingles. If you want to shingle a hip roof, consult a professional.

TOOLS & MATERIALS

• Utility knife	• Cedar shingles	• Cedar (1 × 4, 1 × 6)
• Chalk line	• 2 × 4 lumber	• Caulk/Sealant
• Circular saw	• Roofing nails (1¼", 2")	• 15# building paper
• Table saw	• 6d galvanized nails	• Tape measure
• T-bevel		

HOW TO INSTALL CEDAR SHINGLE ROOFING

Step A: Install the Starter Course

1. Apply building paper to the entire roof, overhanging the eaves by ⅜" (see page 379).

2. Position the first shingle in the starter course so it overhangs the gable edge by 1" and the eave edge by 1½". Tack or clamp a 2 × 4 spacer to the fascia to help set the overhang. Make sure the butt (thick) end of the shingle is pointing down. Fasten the shingle with two 1¼" roofing nails, driven 4" up from the butt end and at least 1" from the side edges. Drive the nails just flush with the surface—countersinking creates a cavity that collects water.

3. Install the remaining shingles in the starter course, maintaining a ¼ to ⅜" gap between shingles. If necessary, trim the last shingle to width.

Step B: Install the Remaining Courses

1. Set the first shingle in the first course so its butt and outside edges are flush with the shingles in the starter course and it overlaps the shingle gap below by 1½". Fasten the shingle 1 to 2" above the exposure line and 1" from the side edges.

A. Install the starter row of shingles, overhanging the gable end by ⅜" and the eave by 1½".

C. Install the first course of shingles on top of the starter course, offsetting the shingle gaps 1½" between the courses.

2. Install the remaining shingles in the first course, maintaining a ¼ to ⅜" gap between shingles.

3. Snap a chalk line across the shingles at the exposure line (5½" in this example). Install the second course, aligning the butt ends with the chalk line. Make sure shingle gaps are offset with the gaps in the first course by 1½".

4. Install the remaining courses, using chalk lines to set the exposure. Measure from the ridge periodically to make sure the courses are parallel to the ridge. Offset the shingle gaps by 1½" with the gaps in the preceding three courses—that is, any gaps that are aligned must be four courses apart. Add courses until the top (thin) ends of the shingles are within a few inches of the ridge.

5. Shingle the opposite side of the roof.

Step C: Shingle the Ridge

1. Cut a strip of building paper to 24" wide and as long as the ridge. Fold the paper in half and lay it over the ridge so it overlaps the shingles on both sides of the roof; tack it in place with staples.

2. Install another course of shingles on each side, trimming the top edges so they are flush with the ridge. Cut another strip of building paper 12" wide, fold it, and lay it over these shingles.

3. Install the final course on each side, trimming the ends flush with the ridge. Nail the shingles about 2½" from the ridge.

Step D: Install the Ridge Cap

1. Find the angle of the ridge using a T-bevel and two scraps of 1× board: position the boards along the ridge with their edges butted together. Set the T-bevel to match the angle.

2. Transfer the angle to a table saw or circular saw and rip test pieces of 1×. Test-fit the pieces on the ridge and adjust the angles as needed.

3. Cut the 1 × 6 and 1 × 4 cap boards to run the length of the ridge. Join the boards with sealant and 6d galvanized box nails. Attach the cap to the ridge with 2" roofing nails driven every 12".

B. *Cover the ridge with 24" of building paper, then a course of trimmed shingles. Repeat with 12" of paper and shingles.*

D. *Use a T-bevel and scrap boards to find the ridge angles, then cut the 1 × 4 and 1 × 6 for the ridge cap.*

Siding & Trim

The siding and exterior trim not only provide an attractive skin for your building, but they protect the structure from the weather. It's important to keep this function in mind as you install them. Watch for areas where water can pool or trickle in, and make sure all unfinished edges and seams are covered or sealed with caulk.

Apply a protective finish—stain, paint, or varnish—to your siding and trim as soon as possible after installing them. Since conditions vary by region, ask your supplier about the best treatment for your siding, or contact the manufacturer.

Plywood Siding

Plywood siding is the least expensive and easiest to install of all the standard exterior finishes. It's available in 4 × 8-ft., 9-ft., and 10-ft. sheets; ⅜", ½", or ⅝" thicknesses; and in several styles, including striated, rough sawn, channel groove, and board-&-batten. The most common style, Texture 1-11 (shown here), is made to resemble vertical board siding and typically has ship-lap edges that form weatherproof vertical seams.

Plywood siding is exterior-grade, but the layered edges must be protected from moisture. For types with unmilled (square) edges, caulk the gap at vertical seams or install a 1 × 2 batten strip over the joint. All horizontal joints must have metal Z-flashing for moisture protection.

A. *Install the plywood siding vertically. Plumb each sheet and fasten it to the framing with 8d galvanized finish nails.*

B. *Add galvanized metal flashing between rows of siding to prevent water from entering the seam.*

TOOLS & MATERIALS

- Basic tools
- Chalk line
- Level
- Circular saw
- Jigsaw
- Plywood siding
- 8d galvanized finish nails
- 6d galvanized box nails
- Galvanized Z-flashing
- Pencil

HOW TO INSTALL PLYWOOD SIDING

Step A: Install the First Row of Siding

1. Snap a chalk line for the top edges of the siding, accounting for the overhang at the bottom edge: For wood floors, overhang the bottom of the floor frame by ¾ to 1"; for slabs, overhang the top of the slab by 1".

2. Position the first sheet—vertically—at a corner so one side edge is flush with the corner framing and the other breaks on the center of a stud; hold the top edge on the chalk line. Check with a level to make sure the sheet is plumb, then fasten it with 8d galvanized finish nails, driven every 6" along the perimeter and every 12" in the field of the sheet.

3. Install the remaining sheets, checking each one for plumb and leaving a ⅛" gap between sheets. (For ship-lap edges, first fit the sheets tight, then draw a pencil line along the upper sheet's edge. Slide over the upper sheet ⅛", using the mark as a gauge.) At the joints, do not nail through both sheets with one nail. Overlap the sheets at the corners, if desired (they will

be covered by trim, in any case). Apply siding over door and window openings, but do not nail into the headers if you will install flashing. If you start with a trimmed sheet, place the cut edge at the corner.

Step B: Install the Flashing & Second Row

1. Install Z-flashing along the top edge of siding using 6d galvanized box nails.

2. Install the upper row of siding, leaving a ⅛" gap above the flashing.

3. Cut out the door and window openings with a circular saw, jigsaw, or reciprocating saw.

4. Install trim over the flashed joints and at the building corners (see page 387).

Trim

Trim includes the boards that conceal building seams, cover gaps around window and doorframes, finish corners, and perform other decorative and weatherproofing functions. For sheds and outbuildings, simple trim details with 1 × 3, 1 × 4, or 1 × 6 cedar boards work well.

If your building has plywood siding, install the trim after the siding. When installing trim around doors and windows, the simplest method is to use butt joints (photo A). A slightly fancier alternative is to miter them (photo B).

To install window and door trim with butt joints, add the head trim first, then cut the two side pieces to fit. Install mitered trim pieces on opposing sides, (that is, top-bottom, then sides, or vice versa). Leave a ¼" reveal for all window and door trim. This adds interest and makes bowed jambs less noticeable. Exposed doors and windows must have flashing above the trim.

To install corner trim (photo C), cut two pieces to length, then nail them together at a right angle, using 6d or 8d galvanized box nails or finish nails. Set the trim on the corner, plumb it with a level, and nail it to the framing with 8d galvanized box nails or finish nails.

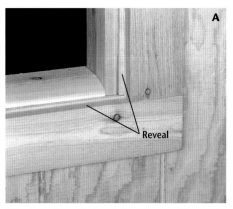

Window trim with butt joints. *Leave a ¼" reveal between the trim and the inside edge of the frame.*

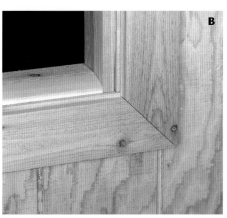

Window trim with miter joints. *Cut all miters at 45° and test-fit the joints before nailing the pieces.*

Install corner trim *by nailing the two pieces together then attaching the assembly to the building.*

FINISHING ROOF OVERHANGS

A common method for finishing the underside of a roof overhang is to install soffit panels that enclose the rafter ends. Soffits can be attached directly to the rafters or to horizontal blocking that extends back to the wall. An alternative to soffitting is leaving the rafter ends exposed. With this application, the wall siding is notched to fit around the rafters.

A roof overhang should also include means for ventilating the building. With soffits, this can be achieved with soffit vents—metal grates (available in rectangular, plug, and strip styles) that cover holes cut into the soffit panels. Exposed overhangs are by nature ventilated but should have bug screen to seal the gaps between the walls and the roof sheathing. To increase ventilation, you can also install roof vents (see page 377).

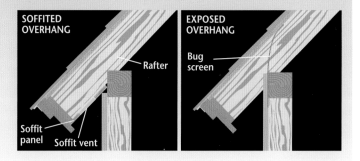

Doors & Windows

Shed doors and windows can be either prehung (factory-built) or homemade. Three of the shed projects in this section include plans for making your own doors and windows. They're simple designs using basic materials and can be built in an hour or two.

Prehung Doors & Windows

Prehung door and window units come in standard sizes, or they can be ordered in custom sizes, though at a higher price. Before framing the walls of your shed, select a door or window and confirm its exact dimensions before sizing the rough openings; be sure to use the outer dimensions of the unit's frame, not of the door or window itself.

Most exterior doors have preattached trim, called *brick molding*, on the outsides of the jambs. You can remove this if you want to add your own trim.

TOOLS & MATERIALS

- Basic tools
- Level
- Handsaw
- Nail set
- Door or window unit
- Tapered cedar shims
- 1¾" roofing nails
- Caulking gun
- Construction adhesive
- Utility knife
- 16d galvanized casing nails
- Hammer

To keep water out, install flashing above the trim of any doors or windows that are exposed—that is, without a roof overhang above. If security is a concern, install a deadbolt for a prehung door or a hasp latch and padlock for a homemade door.

HOW TO INSTALL A PREHUNG WINDOW

NOTE: Window installations vary by product and manufacturer; follow the specific instructions provided for your window, including the steps for preparing the rough opening, shimming, flashing, etc. Shown here are the basic steps for installing a utility window with a nailing flange.

Step A: Set & Shim the Window

1. Set the window into the rough opening and center it between the sides. Place pairs of tapered shims directly beneath the side jambs and at the center of the sill; position the shims so the tapered ends are opposed to form a flat surface.

2. From outside, drive one 1¾" roofing nail through the nailing flange at one of the lower corners of the window, but do not drive the nail completely.

Step B: Level & Fasten the Window

1. Place a level across the sill or top of the jamb, and adjust the shims until the window is perfectly level.

A. *Add pairs of tapered shims under the side window jambs and under the center of the sill.*

B. *Level the window, then fasten the unit in place with roofing nails driven through the nailing flange.*

2. Drive one nail through the nailing flange at each corner of the window. Check the window operation to make sure it's smooth, then complete the nailing, following the manufacturer's instructions for spacing.

3. If the manufacturer recommends leaving the shims in place, trim the shims with a utility knife, then glue them in place with construction adhesive.

HOW TO INSTALL A PREHUNG DOOR
Step A: Plumb & Fasten the Hinge Jamb
1. Cut out the bottom plate inside the rough opening using a handsaw. Remove any bracing or nails installed to protect the door during shipping.

2. Set the door into the opening and center it between the sides. Push the brick molding flat against the sheathing or siding; if there's no molding, position the outside edge of the jamb flush with the siding or sheathing. Insert pairs of tapered shims (with the tapered ends opposed to form a flat surface) between the hinge jamb and the framing. Add shims at the top and bottom and at each hinge location.

3. Starting with the top shims, check the hinge jamb with a level to make sure it's plumb, and adjust the shims as needed. Nail through the jamb and shims and into the framing with one 16d casing nail. Repeat at the remaining shim locations.

Step B: Secure the Latch & Head Jambs
1. Standing inside the shed, close the door, and examine the gap between the door and latch jamb. Starting at the top of the latch jamb, install shims between the jamb and the framing. Check the gap to make sure you're not bowing the jamb. Fasten the jamb and shims with one 16d casing nail.

2. Shim and fasten the latch jamb at four more locations, level with the hinge-side shims, making sure the gap along the door remains consistent.

3. Shim and fasten the head jamb at two locations. For added support, you can replace one screw on each hinge with a 3½" screw, but be careful not to overtighten them and pull the frame out of square.

4. Nail through the brick molding and into the sheathing (or siding) and framing with 16d casing nails driven every 16".

5. Cut off the shims flush with the framing using a utility knife. Set all nails with a nail set.

A. *Plumb the doorjamb, working from the top down. Fasten through the jamb and each shim pair with a casing nail.*

B. *Shim the latch jamb, using the gap between the door and the jamb as a gauge. Make sure the gap is consistent.*

Simple Storage Shed

The name of this practical outbuilding says it all. It's an easy-to-build, sturdy, 8 × 10-ft. shed with plenty of storage space. With no windows it also offers good security. The clean, symmetrical interior and centrally located double doors make for easy access to your stuff. The walls are ready to be lined with utility shelves, and you can quickly add a ramp to simplify parking the lawnmower, wheelbarrow, and other yard equipment.

This shed is indeed basic, but it's also a nicely proportioned building with architecturally appropriate features like overhanging eaves and just enough trim to give it a quality, hand-built appearance. Without getting too fancy—remember, simplicity is the central design idea—you might consider finishing the exterior walls and roof of the shed with the same materials used on your house. This easy modification visually integrates the shed with the rest of the property and provides a custom look that you can't get with kit buildings.

Inside the shed, you can maximize storage space by building an attic: Install full-length 2 × 4 or 2 × 6 joists (which also serve as rafter ties) and cover them with ½" plywood. Include one or more framed-in access openings that you can easily reach with a stepladder. This type of storage space is ideal for seldom-used household items—like winter clothing and holiday decorations—that you can stow in covered plastic bins.

The simplicity and economy of this shed design also make it a great choice for cabins, vacation homes, and other remote locations. A heavy-duty hasp latch and padlock on the door, along with head and foot slide bolts inside, will provide the security you need when you're away for long periods.

This simple storage shed is a perfect home for yard and gardening equipment, out-of-season decorations, or shelving for tools or bins.

The double doors allow for extra width getting in and out of the shed, and, with the right latch and padlock, reliable security for valuable equipment.

Cutting List

Description	Quantity/Size	Material
Foundation		
Drainage material	1.25 cu. yd.	Compactable gravel
Skids	2 @ 10'	4 × 6 pressure-treated landscape timbers
Floor		
Rim joists	2 @ 10'	2 × 8 pressure-treated, rated for ground contact
Joists	9 @ 8'	2 × 8 pressure-treated
Floor sheathing	3 sheets @ 4 × 8'	¾" tongue-&-groove ext.-grade plywood
Wall Framing		
Bottom plates	2 @ 10', 2 @ 8'	2 × 4
Top plates	4 @ 10', 4 @ 8'	2 × 4
Studs	36 @ 8'	2 × 4
Door header	1 @ 10'	2 × 6
Roof Framing		
Rafters	6 @ 12'	2 × 6
Rafter blocking	2 @ 10'	2 × 6
Ridge board	1 @ 10'	1 × 8
Collar ties	2 @ 12'	2 × 4
Exterior Finishes		
Siding	11 sheets @ 4 × 8'	½" Texture 1-11 plywood siding
Fascia	4 @ 12'	1 × 8
Corner trim	8 @ 8'	1 × 2
Gable wall trim	2 @ 8'	1 × 4
Siding flashing	16 linear ft.	Metal Z-flashing

Description	Quantity/Size	Material
Roofing		
Sheathing (& door header spacer)	5 sheets @ 4 × 8'	½" exterior-grade plywood roof sheathing
15# building paper	1 roll	
Shingles	1¼ squares	Asphalt shingles—250# per sq. min.
Drip edge	45 linear ft.	Metal drip edge
Door		
Frames	7 @ 8'	2 × 4 pressure-treated
Panels	1 sheet @ 4 × 8'	½" Texture 1-11 plywood siding
Stops & overlap trim	4 @ 8'	1 × 2 pressure-treated
Fasteners & Hardware		
16d galvanized common nails	4 lbs.	
16d common nails	10 lbs.	
10d common nails	2 lbs.	
8d galvanized common nails	3 lbs.	
8d box nails	3 lbs.	
8d galvanized siding or finish nails	9 lbs.	
1" galvanized roofing nails	5 lbs.	
Door hinges with screws	6 @ 3½"	Galvanized metal hinges
Door handle	1	
Door lock (optional)	1	
Door head bolt	1	
Door foot bolt	1	
Construction adhesive		

TOOLS & MATERIALS

- Compacted gravel
- Circular saw
- 4 × 6 timber skids
- Level
- 2 × 8 rim joists
- 16d galvanized common nails
- Tongue-and-groove plywood flooring
- 8d galvanized common nails
- Pressure-treated lumber
- Cripple studs
- Hammer
- Z-flashing
- 10d common nails
- Roof sheathing
- Metal drip edge
- Building paper
- Asphalt shingle roofing

ELEVATION

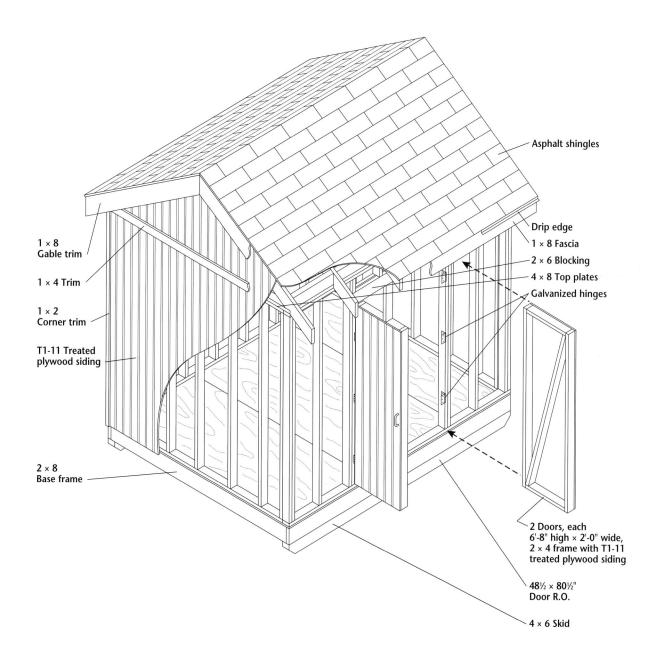

1 × 8
Gable trim

1 × 4 Trim

1 × 2
Corner trim

T1-11 Treated
plywood siding

2 × 8
Base frame

Asphalt shingles

Drip edge

1 × 8 Fascia

2 × 6 Blocking

4 × 8 Top plates

Galvanized hinges

2 Doors, each
6'-8" high × 2'-0" wide,
2 × 4 frame with T1-11
treated plywood siding

48½ × 80½"
Door R.O.

4 × 6 Skid

FRAMING ELEVATION

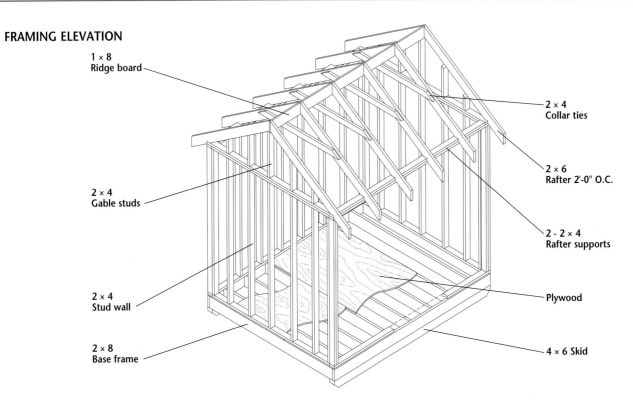

1 × 8
Ridge board

2 × 4
Collar ties

2 × 6
Rafter 2'-0" O.C.

2 × 4
Gable studs

2 - 2 × 4
Rafter supports

2 × 4
Stud wall

Plywood

2 × 8
Base frame

4 × 6 Skid

SIDE FRAMING

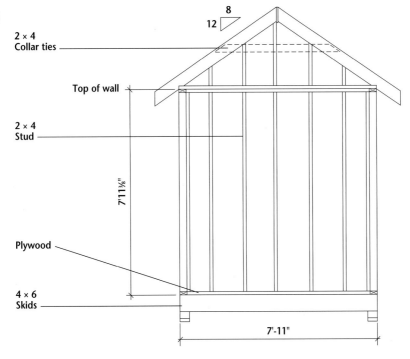

8

12

2 × 4
Collar ties

Top of wall

2 × 4
Stud

7'11³⁄₈"

Plywood

4 × 6
Skids

7'-11"

FLOOR FRAMING

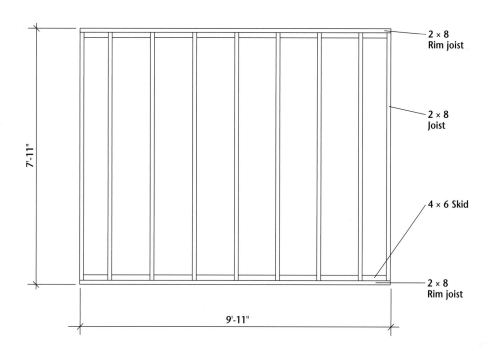

2 × 8
Rim joist

2 × 8
Joist

4 × 6 Skid

2 × 8
Rim joist

7'-11"

9'-11"

REAR FRAMING

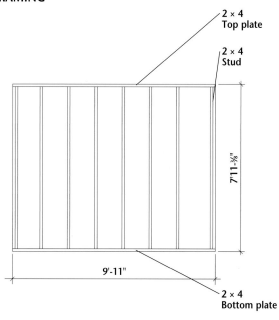

2 × 4
Top plate

2 × 4
Stud

7'11-³⁄₈"

9'-11"

2 × 4
Bottom plate

FRONT FRAMING

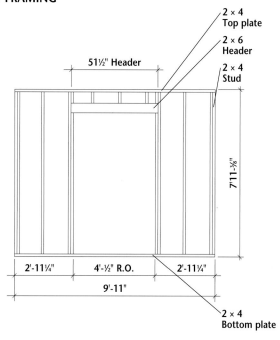

2 × 4
Top plate

2 × 6
Header

2 × 4
Stud

51½" Header

7'11-³⁄₈"

2'-11¼"   4'-½" R.O.   2'-11¼"

9'-11"

2 × 4
Bottom plate

ROOF PLAN

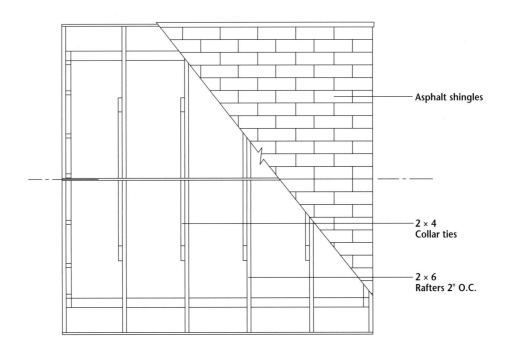

Asphalt shingles

2 × 4
Collar ties

2 × 6
Rafters 2" O.C.

FLOOR PLAN

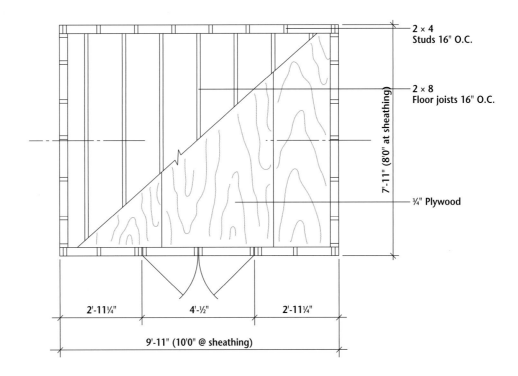

2 × 4
Studs 16" O.C.

2 × 8
Floor joists 16" O.C.

7'-11" (8'0" at sheathing)

¾" Plywood

2'-11¼"   4'-½"   2'-11¼"

9'-11" (10'0" @ sheathing)

RAFTER TEMPLATE

8

12

6"

4'-9¹¹⁄₁₆"

2"

4½"

2 × 6

DOOR DETAIL

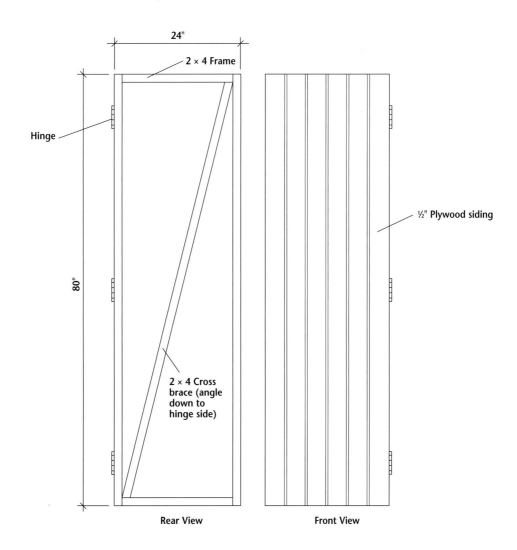

24"

2 × 4 Frame

Hinge

80"

½" Plywood siding

2 × 4 Cross
brace (angle
down to
hinge side)

Rear View

Front View

HOW TO BUILD A SIMPLE STORAGE SHED

1. *Prepare the foundation site with a 4" layer of compacted gravel where the skids will be located. Cut the two 4 × 6 timber skids at 119". Position the skids on the gravel beds so their outside edges are 95" apart, making sure they are level and parallel.*

2. *Cut two 2 × 8 rim joists at 119". Cut nine 2 × 8 joists at 92". Assemble the floor frame following the FLOOR FRAMING plans (page 395), then set it on the skids and measure the diagonals to make sure the frame is square. Fasten the joists to the skids with 16d galvanized common nails.*

3. *Attach tongue-and-groove plywood flooring to the floor frame, starting at the left front corner of the shed. Begin the second row of plywood with a full sheet in the right rear corner to stagger end joints. Make sure the tongues are fully seated in the mating grooves. Fasten the sheathing with 8d galvanized common nails.*

4. *Frame the rear wall: Cut one 2 × 4 bottom plate and one top plate at 119". Cut ten 2 × 4 studs at 92⅜". Assemble the wall using 16" on-center spacing, as shown in the REAR FRAMING plans (page 395). Raise the wall and fasten it flush to the rear edge of the floor, then brace the wall in position with 2 × 4 braces.*

Position your shed *near your home, garage, or another structure on your property. However, since the bin will shift in freeze-thaw cycles, do not attach this structure to your home if you live in a cold climate.*

Cutting List

Description	Quantity/Size	Material
Foundation		
Drainage material	0.5 cu. yd.	Compactable gravel
Skids	2 @ 6'	4 × 4 treated timbers
Floor Framing		
Rim joists	2 @ 6'	2 × 6 pressure-treated
Joists	3 @ 8'	2 × 6 pressure-treated
Floor sheathing	1 sheet @ 4 × 8	¾" tongue-&-groove ext.-grade plywood
Joist clip angles	4	3 × 3 × 3" × 16-gauge galvanized
Wall Framing		
Bottom plates	1 @ 8', 2 @ 6'	2 × 4
Top plates	1 @ 8', 3 @ 6'	2 × 4
Studs	14 @ 8', 8 @ 6'	2 × 4
Header*	2 @ 6'	2 × 6
Header spacer	1 piece @ 6'	½" plywood—5" wide
Roof Framing		
Rafters*	6 @ 6'	2 × 6
Ledger*	1 @ 6'	2 × 6
Roofing		
Roof sheathing	2 sheets @ 4 × 8'	½" ext.-grade plywood
Shingles	30 sq. ft.	250# per square min.
Roofing starter strip	7 linear ft.	
15# building paper	30 sq. ft.	
Metal drip edge	24 linear ft.	Galvanized metal
Roofing cement	1 tube	
Exterior Finishes		
Plywood siding	4 sheets @ 4 × 8'	⅝" Texture 1-11 plywood siding, grooves 8" O.C.

Description	Quantity/Size	Material
Door trim	2 @ 8' 2 @ 6'	1 × 10 S4S cedar 1 × 8 S4S cedar
Corner trim	6 @ 8'	1 × 4 S4S cedar
Fascia	3 @ 6" 1 @ 6'	1 × 8 S4S cedar 1 × 4 S4S cedar
Bug screen	8" × 6'	Fiberglass
Doors		
Frame	3 @ 6'	¾" × 3½" (actual) cedar
Stops	3 @ 6'	1 × 2 S4S cedar
Panel material	12 @ 6'	1 × 6 T&G V-joint S4S cedar
Z-braces	2 @ 10'	1 × 6 S4S cedar
Construction adhesive	1 tube	
Interior trim (optional)	3 @ 6'	1 × 3 S4S cedar
Strap hinges	6, with screws	
Fasteners		
16d galvanized common nails	3½ lbs.	
16d common nails	3½ lbs.	
10d common nails	12 nails	
10d galvanized casing nails	20 nails	
8d galvanized box nails	½ lb.	
8d galvanized finish nails	2 lbs.	
8d common nails	24 nails	
8d box nails	½ lb.	
1½" joist hanger nails	16 nails	
⅞" galvanized roofing nails	¼ lb.	
2½" deck screws	6 screws	
1¼" wood screws	60 screws	

*NOTE: 6-foot material is often unavailable at local lumber stores, so buy half as much of 12-foot material.

TOOLS & MATERIALS

- Compacted gravel
- Pressure-treated lumber
- Circular saw
- Level
- 4 × 4 skids
- 2 × 6 rim joists
- Joist clip angles
- ¼" plywood
- Pencil
- Hammer
- Plumb bob
- Building paper
- Asphalt shingles
- Shims
- 10d casing nails
- Construction adhesive
- 1¼" screws
- Door hinges
- Fiberglass insect mesh

FLOOR FRAMING PLAN

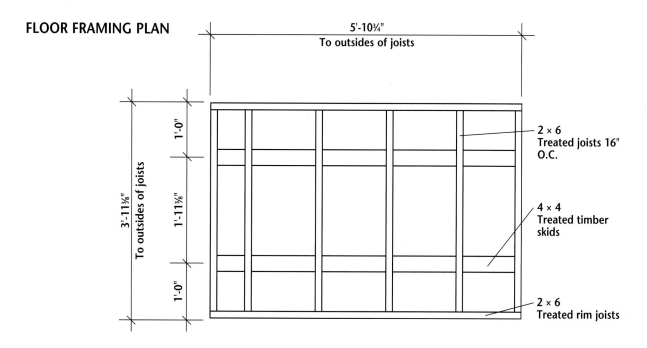

5'-10¾"
To outsides of joists

3'-11⅜"
To outsides of joists

1'-0"

1'-11⅜"

1'-0"

2 × 6
Treated joists 16"
O.C.

4 × 4
Treated timber
skids

2 × 6
Treated rim joists

ROOF FRAMING PLAN

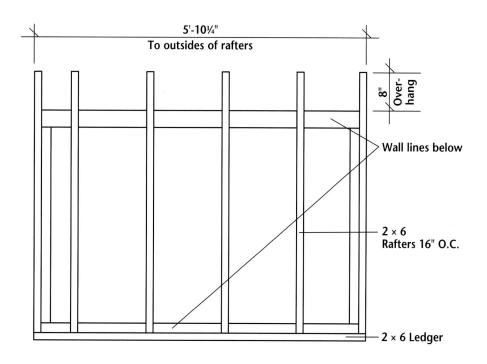

5'-10¾"
To outsides of rafters

8" Over-hang

Wall lines below

2 × 6
Rafters 16" O.C.

2 × 6 Ledger

FRONT FRAMING ELEVATION

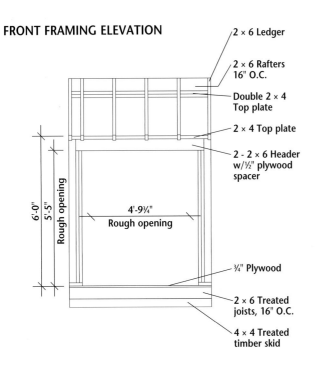

2 × 6 Ledger

2 × 6 Rafters 16" O.C.

Double 2 × 4 Top plate

2 × 4 Top plate

2 - 2 × 6 Header w/½" plywood spacer

¾" Plywood

2 × 6 Treated joists, 16" O.C.

4 × 4 Treated timber skid

6'-0"

5'-5" Rough opening

4'-9¾" Rough opening

LEFT FRAMING ELEVATION

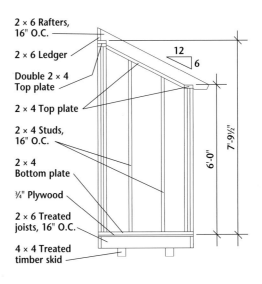

2 × 6 Rafters, 16" O.C.

2 × 6 Ledger

Double 2 × 4 Top plate

2 × 4 Top plate

2 × 4 Studs, 16" O.C.

2 × 4 Bottom plate

¾" Plywood

2 × 6 Treated joists, 16" O.C.

4 × 4 Treated timber skid

12 / 6

6'-0"

7'-9½"

REAR SIDE FRAMING ELEVATION

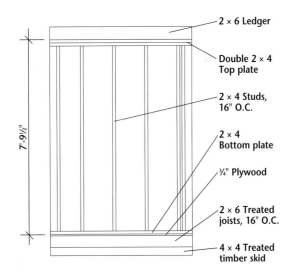

2 × 6 Ledger

Double 2 × 4 Top plate

2 × 4 Studs, 16" O.C.

2 × 4 Bottom plate

¾" Plywood

2 × 6 Treated joists, 16" O.C.

4 × 4 Treated timber skid

7'-9½"

RIGHT SIDE FRAMING ELEVATION

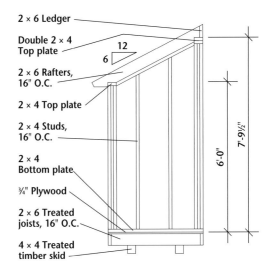

2 × 6 Ledger

Double 2 × 4 Top plate

2 × 6 Rafters, 16" O.C.

2 × 4 Top plate

2 × 4 Studs, 16" O.C.

2 × 4 Bottom plate

¾" Plywood

2 × 6 Treated joists, 16" O.C.

4 × 4 Treated timber skid

6 / 12

6'-0"

7'-9½"

BUILDING SECTION

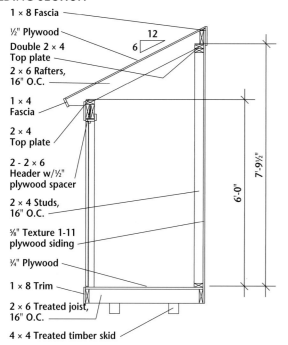

1 × 8 Fascia

½" Plywood

Double 2 × 4 Top plate

2 × 6 Rafters, 16" O.C.

1 × 4 Fascia

2 × 4 Top plate

2 - 2 × 6 Header w/½" plywood spacer

2 × 4 Studs, 16" O.C.

⅝" Texture 1-11 plywood siding

¾" Plywood

1 × 8 Trim

2 × 6 Treated joist, 16" O.C.

4 × 4 Treated timber skid

12
6

7'-9½"

6'-0"

SIDE ELEVATION

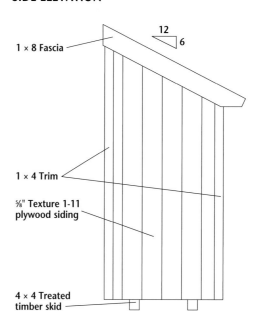

1 × 8 Fascia

12
6

1 × 4 Trim

⅝" Texture 1-11 plywood siding

4 × 4 Treated timber skid

FRONT ELEVATION

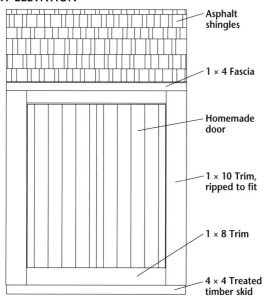

Asphalt shingles

1 × 4 Fascia

Homemade door

1 × 10 Trim, ripped to fit

1 × 8 Trim

4 × 4 Treated timber skid

REAR ELEVATION

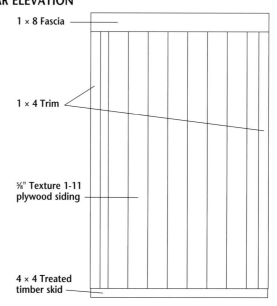

1 × 8 Fascia

1 × 4 Trim

⅝" Texture 1-11 plywood siding

4 × 4 Treated timber skid

407

Wall Plan

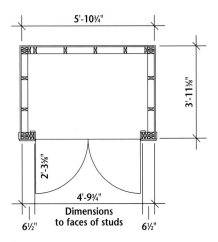

5'-10¾"

3'-11⅜"

2'-3⅝"

4'-9¾"

Dimensions
to faces of studs

6½" 6½"

RAFTER TEMPLATE

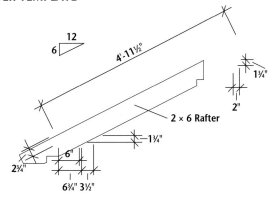

12
6

4'-11½"

1¾"

2"

2 × 6 Rafter

1¾"

2¾"

6"

6¾" 3½"

SIDE ROOF EDGE DETAIL

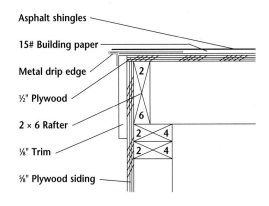

Asphalt shingles

15# Building paper

Metal drip edge

½" Plywood

2 × 6 Rafter

⅛" Trim

⅝" Plywood siding

2
6
2 4
2 4

OVERHANG DETAIL

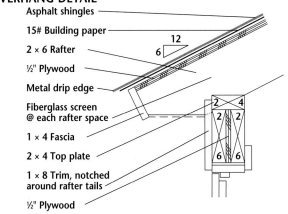

Asphalt shingles

15# Building paper

2 × 6 Rafter

½" Plywood

Metal drip edge

Fiberglass screen
@ each rafter space

1 × 4 Fascia

2 × 4 Top plate

1 × 8 Trim, notched
around rafter tails

½" Plywood

12
6

2 4
2 2
6 6

DOORJAMB DETAIL

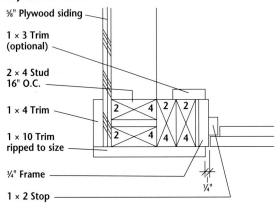

⅝" Plywood siding

1 × 3 Trim
(optional)

2 × 4 Stud
16" O.C.

1 × 4 Trim

1 × 10 Trim
ripped to size

¾" Frame

1 × 2 Stop

2 4 2 2
2 4 4

¼"

DOOR ELEVATION

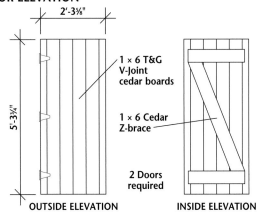

2'-3⅝"

5'-3¾"

1 × 6 T&G
V-Joint
cedar boards

1 × 6 Cedar
Z-brace

2 Doors
required

OUTSIDE ELEVATION   INSIDE ELEVATION

HOW TO BUILD THE LEAN-TO TOOL BIN

1. *Prepare the site with a 4" layer of compacted gravel. Cut the two 4 × 4 skids at 70¾". Set and level the skids following FLOOR FRAMING PLAN (page 405). Cut two 2 × 6 rim joists at 70¾" and six joists at 44⅛". Assemble the floor and set it on the skids as shown in the FLOOR FRAMING PLAN. Check for square, and then anchor the frame to the skids with four joist clip angles (INSET photo). Sheath the floor frame with ¾" plywood.*

2. *Cut plates and studs for the walls: Side walls—two bottom plates at 47⅜", four studs at 89", and four studs at 69"; Front wall—one bottom plate at 63¾", one top plate at 70¾", and four jacks studs at 63½". Rear wall—one bottom plate at 63¾", two top plates at 70¾", and six studs at 89". Mark the stud layouts onto the plates.*

3. *Fasten the four end studs of each side wall to the bottom plate. Install these assemblies. Construct the built-up 2 × 6 door header at 63¾". Frame and install the front and rear walls, leaving the top plates off at this time. Nail together the corner studs, making sure they are plumb. Install the rear top plates flush to the outsides of the side wall studs. Install the front top plate in the same fashion.*

4. *Cut the six 2 × 6 rafters following the RAFTER TEMPLATE (page 408). Cut the 2 × 6 ledger at 70¾" and bevel the top edge at 26.5° so the overall width is 4⁵⁄₁₆". Mark the rafter layout onto the wall plates and ledger, as shown in the ROOF FRAMING PLAN (page 405), then install the ledger flush with the back side of the rear wall. Install the rafters.*

5. *Complete the side wall framing: cut a top plate for each side to fit between the front and rear walls, mitering the ends at 26.5°. Install the plates flush with the outsides of the end rafters. Mark the stud layouts onto the side wall bottom plates, then use a plumb bob to transfer the marks to the top plate. Cut the two studs in each wall to fit, mitering the top ends at 26.5°. Install the studs.*

6. *Sheath the side walls and rear walls with plywood siding, keeping the bottom edges ½" below the floor frame and the top edges flush with the tops of the rafters. Overlap the siding at the rear corners, and stop it flush with the face of the front wall.*

7. *Add the 1 × 4 fascia over the bottom rafter ends as shown in the OVERHANG DETAIL (page 408). Install 1 × 8 fascia over the top rafter ends. Overhang the front and rear fascia to cover the ends of the side fascia, or plan to miter all fascia joints. Cut the 1 × 8 side fascia to length, and then clip the bottom front corners to meet the front fascia. Install the side fascia.*

8. *Install the ½" roof sheathing, starting with a full-width sheet at the bottom edge of the roof. Fasten metal drip edge along the front edge of the roof. Cover the roof with building paper, then add the drip edge along the sides and top of the roof. Shingle the roof, and finish the top edge with cut shingles or a solid starter strip.*

9. Cut and remove the bottom plate inside the door opening. Cut the 1 × 4 head jamb for the doorframe at 57⅛" and cut the side jambs at 64". Fasten the head jamb over the sides with 2½" deck screws. Install 1 × 2 door stops ¾" from the front edges of jambs, as shown in the DOORJAMB DETAIL (page 408). Install the frame in the door opening, using shims and 10d casing nails.

10. For each door, cut six 1 × 6 tongue-and-groove boards at 63¾". Fit them together, then mark and trim the two end boards so the total width is 27⅝". Cut the 1 × 6 Z-brace boards following the DOOR ELEVATION (page 408). The ends of the horizontal braces should be 1" from the door edges. Attach the braces with construction adhesive and 1¼" screws. Install each door with three hinges.

11. Staple fiberglass insect mesh along the underside of the roof from each side 2 × 6 rafter. Cut and install the 1 × 8 trim above the door, overlapping the side doorjambs about ¼" on each side (see the OVERHANG DETAIL, page 408).

12. Rip vertical and horizontal trim boards to width, then notch them to fit around the rafters, as shown in the DOORJAMB DETAIL (page 408). Notch the top ends of the 1 × 10s to fit between the rafters and install them. Add 1 × 8 trim horizontally between the 1 × 10s below the door. Install the 1 × 4 corner trim, overlapping the pieces at the rear corners.

Service Shed

This versatile shelter structure is actually two projects in one. Using the same primary design, you can build an open-sided firewood shelter, or you can add doors and a shelf and create a secured shed that's perfect for trash cans or recyclables. Both projects have four vertical corner posts, a rectangular floor frame decked with 2 × 6s, and gapped side slats that provide cross ventilation. The plywood, shed-style roof is covered with cedar shingles, but you can substitute with any type of roofing.

To adapt the service shed for use as a closed storage shed, you can add a center post (mostly to function as a nailer) and attach slats to create a rear wall. With two more posts in the front,

you may define door openings. The adapted shed won't offer secure storage for valuable items like tools, but it will prevent dogs, squirrels, raccoons, and other pests from getting into your trash cans.

As for materials, you can save a lot of money by building this project with pressure-treated lumber. Stain or paint the greenish lumber to change its coloring or leave it bare and allow it to weather to a silvery gray. If you prefer the look of cedar lumber, use it for everything but the shelter's floor frame and decking. Also, you might want to set the corner posts on concrete blocks or stones to prevent the cedar from rotting prematurely due to ground contact.

With simply constructed doors, this shed is a perfect home for trash cans, recycling bins, or inexpensive gardening implements.

The cross-ventilation *the gapped side slats provide makes this structure perfect for drying firewood.*

SEASONING FIREWOOD

Proper seasoning, or drying, of firewood takes time. After freshly cut logs are split, the drying process can take six to 12 months, given the right conditions. Stacking split wood under a shelter with one or more open sides is ideal because it protects the wood from rain and snow moisture while letting airflow through the stack to hasten drying.

You can test wood for seasoning by its look and feel and by how it burns. The ends of dry logs show cracks and typically have a grayish color, while unseasoned wood still looks freshly cut and may be moist to the touch. Fresher wood also makes a heavy, dull thud when pieces are knocked together. When it comes to burning, dry wood lights easily and burns consistently, while wet wood tends to burn out if unattended and often smokes excessively as the internal moisture turns to steam.

If you order split firewood from a supplier and can't guarantee how well seasoned it is, have it delivered at least six months before the start of the burning season. This gives the wood plenty of time to dry out. Regarding quantity, a "cord" of neatly stacked split logs measures 128 cubic feet—a stack that's 4 ft. high, 4 ft. deep, and 8 ft. long. A "half cord" measures 64 cubic feet.

413

Cutting List

Part	Quantity/Size Firewood Shed	Quantity/Size Garbage Shed	Material
Framing			
Side & end floor supports	2 @ 10'	2 @ 10'	2 × 4 pressure-treated
Center floor support	1 @ 8'	1 @ 8'	2 × 4 pressure-treated
Floorboards	3 @ 10'	3 @ 10'	2 × 6 pressure-treated
Corner posts	4 @ 8'	4 @ 8'	2 × 4 cedar
Headers	2 @ 8'	2 @ 8'	2 × 4 cedar
Rafters	1 @ 8' 1 @ 4'	1 @ 8' 1 @ 4'	2 × 4 cedar
Rear center post		1 @ 4'	2 × 4 cedar
Doorposts		1 @ 8'	2 × 4 cedar
Door ledger		1 @ 8'	2 × 4 cedar
Slats			
End slats	5 @ 8'	5 @ 8'	1 × 6 cedar
Back slats		5 @ 8'	1 × 6 cedar
Roofing			
Sheathing	1 sheet @ 4 × 8'	1 sheet @ 4 × 8'	¾" CDX plywood
Roof edging	2 @ 10'	2 @ 10'	1 × 2 T
15# building paper	37 sq. ft.	37 sq. ft.	
Shingles	25 sq. ft	25 sq. ft.	18" cedar shingles
Roof cap	1 @ 8' 1 @ 8'	1 @ 8' 1 @ 8'	1 × 4 cedar 1 × 3 cedar

Part	Quantity/Size Firewood Shed	Quantity/Size Garbage Shed	Material
Shelf & Doors			
Shelf		1 @ 24⅝ × 28⅛"	¾" ext.-grade plywood
Shelf cleats		1 @ 6'	1 × 3 cedar
Door panels		1 sheet @ 4 × 8'	¾" ext.-grade plywood
Stiles		3 @ 8' (wide doors) 1 @ 10' (narrow door)	1 × 4 cedar
Hinges		6	Exterior hinges
Door handle		3	Exterior handles
Fasteners			
¼" × 3" lag screws	8, with washers	10, with washers	
Deck screws			
3½"	12	12	
3"	62	62	
2½"	36	48	
2"	50	62	
1⅝"	100	160	
1¼"		116	
6d galvanized finish nails	30	30	
3d galvanized roofing nails	1 lb.	1 lb.	

TOOLS & MATERIALS

- Pressure-treated lumber or cedar
- Drill
- Deck screws (1¼", 1⅝", 2", 2½", 3", 3½")
- Circular saw
- Framing square
- Clamps
- 3" lag screws & washers
- Cutting guide
- Ratchet wrench
- ¾" exterior plywood
- 6d galvanized finish nails
- Building paper
- Cedar shingles
- ¾" interior plywood shelf (optional)

FLOOR FRAMING PLAN

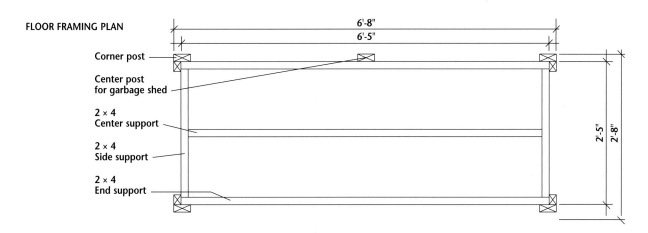

Corner post

Center post
for garbage shed

2 × 4
Center support

2 × 4
Side support

2 × 4
End support

6'-8"
6'-5"
2'-5"
2'-8"

FLOOR PLAN

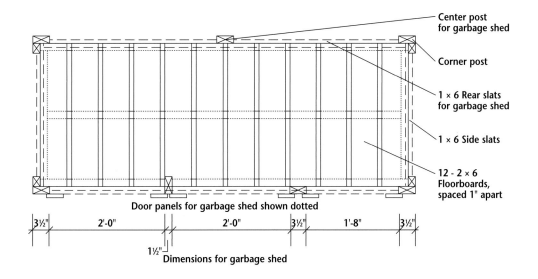

Center post
for garbage shed

Corner post

1 × 6 Rear slats
for garbage shed

1 × 6 Side slats

12 - 2 × 6
Floorboards,
spaced 1" apart

Door panels for garbage shed shown dotted

3½"   2'-0"   2'-0"   3½"   1'-8"   3½"

1½"
Dimensions for garbage shed

ROOF FRAMING PLAN

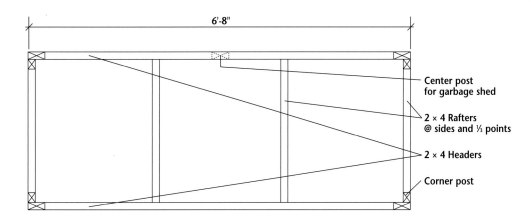

6'-8"

Center post
for garbage shed

2 × 4 Rafters
@ sides and ⅓ points

2 × 4 Headers

Corner post

BUILDING SECTION

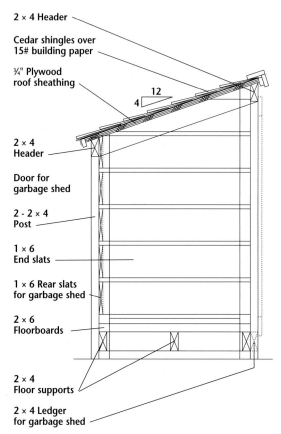

- 2 × 4 Header
- Cedar shingles over 15# building paper
- ¾" Plywood roof sheathing
- 2 × 4 Header
- Door for garbage shed
- 2 - 2 × 4 Post
- 1 × 6 End slats
- 1 × 6 Rear slats for garbage shed
- 2 × 6 Floorboards
- 2 × 4 Floor supports
- 2 × 4 Ledger for garbage shed

RAFTER TEMPLATES

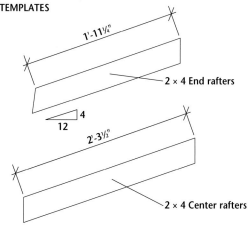

- 1'-11¼"
- 2 × 4 End rafters
- 4 / 12
- 2'-3½"
- 2 × 4 Center rafters

UPPER ROOF EDGE DETAIL

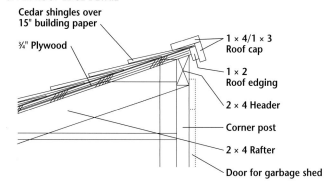

- Cedar shingles over 15" building paper
- ¾" Plywood
- 1 × 4/1 × 3 Roof cap
- 1 × 2 Roof edging
- 2 × 4 Header
- Corner post
- 2 × 4 Rafter
- Door for garbage shed

DOOR ELEVATION

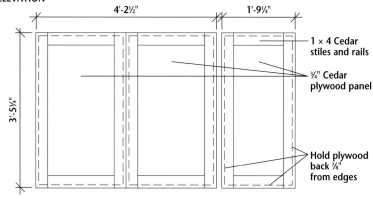

- 4'-2½"
- 1'-9¼"
- 3'-5¾"
- 1 × 4 Cedar stiles and rails
- ¾" Cedar plywood panel
- Hold plywood back ⅞" from edges

DOOR EDGE & CORNER POST DETAIL

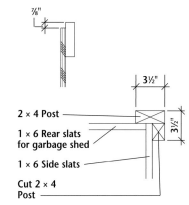

- ⅞"
- 3½"
- 3½"
- 2 × 4 Post
- 1 × 6 Rear slats for garbage shed
- 1 × 6 Side slats
- Cut 2 × 4 Post

FRONT ELEVATION

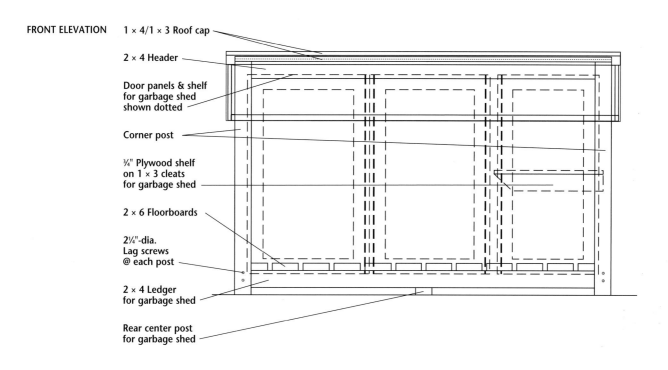

1 × 4/1 × 3 Roof cap

2 × 4 Header

Door panels & shelf
for garbage shed
shown dotted

Corner post

¾" Plywood shelf
on 1 × 3 cleats
for garbage shed

2 × 6 Floorboards

2¼"-dia.
Lag screws
@ each post

2 × 4 Ledger
for garbage shed

Rear center post
for garbage shed

REAR ELEVATION

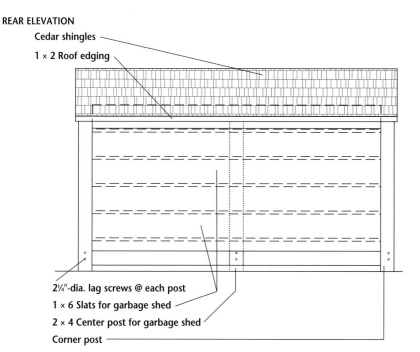

Cedar shingles

1 × 2 Roof edging

2¼"-dia. lag screws @ each post

1 × 6 Slats for garbage shed

2 × 4 Center post for garbage shed

Corner post

SIDE ELEVATION

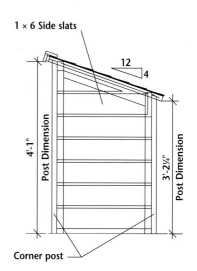

1 × 6 Side slats

12

4

4'-1"
Post Dimension

3'-2¼"
Post Dimension

Corner post

417

HOW TO BUILD THE SERVICE SHED

1. Construct the floor frame: Cut the side supports, end supports, and one center support. Fasten the end supports between the sides with 3½" deck screws, as shown in the FLOOR FRAMING PLAN (page 415); locate the screws where they won't interfere with the corner post lag screws (see Step 4). Fasten the center support between the end supports, centered between the side supports.

2. Cut twelve 2 × 6 floorboards to length. Make sure the floor frame is square, then install the first board at one end, flush with the outsides of the frame using 3" deck screws. Use 1" spacers to set the gaps as you install the remaining boards. Rip the last board as needed. (For the closed shed, create a 1½ × 2" notch for the left doorpost, starting 26" from the left end of the floor frame).

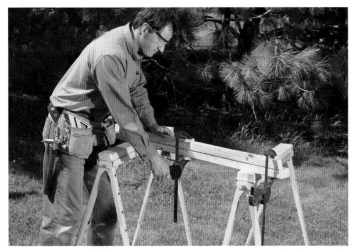

3. Build the corner posts: rip two 8-ft. 2 × 4s to 2" in width. Make an 18° cut at about 53", leaving a 43" piece from each board. Cut two full-width 2 × 4 pieces at 53" and two at 43", beveling the top ends at 18°. Assemble each front post to form an "L", using the 53" pieces and keeping the angled ends flush; use 2½" deck screws. Assemble the rear posts the same way using the 43" pieces.

4. Trim the corner posts to length: First, cut the front posts at 49", measuring from the longest point of the angled ends. Cut the rear posts at 38¼", measuring from the shortest point of the angled ends. Mark the insides of the posts 1½" from the bottom ends. Set each post on the floor frame so the mark is aligned with the bottom of the frame, then anchor the post with two 3" lag screws and washers, driven through counterbored pilot holes.

5. *To begin framing the roof, cut two 2 × 4 roof headers at 73". Bevel the top edges of the headers at 18° using a circular saw and cutting guide or a tablesaw. (The broad face of the header should still measure 3½".) Position the headers between the corner posts, flush with the outsides of the posts. Also, the beveled edges should be flush with the post tops. Fasten the headers to the posts with 2½" deck screws.*

6. *Cut two upper and two lower rafters, following the RAFTER TEMPLATES (page 416). Install the end rafters between the corner posts, flush with the tops of the posts, using 2½" deck screws. Install the two center rafters between the headers, 25" in from the end rafters. For the closed shed, cut the 2 × 4 rear center post to run from the bottom of the rear header down to 1½" below the bottom of the floor frame (as shown). Install the center post centered between the corner posts.*

7. *Plan the layout of the 1 × 6 slats, gapping the slats as desired. On each side, the bottom slat mounts to the outside of the floor, covering the floor from view. The remaining slats mount to the insides of the corner posts. Cut the side slats to fit and install them with 1⅝" deck screws. For the closed shed, cover the rear side with slats using the same techniques.*

8. Sheath the roof with a piece of ¾" exterior plywood cut to 35½ × 81½". Overhang the posts by ¾" on all sides and fasten the sheathing to the posts, headers, and rafters with 2" deck screws. Add 1 × 2 trim along all edges of the sheathing, mitering the ends at the corners. Fasten the trim with 6d galvanized finish nails so the top edges are flush with the sheathing.

9. Apply building paper over the sheathing and trim, overhanging the bottom roof edge by 1" and the sides by ½". Install the cedar shingles (see page 384). Construct the roof cap with 1 × 3 and 1 × 4 trim boards. Join the boards to form an "L" using 6d finish nails. Fasten the cap along the top edge of the roof with 6d nails.

For the closed shed only, complete the following four steps:

10. Cut the 2 × 2 door ledger at 73". Install the ledger flush with the top of the floor frame, screwing through the back of the side support with 2½" screws. Cut the 2 × 4 doorposts to fit between the ledger and door header, as shown in the FLOOR PLAN (page 415). NOTE: The left post is on edge, and the right post is flat. Make sure the posts are plumb and fasten them with 2½" screws.

11. Install 1 × 3 shelf cleats at the desired height, fastening them to the rear and side slats and the right doorpost. Cut the ¾" plywood shelf to fit the space and install it with 1⅝" deck screws.

12. For the door trim, cut four stiles at 41¾" and four rails at 18¼" from three 8-ft. 1 × 4s. Cut two stiles at 41¾" and two rails at 14¼" from one 10-ft. 1 × 4. Cut two ¾" plywood panels at 23½ × 40" and one panel at 19½ × 40".

13. Fasten the rails and stiles to the door panels with 1¼" deck screws, following the DOOR ELEVATION (page 416). Screw through the backsides of the panels. Install the doors with two hinges each. Use offset sash hinges mounted to the shed posts, or use standard strap hinges mounted to ¾"-thick blocks.

Kit Sheds

The following pages walk you through the steps of building two new sheds from kits. The metal shed measures 8 × 9 feet and comes with every piece in the main building precut and predrilled. The wood shed is a cedar building with panelized construction—most of the major elements come in preassembled sections. The walls panels have exterior siding installed, and the roof sections are already shingled.

The metal shed can be built on top of a patio surface or out in the yard, with or without a floor. The wood shed comes with a complete wood floor, but the building needs a standard foundation (wooden skid, concrete block, or concrete slab). To help keep either type of shed level and to reduce moisture from ground contact, it's a good idea to build it over a bed of compacted gravel. A 4"-deep bed that extends about 6" beyond the building footprint makes for a stable foundation.

Before you purchase a shed kit, check with your local building department to learn about restrictions that affect your project. It's recommended—and often required—that lightweight metal sheds be anchored to the ground. Shed manufacturers offer different anchoring systems, including cables for tethering the shed into soil and concrete anchors for tying into a concrete slab.

TOOLS & MATERIALS

- Metal shed kit or wood shed kit
- Compacted gravel
- Landscape fabric
- Tamper
- Level
- 2 × 4
- Work gloves
- Eye protection
- Tape measure
- Drill
- Weatherstripping tape
- Plywood flooring
- Anchor kit

HOW TO ASSEMBLE A METAL KIT SHED

1. *Prepare the building site by leveling and grading as needed, and then excavating and adding a 4"-thick layer of compactable gravel. If desired, apply landscape fabric under the gravel to inhibit weed growth. Compact the gravel with a tamper and use a level and a long, straight 2 × 4 to make sure the area is flat and level.*

2. *Begin by assembling the floor kit according to the manufacturer's directions—these will vary quite a bit among models, even within the same manufacturer. Be sure that the floor system parts are arranged so the door is located where you wish it to be. Do not fasten the pieces at this stage. NOTE: Always wear work gloves when handling shed parts—the metal edges can be very sharp.*

3. Once you've laid out the floor system parts, check to make sure they're square before you begin fastening them. Measuring the diagonals to see if they're the same is a quick and easy way to check for square.

4. Fasten the floor system parts together with kit connectors once you've established that the floor is square. Anchor the floor to the site if your kit suggests. Some kits are designed to be anchored after full assembly is completed.

5. Begin installing the wall panels according to the instructions. Most panels are predrilled for fasteners, so the main trick is to make sure the fastener holes align between panels and with the floor.

6. Tack together mating corner panels on at least two adjacent corners. If your frame stiffeners require assembly, have them ready to go before you form the corners. With a helper, attach the frame stiffener rails to the corner panels.

7. Install the remaining fasteners at the shed corners once you've established that the corners all are square.

8. Lay out the parts for assembling the roof beams and the upper side frames and confirm that they fit together properly. Then, join the assemblies with the fasteners provided.

9. Attach the moving and nonmoving parts for the upper door track to the side frames if your shed has sliding doors.

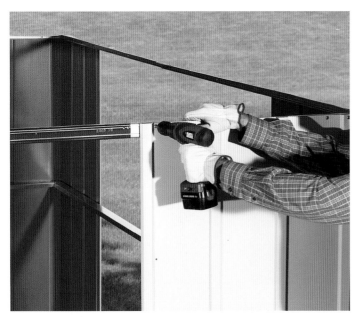

10. Fasten the shed panels to the top frames, making sure that any fasteners holes are aligned and that crimped tabs are snapped together correctly.

11. Fill in the wall panels between the completed corners, attaching them to the frames with the provided fasteners. Take care not to overdrive the fasteners.

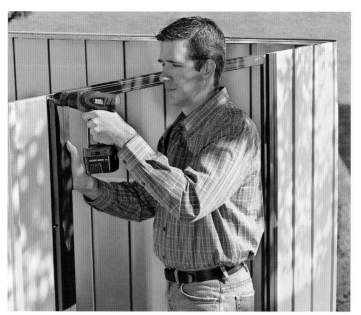

12. Fasten the doorframe trim pieces to the frames to finish the door opening. If the fasteners are colored to match the trim, make sure you choose the correct ones.

13. Insert the shed gable panels into the side frames and the door track and slide them together so the fastener holes are aligned. Attach the panels with the provided fasteners.

14. Fit the main roof beam into the clips or other fittings on the gable panels. Have a helper hold the free end of the beam. Position the beam and secure it to both gable ends before attaching it.

15. Drive fasteners to affix the roof beam to the gable ends and install any supplementary support hardware for the beam, such as gussets or angle braces.

16. *Begin installing the roof panels at one end, fastening them to the roof beam and to the top flanges of the side frames.*

17. *Apply weatherstripping tape to the top ends of the roof panels to seal the joints before you attach the overlapping roof panels. If your kit does not include weatherstripping tape, look for adhesive-backed foam tape in the weatherstripping products section of your local building center.*

18. *As the overlapping roof panels are installed and sealed, attach the roof cap sections at the roof ridge to cover the panel overlaps. Seal as directed.* NOTE: *Completing one section at a time allows you to access subsequent sections from below so you don't risk damaging the roof.*

TIPS FOR MAINTAINING A METAL SHED

Touch up scratches or any exposed metal as soon as possible to prevent rust. Clean the area with a wire brush, and then apply a paint recommended by the shed's manufacturer.

Inspect your shed once or twice a year and tighten loose screws, bolts, and other hardware. Loose connections lead to premature wear.

Sweep off the roof to remove wet leaves and debris, which can be hard on the finish. Also clear the roof after heavy snowfall to reduce the risk of collapse.

Seal open seams and other potential entry points for water with silicone caulk. Keep the shed's doors closed and latched to prevent damage from wind gusts.

20. *Assemble the doors, paying close attention to right/left differences on double doors. Attach hinges for swinging doors and rollers for sliding doors.*

19. *Attach the peak caps to cover the openings at the ends of the roof cap and then install the roof trim pieces at the bottoms of the roof panels, tucking the flanges or tabs into the roof as directed. Install plywood floor, according to manufacturer instructions.*

21. *Install door tracks and door roller hardware on the floor as directed and then install the doors according to the manufacturer's instructions. Test the action of the doors and make adjustments so the doors roll or swing smoothly and are aligned properly.*

ANCHOR THE SHED

Metal sheds tend to be light in weight and require secure anchoring to the ground, generally with an anchor kit that may be sold separately by your kit manufacturer. There are many ways to accomplish this. The method you choose depends mostly on the type of base you've built on, be it concrete or wood or gravel. On concrete and wood bases, look for corner gusset anchors that are attached directly to the floor frame and then fastened with landscape screws (wood) or masonry anchors driven into concrete. Sheds that have been built on a gravel or dirt base can be anchored with auger-type anchors that are driven into the ground just outside the shed. You'll need to anchor the shed on at least two sides. Once the anchors are driven, cables are strung through the shed so they are connected to the roof beam. The ends of the cables should exit the shed at ground level and then be attached to the anchors with cable clamps.

HOW TO BUILD A WOOD KIT SHED

1. *Prepare the base for the shed's wooden skid foundation with a 4" layer of compacted gravel. Make sure the gravel is flat, smooth, and perfectly level.* Note: *For a sloping site, a concrete block foundation may be more appropriate (check with your shed's manufacturer).*

2. *Assemble a frame of 4 × 4 or 6 × 6 timbers cut to match the length and width of the shed's floor frame. Make sure the frame is square and level.*

PREPARE FOR THE DELIVERY

Panelized shed kits are shipped on pallets. The delivery truck may have a forklift, and the driver can take off the load by whole pallets. Otherwise, you'll have to unload the pieces one at a time. Make sure to have two helpers on hand to help you unload (often drivers aren't allowed to help due to insurance liability).

Once the load is on the ground, carry the pieces to the building site and stack them on pallets or scrap-wood skids to keep them clean and dry. Look through the manufacturer's instructions and arrange the stacks according to the assembly steps.

3. *Assemble the floor frame pieces with screws. First, join alternating pairs of large and small pieces to create three full-width sections. Fasten the sections together to complete the floor frame.*

4. *Attach the floor runners to the bottom of the floor frame using exterior screws. Locate the side runners flush to the outsides of the frame, and center the middle runner in between. Set the frame on the skids with the runners facing down. Check the frame to make sure it is level. Secure the floor to the skids following the manufacturer's recommendations.*

5. *Cover the floor frame with plywood, starting with a large sheet at the left rear corner of the frame. Fasten the plywood with screws. Install the two outer deck boards. Lay out all of the remaining boards in between, then set even gapping for each board. Fasten the remaining deck boards.*

6. *Lay out the shed's wall panels in their relative positions around the floor. Make sure you have them right-side-up: the windows are on the top half of the walls; on the windowless panels, the siding tells you which end is up.*

7. Position the two rear corner walls upright onto the floor so the wall framing is flush with the floor's edges. Fasten the wall panels together. Raise and join the remaining wall panels one at a time. Do not fasten the wall panels to the shed floor in this step.

8. Place the door header on top of the narrow front wall panel so it's flush with the wall framing. Fasten the header with screws. Fasten the doorjamb to the right-side wall framing to create a ½" overhang at the end of the wall. Fasten the header to the jamb with screws.

9. Confirm that all wall panels are properly positioned on the floor. The wall framing should be flush with edges of the floor frame; the wall siding overhangs the outsides of the floor. Fasten the wall panels by screwing through the bottom wall plate, through the plywood flooring, and into the floor framing.

10. Install the wall's top plates starting with the rear wall. Install the side wall plates as directed—these overhang the front of the shed and will become part of the porch framing. Finally, install the front wall top plates.

11. *Assemble the porch rail sections using the screws provided for each piece. Attach the top plate extension to the 4 × 4 porch post, and then attach the wall trim/support to the extension. Fasten the corner brackets, centered on the post and extension. Install the handrail section 4" up from the bottom of the post.*

12. *Install each of the porch rail sections: Fasten through the wall trim/support and into the side wall, locating the screws where they will be least visible. Fasten down through the wall top plate at the post and corner bracket locations to hide the ends of the screws. Anchor the post to the decking and floor frame with screws driven through angled pilot holes.*

13. *Hang the Dutch door using two hinge pairs. Install the hinges onto the door panels. Use three pairs of shims to position the bottom door panel: ½" shims at the bottom, ⅜" shims on the left side, and ⅛" shims on the right side. Fasten the hinges to the wall trim/support. Hang the top door panel in the same fashion, using ¼" shims between the door panels.*

14. *Join the two pieces to create the rear wall gable, screwing through the uprights on the back side. On the outer side of the gable, slide in a filler shingle until it's even with the neighboring shingles. Fasten the filler with two finish nails located above the shingle exposure line, two courses up. Attach the top filler shingle with two (exposed) galvanized finish nails.*

15. *Position the rear gable on top of the rear wall top plates and center it from side to side. Use a square or straightedge to align the angled gable supports with the angled ends of the outer plates. Fasten the gable to the plates and wall framing with screws. Assemble and install the middle gable wall.*

16. *Arrange the roof panels on the ground according to their installation. Flip the panels over and attach framing connectors to the rafters at the marked locations using screws.*

17. *With one or two helpers, set the first roof panel at the rear of the shed, then set the opposing roof panel in place. Align the ridge boards of the two panels, and then fasten them together with screws. Do not fasten the panels to the walls at this stage.*

18. Position one of the middle roof panels, aligning its outer rafter with that of the adjacent rear roof panel. Fasten the rafters together with screws. Install the opposing middle panel in the same way. Set the porch roof panels into place one at a time—these rest on a ½" ledge at the front of the shed. From inside the shed, fasten the middle and porch panels together along their rafters.

19. Check the fit of all roof panels at the outside corners of the shed. Make any necessary adjustments. Fasten the panels to the shed with screws, starting with the porch roof. Inside the shed, fasten the panels to the gable framing, then anchor the framing connectors to the wall plates.

20. Install the two roof gussets between the middle rafters of the shed roof panels (not the porch panels). First measure between the side walls—this should equal 91" for this kit. If not, have two helpers push on the walls until the measurement matches your requirement. Hold the gussets level, and fasten them to the rafters with screws.

21. *Add filler shingles at the roof panel seams. Slide in the bottom shingle and fasten it above the exposure line two courses up using two screws. Drive the screws into the rafters. Install the remaining filler shingles the same way. Attach the top shingle with two galvanized finish nails.*

22. *Cover the underside of the rafter tails (except on the porch) with soffit panels, fastening to the rafters with finish nails. Cover the floor framing with skirting boards, starting at the porch sides. Hold the skirting flush with the decking boards on the porch and with the siding on the walls, and fasten it with screws.*

23. *Add vertical trim boards to cover the wall seams and shed corners. The rear corners get a filler trim piece, followed by a wide trim board on top. Add horizontal trim boards at the front wall and along the top of the door. Fasten all trim with finish nails.*

24. *At the rear of the shed, fit the two fascia boards over the ends of the roof battens so they meet at the roof peak. Fasten the fascia with screws. Install the side fascia pieces over the rafter tails with finish nails. The rear fascia overlaps the ends of the side fascia. Cover the fascia joints and the horizontal trim joint at the front wall with decorative plates.*

25. Place the two roof ridge caps along the roof peak, overlapping the caps' roofing felt in the center. Fasten the caps with screws. Install the decorative gusset gable underneath the porch roof panels using mounting clips. Finish the gable ends with two fascia pieces installed with screws.

26. Complete the porch assembly by fastening each front handrail section to a deck post using screws. Fasten the handrail to the corner porch post. The handrail should start 4" above the bottoms of the posts, as with the side handrail sections. Anchor each deck post to the decking and floor frame with screws (see Drilling Counterbored Pilot Holes, this page).

DRILLING COUNTERBORED PILOT HOLES

Use a combination piloting/counterbore bit to predrill holes for installing posts. Angle the pilot holes at about 60°, and drive the screws into the framing below whenever possible. The counterbore created by the piloting bit helps hide the screw head.

Hard-sided Greenhouse

Building a greenhouse from a prefabricated kit offers many advantages. Kits are usually very easy to assemble because all parts are prefabricated and the lightweight materials are easy to handle. The quality of greenhouse kits varies widely, though, and buying from a reputable manufacturer will help ensure that you get many years of service from your greenhouse.

If you live in a snowy climate, you may need to either provide extra support within the greenhouse or be ready to remove snow whenever there is a significant snowfall because the lightweight aluminum frame members can easily bend under a heavy load. Before buying a kit, make sure to check on how snowfall may affect it.

Greenhouse kits are offered by many different manufacturers, and the exact assembly technique you use will depend on the specifics of your kit. Make sure you read the printed instructions carefully, as they may vary slightly from this project.

The kit we're demonstrating here is made from aluminum frame pieces and transparent polycarbonate panels and is designed to be installed over a base of gravel about 5" thick. Other kits may have different base requirements.

When you purchase your kit, make sure to uncrate it and examine all the parts before you begin. Make sure all the pieces are there and that there are no damaged panels or bent frame members.

A perfectly flat and level base is crucial to any greenhouse kit, so make sure to work carefully. Try to do the work on a dry day with no wind, as the panels and frame pieces can be hard to manage on a windy day. Never try to build a greenhouse kit by yourself. At least one helper is mandatory, and you'll do even better with two or three.

Construction of a greenhouse kit consists of four basic steps: laying the base, assembling the frame, assembling the windows and doors, and attaching the panels.

TOOLS & MATERIALS

- Mason's string & stakes
- Shovel
- 2 × 4
- Eye protection
- 4' level
- Gravel
- Drill or driver
- Greenhouse kit

Greenhouse kits come in a wide range of shapes, sizes, and quality. The best ones have tempered-glass glazing and are rather expensive. The one pictured here is glazed with corrugated polyethylene and is at the low end of the cost spectrum.

The familiar gambrel profile is tricky to create from scratch, but when purchased as a kit a gambrel greenhouse is a snap to assemble.

Some greenhouse kits include only the hardware necessary to create the frame structure. The glazing, which is normally some variety of plastic sheeting, is acquired separately.

Kit greenhouses (and other types, too) can be built in groups so you may create a variety of growing climates. This lets you raise species that may not have compatible needs for light, moisture, and heat.

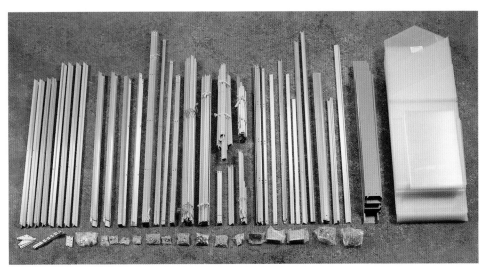

Organize and inspect the contents of your kit cartons to make sure all of the parts are present and in good condition. Most manuals will have a checklist. Staging the parts makes for a more efficient assembly. Be sure not to leave any small parts loose, and do not store parts in high-traffic areas.

A cordless drill/driver with a nut-driver accessory will trim hours off of your assembly time compared with using only hand tools.

Rent outdoor power equipment if you need to do significant regrading to create a flat, level building base. Be sure to have your local utility company inspect for any buried utility lines first. (You may prefer to hire a landscaping company to do regrading work for you.)

HOW TO BUILD A GREENHOUSE KIT

1. Create an outline for the base of the greenhouse using stakes and string. The excavation should be about 2" wider and longer than the overall dimensions of your greenhouse. To ensure that the excavation is perfectly square, measure the diagonals of the outline. If diagonals are equal, the outline is perfectly square. If not, reposition the stakes until the outline is square.

2. Excavate the base area to a depth of 5". Use a long 2 × 4 and a 4-ft. level to periodically check the excavation and to make sure it is level and flat. You can also use a laser level for this job.

3. Assemble the base of the greenhouse using the provided corner connectors and end connectors, attaching them with base nuts and bolts. Lower the base into the excavation area, and check to make sure it's level. Measure the diagonals to see if they are equal; if not, reposition the base until the diagonals are equal, which ensures that the base is perfectly square. Pour a layer of gravel or other fill material into the excavation to within about 1" of the top lip of the base frame. Smooth the fill with a long 2 × 4.

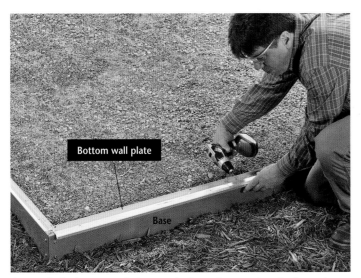

4. *Attach the bottom wall plates to the base pieces so that the flanged edges face outside the greenhouse. In most systems, the floor plates will interlock with one another, end to end, with built-in brackets.*

5. *Fasten the four corner studs to the bottom wall plates using hold-down connectors and bolts. In this system, each corner stud is secured with two connectors.*

6. *Assemble the pieces for each side ceiling plate, then attach one assembled side plate against the inside of the two corner studs, making sure the gutter is positioned correctly. Now attach the front ceiling plate to the outside of the two corner studs that are over the front floor plate.*

BACKWARD & FORWARD

With some kits you need to go backward to go forward. Because the individual parts of your kit depend upon one another for support, you may be required to tack all the parts together with bolts first and then undo and remake individual connections as you go before you can finalize them. For example, in this kit you must undo the track/brace connections one at a time so you can insert the bolt heads for the stud connectors into the track.

7. Attach the other side ceiling plate along the other side, flat against the inside of the corner studs. Then attach corner brackets to the rear studs, and construct the back top plate by attaching the rear braces to the corners and joining the braces together with stud connectors.

8. Fasten the left and right rear studs to the outside of the rear floor plate, making sure the top ends are sloping upward, toward the peak of the greenhouse. Attach the center rear studs to the rear floor plate, fastening them to the stud connectors used to join the rear braces.

9. Attach the side studs on each side wall using the provided nuts and bolts. Then attach the doorway studs to the front wall of the greenhouse.

10. *Attach diagonal struts as specified by the manufacturer. Periodically take diagonal measurements between the top corners of the greenhouse, adjusting as necessary so that the measurements are equal and the greenhouse is square.*

11. *Fasten the gable-end stud extensions to the front and back walls of the greenhouse. The top ends of the studs should angle upward toward the peak of the greenhouse.*

Rafter

Crown

Crown beam

12. *Assemble the roof frame on a flat area near the wall assembly. First assemble the crown-beam pieces; then attach the rafters to the crown, one by one. The end rafters, called the crown beams, have a different configuration, so make sure not to confuse them.*

13. With at least one helper, lift the roof into place onto the wall frames. The gable-end studs should meet the outside edges of the crown beams, and the ends of the crown beams rest on the outer edge of the corner bracket. Fasten in place with the provided nuts and bolts.

Side braces

Roof support window

14. Attach the side braces and the roof support window beams to the underside of the roof rafters as specified by the manufacturer's instructions.

15. Attach the front braces between the corner studs and the doorway studs on the front wall of the greenhouse.

16. *Build the roof windows by first connecting the two side window frames to the top window frame. Slide the window panel into the frame; then secure it by attaching the bottom window frame. Slide the window into the slot at the top of the roof crown; then gradually lower it in place. Attach the window stop to the window support beam.*

17. *Assemble the doors, making sure the top slider/roller bar and the bottom slider bar are correctly positioned. Lift the door panels up into place onto the top and bottom wall plates.*

18. *Install the panels one-by-one using panel clips. Begin with the large wall panels. Position each panel and secure it by snapping a clip into the frame at the intervals specified by the manufacturer's instructions.*

19. *Add the upper panels. At the gable ends, the upper panels will be supported by panel connectors that allow the top panel to be supported by the bottom panel. The lower panels should be installed already.*

20. *Install the roof panels and roof-window panels so that the top edges fit up under the edge of the crown or window support and the bottom edges align over the gutters.*

21. *Test the operation of the doors and roof windows to make sure they operate smoothly.*

A-Frame Greenhouse

A greenhouse can be a decorative and functional building that adds beauty to your property. A greenhouse also can be a quick-and-easy, temporary structure that serves a purpose and then disappears. The wood-framed greenhouse seen here fits somewhere between these two types. The sturdy wood construction will hold up for many seasons. The plastic sheeting covering will last one to four or five seasons, depending on the materials you choose (see next page), and it is easy to replace when it starts to degrade.

The five-foot-high kneewalls in this design provide ample space for installing and working on a conventional-height potting table. The walls also provide some space for plants to grow. For a door, this plan simply employs a sheet of weighted plastic that can be tied out of the way for entry and exit. If you plan to go in and out of the greenhouse frequently, you can purchase a prefabricated greenhouse door from a greenhouse materials supplier. To allow for ventilation in hot weather, we built a wood-frame vent cover that fits over one rafter bay and can be propped open easily.

You can use hand-driven nails or pneumatic framing nails to assemble the frame if you wish, although deck screws make more sense for a small structure like this.

A wood-frame greenhouse with sheet-plastic cover is an inexpensive, semipermanent gardening structure that can be used as a potting area as well as a protective greenhouse.

Cutting List

KEY	NO.	PART	DIMENSION	MATERIAL
A	2	Base ends	3½ x 3½ x 96"	4 x 4 landscape timber
B	2	Base sides	3½ x 3½ x 113"	4 x 4 landscape timber
C	2	Sole plates end	1½ x 3½ x 89"	2 x 4 pressure-treated
D	2	Sole plates side	1½ x 3½ x 120"	2 x 4 pressure-treated
E	12	Wall studs side	1½ x 3½ x 57"	2 x 4
F	1	Ridge support	1½ x 3½ x 91"	2 x 4
G	2	Back studs	1½ x 3½ x 76" *	2 x 4
H	2	Doorframe sides	1½ x 3½ x 81" *	2 x 4
I	1	Cripple stud	1½ x 3½ x 16"	2 x 4
J	1	Door header	1½ x 3½ x 32"	2 x 4
K	2	Kneewall caps	1½ x 3½ x 120"	2 x 4
L	1	Ridge pole	1½ x 3½ x 120"	2 x 4
M	12	Rafters	1½ x 3½ x 60" *	2 x 4

*Approximate dimension; take actual length and angle measurements on structure before cutting.

TOOLS & MATERIALS

- (1) 20 x 50 roll 4 or 6-mil polyethylene sheeting or greenhouse fabric, tack strips
- (12) 24"-long pieces of #3 rebar
- (4) 16' pressure-treated 2 × 4
- (2) exterior-rated butt hinges

- (1) screw-eye latch
- (8) 8" timber screws
- Circular saw
- Drill or driver
- Metal cutoff saw or reciprocating saw
- Maul or sledgehammer
- 3" deck screws
- Exterior panel adhesive

- Level
- Jigsaw
- Pencil
- Tape measure
- Utility knife

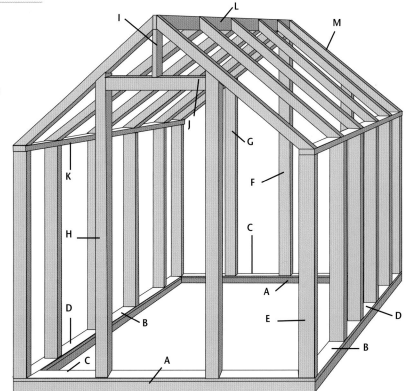

HOW TO BUILD AN A-FRAME GREENHOUSE

1. *Prepare the installation area so it is flat and well drained; then cut the base timbers (4 x 4 landscape timbers) to length. Arrange the timbers so they are flat and level and create a rectangle with square corners. Drive a pair of 8" timber screws at each corner, using a drill/driver with a nut-driver bit.*

2. *Cut 12 pieces of #3 rebar (find it in the concrete supplies section of any building center) to 24" in length to use as spikes for securing the timbers to the ground. A metal cutoff saw or a reciprocating saw with a bimetal blade can be used to make the cuts. Drill a ⅜" guide hole through each timber near each end and in the middle. Drive a rebar spike at each hole with a maul or sledge hammer until the top is flush with the wood.*

3. *Cut the plates and studs for the two side walls (called kneewalls). Arrange the parts on a flat surface and assemble the walls by driving three 3" deck screws through the cap and base plates and into the ends of the studs. Make both kneewalls.*

4. Set the base plate of each kneewall on the timber base and attach the walls by driving 3" deck screws down through the base plates and into the timbers. For extra holding power, you can apply exterior panel adhesive to the undersides of the plates, but only if you don't plan to relocate the structure later.

5. Cut the ridge support post to length and attach it to the center of one end base plate, forming a T. Cut another post the same length for the front (this will be a temporary post) and attach it to a plate. Fasten both plates to front and back end timbers.

6. Set the ridge pole on top of the posts and check that it is level. Also check that the posts are level and plumb. Attach a 2 x 4 brace to the outer studs of the kneewalls and to the posts to hold them in square relationship. Double-check the pole and posts with the level.

7. Cut a 2 x 4 to about 66" to use as a rafter template. Hold the 2 x 4 against the end of the ridge pole and the top outside corner of a kneewall. Trace along the face of the ridge and the top plate of the wall to mark cutting lines. Cut the rafter and use it as a template for the other rafters on that side of the roof. Create a separate template for the other side of the roof.

449

8. Mark cutting lines for the rafters using the templates and cut them all. You'll need to use a jigsaw or handsaw to make the bird's-mouth cuts on the rafter ends that rest on the kneewall.

9. Attach the rafters to the ridge pole and the kneewalls with deck screws driven through pilot holes. Try to make the rafters align with the kneewall studs.

10. Mark the positions for the remaining end wall studs on the base plate. At each location, hold a 2 x 4 on end on the base plate and make it level and plumb. Trace a cutting line at the top of the 2 x 4 where it meets the rafter. Cut the studs and install them by driving screws toenail-style.

11. Measure up 78" (or less if you want a shorter door) from the sole plate in the door opening and mark a cutting line on the temporary ridge post. Make a square cut along the line with a circular saw or cordless trim saw (Inset). Then cut the door header to fit between the vertical doorframe members. Screw the header to the cut end of the ridge post and drive screws through the frame members and into the header.

12. *Begin covering the greenhouse with your choice of cover material. (We used 6-mil polyethylene sheeting.) Start at the ends. Cut the sheeting to size and then fasten it by attaching screen retainer strips to wood surfaces at the edges of the area being covered. Tack the sheeting first at the top, then at the sides, and finally at the bottom. After the strips are installed (use wire brads), trim the sheeting along the edges of the strips with a utility knife.*

13. *Attach the sheeting to the outside edge of the base plate on one side. Roll sheeting over the roof and down the other side. Draw it taut and cut it slightly overlong with scissors. Attach retainer strips to the other base plate and then to the outside edges of the corner studs.*

14. *Make and hang a door. We simply cut a piece of sheet plastic a little bigger than the opening (32") and hung it with retainer strips from the header. Attach a piece of 2 x 4 to the bottom of the door for weight.*

OPTION: *Make a vent window. First, cut a hole in the roof in one rafter bay and tack the cut edges of the plastic to the faces (not the edges) of the rafters, ridge pole and wall cap. Then build a frame from 1 x 2 stock that will span from the ridge to the top of the kneewall and extend a couple of inches past the rafters at the side of the opening. Clad the frame with plastic sheeting and attach it to the ridge pole with butt hinges. Install a screw-eye latch to secure it at the bottom. Make and attach props if you wish.*

451

Accessories & Recreation Structures

With your larger projects (such as decks, porches, and sheds) completed, there are many other elements you can add to your outdoor home that will not only make it a more functional and usable space, but also a more enjoyable one.

Building an arbor over a patio or deck can help block out the glaring sun and provide shade for wide-open, treeless yards. Garden ponds and ornamental fountains can be used to establish unique focal points and help create a tranquil setting. Installing a fire pit in the backyard can create a cozy campfire retreat—the perfect way to end a day with family and friends.

When choosing a site, consider the ways you will use the element. A play structure may be better suited farther back in the yard, but within view of an accessible window in the house so you can keep an eye on the kids.

Also research your local building codes—they can be determining factors in where and how you install certain projects. For instance, most codes require that a fire pit be positioned a minimum distance from the house or any other combustible materials, such as a wood fence or deck.

Adding elements such as these increase the overall value of your entire home, and make it a much more comfortable place to live.

IN THIS CHAPTER:

- Children's Play Structure
- Tree House
- A-Frame Swing Set with Climbing Wall
- Raised Garden Bed
- Fire Pit
- Outdoor Kitchen
- Brick Barbecue
- Garden Pond & Fountain
- Free-form Meditation Pond
- Backyard Putting Green
- Arbor
- Classical Pergola

Children's Play Structure

Children like to be active, and a play structure provides them with a space all their own, designed specifically with playtime in mind. Play structures provide places for children to have fun, and help them develop physical strength and skills, such as balance and agility.

The play structure shown here has been carefully designed to provide a fun and safe activity area for your children. The ladders leading up to the clubhouse tower are angled to maximize the play areas above and below the structure. Balusters and stringers frame all entrances and exits to enclose the clubhouse, reducing the risk of injuries due to falls. Also, milled cedar timbers are used in the construction to soften sharp corners and prevent splintering.

Though the play structure is installed on a grass surface, it can easily be adapted for a softer, loose-fill floor, such as sand, pea gravel, or wood chips. Just add the depth of the loose-fill flooring material—typically 8 to 12"—to the length of the ladder legs, and anchor the structure at the solid subbase level. Refer to pages 32 to 33 for information on installing loose-fill material. NOTE: Page 523 provides resources for play structure hardware—such as metal gussets—and full kits.

TOOLS & MATERIALS

- Tape measure
- Reciprocating saw or handsaw
- Drill
- 1⅜₆" Forstner bit or spade bit
- Round file
- Scrap 2 × 4
- Mallet
- Framing square
- Spade bits (⅞", 1⅛", 1⅜")
- Ratchet wrench
- Circular saw
- Straightedge
- Bar clamps

- (various sizes)
- Level
- Combination square
- 6-ft. steel fence post
- 36¼" tubular steel ladder rungs (10)
- Carriage bolts with washers (4", 5", 6½", 7", 7½", 11")
- Galvanized lag screws with washers (⁵⁄₁₆ × 1½", ⁵⁄₁₆ × 2½", ⁵⁄₁₆ × 3½", ⅜ × 1½", ⅜ × 4", ⅜ × 5½")
- Galvanized deck screws (2", 2½", 3")

- Angled metal braces (4)
- 16" 2 × 2 green-treated stakes (6)
- Metal A-frame gusset
- Swing hanger clamps (6)
- #10 × 1½" sheet metal screws
- String
- ¾" galvanized hex bolts with lock washers
- Angle irons with ¾" screws (2)
- 4" mending plates with ¾" screws (2)
- ¼", ⁵⁄₁₆", ⅜" twist bits

EXPLODED VIEW

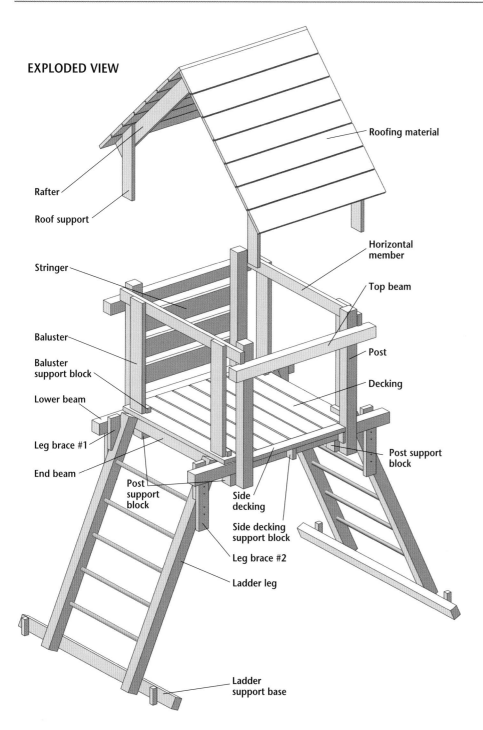

Rafter

Roof support

Stringer

Baluster

Baluster
support block

Lower beam

Leg brace #1

End beam

Post
support
block

Roofing material

Horizontal
member

Top beam

Post

Decking

Post support
block

Side
decking

Side decking
support block

Leg brace #2

Ladder leg

Ladder
support base

Lumber List

Qty.	Size	Part
4	4 × 4" × 70"	Ladder leg
2	3 × 4" × 72"	Ladder support base*
2	4 × 4" × 71"	Lower beam
4	2 × 4" × 12¾"	Leg brace #1
4	2 × 4" × 15¼"	Leg brace #2
8	¾ × 6" × 47"	Decking
3	4 × 4" × 41"	Deck end beam, mid-beam (not shown)
4	4 × 4" × 44"	Post
4	4 × 4" × 7"	Post support block
2	4 × 4" × 51"	Top beam
2	2 × 4" × 56"	Horizontal member
4	2 × 4" × 18"	Roof support **
2	1 × 4" × 34"	Side decking
4	1 × 4" × 2¼"	Side decking support block
2	2 × 4" × 3½"	Side decking mid-support block
3	¾ × 6" × 37"	Stringer
4	¾ × 6" × 34"	Baluster
4	2 × 2" × 7"	Baluster support block
2	4 × 4" × 113"	Double swing beam
2	4 × 4" × 96"	A-frame leg
1	2 × 4" × 41"	A-frame brace
1	3 × 4" × 96"	A-frame support base *
4	2 × 4" × 39"	Rafter **
14	1 × 6" × 66"	Roofing material ***

Use cedar building materials unless otherwise noted

*Landscape timber stock

**Green-treated

***Tongue-and-groove cedar

NOTICE: The tubular steel ladder rungs shown here may be difficult to locate as individual parts from play structure systems retailers. If you experience difficulty finding them, you may substitute a cargo-net style chain ladder, or add an intermediate ladder leg between each leg pair and install 17¾" overhead monkey bars to function as ladder rungs.

FIGURE 1

8¾"

7⅝"

Lower beam

6"

Reference line

FIGURE 3

Leg brace #1

4¼"

2"

12¾"

FIGURE 2

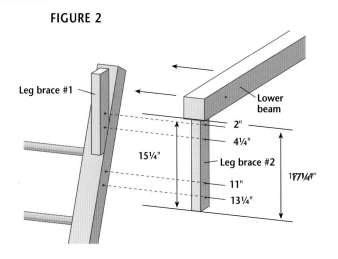

Leg brace #1

Lower beam

2"

4¼"

15¼"

Leg brace #2

17¼"

11"

13¼"

FIGURE 5

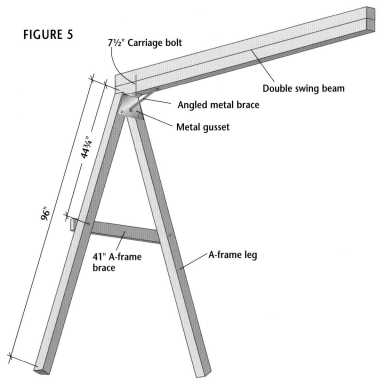

7½" Carriage bolt

Double swing beam

Angled metal brace

Metal gusset

44¾"

96"

41" A-frame brace

A-frame leg

FIGURE 4

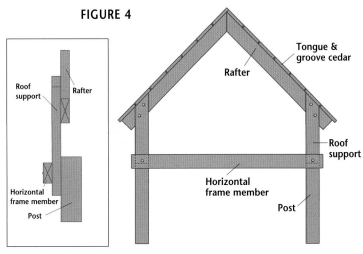

Roof support

Rafter

Horizontal frame member

Post

Tongue & groove cedar

Rafter

Roof support

Horizontal frame member

Post

FIGURE 6

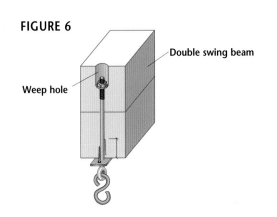

Double swing beam

Weep hole

HOW TO BUILD A CHILDREN'S PLAY STRUCTURE

Step A: Assemble the Ladders

1. Cut four 4 × 4 ladder legs at 70" using a reciprocating saw. Draw a reference line down the middle of each leg using a straightedge. Measuring from one end, mark each leg along the reference line at 3¾", 13", 24", 35", 46", and 57".

2. At the 3¾" mark, drill a ⅜" hole through each ladder leg. At the remaining marks, drill 1⅜"-deep holes using a 1⁵⁄₁₆" Forstner bit or spade bit, then round over the edges of each to a ¼" radius using a round file.

3. Drive five 36¾" tubular steel ladder rungs into the holes of one ladder leg using a scrap 2 × 4 and a mallet. Check the alignment of the rungs with a framing square to make sure they are straight. If the rungs are difficult to insert, apply petroleum jelly to the inside of the holes. NOTE: Loose rungs can be tightened by inserting aluminum flashing into holes. Cut flashing into ¾ × 2" strips, and install so edges are ⅛" below the edges of the holes.

4. Align the rungs with the holes of the second ladder leg, and fit them in place. Place a scrap 2 × 4 over the leg, and use a mallet to drive the rungs into the holes of the second leg, creating a 41"-wide ladder. Repeat to build the second ladder.

Step B: Build the Clubhouse Leg Assembly

1. Cut two 4 × 4 lower beams to 71". Measure in from each end and mark at 8¾", centered on the beams. Drill ⅜"-deep counterbore holes at each, using a 1⅜" spade bit, then ⅜" holes through the lower beams.

2. On the side of the beams opposite the counterbore holes, measure from each end along the top edge and mark at 7⅜". Measure along the bottom edge and mark at 6". Connect the marks with a straightedge and draw a reference line. (Refer to Figure 1 on page 456.)

3. Place the ladders between the lower beams with the counterbore holes facing out. Align the counterbore holes with the pilot holes at the tops of the ladder legs. Use a ratchet wrench to loosely fasten the structure together using 7" galvanized carriage bolts with washers.

Step C: Assemble the Leg Braces

NOTE: refer to Figure 2 on page 456 for the leg brace assembly detail.

1. Cut four 2 × 4 leg brace #1s, following Figure 2 on page 456. Also cut four leg brace #2s to 15¼" using a circular saw.

2. Align the ladder legs with the reference lines drawn on the beams; then clamp leg brace #1 in place so the angled edge rests on the ladder leg and the top is 1¼" above the top face of the lower beam.

3. From the top of leg brace #1, measure down and mark at 2 and 4" on center. Drill ¼"-deep counterbore holes at each location using a 1⅛" spade bit, then drill ⁵⁄₁₆" pilot holes through the braces. Drive ⁵⁄₁₆ × 2½" galvanized lag screws with washers through brace #1 and into the lower beam using a ratchet wrench.

A. Insert the rungs into one ladder leg using a mallet and scrap board. Lift the assembly and fit the rungs into the holes of the second leg.

B. Position the two ladders between the lower beams, align the pilot holes, and loosely fasten with carriage bolts.

C. Clamp the leg braces in place, drill counterbored pilot holes, and fasten to the ladder with lag screws with washers.

457

4. Clamp leg brace #2 to leg brace #1, so leg brace #2 is flush with leg brace #1 and butted to the bottom face of the beam. From the top of leg brace #2, measure down and mark at 2", 4¼", 11", and 13¼", centered on the brace.

5. Drill ¼"-deep counterbore holes at each mark using a 1⅛" spade bit, then 5⁄16" pilot holes through the braces. Fasten with 5⁄16 × 2½" galvanized lag screws with washers using a ratchet wrench.

6. Brace the next corner, then raise and brace the other side of the structure. Fully tighten the carriage bolts joining the lower beams to the ladder legs.

Step D: Install the End Beams & Mid-Beam

1. Cut eight ¾ × 6 decking boards to 47" using a circular saw. Lay one decking board across the lower beams at each end, tight against the tops of the ladders, and aligning one end flush with the edge of one beam. Drill a pair of 5⁄16" pilot holes, and use 2½" galvanized deck screws to fasten only this one end of the decking boards to the lower beams.

2. Cut two 4 × 4 end beams to 41". Clamp the end beams to the underside of the decking boards, between the lower beams and tight against the ladder legs.

3. Drill pairs of ⅝"-deep counterbore holes, using a 1⅜" spade bit, then drill ¼" pilot holes through the lower beams and into the ends of the end beams. Also drill ⅜" clearance holes for lag screw shanks to a 1" depth. Fasten the beams with ⅜ × 1½" galvanized lag screws with washers, using a ratchet wrench, until the unattached ends of the decking boards are flush with the edge of the other lower beam.

4. Drill pairs of 5⁄16" pilot holes through the unattached ends of the decking boards, and fasten to the other lower beam using 2½" galvanized deck screws.

5. Cut one 4 × 4 mid-beam at 41". Center it between the end beams and clamp to the decking boards. Drill pairs of ½"-deep counterbore holes using a 1⅜" spade bit, then drill ¼" pilot holes through the end beams and into the mid-beam. Also drill ⅜" clearance holes, 1" deep, for the lag screw shanks. Fasten with ⅜ × 5½" galvanized lag screws with washers using a ratchet wrench.

6. Drill 5⁄16" pilot holes and fasten the decking boards to the mid-beam using 2½" galvanized deck screws.

Step E: Add the Ladder Support Base

1. Cut two 3 × 4 landscape timbers at 72" for ladder support bases using a reciprocating saw.

2. Check to make sure the clubhouse is level. Center the ladder support bases against the inside faces of the ladder legs. Set each base into the ground using a mallet.

3. Clamp the support bases to the ladders. Drill a ½"-deep counterbore hole using a 1⅜" spade bit, then drill a ¼" pilot hole through each leg and into the base. Also drill ⅜" shank clearance holes 1" deep at each counterbore hole. Fasten with ⅜ × 5½" galvanized lag screws with washers using a ratchet wrench.

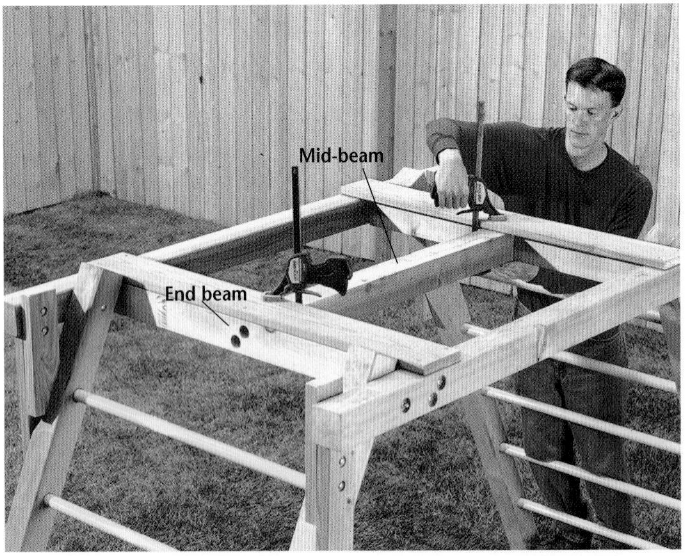

D. *Attach decking boards on top of the lower beams, set tightly against each ladder. Fasten on one side only. Position and secure the end beams and mid-beam, then fasten the other ends of the decking boards.*

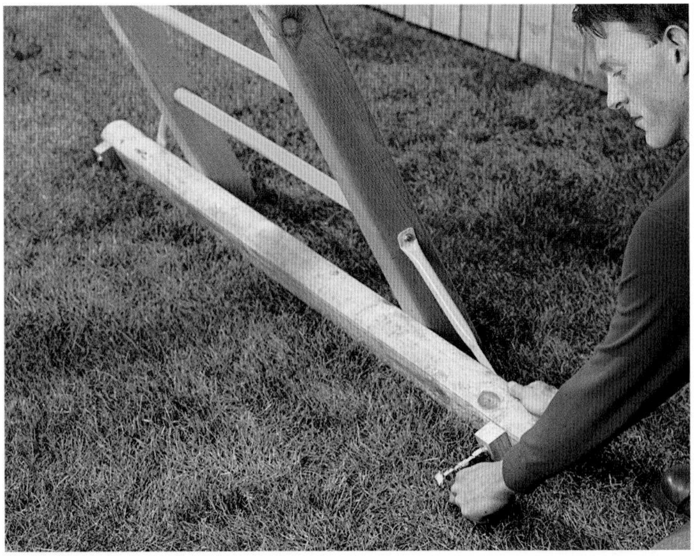

E. *With the lower structure on level ground and the ladder support bases attached to the bottom of the ladders, drive anchor stakes into the ground at each end of the base, then attach the stakes to the bases with lag screws.*

4. To add strength and stability, attach angled metal braces between the ladders and bases using 5⁄16 × 1½" galvanized lag screws. Also drive 16"-long 2 × 2 green-treated stakes into the ground at each end of the bases, and attach to the support bases with 5⁄16 × 3½" galvanized lag screws.

Step F: Install the Decking & Posts

1. Evenly space the six remaining decking boards across the lower beams and mid-beam. Drill pairs of 5⁄16" pilot holes, then fasten with 2½" galvanized deck screws.

2. Cut four 7"-long 4 × 4 blocks. Measure along one side of each post support block and mark the midpoint.

3. From one end, measure along each lower beam and mark at 16¾ and 54¼". Clamp the blocks to the underside of the lower beams, aligning the midpoint with each mark on the beams.

4. Drill 1¼"-deep counterbore holes using a 1⅜" spade bit, then drill ¼" pilot holes through the bottom of the blocks, up into the clubhouse. Also drill 1"-deep, ⅜" shank clearance holes. Fasten with ⅜ × 4" lag screws with washers using a ratchet.

5. Cut four 4 × 4 posts at 44". Center the posts against the lower beams and blocks at the midpoint and flush with the bottom of the blocks. Square the posts to the clubhouse using a combination square, and clamp in place.

6. At each post, drill two ⅝"-deep counterbore holes using a 1⅜" spade bit, then drill ¼" pilot holes, one through the post and into the lower beams and one into the blocks. Also drill ⅜" shank clearance holes to a 1" depth. Fasten the posts to the lower beams with 7" galvanized carriage bolts with washers, and to the blocks using ⅜ × 5½" galvanized lag screws with washers using a ratchet wrench.

Step G: Install the Top Beams & Horizontal Members

1. On the front side of the posts, measure down from the top and mark at 6".

2. Cut two 4 × 4 top beams at 51". Position the top beams across two posts, parallel to the lower beams, and with the top edge of the top beams at the reference marks. Make sure the ends evenly overhang the sides of the posts, check for level, and clamp in place.

3. Drill ⅝"-deep counterbore holes, using a 1⅜" spade bit, then drill ¼" pilot holes through the top beams and into the posts. Also drill ⅜" shank clearance holes to a 1" depth. Fasten the top beams to the posts with 7" galvanized carriage bolts with washers using a ratchet wrench.

4. Cut two 2 × 4 horizontal members at 56". Also cut four 2 × 4 roof supports at 18" and angle one end at a 45° angle.

5. On the ladder sides of the posts, measure down 1½" from the tops and mark. Position the horizontal members across the posts, aligning the top edge with the marks, and sandwiching the roof supports between the members and posts (refer to Figure 4 on page 456). Make sure the members are level, then clamp in place, so the ends evenly overhang the posts.

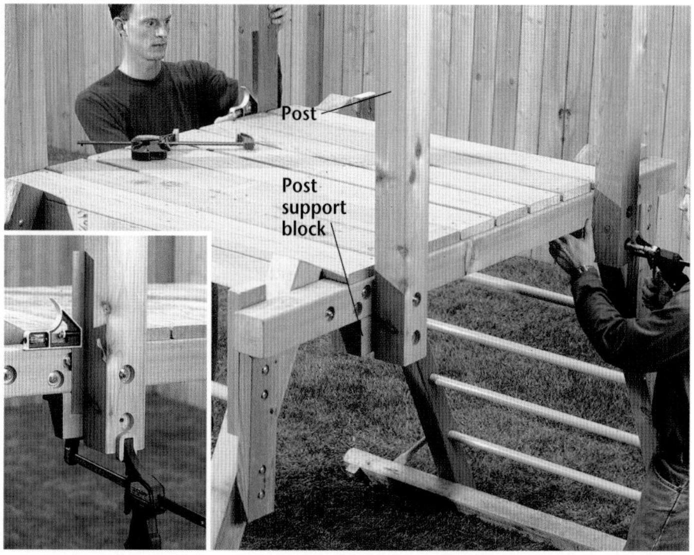

F. *Clamp the posts in place, make sure they are properly aligned, and plumb (Inset), then attach to the lower beams and support blocks with lag screws.*

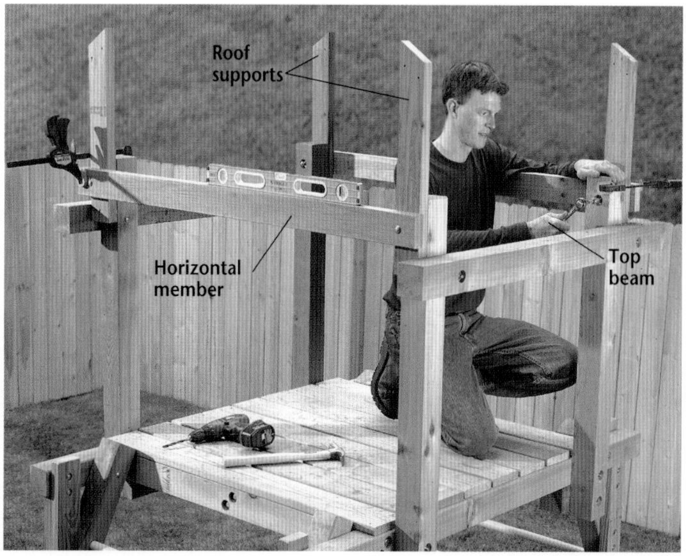

G. *Attach the top beams to the posts with 7" carriage bolts. Also attach the horizontal members and roof supports in place using 6½" carriage bolts.*

6. On the deck side of the posts, drill ½"-deep counterbore holes using a 1⅜" spade bit, then drill ⅜" pilot holes through posts and roof supports and into the horizontal members. Also drill ⅜" shank clearance holes to a 1" depth. Fasten using 6½" galvanized carriage bolts with washers using a ratchet wrench.

Step H: Install the Side Decking

1. Cut two 2¼"-long 1 × 4 side decking support blocks. On the swing side of the clubhouse, place one block against each post so it is flush with the top of the lower beam. Drill two ⁵⁄₁₆" pilot holes, then fasten each with 2" galvanized deck screws.

2. Cut a 1 × 4 side decking boards at 34". Position the board on the blocks, drill a ⁵⁄₁₆" pilot hole at each end, and fasten with 2" galvanized deck screws.

3. Cut a 3½"-long 2 × 4 side decking mid-suport block. Center the block against the lower beam with the top flush against the underside of the side decking board. Drill a 1½"-deep counterbore hole using a ⅞" spade bit, then drill a ⁵⁄₁₆" pilot hole through the block and into the lower beam. Fasten with a 3" galvanized deck screw.

4. Drill a ⁵⁄₁₆" pilot hole through the top of the side decking board into the block. Fasten with a 2" galvanized deck screw.

5. Repeat the steps to install side decking on the opposite side of the clubhouse.

Step I: Install the Stringers & Balusters

1. Cut three ¾ × 6 stringers at 37". On the side of the clubhouse with the side decking, clamp the stringers to the posts, spaced 2½" apart. Rip a scrap board to use as a spacer.

2. Drill pairs of ⁵⁄₁₆" pilot holes through each stringer, into the posts. Fasten with 2" galvanized deck screws.

3. Cut four ¾ × 6 balusters at 34" and four 7"-long 2 × 2 baluster support blocks. At one end of each baluster, fasten a block to the interior face, flush with the bottom edge. Drill a pair of ⁵⁄₁₆" pilot holes, then fasten with 2" galvanized deck screws.

4. Position the balusters so they do not obstruct the ladder entrances to the clubhouse, with the block ends on the deck and the tops against the horizontal members. Loosely fasten the top ends with 2" galvanized deck screws.

5. Check the balusters for plumb, then drill a ⁵⁄₁₆" pilot hole through the blocks and into the decking. Fasten using 2½" galvanized deck screws, then fully tighten the screws at the top ends.

Step J: Build the Swing A-frame & Beam

NOTE: refer to Figure 5 on page 456 for the A-frame and beam assembly.

1. On the swing side of the clubhouse, install two angled metal braces extending from the lower beam to the posts using ⁵⁄₁₆ × 1½" galvanized lag screws.

2. Cut two 4 × 4 A-frame legs at 96" and one 2 × 4 A-frame brace at 41".

H. *Position a support block flush with the bottom of the side decking and attach to the lower beam with a 3" deck screw. Attach the side decking to the block with 2½" deck screws.*

I. *Install stringers between the posts in the clubhouse tower over any opening that does not house any accessories. Fasten to the posts with deck screws.*

3. Lay the legs on a flat surface, and mark on top at 1¾ and 44¾"—this will be the inside face of the A-frame when the legs are installed. At the 1¾" mark, drill ⅜" through holes centered on the legs. At the 44¾" mark, drill ½"-deep counterbore holes using a 1⅜" spade bit, then drill ⅜" through holes. Also drill ⅜" through holes in each end of the brace, 1¾" in from each end.

4. Attach the metal gusset to the inside faces of the legs so the gusset flange faces up. Align the top screw holes of the gusset with the 1¾" through holes on the ends of the legs. Attach the gusset with 4" galvanized carriage bolts so the washers and nuts are at the inside face. Loosely tighten each nut.

5. Position the brace against the outside face of the legs, aligning the through holes of the brace with the through holes at 44¾" on the legs. Fasten the brace to the legs with 5" galvanized carriage bolts, so the washers and nuts fit in the counterbore hole. Loosely tighten each nut.

6. Adjust the A-frame legs to create a symmetrical triangle, then tighten all the nuts. Drill a 7⁄32" pilot hole into each leg at the two remaining screw holes in the gusset, then secure with ⅜ × 1½" galvanized lag screws with washers.

7. Cut two 4 × 4 swing beams at 113". Clamp the beams together, then measure and mark at 5¼", 19¾", 26⅞", 34", 49⅜", 56½", 63⅝", 79", 86⅛", 93¼", and 107¾".

8. Drill 1½"-deep counterbore holes using a 1⅜" spade bit at the marks for 19¾", 34", 49⅜", 63⅝", 79", and 93¼", then ⅜" holes through the beams at all of the locations. Also drill ¼" weep holes from the bottom edge of each counterbore hole out to the outer face of the beam for water drainage.

9. At the three pilot holes between the counterbore holes, use 7½" galvanized carriage bolts with washers to fasten the beams together.

10. Turn the beam so the bottom faces up. Install swing hanger clamps at the six counterbore pilot holes (refer to Figure 6 on page 456). Align each hanger clamp and fasten to the bottom beam with #10 × 1½" sheet metal screws. Secure the hangers at the top beam with washers and nuts.

Step K: Install the Swing A-frame & Beam

1. On the swing beam side of the clubhouse, run a level string between the two ladders at the bottom of their outside legs. Measure along the string from one end and mark the midpoint with masking tape.

2. Place the double swing beam on the ground, perpendicular to and 3½" out from the midpoint of the string. Check that the beam is square with the string using a framing square.

3. Drive a fence stake in the ground 1½" away from the far end of the beam. Position the A-frame in front of the stake so it is perpendicular to and centered on the swing beam using a framing square. Secure the A-frame to the stake with string.

4. With a helper, lift the beam into place, with one end on the gusset and the other end on the top beam of the clubhouse.

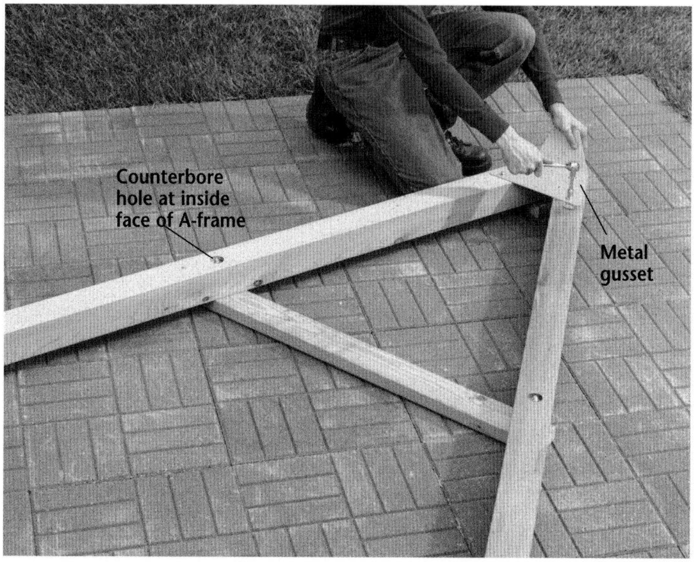

J. *After adjusting the A-frame legs to form a symmetrical triangle, fully tighten all the carriage bolts and install ⅜ × 1½" lag screws at the remaining screw holes in the gusset to secure the A-frame.*

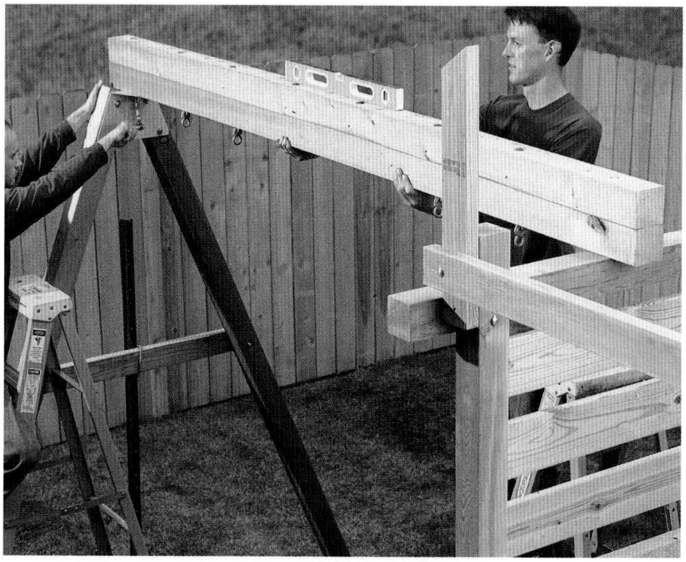

K. *With someone's help, lift the double swing beam into position. Make sure it is level and square, then fasten it to the gusset with a 7½" carriage bolt and to the clubhouse with an 11" carriage bolt.*

5. Check that the swing beam is square and level, then align the hole in the end of the beam with the screw hole on the top of the gusset and fasten using a 7½" galvanized carriage bolt and washer.

6. At the clubhouse, make sure the beam is centered on and squared to the top beam. Using the pilot hole in the beam as a guide, drill a ⅜" pilot hole through the top beam. Fasten together using an 11" galvanized carriage bolt with washer.

7. Position angled metal braces to connect the swing beam and top beam. Drill ⁷⁄₃₂" pilot holes, then fasten using ⅜ × 1½" galvanized lag screws with washers.

8. Drill a ⁷⁄₃₂" pilot hole into the bottom swing beam at the second screw hole of the gusset, then fasten using a ⅜ × 1½" galvanized lag screw. Attach an angled metal brace to the gusset and beam using a ¾" hex bolt, lock washer, and nut at the gusset, and drill a ⁷⁄₃₂" pilot hole at the beam location and use a ⅜ × 1½" galvanized lag screw.

9. Connect the beam to the A-frame legs using brace plates. Drill ⁷⁄₃₂" pilot holes, then fasten the plates using ⅜ × 1½" galvanized lag screws.

10. With the beam and A-frame in place, check to make sure the beam is level and the A-frame plumb. Cut and install a 96"-long 3 × 4 landscape timber leg support base, following the same techniques in step E.

Step L: Build the Rafters

1. Cut four 2 × 4 rafters at 39". Mark and cut one end of each at a 45° angle. Butt the angled ends of two rafters together, install an angle iron at the bottom edge of the joint, and fasten it using ¾" screws. Also center a 4" mending plate over the joint and fasten it with ¾" screws.

2. Place the rafter assemblies against the inside face of the roof supports, with the mending plate facing into the structure and so the top edge of the rafters are flush with the top of the roof supports. Clamp in place.

3. Drill pairs of ⁵⁄₁₆" pilot holes and fasten the rafters to the roof supports with 2½" galvanized deck screws.

Step M: Install the Roofing

1. Cut fourteen 1 × 6 tongue and groove cedar boards at 66". Position one board on top of the rafters, flush with the ends, and with the tongue pointing toward the peak. Allow the ends to overhang the outside edges of the rafters by 6" on both sides, then clamp in place. Drills pairs of ⁵⁄₁₆" pilot holes, then fasten with 2" galvanized deck screws.

3. Working toward the peak, position subsequent boards so the groove fits over the tongue of the previous board, and so they overhang the rafters by 6" on each end. Drills pairs of ⁵⁄₁₆" pilot holes, then fasten with 2" galvanized deck screws.

4. If the last board overhangs the peak, position the board and mark the backside at the peak, then rip to size. Repeat for the other side of the roof.

L. *Cut the ends of the rafters at 45° angles, butt the ends together, and secure the joint with an angle iron and a mending plate (INSET). Align the rafter assembly with the roof supports, and secure with deck screws.*

M. *Use tongue and groove cedar to cover the roof, fastening it to the rafters with deck screws. Allow the ends to overhang the rafters by 6".*

A play structure is most fun when it provides a range of options. A wide variety of play equipment is available, from simple favorites, such as swings and slides, to more elaborate equipment, such as gliders, horizontal ladders, cargo nets, and rock climbing walls.

Other accessory items are designed to make play areas safer. Handles and railings help to direct appropriate play routes, while shade walls and enclosures provide shaded areas for less active play. Most equipment and accessories are made of plastics or use powder-coat paints to provide nonslip, grippable surfaces.

Many of these items can be purchased at home centers or ordered directly from the manufacturer. Always follow the manufacturer's installation instructions when installing play structure accessories.

A sturdy slide is a play structure standard, providing a thrilling ride out of the clubhouse.

A shade wall shades the play area and provides a colorful alternative to wooden balusters or rails.

A glider is built to seat two, allowing children to swing together.

A rock climbing wall is a fun addition that creates a greater climbing challenge than a ladder.

Tree House

No other structure lends itself to outdoor play quite like a tree house. There's something magical about playing in a tree. There's also the added thrill of being able to play in a miniature house above the ground.

Tree houses come in all shapes, sizes, models, and designs, some more professional looking than others. While tree houses should be fun, they also need to be safe. The tree house featured here is both. The front half is open at the top to allow children to look out at their surroundings. The support system holds the tree house securely in place, the railing prevents falls, and the ladder ensures a safe entrance and exit. The roof is constructed with fiberglass panels that allow light to enter.

While almost any full-size tree will serve as a host for the tree house, there are a few important precautions to take. Make sure the tree has a strong base of at least 12" in diameter. It must be alive and healthy. If the leaves on the tree are brown and starting to wither, and it's not autumn yet, the tree could have a disease and should not be used. Choose a tree that doesn't produce a lot of sap so your children will not get covered in it. Caution your kids not to peel bark off the tree or it will eventually kill the tree.

This project calls for the tree house to sit six feet off the ground. You can adjust this height to suit your particular tree, but be careful not to place the structure too low or the diagonal braces will run into the ground before touching the tree. The diagonal braces are tricky to cut. Nevertheless, it's important they are done correctly and properly fastened to the tree house and the tree.

Material List

DESCRIPTION	QTY./SIZE	MATERIAL
Support System		
Timber diagonal support	4 @ 8'-0"	4 × 6 treated timber
Spikes	8 @ 12"	Timber to tree (2 per timber)
Adjustable angles	8	Simpson S50
Floor Framing		
Rim joists	7 @ 8'-0"	2 × 8 treated
Rim joist	1 @ 10'-0"	2 × 8 treated
Joists and joist supports	8 @ 8'-0"	2 × 8 treated
Joist hangers	4 with nails	Simpson U26
Beam hangers	4 with nails	Simpson U26-2
Spikes	6 @ 8"	Support to tree (3 per support)
Spikes	6 @ 8"	Joists to tree (3 per joist)
Decking	17 @ 8'-0"	2 × 6 treated
Wall Framing		
Girts/studs/top plates	8 @ 8'-0"	2 × 4 SPF construction grade no. 2
Posts	9 @ 6'-0"	4 × 4 treated
Metal connectors	9 with nails	Posts to joist rims – Simpson 88L
Metal connectors	9 with nails	Posts to roof timbers – Simpson 88L
Roof Framing		
Timber beams	4 @ 8'-0"	4 × 6 treated
Rafters	2 @ 8'-0"	2 × 6 SPF construction grade no. 2
Metal connectors	8 with nails	Beam to beam – Simpson A34
Spikes	6 @ 8"	Rafters to tree (3 per rafter)
Roofing panels	5 @ 2'-0" × 10'-0"	Corrugated fiberglass panels
Closure strips	4 @ 9'-0"	Wood strips

DESCRIPTION	QTY./SIZE	MATERIAL
Ladder		
Stringer	2 @ 10'-0"	2 × 8 treated
Rungs	3 @ 8'-0"	2 × 6 treated
Ladder footing	1 @ 4'-0"	2 × 12 treated
Tread clip	18	1½" × 1½" × 5" 16-gauge angle
Galvanized wood screws	120 @ 1¼"	Angle to treads
Exterior Finishes		
Siding	40 @ 8'-0"	1 × 6 T&G V-JT cedar boards
Pickets	15 @ 8'-0"	1 × 6 S4S cedar
Galvanized wood screws	120 @ 1¼"	Pickets
Railing		
Top rail	2 @ 9'-0"	2 × 6 S4S cedar
Galvanized wood screws	75 @ 1½"	Railing
Miscellaneous		
Galvanized box nails	16d – 3 pounds	Lumber to lumber
Box nails	8d – 2 pounds	Lumber to lumber
Finish nails	6d	Closure strips to rafters
Galvanized finish nails	6d – 1½ pound	Siding
Galvanized	96 @ 1¼"	Panels to closure strips hex-headed panel screws
Galvanized wood screws	210 @ 2½"	Decking

HOW TO BUILD A TREE HOUSE
Step A: Install the Joist Supports

1. Measure 63¼" from the bottom of the tree and make a mark. NOTE: this measurement is for a deck height of 72" from the ground. If you want a different deck height, adjust as necessary.

2. Cut a 2 × 8 joist support at 96" using a circular saw. Place the top edge of the support flush with the mark on the tree, centering the support with the middle of the tree. Drive an 8" spike through the support into the tree, but don't nail it tight. Place a level on the top edge of the support, level it, then finish driving the spike. Nail two more spikes through the support.

3. Use a level to mark the location of the second support on the opposite side of the tree. Tack the 120" rim joist support in place at the mark, level it, then fasten it to the tree using three 8" spikes. The ends of this support should run past the ends of the first support.

4. Place a large framing square at the end of the first support and mark the end on the second support. Do this on each end, then cut the second support at the marks using a circular saw.

Step B: Build the Floor Frame

1. Cut eight 2 × 8 joists at 90". Place one joist on each side of the tree, perpendicular to the supports. Use a carpenter's square to square the joists with the supports and each other. Center the joists over the supports, then tack them to the tree using 16d nails.

2. Place a second joist against each joist on the tree, flush on the top and ends, and drive three 8" spikes through the second joist, through the first joist, and into the tree. Facenail the sets of joists together using 16d box nails driven at a slight angle so they don't come out the other side.

3. Center a joist over the supports so the outside edge of the joist is 1½" from the ends of the supports. Toenail the joist to the supports using 8d box nails. Do this on the front and back sides.

4. Cut two rim joists at 93" and place them over the ends of the joists installed in the last step. Keep the joists flush at the top. Endnail the joists together using 16d nails. Install beam hangers on the rim joists where they intersect the joists on the tree. Fasten the hangers using joist hanger nails.

5. Measure the distance between the joists nailed to the tree and the joists at the ends of the supports. Mark the right and left side rim joists at the midpoints and install joist hangers over the marks using joist hanger nails. The nails will go through the joist, but will be covered by the outside rim joist.

6. Set joists in the hangers, then fasten them in place using 1½" joist hanger nails.

NOTE: Don't stand on the frame until the diagonal supports are installed.

Step C: Attach Diagonal Supports & Complete the Floor Frame

1. Cut a 45° angle on one end of the four 4 × 6 timber diagonal supports. Mark the angled ends following the Diagonal Support drawing (on opposite page), then carefully cut the angles and notches using a jigsaw and miter saw.

2. Set a support under a corner of the floor framing and mark the other end where it crosses the tree. Cut a 45° angle at the mark. NOTE: You may have to set the support in place, mark the end, and make the cut several times before finding a perfect fit. Be careful not to cut the brace too short. Fasten the support

FLOOR FRAMING PLAN

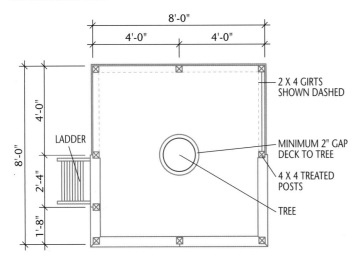

A. *Fasten the second support in place, level with the first one, then cut the ends flush with the first support.*

in place by driving 16d nails through the joists into the support and driving two 12" spikes through the support into the tree. Reinforce the connections by fastening LS50 adjustable angles to the support and tree and to the support and rim joist using 8d nails. The angles adjust from 0 to 135°. You can bend the angle one time only. Do this for all four corners.

3. Cut two rim joists at 93" and place them on the outside of the front and rear joists. These rim joists sit on the edge of the 2 × 8 supports. Align the ends of the rim joists with the outside edges of the side rim joists. Facenail the rim joists to the front and back joists and endnail to the side rim joists using 16d nails.

4. Cut two more rim joists at 96" and facenail them to the side rim joists, overlapping the ends of the joists installed in the last step. Nail the corners together using 16d nails.

Step D: Install Corner Posts & Timber Beams

1. Cut two 4 × 4 back corner posts at 66" and two front corner posts at 54½" using a reciprocating saw.

2. Set a piece of plywood over the floor framing to stand on. Place the back posts in the rear corners and the front posts in the front corners, flush with the outside edges of the rim joists. Plumb the posts using a level, then toenail them to the joists using 16d nails. Reinforce the connections by fastening a Simpson 88L metal connector to each post and outer rim joist using 16d nails.

3. Cut two 4 × 6 timber beams at 96". Set one beam on the rear corner posts and the other beam on the front corner posts, flush with the outside edges of the posts. Toenail the beams in place, then fasten Simpson 88L metal connectors to the posts and the beams.

4. Nail 2 × 4 scrap lumber on the ends of the beams installed in the last step. Clamp a 4 × 6 side beam against the ends of the front and rear beams using the scrap lumber, making sure the ends of the side beam extend past the inside edge of the two installed beams. Align the side beam with the top inside face of the front and rear beams, then draw a line along the inside edge of the front and rear beams onto the side beam. Do this on both front and rear sides.

DIAGONAL SUPPORT

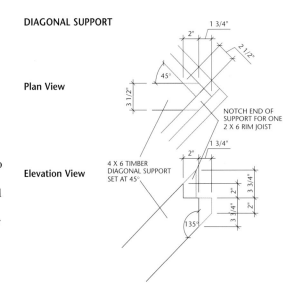

Plan View

Elevation View

1 3/4"
2"
2 1/2"
45°
3 1/2"
NOTCH END OF
SUPPORT FOR ONE
2 X 6 RIM JOIST
1 3/4"
2"
4 X 6 TIMBER
DIAGONAL SUPPORT
SET AT 45°
2"
3 3/4"
3 3/4"
2"
135°

B. *Mark the midpoints between the joists, install joist hangers, then set the joists in the hangers and nail them in place.*

C. *Notch one end of each support brace to fit under the rim joist. Fasten one end under a corner of the floor and the other end to the tree.*

LEFT SIDE FRAMING

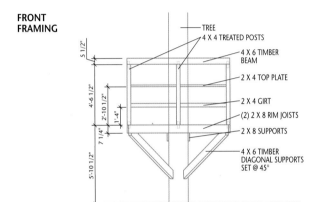

- TREE
- 4 X 4 TREATED POSTS
- 4 X 6 TIMBER BEAM
- 2 X 4 TOP PLATES
- 5 1/2"
- 5'-6"
- 2'-8 1/4"
- 5'-0 3/4"
- 4'-6 1/2"
- 2'-10 1/2"
- 1'-4"
- 7 1/4"
- 5'-10 1/2"
- 2 X 4 GIRT
- 2 X 4 GIRT
- (2) 2 X 8 RIM JOISTS
- 2 X 8 SUPPORTS
- 4 X 6 TIMBER DIAGONAL SUPPORTS SET @ 45°

RIGHT SIDE FRAMING

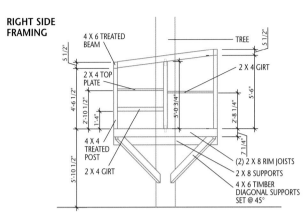

- 4 X 6 TREATED BEAM
- TREE
- 5 1/2"
- 2 X 4 GIRT
- 2 X 4 TOP PLATE
- 5'-6"
- 4'-6 1/2"
- 2'-10 1/2"
- 1'-4"
- 5'-0 3/4"
- 2'-8 1/4"
- 7 1/4"
- 4 X 4 TREATED POST
- 2 X 4 GIRT
- 5'-10 1/2"
- (2) 2 X 8 RIM JOISTS
- 2 X 8 SUPPORTS
- 4 X 6 TIMBER DIAGONAL SUPPORTS SET @ 45°

FRONT FRAMING

- TREE
- 4 X 4 TREATED POSTS
- 5 1/2"
- 4'-6 1/2"
- 2'-10 1/2"
- 1'-4"
- 7 1/4"
- 5'-10 1/2"
- 4 X 6 TIMBER BEAM
- 2 X 4 TOP PLATE
- 2 X 4 GIRT
- (2) 2 X 8 RIM JOISTS
- 2 X 8 SUPPORTS
- 4 X 6 TIMBER DIAGONAL SUPPORTS SET @ 45°

D. *Place a side beam between the front and back beams, mark the side beam, cut it to length, then fasten it in place using metal connectors.*

BACK FRAMING

- POST TO BEAM LOAD DOWN CLIPS
- TREE
- 4 X 4 TREATED POSTS
- 5 1/2"
- 1'-10 3/4"
- 1 1/2"
- 8"
- 5'-6"
- 2'-8 1/4"
- 1 1/2"
- 7 1/4"
- 1'-5" 1'-4" 2'-6" 1'-4" 1'-5"
- 4 X 6 TIMBER BEAM
- 2 X 4 STUD
- 2 X 4 GIRTS
- (2) 2 X 8 RIM JOISTS
- 2 X 8 SUPPORTS
- 4 X 6 TIMBER DIAGONAL SUPPORTS SET @ 45°
- POST HOLD DOWN CLIPS

E. *Mark the middle posts where they cross the timber beams. Cut the posts at the marks, then fasten them in place using metal connectors.*

5. Clamp a 2 × 6 rafter on the end of the beams and repeat the last step to draw a line onto the rafters along the inside edge of the beams. Cut the rafter at the marks using a circular saw, then use it as a template to mark and cut the second rafter. Place the rafters on either side of the tree, flush with the top of the timber beams. Toenail the rafters to the beams using 16d nails. Drive three 8" spikes through each rafter into the tree.

6. Cut the side beams at the marks using a reciprocating saw. Set the side beams in place between the front and back beams. Toenail the beams in place. Install Simpson A34 metal connectors on the inside corners of the beams using 8d × 1½" nails.

Step E: Attach the Middle Posts

1. Cut a 4 × 4 post at 54½". Mark the center point between the front corner posts and install the post over the mark. Align the outside of the post with the outside edges of the rim joist and the timber beam. Use a level to plumb the post, then toenail it in place. Secure the post to the rim joist and timber beam using Simpson 88L metal connectors.

2. Cut a post at 66" and install it at the center of the back side by repeating step 1.

3. Place a post at the center of the right side. Keep the bottom end on the rim joist, plumb the post using a level, and mark along the top edge of the post where it crosses the timber beam. Cut the post at the mark, then toenail it to the rim joist and the timber beam. Secure the connections by installing metal connectors. Repeat this step for the left side.

4. On the left side, measure 24" from the front edge of the middle post and mark the rim joist. Set a post in front of the mark, then mark the top of the post where it crosses the timber beam. Cut the post at the mark, then install it at the mark on the rim joist using metal connectors.

Step F: Build the Floor

1. Use a jigsaw to cut a 3½ × 3½" notch on each end of the first deck board to fit around the posts. Place the board on the right side of the tree house, aligning the ends with the outside edges of the rim joists, then mark the board at the middle post location. Cut a 3½ × 3½" notch at the mark.

2. Set the first deck board in place. Drill two ³⁄₃₂" pilot holes at both ends of the deck board, then fasten it to the rim joists using ½" galvanized wood screws. Install two screws in the deck board where it crosses each joist and every 16" along the side.

3. Fasten the remaining boards to the frame. Since the boards are precut to 96", they should align with the outside edges of the front and back rim joists. Space the boards about ⅛" apart. Drill ³⁄₃₂" pilot holes in the ends of the boards where they cross the rim joists. Fasten each board using two screws per joist. If necessary, add blocking to support ends of boards that fall in line with middle posts.

4. Every three or four boards, measure the distance to the outside edge of the left side rim joist. Take a measurement from both ends of the board to make sure they're equal. Make sure the distance to the edge will allow the last board to sit flush

F. *Install the decking, cutting the boards to fit around the tree and posts. Fasten the boards to the joists using galvanized wood screws.*

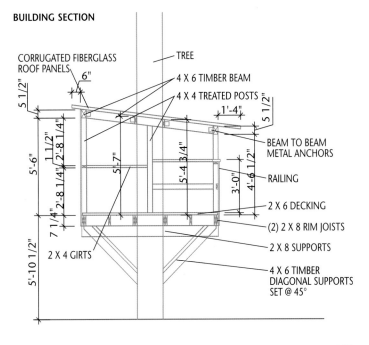

BUILDING SECTION

CORRUGATED FIBERGLASS ROOF PANELS

6"

TREE

4 X 6 TIMBER BEAM

4 X 4 TREATED POSTS

5 1/2"

1'-4"

5 1/2"

BEAM TO BEAM METAL ANCHORS

RAILING

2 X 6 DECKING

(2) 2 X 8 RIM JOISTS

2 X 8 SUPPORTS

4 X 6 TIMBER DIAGONAL SUPPORTS SET @ 45°

5 1/2"

5'-6"

11 1/2"

2'-8 1/4"

2'-8 1/4"

5'-7"

5'-4 3/4"

3'-0"

4'-6 1/2"

7 1/4"

5'-10 1/2"

2 X 4 GIRTS

FLOOR PLAN

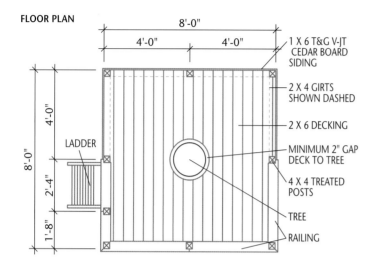

1 X 6 T&G V-JT
CEDAR BOARD
SIDING

2 X 4 GIRTS
SHOWN DASHED

2 X 6 DECKING

MINIMUM 2" GAP
DECK TO TREE

4 X 4 TREATED
POSTS

TREE

RAILING

LADDER

with the outside edge of the rim joist. If needed, make slight adjustments to the spacing between deck boards.

5. Measure and mark each board to fit around the tree. Keep the decking 2" away from the tree. Cut the boards at the marks using a jigsaw then install them.

Step G: Lay Out the Stringers

1. Measure from the top of the deck and mark the posts on either side of the ladder opening at 18¾" and 34½".

2. Cut an 80° angle at the bottom of a 2 × 8 stringer using a circular saw. Set the stringer inside the ladder opening so the edge of the stringer butts against the deck and crosses the inside edge of the post at the 18¾" mark. Mark the stringer along the inside edge of the post and along the 34½" mark on the post.

3. Remove the stringer and cut it at the marks. Using the stringer as a template, place it over the second 2 × 8 stringer, make sure the edges are flush, trace the first stringer onto the second one, and cut along the marks.

4. Outline the rise and run locations for the rungs on the stringers following illustration G. The ladder is assembled and installed in step K.

NOTE: These measurements are for a 72" deck height. If your deck height is different, make the necessary adjustments to your stringers.

Step H: Install the Girts and Top Plates

1. Cut nine 2 × 4 girts and three 2 × 4 top plates at 42¾" using a circular saw.

2. On the front side of the tree house, measure from the top of the deck boards and mark the posts at 14½" and 33". Set a girt on-edge above the 14½" marks on each side of the middle post.

Align the outside edge of the girts with the outside edges of the posts, then toenail the girts in place with 8d nails.

3. Set a top plate flat above the 33" marks on both sides of the middle post. Align the outside edges of the plates and the posts, then toenail the plates in place.

4. On the back side, measure from the deck and mark the posts at 30¾" and 40¼". Position girts flat and toenail them to the posts above the marks, keeping the outside edges flush.

5. Cut four 2 × 4 studs at 8". Measure from the outside edge of the corner posts and mark the girts installed in the last step at 15½" and 33". Fasten the studs at the marks using 16d nails.

6. On the right side, mark the front and middle posts at 14½" and 33" above the deck. Toenail a girt on-edge above the 14½" marks on the front and middle posts. Toenail a top plate flat above the 33" marks on the posts. On the back and middle posts, make a mark 30¾" above the deck. Toenail a girt flat to the posts above the marks.

7. On the left side, mark the back and middle posts at 30¾" above the deck and install a girt flat above the marks.

8. Cut one 2 × 4 top plate at 24" and one at 15¼". Cut a 2 × 4 girt at 15¼". Mark the two middle rails and the front rail 14½" and 33" from the top of the deck. Install the 24" top plate flat between the two middle posts above the 33" marks. Install the 15¼" top plate flat between the middle and front corner posts at the same height. Install the girt on-edge above the 14½" marks.

Step I: Install the Siding

1. Starting in a back corner, place a 1 × 6 tongue-and-groove cedar board flush with the outside edge of the post and the bottom edge of the rim joist. Allow the top to extend past the timber beam. Nail the board at the top, bottom, and girt locations using 6d galvanized finish nails. Nail the board to the corner post every 16".

2. Install the next board, fitting together the tongue-and-groove joint. Install the remaining boards, checking every third board with a level to make sure it's plumb and making any necessary adjustments in small increments. Install the siding on the back ends of the left and right sides of the tree house, overlapping the siding at the back corners. Rip the last board on the left and right sides to cover half of the middle posts.

3. Cut the siding flush with the top edge of the timber beams and cut out the window openings using a reciprocating saw.

4. Cut the 1 × 6 cedar picket boards for the front at 43¼" using a circular saw. Cut two boards from each piece of lumber. Align the first board with the outside edge of a front corner post and the bottom edge of the rim joist, drill ³⁄₃₂" pilot holes, then insert 1¼" wood screws. Install the remaining boards on the front and sides 6" on center, giving ½" gap between boards.

5. Butt a cedar board against the tongue-and-groove siding on the right side middle post, and align the last board on the left side with the inside edge of the front ladder support.

LEFT SIDE ELEVATION

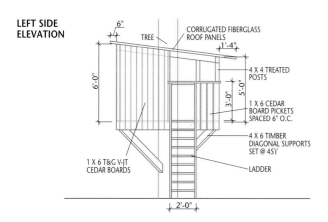

6"

TREE

CORRUGATED FIBERGLASS ROOF PANELS

1'-4"

4 X 4 TREATED POSTS

6'-0"

3'-0"

5'-0"

1 X 6 CEDAR BOARD PICKETS SPACED 6" O.C.

4 X 6 TIMBER DIAGONAL SUPPORTS SET @ 45Ý

1 X 6 T&G V-JT CEDAR BOARDS

LADDER

2'-0"

RIGHT SIDE ELEVATION

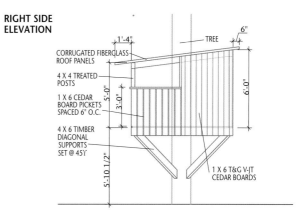

TREE

6"

CORRUGATED FIBERGLASS ROOF PANELS

4 X 4 TREATED POSTS

1'-4"

5'-0"

3'-0"

6'-0"

1 X 6 CEDAR BOARD PICKETS SPACED 6" O.C.

4 X 6 TIMBER DIAGONAL SUPPORTS SET @ 45Ý

5'-10 1/2"

1 X 6 T&G V-JT CEDAR BOARDS

FRONT ELEVATION

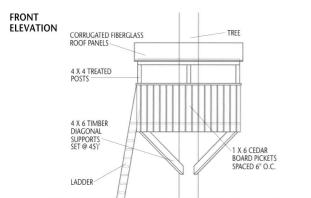

CORRUGATED FIBERGLASS ROOF PANELS

TREE

4 X 4 TREATED POSTS

4 X 6 TIMBER DIAGONAL SUPPORTS SET @ 45Ý

1 X 6 CEDAR BOARD PICKETS SPACED 6" O.C.

LADDER

BACK ELEVATION

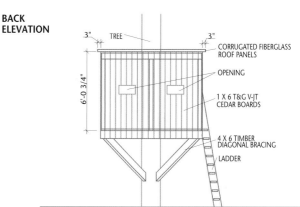

3"

TREE

3"

CORRUGATED FIBERGLASS ROOF PANELS

OPENING

6'-0 3/4"

1 X 6 T&G V-JT CEDAR BOARDS

4 X 6 TIMBER DIAGONAL BRACING

LADDER

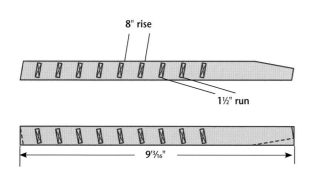

8" rise

1½" run

9¹³⁄₁₆"

G. Cut the stringers and mark them with the rise and run locations for the ladder rungs.

H. Install the girts and top plates between the rails on all four sides of the tree house.

I. *Butt the tongue-and-groove siding and the cedar board together at the middle post on the right side.*

ROOF FRAMING PLAN

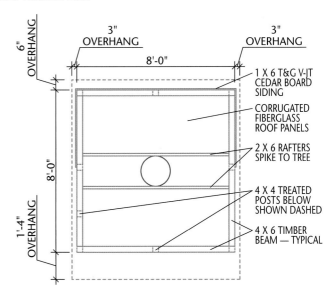

Step J: Attach the Roof

1. Cut four closure strips at 98". Place the closure strips over the rafters and timber beams so they have a 1" overhang on each end. Attach the strips using 6d finish nails.

2. Place the first fiberglass roof panel over the closure strips so it overhangs the side by 3". The panel should overhang the back by approximately 6" and the front by 16", depending on how the panel sits in the closure strips. The panels are 120" long, so you have an extra two inches on the ends to work with. Attach the panel by drilling ⅛" holes through the peaks, not the troughs, and inserting 1¼" hex-headed panel screws with rubber gaskets at every fourth or fifth peak.

3. Set the next panel in place, overlapping the end by 3 to 4". Mark the panel where it crosses the tree. Cut out the mark, allowing a 3" gap for the tree, using a jigsaw. Apply caulk to the last trough of the first panel, then set the second panel in place, drill pilot holes, and insert screws. Install the remaining panels the same way.

Step K: Build & Install the Ladder

1. Attach tread clips to the stringers, flush with the bottom of each rung outline. Drill ³⁄₃₂" pilot holes through the holes in the clips and fasten them to the stringers using 1¼" wood screws.

2. Cut nine 2 × 6 ladder rungs at 20½". This allows a ¼" gap on each end for the tread clips. Keep the outside edges of the stringers 24" apart and fasten the rungs to the clips using 1¼" wood screws.

3. Cut a 2 × 12 ladder footing at 36". Center the footing from back to front and side to side on the bottom of the ladder. Drill pilot holes into the footing, then fasten the footing to the stringers using 2½" wood screws.

4. Set the ladder in place with half of the footing below grade. Attach the ladder to the posts using 16d nails.

Step L: Attach the Top Rails

1. Cut two 2 × 6 top rails at 49½". Cut one end square and one end with a 45° angle, using a circular saw. Cut a top rail at 99" with a 45° angle on both ends.

2. Mark the ends of the rails following the Top Rail Corner and Top Rail @ Wall illustrations and cut the notches using a jigsaw. Cut a notch in the left side top rail for the post at the top of the ladder.

3. Place the rails on the top plates, fitting the notches around the posts. Make sure the angles fit together tightly. Make any necessary cuts to get a tight fit, then secure the top rails in place by drilling pilot holes and inserting 2½" galvanized wood screws.

Step M: Celebrate with Your Kids!

Bring blankets and pillows and have a sleep out. Ghost stories are optional.

LADDER DETAIL

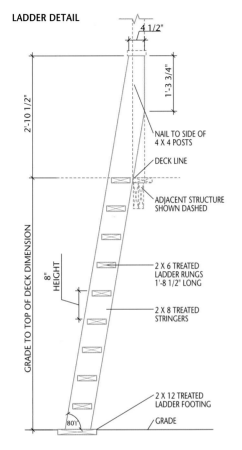

4 1/2"

1'-3 3/4"

2'-10 1/2"

NAIL TO SIDE OF
4 X 4 POSTS

DECK LINE

ADJACENT STRUCTURE
SHOWN DASHED

GRADE TO TOP OF DECK DIMENSION

8"
HEIGHT

2 X 6 TREATED
LADDER RUNGS
1'-8 1/2" LONG

2 X 8 TREATED
STRINGERS

2 X 12 TREATED
LADDER FOOTING

GRADE

80°

TOP RAIL @ WALL

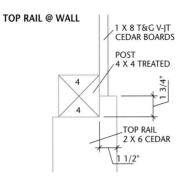

1 X 8 T&G V-JT
CEDAR BOARDS

POST
4 X 4 TREATED

4

4

1 3/4"

TOP RAIL
2 X 6 CEDAR

1 1/2"

TOP RAIL CORNER

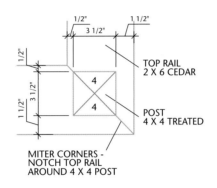

1/2"

3 1/2"

1 1/2"

1/2"

1 1/2"

3 1/2"

TOP RAIL
2 X 6 CEDAR

4

4

POST
4 X 4 TREATED

MITER CORNERS -
NOTCH TOP RAIL
AROUND 4 X 4 POST

RAIL DETAIL

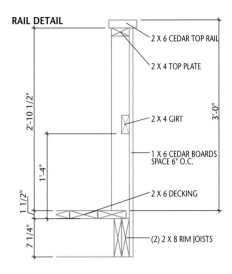

2 X 6 CEDAR TOP RAIL

2 X 4 TOP PLATE

2 X 4 GIRT

1 X 6 CEDAR BOARDS
SPACE 6" O.C.

2 X 6 DECKING

(2) 2 X 8 RIM JOISTS

2'-10 1/2"

3'-0"

1'-4"

1 1/2"

7 1/4"

LADDER STRINGER

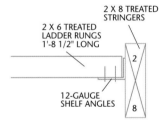

2 X 8 TREATED
STRINGERS

2 X 6 TREATED
LADDER RUNGS
1'-8 1/2" LONG

12-GAUGE
SHELF ANGLES

2

8

J. Cut the roof panel to fit around the tree, then set the panel in place over the first panel, drill pilot holes, and fasten the panel to the beams and rafters.

K. Assemble the ladder, then nail it to the insides of the posts.

L. Fit the top rails together at the angles so the posts fit inside the notches. Attach the rails to the top plates.

A-Frame Swing Set with Climbing Wall

An A-frame swing set is a staple on playgrounds and in backyards. It's a structure we remember from our childhoods and one we want our kids to remember as they grow up. A-frame swing sets are popular because they're easy to build, appeal to kids of every age group, and look nice in the yard.

One of the benefits of A-frame swing sets is that you can choose from a variety of accessories to include on them. While this particular A-frame contains a climbing wall, swings, and gym rings, there are a host of other options available, such as trapeze bar, child's telescope, steering wheel, and gliders, just to name a few.

Just as there are a lot of accessories for A-frames, there are also a lot of gussets and brackets for building the structure. The ones suggested in this project are similar to most types of hardware on the market.

TOOLS & MATERIALS

- ¼ × 4" galvanized eye bolts with washers and nuts (3)
- ⅜ × 5" galvanized carriage bolts with washers and nuts (12)
- ⅜ × 6" galvanized carriage bolts with washers and nuts (4)
- A-frame bracket (4)
- Truss bracket w/screws (2)
- ⁵⁄₁₆ × 7" swing hanger unit (6)

- Galvanized nails (8d, 10d)
- ¼ × 2" lag screws
- Fence stakes (2)
- Swings w/chairs (2)
- Gym rings (1 set)
- Climbing net
- Leg anchors (6)
- 2 × 6 × 96" cedar (2)
- 4 × 4 × 96" cedar (6)
- 4 × 6 × 168" cedar (1)
- Step ladder

- Hand maul or sledge hammer
- Basic tools (page 18)
- Drill
- Twist bit (¼", ⅜", ⁵⁄₁₆")
- Spade bit (¾", 1")
- String or tie wire
- Circular saw
- Clamps
- Ratchet wrench
- Reciprocating saw

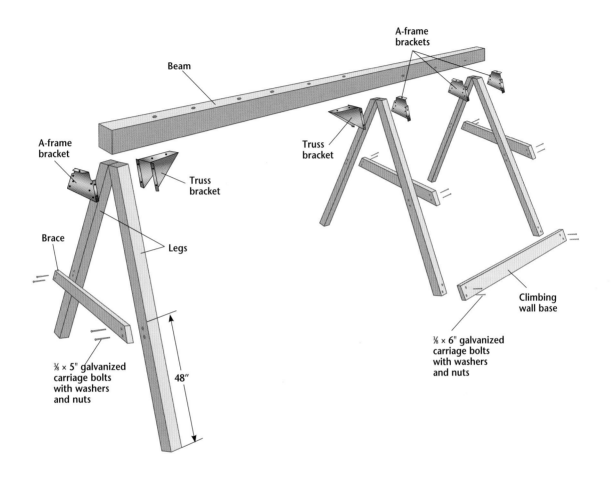

Beam

A-frame
brackets

A-frame
bracket

Truss
bracket

Truss
bracket

Brace

Legs

Climbing
wall base

⅜ × 5" galvanized
carriage bolts
with washers
and nuts

48″

⅜ × 6" galvanized
carriage bolts
with washers
and nuts

Cutting List

Part	Qty.	Size
Legs	6	4 x 4 x 96"
Beam	1	4 x 6 x 168"
Braces	3	2 x 6 cut to fit
Climbing wall base	1	2 x 6 x 54"

HOW TO BUILD AN A-FRAME SWING SET WITH CLIMBING WALL

Step A: Build the A-frames

1. Place a steel A-frame bracket at the top of a 4 × 4 leg so the inside of the leg is flush with the top of the bracket. (The outside of the leg will stick out over the top of the bracket.) Attach the bracket using 10d galvanized nails. Insert a second leg into the bracket and fasten it in place using 10d nails.

2. Turn the legs over and fasten a truss bracket at the top of the legs opposite the A-frame bracket using ¼ × 2" lag screws driven through pilot holes.

3. Turn the leg assembly over so the truss bracket is facing down. Measure 48" from the bottom of each leg and make a mark. Place a 2 × 6 brace across the legs with the top of the brace flush with the marks. Draw a line along each end of the brace where it crosses the outsides of the legs. Cut the brace at the lines using a circular saw.

4. Clamp the brace to the legs at the marks, flush with the outsides of the legs. Drill two ⅜" holes at each end of the brace, offsetting the holes. Drill all the way through the legs. Turn the frame over. Using the holes as a guide, drill ½"-deep recesses into the legs using a 1" spade bit. Insert ⅜ × 5" galvanized carriage bolts through the holes from the brace side. Place a washer and nut on the end of each bolt in the recesses. Tighten the nuts using a ratchet wrench.

5. Cut the top of the legs flush with the top of the A-frame and truss brackets using a reciprocating saw.

6. Repeat steps 1 through 5 to build another A-frame. Build a third one with an A-frame bracket on both sides of the leg assembly.

Step B: Prepare the Swing Beam

1. On the 4 × 6 beam, mark the locations for the swing hangers. From the end of the beam, mark the bottom of the beam at 18", 36", 50", 68", 82", and 100".

2. Drill a ⁵⁄₁₆" hole at each of the marks, centered from front to back. Insert a ⁵⁄₁₆ × 7" swing hanger unit into each hole so the nailing plate covers the hook at the end of the hanger. Fasten a washer and nut on the end of each bolt using a ratchet wrench. Attach the nailing plate to the beam using 8d galvanized nails.

3. Measuring from the same end of the beam as in step 1, make a mark for the middle leg assembly at 110½ and 114". Make a mark on the face of the beam at 121½", 137½", and 153½" for the climbing wall.

4. Drill ¼" holes at the marks for the climbing wall 2" from the bottom edge of the beam. Insert ¼ × 4" eye bolts through the holes and fasten them with washers and nuts.

Step C: Assemble the Structure

1. Drive two fence stakes in the ground 164" apart at the location you want to place the swing set. Stand an A-frame leg

A. Insert carriage bolts through the brace and legs. Fasten a washer and nut in the recesses, then tighten the nut.

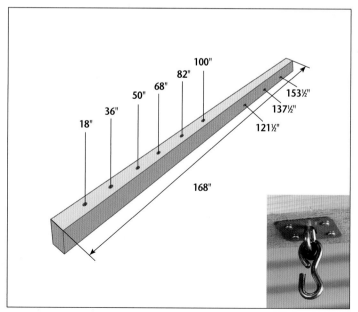

B. Drill pilot holes and install swing hangers and eye bolts (INSET) on the beam at the proper locations.

assembly with truss bracket in front of a stake (this is the swing set end) and the leg assembly with A-frame brackets on both sides in front of the other stake (this is the climbing wall end). Make sure the A-frames are level. The leg assemblies should be parallel with each other. Tie the assemblies to the stakes using thick string or wire.

2. Place the beam on top of the brackets on the leg assemblies. Center the beam so the ends overhang the outsides of the leg assemblies by 3½".

3. Fasten the beam in place by drilling pilot holes through the truss bracket and A-frame brackets and inserting ¼ × 2" lag screws.

4. Place the remaining leg assembly between the 110½ and 114" marks so the truss bracket faces the swing set side. Drill pilot holes through the truss bracket and insert ¼ × 2" lag screws.

5. Measure from one end of the climbing wall base and make a mark at 11", 21½", 32", and 43". Drill a ¾" hole at each mark, centered from top to bottom. NOTE: The climbing wall has three connections at the top, but four at the bottom.

6. Clamp the climbing wall base to the bottom front of the two legs that sit on either side of the climbing wall. Align the base

with the bottoms and the sides of the legs. Drill two ⅜" holes at both ends of the base through the legs, staggering the holes. Drill all the way through the legs. Insert a ⅜ × 6" galvanized carriage bolt through each hole and tighten a washer and nut on the end of each bolt.

Step D: Attach the Accessories

1. Attach the swings and gym rings to the swing hangers, adjusting the chains so the accessories are level and at a proper height. Once the swings and gym rings are in place, use pliers to crimp the S-hooks on the hangers closed.

2. Attach the top of the climbing net to the eye bolts on the beams. Fasten the bottom of the net to the climbing wall base by inserting the loose ends of the rope through the holes in the base, pulling the rope tight, then tying the ends in knots.

Step E: Anchor the Structure

1. Fasten an anchor bracket approximately 2" from the bottom of a leg using the screw that came with the bracket.

2. Drive the auger anchor into the ground an appropriate distance from the bracket. Once the anchor is firmly planted in the ground, connect it to the anchor bracket. Do this for all six legs to help ground the structure.

C. *Tie the leg assemblies to fence stakes, then center the beam on the brackets and fasten it in place.*

D. *Attach the swings, gym rings, and climbing wall to the hangers and eye bolts.*

E. *Fasten anchors to the legs of the structure to keep them from moving.*

477

Raised Garden Bed

Raised garden beds are attractive, functional, and easy to build and maintain. Especially if your yard has poor soil, raised beds are an ideal way to add ornamental or vegetable gardens to your outdoor home. If you build a raised bed properly, fill it with high-quality topsoil and water it frequently, growing healthy plants is practically foolproof.

In addition to their functional appeal, raised beds can serve as strong design features. They provide excellent opportunities to repeat materials used in other landscape elements. You can build raised beds from a variety of materials, including brick, cut stone, interlocking block, and landscape timbers. As you plan your raised bed, think about the types of plants you want to grow and the amount of sunlight they need.

Our version of a raised bed is 5 × 3 ft., 9" deep. To build this bed, you simply stack 4 × 4 cedar timbers flush on top of one another in three layers, and secure them with galvanized nails. Then drill holes into the frame to provide drainage, which helps keep the plants healthy. Once the frame is complete, line the bed and frame with landscape fabric to prevent weed growth and keep dirt from clogging the drainage holes. If you're planting shrubs or vegetables in your raised bed, put landscape fabric on the sides only, since these plants typically have deeper root growth than flowers.

TOOLS & MATERIALS

- Basic tools
- Reciprocating saw
- Drill with ³/₁₆", ½" bits
- Stakes and string
- 8-ft. 4 × 4 timbers (6)
- 6" galvanized nails
- Landscape fabric
- Galvanized roofing nails
- Topsoil
- Plantings
- Mulch
- Wood sealer/protectant
- Shovel
- Paintbrush

HOW TO BUILD A RAISED BED

Step A: Prepare the Site

1. Outline a 5 × 3 ft. area with stakes and string to mark the location of the bed. Use a shovel to remove all of the grass or weeds inside the area.

2. Dig a flat, 2"-deep, 6"-wide trench around the perimeter of the area, just inside the stakes.

Step B: Build & Level the Base

1. Measure and mark one 54" piece and one 30" piece on each 4 × 4. Hold each timber steady on sawhorses while you cut it using a reciprocating saw.

2. Coat each timber with a wood sealer/protectant. Let the sealer dry completely.

3. Lay the first row of the timbers in the trench. Position a level diagonally across a corner, then add or remove soil to level it. Repeat with remaining corners.

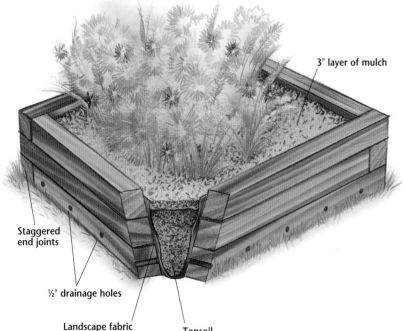

3" layer of mulch

Staggered end joints

½" drainage holes

Landscape fabric

Topsoil

TIP: PLANTING & MAINTAINING A RAISED GARDEN BED

Raised-bed gardens freeze faster and deeper than in-ground planting beds. Because the outside edges of the bed are more sensitive to temperature fluctuations, use this space for annuals and hardy perennials. Plant sensitive perennials and bulbs closer to the center, where the soil temperature is more stable.

If you live in an area with below-freezing winter temperatures, limit your plant choices to winter-hardy perennials, annual flowers, and vegetables.

Raised beds also dry out faster than garden beds and require frequent waterings. Water the bed whenever the top 2 to 4" of soil is dry (depending on the depth of your bed) and before you see the soil shrink away from the sides of the bed.

Step C: Complete the Raised Bed

1. Set the second layer of timbers in place, staggering the joints with the joint pattern in the first layer.

2. Drill ³⁄₁₆" pilot holes near the ends of the timbers, then drive in the galvanized barn nails.

3. Lay the third row of timbers, repeating the pattern of the first row to stagger the joints.

4. Drill pilot holes through the third layer, offsetting them to avoid hitting the underlying nails. Drive the nails through the pilot holes.

5. Drill ½" drainage holes, spaced every 2 ft., horizontally through the bottom layer of timbers.

6. Line the bed with strips of landscape fabric, overlapping the strips by 6".

7. Drive galvanized roofing nails through the fabric, attaching it to the timbers.

Step D: Fill with Soil & Plants

1. Fill the bed with topsoil to within 4" of the top. Tamp the soil lightly with a shovel.

2. Add plants, loosening their root balls before planting. Apply a 3" layer of mulch, and water the plants.

A. *Use a shovel to remove the grass inside the outline, then dig a trench for the first row of timbers.*

B. *Level timbers in the trench, then lay the next layer, staggering the joints. Drill holes and drive nails through them.*

C. *Place the third layer of landscape timbers over the second, staggering the joints. Secure the timbers in place with nails. Drill 1" drainage holes through the bottom row of the timbers. Line the bed with landscape fabric.*

D. *Fill the bed with topsoil, then plant your garden. Apply a 3" layer of mulch, and water the garden.*

Fire Pit

A fire pit creates a unique space for enjoying fun and safe recreational fires. When determining a location for a fire pit, choose a spot where the ground is relatively flat and even, and at least 25 ft. from your home, garage, shed, or any other fixed, combustible structures in your yard. It is also important that a garden hose or other extinguishing device be accessible at the location.

In this project, two courses of 6" manhole block are used to create a fire pit with a 26" interior diameter, ideal for backyard settings within city limits. Manhole blocks are designed specifically to create rounded tunnels and walls and can be purchased from most concrete block manufacturers.

Three ¾" gaps have been factored into this design to act as air vents, allowing the natural airflow to stoke the fire. This layout makes the circumference of the second course roughly ½" smaller than the first. A slightly thicker layer of surface-bonding cement is added to the top course to make up the difference.

Surface-bonding cement starts out as a white paste and can be tinted to match or complement any color of capstone. The 8 × 16" landscape pavers used here are cut at angles to allow 10 pieces to fit around the rim of the fire pit (see illustration on next page).

There are usually heavy restrictions for pit fires within city limits, regarding pit size, seasonal burning, waste burning, and more. Many municipalities also require that you purchase a recreational burning permit issued by an inspector from the fire department. Check with your local building department for restrictions specific to your area.

When not in use or during winter months, you may want to cover the top of the fire pit to prevent damage that may occur in inclement weather.

Building a fire pit in your yard can transform your space from an open expanse, to a cozy, social gathering place.

NOTE: It is important to allow your fire pit to cure for at least 30 days before building a fire in it. Heat can cause concrete with a high moisture content to greatly expand and contract, causing the material to severely crack or fragment.

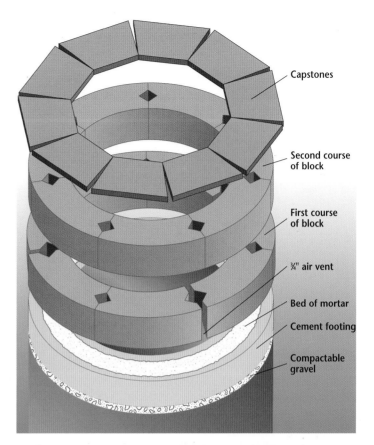

TOOLS & MATERIALS

- Hammer or hand maul
- Tape measure
- Shovel
- Hand tamp
- Wheelbarrow or mixing box
- 2 × 4
- Mason's trowel
- Spray bottle
- Jointing tool
- Square-end trowel

- Tuck-point trowel
- Circular saw with an abrasive masonry blade
- Eye & ear protection
- Wire brush
- 2 × 2 wooden stakes (2)
- Mason's string
- Spray paint
- Compactable gravel
- 60-lb. concrete (12)
- Sheet plastic

- 6" manhole blocks
- ¾" wood spacers (3)
- Chalk
- Refractory mortar
- Surface-bonding cement
- Mortar tinting agent
- ½" plywood
- 8 × 16" landscape pavers (10)

HOW TO BUILD A FIRE PIT

Step A: Excavate the Site

1. Use a hammer or a hand maul to drive a wooden stake into the centerpoint of the planned fire pit location. Then drive a temporary stake into the ground 10½" from the center stake.

2. Tie a mason's string to the center stake—the string should be just long enough to reach the temporary stake. Hold or tie a can of spray paint to the end of the string. Pull the string taut and spray paint a circle on the ground.

3. Remove the temporary stake and drive it into the ground 22½" from the center stake. Pull the string taut, and spray a second circle on the ground.

4. Strip away the grass between the two circles and dig a trench 10" deep.

5. Fill the base of the trench with 2" of compactable gravel. Tamp the gravel thoroughly.

Step B: Pour the Footing

1. Mix concrete in a wheelbarrow or mixing box and shovel it into the trench until the concrete reaches ground level. Work the concrete with a shovel to remove any air pockets.

2. Screed the surface of the concrete by dragging a short 2 × 4 along the top of the natural form. Add concrete to any low areas and screed the surface again. Finish the concrete with a trowel.

3. When the concrete is hard to the touch, cover it with a sheet of plastic and let it cure for 2 to 3 days. Remove the plastic and let the concrete cure for an additional week.

4. Fill center of the concrete circle with compactable gravel.

Step C: Lay the First Course

1. When the concrete has sufficiently cured, lay out the first course of 6" manhole blocks with three ¾" gaps for air vents using ¾" wood spacers.

A. *Outline the location of the footing using spray paint and a piece of string. Then dig a circular trench 10" deep.*

481

2. Mark the internal and external circumference of the first course on the footing with chalk, and remove the blocks. Take note of any low or high spots on the footing, remembering that low spots can be leveled out with extra mortar at the base.

3. Mix a batch of refractory mortar and lightly mist the footing area with water. Throw a bed of mortar on the misted area, covering only the area inside the reference lines.

4. Set a manhole block into the bed of mortar, centering it on the footing and the chalk reference lines. Press the block into the mortar until the joint is approximately ⅜" thick. Place the second block directly against the first block with no spacing between the blocks and press it in place until the tops of the blocks are flush. Use a scrap of 2 × 4 to help you position the tops of the blocks evenly along the first course.

5. Continue laying the blocks, making sure the spaces for the three air vents are correctly positioned with the ¾" wood scraps. Do not allow the wood spacers to become set in the mortar.

6. Continue laying blocks until the first course is set. Remove any excess mortar with a trowel and finish the joints with a jointing tool.

Step D: Lay the Second Course

Dry-lay the second course of blocks over the first, offsetting the layout of the joints between the blocks. NOTE: Because of the air vents in the first course, the second course is slightly smaller

B. After tamping a 2" layer of compactable gravel in the bottom of the trench, fill with concrete and screed it with a scrap of 2 × 4. Float the surface with a trowel.

C. Mist the footing with water and spread a bed of mortar inside the reference lines. Place the blocks of the first course in position, with three ¾" spacers in the course to create air vents.

D. Dry-lay the second course of block ⅜" from the outside edge of the first course. Fill any block hollows with mortar.

in diameter. When laying the second course, line up the internal edges of the blocks, leaving a slight lip along the outer edge.

Step E: Apply Surface-bonding Cement

1. Mix a small batch of surface-bonding cement according to the manufacturer's instructions. Add a mortar tinting agent, if desired.

2. Mist the blocks of the fire pit with water. Apply the surface-bonding cement to the exterior of the fire pit walls using a square-end trowel. Make up the difference in diameter between the two courses with a thicker coating of surface-bonding cement on the second course. To even out the cement, angle the trowel slightly and make broad upward strokes. Keep the top of the fire pit clear of surface-bonding cement to ensure the cap will bond to the wall properly.

3. Use a tuck-point trowel to layer the surface-bonding cement inside the edges of the air vents. Do not cover the air vents completely with surface-bonding cement.

4. Use a wet trowel to smooth the surface to create the texture of your choice. Rinse the trowel frequently, keeping it clean and wet.

Step F: Install the Capstones

1. Make a capstone template from ½" plywood, following the illustration (above right). Use the template to mark ten 8 × 16" landscape pavers to the capstone dimensions.

2. Cut the pavers to size using a circular saw with an abrasive masonry blade and a cold chisel. When cutting brick with a masonry blade, make several shallow passes, and always wear ear and eye protection.

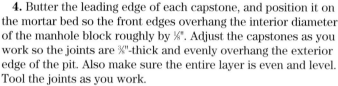

3. Mist the top of the fire pit with water. Mix a batch of mortar and fill in any block hollows, then throw a bed of mortar along the top of the second course.

4. Butter the leading edge of each capstone, and position it on the mortar bed so the front edges overhang the interior diameter of the manhole block roughly by ⅛". Adjust the capstones as you work so the joints are ⅜"-thick and evenly overhang the exterior edge of the pit. Also make sure the entire layer is even and level. Tool the joints as you work.

5. Use a jointing tool to smooth mortar joints within 30 minutes. Cut away any excess mortar pressed from the joints with a trowel. When the mortar is set, but not too hard, brush away excess mortar from the faces of the capstones with a wire brush.

6. Allow the fire pit to cure for 30 days before its first use.

E. *Mist the surface of the walls and apply surface-bonding cement with a square-end trowel. Use more surface-bonding cement on the second course to even out the gap between the courses.*

F. *Lay a bed of mortar on top of the second course and set the cap stones into place, maintaining a uniform overhang.*

Outdoor Kitchen

With its perfect blend of indoor convenience and alfresco atmosphere, it's easy to see why the outdoor kitchen is one of today's most popular home upgrades. In terms of design, outdoor kitchens can take almost any form, but most are planned around the essential elements of a built-in grill and convenient countertop surfaces (preferably on both sides of the grill). Secure storage inside the cooking cabinet is another feature many outdoor cooks find indispensable.

The kitchen design in this project combines all three of these elements in a moderately sized cooking station that can fit a variety of kitchen configurations. The structure is freestanding and self-supporting, so it can go almost anywhere—on top of a patio, right next to a house wall, out by the pool, or out in the yard to create a remote entertainment getaway. Adding a table and chairs or a casual sitting area might be all you need to complete your kitchen accommodations. But best of all, this kitchen is made almost entirely of inexpensive masonry materials.

Concrete and masonry are ideally suited to outdoor kitchen construction. It's noncombustible, not damaged by water, and can easily withstand decades of outdoor exposure. In fact, a little weathering makes masonry look even better. In this project, the kitchen's structural cabinet is built with concrete block on top of a reinforced concrete slab. The countertop is 2"-thick poured concrete that you cast in place over two layers of cementboard. The block sides of the cabinet provide plenty of support for the countertop, as well as a good surface for applying the stucco finish. You could also finish the cabinet with veneer stone or tile.

TOOLS & MATERIALS

- Chalk line
- Pointed trowel
- Masonry mixing tools
- Level
- Mason's string
- Circular saw with masonry blade
- Utility knife
- Straightedge
- Square-notched trowel
- Metal snips
- Wood float
- Steel finishing trowel
- Drill with masonry bit
- Concrete block
- Mortar mix or mason mix
- Metal reinforcement, as required
- Steel angle iron
- ½" cementboard (two 8'-long sheets)
- 2 × 4 and 2 × 6 lumber
- Deck screws (2½", 3")
- Galvanized metal stucco lath
- Silicone caulk
- Vegetable oil or other release agent
- Countertop concrete mix
- Base coat stucco
- Finish coat stucco
- Water sprayer
- Sandpaper
- Food-safe sealer

The outdoor kitchen is one of today's most popular home upgrades. Build in essentials, such as large countertop surfaces, a built-in grill, and secure storage.

Construction Details

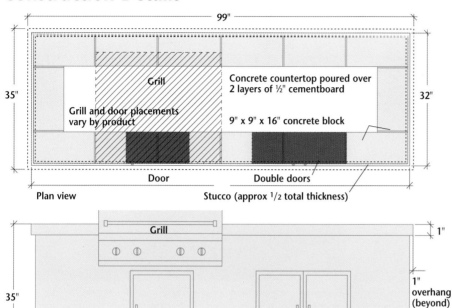

99"

35"   32"

Grill

Grill and door placements vary by product

Concrete countertop poured over 2 layers of ½" cementboard

9" x 9" x 16" concrete block

Door

Double doors

Plan view

Stucco (approx ¹/₂ total thickness)

Grill

35"   Door   Door

1"

1" overhang (beyond) stucco)

Front elevation

Concrete slab (reinforced, as required)

The basic structure of this kitchen consists of five courses of standard 8 x 8 x 16" concrete block. Two mortared layers of ½" cementboard serve as a base for the countertop. The 2"-thick poured concrete layer of the countertop extends 1½" beyond the rough block walls and covers the cementboard edges. The walls receive a two-coat stucco finish, which can be tinted during the mixing or painted after it cures. Doors in the front of the cabinet provide access to storage space inside and to any utility connections for the grill. The kitchen's dimensions can easily be adjusted to accommodate a specific location, cooking equipment, or doors and additional amenities.

PLANNING A KITCHEN PROJECT

Whether you model your project after the one shown here or create your own design, there are a few critical factors to address as part of your initial planning:

Foundation: Check with your local building department about foundation requirements for your kitchen. Depending on the kitchen's size and location, you may be allowed to build on top of a standard 4"-thick reinforced concrete patio slab, or you might need frost footings or a reinforced "floating footing" similar to the one shown on page 492 (Brick Barbecue).

Grill & Door Units: You'll need the exact dimensions of the grill, doors, and any other built-in features before you draw up your plans and start building. When shopping for equipment, keep in mind its utility requirements and the type of support system needed for the grill and other large units. Some grills are drop-in and are supported only by the countertop; others must be supported below with a noncombustible, load-bearing material, such as concrete block or a poured concrete platform.

A grill gas line typically extends up into the cabinet space under the grill and is fitted with a shutoff valve.

Utility Hookups: Grills fueled by natural gas require a plumbed gas line, and those with electric starters need an outdoor electrical circuit, both running into the kitchen cabinet. To include a kitchen sink, you'll need a dedicated water line and a drain connection (to the house system, directly to the city sewer, or possibly to a dry well on your property). Outdoor utilities are strictly governed by building codes, so check with the building department for requirements. Generally, the rough-in work for utilities is best left to professionals.

HOW TO BUILD AN OUTDOOR KITCHEN

1. *Pour the foundation or prepare the slab for the wall construction. See pages 190 to 193 for help with building frost footings and pages 358 to 360 for pouring a concrete slab. To prepare an existing slab, clean the surface thoroughly to remove all dirt, oils, concrete sealers, and paint that could prevent a good bond with mortar.*

2. *Dry-lay the first course of block on the foundation to test the layout. If desired, use 2- or 4"-thick solid blocks under the door openings. Snap chalk lines to guide the block installation, and mark the exact locations of the door openings.*

3. *Set the first course of block into mortar. Cut blocks as needed for the door openings. Lay the second course, offsetting the joints with the first course in a running bond pattern.*

4. *Continue laying up the wall, adding reinforcing wire or rebar if required by local building code. Instead of tooling the mortar joints for a concave profile, use a trowel to slice excess mortar from the blocks. This creates a flat surface that's easier to cover with stucco.*

486

5. *Install steel angle lintels to span over the door openings. If an opening is in line with a course of block, mortar the lintels in place on top of the block. Otherwise, use a circular saw with a masonry blade to cut channels for the horizontal leg of the angle (left). Lintels should span 6" beyond each side of an opening. Slip the lintel into the channels, and then fill the block cells containing the lintel with mortar to secure the lintel in place. Lay a bed of mortar on top of the lintels, then set block into the mortar. Complete the final course of block in the cabinet and let the mortar cure.*

6. *Cut two 8-ft.-long sheets of cementboard to match the outer dimensions of the block cabinet. Apply mortar to the tops of the cabinet blocks and then set one layer of cementboard into the mortar. If you will be installing a built-in grill or other accessories, make cutouts in the cementboard with a utility knife or a jigsaw with a remodeler's blade.*

7. *Cut pieces to fit for a second layer of cementboard. Apply a bed of mortar to the top of the first panel, and then lay the second layer pieces on top, pressing them into the mortar so the surfaces are level. Let the mortar cure.*

8. To create a 1½" overhang for the countertop, build a perimeter band of 2 x 4 lumber; this will serve as the base of the concrete form. Cut the pieces to fit tightly around the cabinet along the top. Fasten the pieces together at their ends with 3" screws so their top edges are flush with the bottom of the cementboard.

9. Cut vertical 2 x 4 supports to fit snugly between the foundation and the bottom of the 2 x 4 band. Install a support at the ends of each wall and evenly spaced in between. Secure each support with angled screws driven into the band boards.

10. Build the sides of the countertop form with 2 x 6s cut to fit around the 2 x 4 band. Position the 2 x 6s so their top edges are 2" above the cementboard, and fasten them to the band with 2½" screws.

11. Form the opening for the grill using 2 x 6 side pieces (no overhang inside opening). Support the edges of the cementboard along the grill cutout with cleats attached to the 2 x 6s. Add vertical supports as needed under the cutout to keep the form from shifting under the weight of the concrete.

12. *Cut a sheet of stucco lath to fit into the countertop form, leaving a 2" space along the inside perimeter of the form. Remove the lath and set it aside. Seal the form joints with a fine bead of silicone caulk and smooth with a finger. After the caulk dries, coat the form boards (not the cementboard) with vegetable oil or other release agent.*

13. *Dampen the cementboard with a mist of water. Mix a batch of countertop mix, adding color if desired (see page 53). Working quickly, fill along the edges of the form with concrete, carefully packing it down into the overhang portion by hand.*

14. *Fill the rest of the form halfway up with an even layer of concrete. Lay the stucco lath on top, then press it lightly into the concrete with a float. Add the remaining concrete so it's flush with the tops of the 2 x 6s.*

15. *Tap along the outsides of the form with a hammer to remove air bubbles trapped against the inside edges. Screed the top of the concrete with a straight 2 x 4 riding along the form sides. Add concrete as needed to fill in low spots so the surface is perfectly flat.*

16. *After the bleed water disappears, float the concrete with a wood or magnesium float. The floated surface should be flat and smooth but will still have a somewhat rough texture. Be careful not to overfloat and draw water to the surface.*

17. *A few hours after floating, finish the countertop as desired. A few passes with a steel finishing trowel yields the smoothest surface. Hold the leading edge of the trowel up and work in circular strokes. Let the concrete set for a while between passes.*

18. *Moist-cure the countertop with a fine water mist for three to five days. Remove the form boards. If desired, smooth the countertop edges with an abrasive brick and/or a diamond pad or sandpaper. After the concrete cures, apply a food-safe sealer to help prevent staining.*

19. *Prepare for door installation in the cabinet. Outdoor cabinet doors are usually made of stainless steel and typically are installed by hanging hinges or flanges with masonry anchors. Drill holes for masonry anchors in the concrete block, following the door manufacturer's instructions.*

TIP

Honeycombs or air voids can be filled using a cement slurry of cement and water applied with a rubber float. If liquid cement color was used in your countertop concrete mix, color should be added to the wet cement paste. Some experimentation will be necessary.

20. *Finish installing and hanging the doors. Test the door operations and make sure to caulk around the edges with high-quality silicone caulk.* NOTE: *Doors shown here are best installed before the stucco finish is applied to the cabinet. Other doors may be easier to install following a different sequence.*

21. To finish the cabinet walls, begin by dampening the contrete block and then applying a ⅜"-thick base coat of stucco. Apply an even layer over the walls; then smooth the surface with a wood float and moist-cure the stucco for 48 hours or as directed by the manufacturer.

22. Apply a finish coat of tinted stucco that's at least ⅛" thick. Evenly saturate the base coat stucco surface with water prior to applying the the finish coat. Texture the surface as desired. Moist-cure the stucco for several days as directed.

23. Set the grill into place, make the gas connection, then check it carefully for leaks. Permanently install the grill following the manufacturer's directions. The joints around grills are highly susceptible to water intrusion; seal them thoroughly with an approved caulk to help keep moisture out of the cabinet space below.

491

Brick Barbecue

The barbecue design shown here is constructed with double walls—an inner wall, made of heat-resistant fire brick set on edge surrounding the cooking area, and an outer wall, made of engineer brick. We chose engineer brick because its stout dimensions mean you'll have fewer bricks to lay. You'll need to adjust the design if you select another brick size. Proper placement of the inner walls is necessary so they can support the grills. A 4" air space between the walls helps insulate the cooking area. The walls are capped with thin pieces of cut stone.

Refractory mortar is recommended for use with fire brick. It is heat resistant and the joints will last a long time without cracking. Ask a local brick yard to recommend a refractory mortar for outdoor use.

The foundation combines a 12"-deep footing supporting a reinforced slab. This structure, known as a floating footing, is designed to shift as a unit when temperature changes cause the ground to shift. Ask a building inspector about local building code specifications.

NOTE: The brick sizes recommended here allow you to build the barbecue without splitting a lot of bricks. If the bricks recommended are not easy to find in your area, a local brick yard can help you adjust the project dimensions to accommodate different brick sizes.

TOOLS & MATERIALS

- Tape measure
- Hammer
- Brickset chisel
- Mason's string & stakes
- Shovel
- Aviation snips
- Reciprocating saw or hack saw
- Masonry hoe
- Shovel, wood float
- Chalk line
- Line level
- Wheelbarrow
- Mason's trowel

- Jointing tool
- 2 × 4 lumber
- 18-gauge galvanized metal mesh
- #4 rebar
- 16-gauge tie wire
- Bolsters
- Fire brick (4½ × 2½ × 9")
- Engineer brick (4 × 3⅕ × 8")
- Type N mortar
- Refractory mortar
- ⅜"-dia. dowel
- Metal ties

- 4" T-plates
- Engineer brick (4 × 2 × 12")
- Brick sealer
- Stainless steel expanded mesh (23¾ × 30")
- Cooking grills (23⅜ × 15½")
- Ash pan
- Vegetable oil or other commercial release agent
- Concrete

The addition of a brick barbecue to your patio is a non-intrusive way to incorporate summer cooking into a four-seasons space, while adding the beauty and stability of brick to your outdoor decorating scheme.

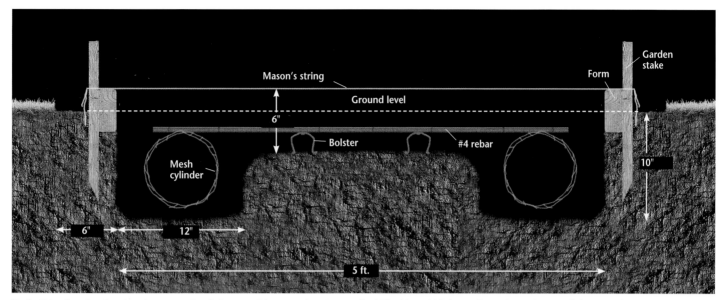

***To build a floating footing,** lay out a 4 × 5-ft. area. Dig a continuous trench, 12" wide × 10" deep, along the perimeter of the area, leaving a rectangular mound in the center. Remove 4" of soil from the top of the mound, and round over the edges.*

HOW TO BUILD A FLOATING FOOTING

1. Lay out a 4 × 5-ft. area with stakes and string. Dig a continuous trench, 12" wide × 10" deep, along the perimeter of the area, leaving a rectangular mound in the center.

2. Remove 4" of soil from the top of the mound, and round over the edges.

3. Set a 2 × 4 wood form around the site so that the top is 1" above the ground along the back and ½" above the ground along the front to create a slope to help shed water. Use a mason's string and a line level to ensure that the forms are level from side to side.

4. Reinforce the footing with metal mesh and five 52"-long pieces of rebar. Roll the mesh into 6"-dia. cylinders and cut them to fit into the trench, leaving a 4" gap between each. Use bolsters where necessary to suspend the rebar.

5. Coat the forms with vegetable oil, and pour the concrete.

HOW TO BUILD A BRICK BARBECUE

Step A: Dry-lay the First Course

1. After the floating footing has cured for one week, use a chalk line to mark the layout for the inner edge of the fire brick wall. Make a line 4" in from the front edge of the footing, and a centerline perpendicular to the first line. Make a 24 × 32" rectangle that starts at the 4" line and is centered on the centerline.

A. *Dry-lay the outer wall, as shown here, using engineer brick. Space the bricks for ⅜" mortar joints.*

2. Dry-lay the first course of fire brick around the outside of the rectangle, allowing for ⅛"-thick mortar joints. Start with a full brick at the 4" line to start the right and left walls. Complete the course with a cut brick in the middle of the short wall.

3. Dry-lay the outer wall, as shown on page 493 using 4 × 3⅕ × 8" engineer brick. Space the bricks for ⅜" joints. The rear wall should come within ⅜" of the last fire brick in the left inner wall.

4. Complete the left wall with a cut brick in the middle of the wall. Mark reference lines for this outer wall.

Step B: Make a Story Pole

1. Make a story pole using a straight 1 × 2 or 2 × 2. On one side of the board, mark eight courses of fire brick, leaving a ⅜" gap for the bottom mortar joint and ⅛" gaps for the remaining joints. The top of the final course should be 36" from the bottom edge. Transfer the top line to the other side of the pole.

2. Lay out 11 courses of engineer brick, spacing them evenly so that the final course is flush with the 36" line. Each horizontal mortar joint will be slightly less than ½"-thick.

B. *To make a story pole, mark one side of a straight board for eight courses of fire brick, leaving a ⅜" gap for the bottom mortar joint and ⅛" gaps for the remaining joints.*

C. *Lay the first course of the outer wall using Type N mortar. Use oiled ⅜" dowels to create weep holes behind the front bricks of the left and right walls.*

D. *Place metal ties between the corners of the inner and outer walls at the second, third, fifth, and seventh courses.*

Step C: Lay the First Course in Mortar

1. Lay a bed of refractory mortar for a ⅜" joint along the reference lines for the inner wall, then lay the first course of fire brick using ⅛" joints between the bricks.

2. Lay the first course of the outer wall, using Type N mortar. Use oiled ⅜" dowels to create weep holes behind the front bricks of the left and right walls.

3. Alternate laying the inner and outer walls, checking your work with the story pole and a level after every other course.

Step D: Lay the Subsequent Courses

1. Start the second course of the outer wall using a half brick butted against each side of the inner wall, then complete the course. Because there is a half brick in the right outer wall, you need to use two three-quarter bricks in the second course to stagger the joints.

2. Continue adding courses offsetting the joists from row to row, and alternate between laying the inner and outer walls. Place metal ties between the corners of the inner and outer walls at the second, third, fifth, and seventh courses. Use ties at the front junctions and along the rear walls.

3. Mortar the joint where the left inner wall meets the rear outer wall.

4. Smooth the mortar joints with a jointing tool when the mortar has hardened enough to resist minimal finger pressure. Check the joints in both walls after every few courses. The different mortars may need smoothing at different times.

Step E: Add T-plates

Add T-plates for grill supports above the fifth, sixth, and seventh courses. Use 4"-wide plates with flanges that are no more than 3/32" thick. Position the plates along the side firebrick walls, centered at 3", 12", 18", and 27" from the rear fire brick wall.

Step F: Add the Capstones

1. Lay a bed of Type N mortar for a ⅜"-thick joint on top of the inner and outer walls for the capstones.

2. Lay the capstone flat across the walls, keeping one end flush with the inner face of the fire brick. Make sure the bricks are level, and tool the joints when they are ready.

3. After a week, seal the capstones and the joints between them with brick sealer. Install the grills.

E. *Add T-plates for grill supports above the fifth, sixth, and seventh courses.*

F. *Install the capstones in a bed of Type N mortar with a ⅜"-thick joint.*

Garden Pond & Fountain

A small pond and fountain add more than the illusion of luxury to landscapes; they also add the sound and sparkle of moving water and invite birds to join the party. Installing a pond and fountain can be heavy work, but it's not at all complicated. If you can use a shovel and read a level, you can install a beautiful fountain like the classic Roman fountain shown here.

Most freestanding fountains are designed to be set into an independently installed water feature. The fountains typically are preplumbed with an integral pump, but larger ones may have an external pumping apparatus. The kind of kit you'll find at your local building or garden center normally comes in at least two parts: the pedestal and the vessel.

The project shown here falls into the luxury-you-can-afford category and is fully achievable for a do-it-yourselfer. If the project you have in mind is of massive scale (with a pond larger than around 8 × 10 ft.) you'll likely need to work with a pondscaping professional to acquire and install the materials needed for such an endeavor.

You can install a fountain in an existing water feature, or you can build a new one with a hard liner, as shown here, or with a soft liner. Have your utility providers mark the locations of all utility lines before beginning this or any project that involves digging.

TOOLS & MATERIALS

- Level
- Shovel or spade
- Hand tamp
- Rope
- Preformed pond liner
- Sand
- Compactable gravel
- Interlocking paving stones
- Rubber floor mat
- Freestanding fountain
- Fountain pedestal
- Tarp
- River stones
- Long, straight 2 × 4
- Trowel
- 5-gallon bucket

The work necessary to install a garden pond and fountain will pay dividends for many years to come. The process is not complicated, but it does involve some fairly heavy labor, such as digging and hauling stones.

Installing Ponds & Fountains

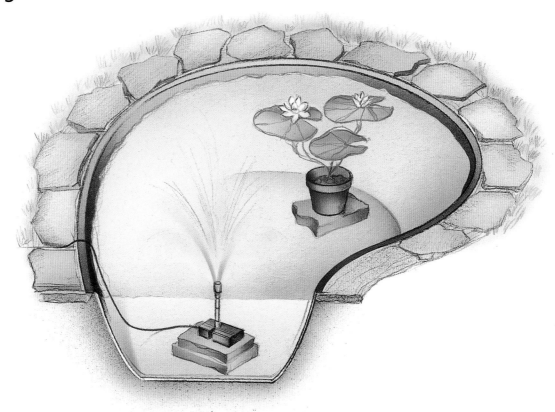

A hard shell-type liner combines well with a fountain because its flat, hard bottom makes a stable surface for resting the fountain base. You may need to prop up the fountain to get it to the optimal level.

If you plan to stock your pond with plant life or livestock, it's important to keep a healthy balance. For stocking with fish, the pond must be at least 24" deep, and you should have at least one submerged water plant to create oxygen.

TIP

Most municipalities require that permanent water features be surrounded by a structure, fence, or wall on all sides to keep small children from wandering in. Good designers view this as a creative challenge, rather than an impediment.

497

HOW TO INSTALL A POND & FOUNTAIN

1. *Choose a flat area of your yard. Set the hard-shell pond liner right-side up in the installation area and adjust it until you are pleased with the location (it should be well away from buried utility lines). Hold a level against the edge of the top of the liner and use it as a guide to transfer the liner shape onto the ground below with a rope.*

2. *Cut away the sod within the outline. Measure the liner at the center and excavate the base area to this depth. Dig the hole 2 to 3" deeper than the liner, and dig past the outline a couple of inches all the way around. If the sides of your liner are sloped, slope the edges of the hole to match.*

3. *Remove any rocks or debris on the bottom of the hole, and add sand to cover the bottom of the hole about 2" deep. Test fit the liner and adjust the sand until the underside of the liner rim is slightly above ground and the liner is level from side to side.*

4. *Cut away the sod beyond the liner excavation area and dig out an area wide enough to accommodate your paving stones (called coping stones), about 1" deeper than the average stone thickness. Flagstone is the most common natural stone choice for coping because it is flat; concrete pavers also may be used easily. Make sure the surface of the excavation is as level as possible.*

5. Fill the liner with 4 to 6" of water. Fill the space between the liner and the sides of the hole with damp sand using a 2 × 4 to tamp it down as you go. Add more water and then more sand; continue until the pond and the gap are filled.

6. Bail about half of the water out of the pond. Place an exterior-rated rubber floor mat (or mats) at least ½" thick on the liner in the spot where you'd like the fountain to rest.

7. Feed the fountain's power cord up through the access holes in the pedestal. Set the fountain in place on top of the pedestal and run the cord to the edge.

8. Check to make sure the pedestal is level. If necessary, shim the pedestal with small flat stones to make the fountain level.

9. Cover the pond and pedestal with a clean tarp, and add an inch of compactable gravel to the excavated area for the paving stones. Tamp down the gravel and check the area with a level. Cut a small channel for the power cord and route it beyond the excavated area toward a power source.

10. Set interlocking pavers in place around lip of liner. Adjust compactable gravel as necessary to make the pavers level.

11. Ponds look more natural if you line the bottoms with rock. Small-diameter (2 to 3") river rock is a good choice. Before putting it into the pond, rinse the rock well. One trick is to put the nozzle of a hose in the bottom of a clean 5-gallon bucket and then fill the bucket with dirty rock. Turn on the hose and let the water run for 15 minutes or so. This will cause impurities to float up and out of the bucket.

12. Remove the tarp from the pond and cover the bottom of the liner with washed river rock. Place the fountain onto the pedestal and submerge the cord, running it out of the pond in an inconspicuous spot, such as between two pavers.

13. *Fill both the pond and the fountain's base with water. If you will not be stocking the pond with fish or plants, add two ounces of chlorine bleach for every 10 gallons of water.*

14. *Allow the water to settle for 30 minutes or so, and then turn on the fountain pump and test. Let the pump run for an hour or so, and then turn it off and remove the fountain head. Use a hose and spray nozzle to clear out any blockages. Perform this maintenance regularly and whenever you notice that the spray from the fountain seems to be restricted.*

POWER CORD MANAGEMENT

There are many ways to provide electrical power to operate the fountain pump. The best way is to add a new outdoor circuit, but this requires an electrician if you are not experienced with home wiring. The easier route is to feed your fountain pump with an exterior-rated extension cord that's plugged into an existing outdoor receptacle. Because having an extension cord laying in your lawn is both a tripping hazard and an electrical hazard (lawn mowers and wiring do not get along), you can bury the cord in a shallow trench. To protect it from digging instruments, either backfill with rocks so you know the exact location of the cord or bury it encased in heavy conduit.

Avoid using this tactic if the pond is located more than 50 feet from the power source.

Dig a trench about 6" deep and 6" wide from the pond to your outdoor power source.

Feed the cord through conduit and lay the conduit in the trench all the way from the pond to the power source. Backfill the trench with dirt.

Free-form Meditation Pond

If your idea of a water garden is more elaborate than most or the shape you have in mind isn't standard round or kidney, a free-form water garden with a soft, pliable pond liner may be the answer for you.

Building a water garden with a soft liner is not difficult or time consuming, but the finished garden will require ongoing maintenance and care. Think carefully about your willingness and ability to provide this care before committing yourself to the project. It's also a good idea to look into local building codes—many municipalities require building permits for ponds over 18" deep.

Before selecting a flexible liner, compare and contrast the available types. PVC (polyvinyl chloride) liners are made from a type of synthetic vinyl that's flexible and stable as long as it does not get direct sunlight exposure. If you choose one, make sure it is not manufactured for swimming pools or roofing.

EPDM (ethylene propylene diene monomer) liners are made from a synthetic rubber that is highly flexible, extremely durable, and fish-friendly. EPDM liners remain flexible at temperatures ranging from -40 to 175°F. They are much easier to find, inexpensive, and overall an excellent choice for do-it-yourselfers. Look for a liner that's at least 45 mil thick. At larger home and garden centers, you can now buy pond liner by the lineal foot.

TOOLS & MATERIALS

- Level
- Shovel or spade
- Hand tamp
- Tape measure
- Garden hose or rope
- Spray paint
- Pond underlayment
- Flexible pond liner
- Sand
- Compactable gravel
- Flagstone pavers

Free-form ponds blend into the landscape, especially with the addition of coping stones set into the edges. Building one involves heavy labor, but no special skills.

HOW TO CREATE A FREE-FORM MEDITATION POND

1. *Select a location well away from buried utility lines. Use a garden hose or a rope to outline the pond. Avoid very sharp turns, and try for a natural looking configuration. When you're satisfied with the pond's shape, lift the hose or rope and use spray paint to mark the perimeter.*

2. *Find the lowest point on the perimeter and flag it for reference as the elevation benchmark. This represents the top of the pond's water-holding capacity, so all depth measurements should be taken from this point. Start digging at the deepest point (usually the middle of the pond) and work out toward the edges. For border plantings, establish one 6- to 8"-wide ledge about 12" down from the benchmark.*

3. *Set a level on the plant shelf to confirm that it is the same elevation throughout. Unless your building site is perfectly level or you have done a lot of earth moving, the edges of the pond are not likely to be at the same elevation, so there may be some pond liner visible between the benchmark and the high point. This can usually be concealed with plants, rocks, or by overhanging your coping more in high areas.*

4. *Dig a 4 × 12" frame around the top of the hole to make room for the coping stones (adjust the width if you are using larger stones). Remove any rocks, debris, roots, or anything sharp in the hole, and add a 2" layer of sand to cover the bottom.*

5. *Cover the bottom and sides of the excavation with pond underlayment. Pond underlayment is a shock-absorbing, woven fabric that you should be able to buy from the same source that provides your liner. If necessary, cut triangles of underlayment and fit them together, overlapping pieces as necessary to cover the contours. This is not a waterproof layer.*

6. *Lay out the liner material and let it warm in the sun for an hour or two. Arrange the liner to cover the excavation, folding and overlapping as necessary. Place rocks around the edges to keep it from sliding into the hole.*

7. *Begin filling the pond with water. Watch the liner as the water level gets higher, and adjust and tuck it to minimize sharp folds and empty pockets.*

8. Add some larger stones to the pond as the water rises, including a flat stone for your pond pump/filter. If the pump/filter has a fountain feature, locate it near the center. If not, locate it near the edge in an easy-to-reach spot.

9. Fill the pond all the way to the top until it overflows at the benchmark. Remove the stones holding the liner in place and begin laying flat stones, such as flagstones, around the perimeter of the pond. Cut and trim flagstones as necessary to minimize gaps.

10. Finish laying the coping stones and fill in gaps with cutoff and shards. If you are in a temperate climate, consider mortaring the coping stones, but be very careful to keep wet mortar out of the water. It kills plants and damages pump/filters. Set flagstone pavers on the ledge at the perimeter of the pond. Add more water and adjust the liner again. Fill the pond to just below the flagstones, and trim the liner.

11. Consult a garden center, an extension agent from a local university, or the Internet to help you choose plants for your pond. Include a mixture of deep-water plants, marginals, oxygenators, and floating plants. Place the plants in the pond. If necessary to bring them to the right height, set the plants on bricks or flat stones. Spread decorative gravel, sand, or mulch to cover the liner at the perimeter of the pond. Install plants along the pond's margins, if desired.

Backyard Putting Green

Serious golfers often say they "drive for show and putt for dough," and most of them practice putting at every opportunity. For these folks, a backyard putting green is the very definition of luxury.

Natural grass putting greens offer the ultimate in luxurious golf environments at home, but they require special breeds of grass and very specialized maintenance that very few people have the time or equipment to provide. But if you are willing to forego the smell of the fresh-cut Bermuda grass and the feel of a well-tended green underfoot, you'll find that there are a number of artificial putting green options that offer a chance to hone your putting stroke.

The panels and turf we used for this project are available from www.backyard-golf.com (See Resources, page 523). The system is easy to install and produces a good practice surface—a fine combination when it comes to putting greens.

TOOLS & MATERIALS

- Line trimmer
- Screwdriver
- Jigsaw
- Spade
- Utility knife
- Hammer
- Graph paper
- Putting green panels
- Artificial turf
- Turf spikes
- Garden hose or rope
- Spray paint
- Sand
- Landscape fabric
- Staples
- Light-colored crayon or chalk
- Double-sided carpet tape

Backyard putting greens give golfers a whole new way to have fun and perfect their game. Special kits, including panels and artificial turf, make building one an easy weekend project.

Designing a Backyard Putting Green

Choose an above-ground green for seasonal use or even to use indoors. They lack a bit of authenticity, but they are very convenient.

Kit accessories, such as pins and edge liners, give a backyard putting green a more genuine flavor. A chipping mat can be positioned around the green to let you work on your close-in short game without destroying your yard. See Resources, page 523.

Artificial turf comes in an array of styles and lengths. Lower nap products, like the two samples to the left, are best for putting greens.

507

HOW TO INSTALL A BACKYARD PUTTING GREEN

1. *Diagram your putting green on graph paper, including cup locations. If you are ordering your kit from an Internet seller, they probably have a mapping and planning program on their site. Order panels and turf as necessary to create your putting green.*

2. *As soon as it arrives, unroll the turf and spray it with water to saturate. Set the turf aside and let it dry for at least 24 hours. This process preshrinks the turf.*

3. *Measure the installation area and mark the perimeter of the putting green using a garden hose or rope. Lift the hose or rope and spray paint the green's outline onto the grass. Some putting green kits are precut to create specific shapes and sizes, while others offer a bit more design flexibility.*

4. *Inside the outlined area, use a line trimmer to scalp the grass down to the dirt. Rake up and remove any debris.*

5. Add sand or remove dirt as necessary to create contours in the putting green. Kit manufacturers suggest that you create the contours that replicate the breaks you most want to practice. For example, if you have trouble hitting uphill and to the right, create a hill and place the cup at the top and to the right.

6. Cover the scalped and contoured installation area with landscape fabric, overlapping seams by at least 2". Trim the fabric to fit inside the outline and secure it to the ground with landscape fabric staples.

7. Starting in the center of the installation area, push two panels together and hold them tightly in place as you insert the fasteners. Use a screwdriver to tighten the fasteners. Install the panels in locations indicated on your diagram.

8. Continue to fill in panels, according to your plan. Take special notice of putting cup locations. In many kits, these require special panels with cups preinstalled. Locate them accurately.

509

9. Where panels go beyond the outline, use a light-colored crayon or chalk to mark a cutting line. Avoid cutting extremely close to panel edges.

10. One panel at a time, cut panels to shape, using a jigsaw with a blade that's slightly longer than the panel thickness. Use panel scraps to fill in open areas in the layout wherever you can, and then mark and cut the scraps to fit.

11. Dig a 4"-wide by 4"-deep trench around the perimeter of the green shape, directly next to the edges of the panels.

12. Unroll the artificial turf on top of the panels. Pay attention to the nap of the turf to make sure it all runs in the same direction. Use a utility knife to cut it to size, 4" larger than the panel assembly.

13. *Install the cups into the panels containing the cup bodies, and then cut holes in the turf with a utility knife.*

14. *Fold back the edges of the turf. Apply double-sided carpet tape to the perimeter of the panel assembly. Peel off the tape's protective cover, then press the turf down onto the tape. Fold the excess turf over the edge of the panel assembly and down into the trench. If the turf bulges around a tight radius, make 3½" slashes in the edge of the turf and ease it around the curve.*

15. *Drive carpet spikes or fabric spikes (provided by the kit manufacturer) through the edges of the turf and into the trench to secure the turf.*

16. *Backfill the trench with the soil you removed earlier. Add landscaping around the edges of the green, if desired. Sweep and hose down the green periodically and as needed.*

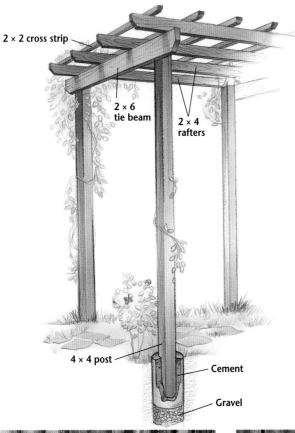

2 × 2 cross strip

2 × 6 tie beam

2 × 4 rafters

4 × 4 post

Cement

Gravel

Arbor

Arbors create a lightly shaded space and add vertical interest to your landscape. For increased shade, you can cover an arbor with meshlike outdoor fabric or climbing vines. You can even transform it into a private retreat by enclosing the sides with lattice.

Our version of a post-and-slat arbor is a 5 × 5-foot, freestanding cedar structure with an extended overhead. You can easily adapt the design to different sizes, but don't space the posts more than 8 feet apart. If you want to build a larger arbor, add additional posts between the corner posts. Before you begin construction, check your local building code for footing depth requirements and setback restrictions.

If you want to add climbing vines, such as clematis or wisteria, plant one vine beside the base of each post. Attach screw eyes to the outside of the posts, then string wire between the eyes. As the vines grow, train them along the wires.

TOOLS & MATERIALS

- Basic tools
- Stakes and string
- Line level
- Posthole digger
- Reciprocating saw
- Paintbrush

- Wood screw clamps
- Concrete mix
- Gravel
- Wood sealer
- 10-ft. 4 × 4 posts (4)
- 6-ft. 2 × 6 tie beams (2)

- Galvanized nails
- 7-ft. 2 × 2 cross strips (7)
- 7-ft. 2 × 4 rafters (4)
- Galvanized deck screws
- 3" lag screws (8)
- Rafter ties (8)

A. *Lay out the location of the arbor posts, then measure the diagonals to check for square.*

B. *Brace the posts into place, then use a level to make sure they are plumb.*

C. *Level and clamp the tie beam against the posts, then secure it with lag screws.*

HOW TO BUILD AN ARBOR

Step A: Dig Holes for the Footings

1. Lay out the location of the posts, 5 ft. apart, using stakes and string. Make sure the layout is square by measuring from corner to corner and adjusting the layout until these diagonal measurements are equal.

2. Dig postholes at the corners to the required depth using a posthole digger.

3. Fill each hole with 6" of gravel.

Step B: Set the Posts

1. Position the posts in the holes. To brace them in a plumb position, tack support boards to the posts on adjoining faces. Adjust the posts as necessary until they're plumb.

2. Drive a stake into the ground, flush against the base of each 2 × 4. Drive galvanized deck screws through the stakes, into the 2 × 4s.

3. Mix one bag of dry concrete to anchor each post. Immediately check to make sure the posts are plumb, and adjust as necessary until the concrete begins to harden. Be sure to let the concrete dry at least 24 hours before continuing.

Step C: Install the First Tie Beam

1. Measure, mark, and cut all the lumber for the arbor. Cut a 3 × 3" notch off the bottom corner of each tie beam, a 2 × 2" notch off the bottom corner of each 2 × 4 rafter, and a 1 × 1" notch off the bottom corner of each cross strip.

2. Position a tie beam against the outside edge of a pair of posts, 7 ft. above the ground. Position the beam to extend about 1 ft. past the post on each side.

3. Level the beam, then clamp it into place with wood screw clamps. Drill two ⅜" pilot holes through the tie beam and into each post. Attach the tie beam to the posts with 3" lag screws.

Step D: Add the Second Tie Beam

1. Use a line level to mark the opposite pair of posts at the same height as the installed tie beam.

2. Attach the remaining tie beam, repeating the process described in #2 and #3 of step C.

3. Cut off the posts so they're level with the tops of the tie beams, using a reciprocating saw or handsaw.

Step E: Attach the Rafters

Attach the rafters to the tops of the tie beams using rafter ties and galvanized nails. Beginning 6" from the ends of the tie beams, space the rafters 2 ft. apart, with the ends extending past each tie beam by 1 ft.

Step F: Install the Cross Strips

1. Position a cross strip across the top of the rafters, beginning 6" from the ends of the rafters. Center the strip so it extends past the outside rafters by about 6". Drill pilot holes through the cross strip and into the rafters. Attach the cross strip with galvanized screws. Add the remaining cross strips, spacing them 1 ft. apart.

2. Finish your arbor by applying wood sealer/protectant.

D. *Attach the other tie beam and trim the tops of the posts flush with the tie beams.*

E. *Attach the rafters to the tie beams with rafter ties and galvanized nails.*

F. *Space the cross strips 1 ft. apart and attach them to the rafters.*

Classical Pergola

Tall and stately, the columned pergola is perhaps the grandest of garden structures. Its minimal design defines an area without enclosing it and makes it easy to place anywhere—from out in the open yard to right up against your house. Vines and flowers clinging to the stout framework create an eye-catching statement of strength and beauty.

In this selected project, Tuscan-style columns supporting shaped beams mimic the column-and-entablature construction used throughout classical architecture. Painting the columns white or adding faux marbling enhances the classical styling. The columns used here are made of structural fiberglass designed for outdoor use. They even adhere to the ancient practice of tapering the top two-thirds of the shaft.

Structural fiberglass columns, like the ones used in this project, are available from architectural products dealers (see Resources, page 523). You can order them over the phone and have them shipped to your door. This type of column is weather-resistant, but most manufacturers recommend painting them for appearance and longevity. Whatever columns you use, be sure to follow the manufacturer's instructions for installation and maintenance.

TOOLS & MATERIALS

- Six 8"-dia. × 8 ft. columns
- Six 16"-dia. concrete tube forms
- Four 2 × 8" × 16 ft. treated pine
- Seven 2 × 6" × 8 ft. treated pine
- One 4 × 4" × 8 ft. treated post
- Compactable gravel
- Concrete (3,000 PSI)
- Six ½" × 6" J-bolts
- Six ½"-dia. × 48" threaded rod and coupling nuts
- Six ½"-dia. × 99" threaded rod and coupling nuts
- Exterior construction adhesive or waterproof wood glue
- 16d galvanized common nails
- Six Corrosion-resistant bearing plates
- Deck screws (2½")
- Coupling nuts
- Paintable caulk
- Paint

Building a pergola is a fairly major carpentry project, but it is also a very rewarding way to put your skills to work and create a beautiful structure in your yard.

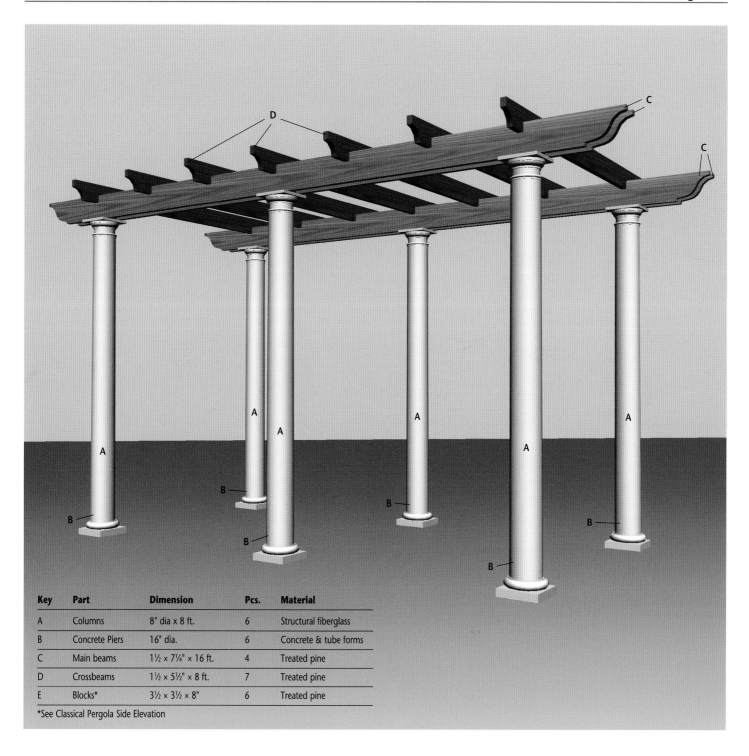

Key	Part	Dimension	Pcs.	Material
A	Columns	8" dia x 8 ft.	6	Structural fiberglass
B	Concrete Piers	16" dia.	6	Concrete & tube forms
C	Main beams	1½ × 7¼" × 16 ft.	4	Treated pine
D	Crossbeams	1½ × 5½" × 8 ft.	7	Treated pine
E	Blocks*	3½ × 3½ × 8"	6	Treated pine

*See Classical Pergola Side Elevation

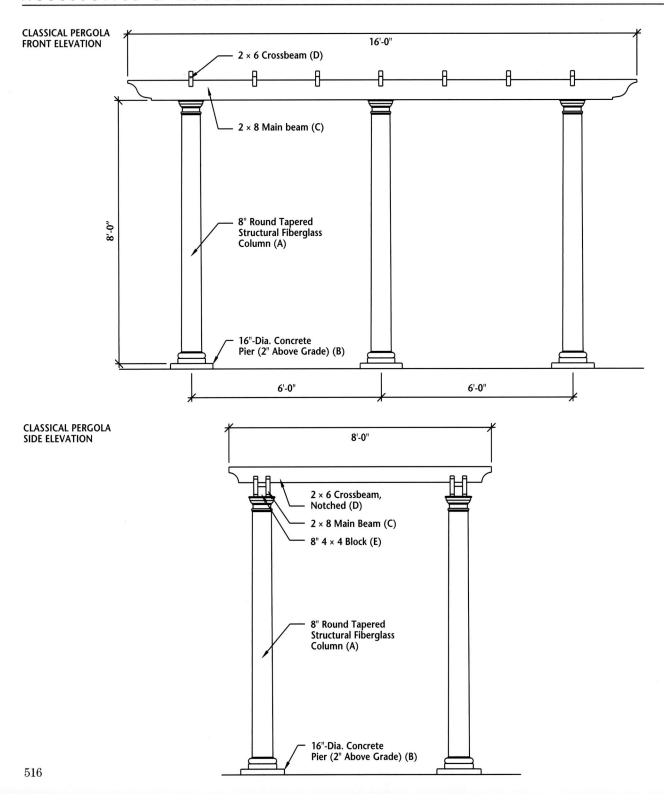

CLASSICAL PERGOLA
FRONT ELEVATION

16'-0"

2 × 6 Crossbeam (D)

2 × 8 Main beam (C)

8'-0"

8" Round Tapered
Structural Fiberglass
Column (A)

16"-Dia. Concrete
Pier (2" Above Grade) (B)

6'-0"

6'-0"

CLASSICAL PERGOLA
SIDE ELEVATION

8'-0"

2 × 6 Crossbeam,
Notched (D)

2 × 8 Main Beam (C)

8" 4 × 4 Block (E)

8" Round Tapered
Structural Fiberglass
Column (A)

16"-Dia. Concrete
Pier (2" Above Grade) (B)

CLASSICAL PERGOLA FOUNDATION PLAN

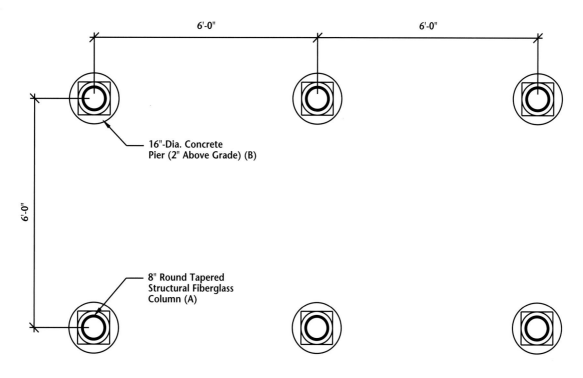

6'-0"   6'-0"

6'-0"

16"-Dia. Concrete
Pier (2" Above Grade) (B)

8" Round Tapered
Structural Fiberglass
Column (A)

CLASSICAL PERGOLA FRAMING PLAN

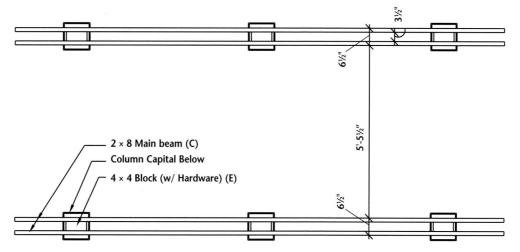

3½"

6½"

5'-5½"

6½"

2 × 8 Main beam (C)

Column Capital Below

4 × 4 Block (w/ Hardware) (E)

CLASSICAL PERGOLA ROOF FRAMING PLAN

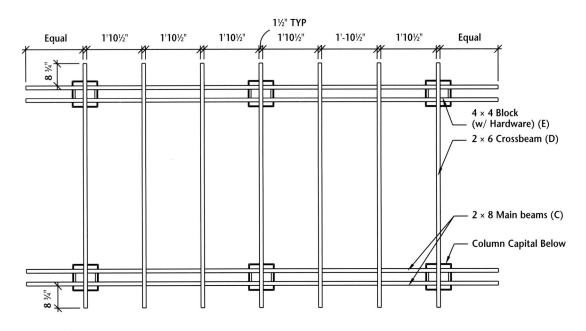

1½" TYP

Equal   1'10½"   1'10½"   1'10½"   1'10½"   1'-10½"   1'10½"   Equal

8 ¾"

8 ¾"

4 × 4 Block (w/ Hardware) (E)

2 × 6 Crossbeam (D)

2 × 8 Main beams (C)

Column Capital Below

CLASSICAL PERGOLA BEAM END TEMPLATES

1" × 1" GRID SHOWN

2 × 8 Main beams

2 × 6 Crossbeams

CLASSICAL PERGOLA COLUMN CONNECTION

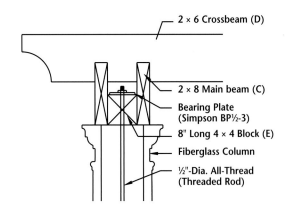

2 × 6 Crossbeam (D)

2 × 8 Main beam (C)

Bearing Plate (Simpson BP½-3)

8" Long 4 × 4 Block (E)

Fiberglass Column

½"-Dia. All-Thread (Threaded Rod)

A. *Finish the tops of the concrete piers using a concrete float after making sure the J-bolt is perpendicular and no more than 2" above the surface.*

HOW TO BUILD THE CLASSICAL PERGOLA
Step A: Pour the Footings

1. Set up batter boards and mason's lines to lay out the pergola columns following the Foundation Plan on page 517. Dig the six holes for the concrete forms. Add a layer of gravel, then set and brace the forms. Make sure the pier depth and gravel layer meet the requirements of the local building code. For this project, the piers are 16" in diameter and extend at least 2" above the ground. You may have to adjust the height of some piers so that all of them are in the same level plane; measure against your level mason's lines to compensate for any unevenness of the ground.

2. Pour the concrete for each form, and set a ½ × 6" J-bolt in the center of the wet concrete. Make sure the bolt is perfectly plumb and extends 1¾ to 2" above the surface of the concrete. Following the concrete manufacturer's instructions, finish the tops of the piers to create a smooth, attractive surface. When painted, the piers become part of the finished project.

Step B: Cut & Shape the Beams

1. Cut the four main beams to length at 192". Cut the seven crossbeams to length at 96". Check all of the beams for crowning—a slight arching shape that's apparent when the board is set on edge. Hold each board flat and sight along its narrow edges. If the board arches, mark the top (convex) side of the arch. This is the crowned edge and should always be installed facing up.

B. *Sight along both narrow edges of the beams. If a beam is arched, mark the beam on the convex side of the arch.*

C. *Sandwich the blocks between the main beams, and fasten the assemblies with exterior adhesive and 16d nails.*

2. Make cardboard patterns for shaping the ends of the main beams and crossbeams; follow the Beam End Templates on page 518. Use the patterns to mark the shapes onto the beam ends. Shape the beam ends using a jigsaw, coping saw, or bandsaw, and then sand the cuts smooth.

Step C: Construct the Main Beam Assemblies

1. Cut six 4 × 4 blocks at 8". Lay each block flat, and drill a ⁹⁄₁₆"-dia. hole through the center of one side. Coat the ends of the blocks and the insides of the holes with wood preservative, following the manufacturer's instructions. The blocks are the main structural connecting points for the pergola, and the preservative helps prevent rotting that may occur over the years.

2. Make a mark 20" in from the end of each main beam. These marks represent the outside ends of the blocks. Construct the main beam assemblies by applying construction adhesive or waterproof wood glue to the side faces of the blocks and sandwiching the beams over the blocks. Make sure the blocks are flush with the bottoms of the beams and their ends are on the reference marks. The holes are face up (vertical). Clamp the assembly, and then fasten the beams to the blocks with 16d common nails. Drive four nails on each side, making sure to avoid the center hole in the blocks. Let the glue dry completely.

3. Mark the crossbeam layout on to the top edges of main beams.

Step D: Prepare & Set the Columns

1. You'll need at least two helpers now. Once you set the columns for one side, continue to the next step to install the main beam. Then, repeat the two steps for the other side of the pergola.

2. Cut the threaded rods to length at 99". Add a corrosion-resistant coupler nut to each J-bolt (threaded anchor rod for patio installation). Lay the columns down next to their respective piers. Slip the base and capital over the ends of the column shafts; these will stay loose so you can slide them out of the way until you secure them.

3. Run the threaded rod through the center of each column. Tip up each column and center it on top of a pier. Check the joint where the column meets the pier; it should make even contact around the column. If necessary, use a rasp to shave the end of the column for even contact.

4. While one person holds the column out of the way, thread the rod into the coupling nut. Adjust the nut so the rod and J-bolt have equal penetration into the nut, and tighten the nut following the manufacturer's instructions. Temporarily brace the column or have a helper hold it upright. Set up the remaining two columns.

D. *Install the columns. Have one person lift up the column while another tightens the coupler nut to the J-bolt and threaded rod.*

E. *Center the column at both ends, then tighten the nut over the bearing plate to secure the entire assembly.*

Step E: Set the Main Beams

1. Using stepladders set up next to the columns, place one of the main beams onto the columns, inserting the rod ends through the blocks. Check for even contact of the beam on all three columns. If necessary, you can trim a column: cut from the bottom end only using a sharp handsaw. NOTE: If there's a slight gap above the center column due to a crowning beam, it will most likely be gone once the beam is anchored.

2. Add bearing plates and nuts to the end of each threaded rod, loosely threading the nuts. Working on one column at a time, make sure the column shaft is centered on the pier and is centered under the beam block at the top end. Place a 2-ft. level along the bottom, untapered section of the column shaft and check the column for plumb. Hold the column plumb while a helper tightens the nut on the rod. Repeat to adjust and secure the remaining columns. Repeat the procedure to install the columns and beam on the other side of the pergola.

Step F: Notch & Install the Crossbeams

1. Place each crossbeam onto the layout marks on top of the main beams so the crossbeam overhangs equally at both ends. Mark each edge where the main beam pieces meet the crossbeam. This ensures that the notches will be accurate for each crossbeam. Number the crossbeams so you can install them in the same order. On your workbench, mark the notches for cutting at 2½" deep.

2. To cut the notches, you can save time by clamping two beams together and cutting both at once. Using a circular saw or handsaw, first cut the outside edges of the notches. Next, make a series of interior cuts at ⅛" intervals. Use a mallet and chisel to remove the waste and smooth the seats of the notches.

3. Set the crossbeams onto the main beams following the marked layout. Drill angled pilot holes through the sides of the crossbeams and into the main beams; drill one hole on each side, offsetting the holes so the screws won't hit each other. Fasten the crossbeams with 2½" deck screws.

Step G: Finish the Columns

1. Secure the base to the pier with masonry screws: First, drill pilot holes slightly larger than the screws through the base. Using a masonry bit, drill pilot holes into the pier. Fasten the base with the screws. Fit each capital against the main beam, drill pilot holes, and fasten the capital with deck screws.

2. Caulk the joints around the capital and base with high quality, paintable caulk. Paint the columns—and beams, if desired—using a primer and paint recommended by the column manufacturer.

F. *Make the notch cuts. Set a circular saw to cut kerfs just above the notch seat; clean up the notch with a chisel and mallet.*

G. *Seal the columns. After fastening the base and capital, caulk all of the joints to hide any gaps and create a watertight barrier.*

Conversion Charts

Metric Equivalents

Inches (in.)	1/64	1/32	1/25	1/16	1/8	1/4	3/8	2/5	1/2	5/8	3/4	7/8	1	2	3	4	5	6	7	8	9	10	11	12	36	39.4
Feet (ft.)																								1	3	3 1/12
Yards (yd.)																									1	1 1/12
Millimeters (mm)	0.40	0.79	1	1.59	3.18	6.35	9.53	10	12.7	15.9	19.1	22.2	25.4	50.8	76.2	101.6	127	152	178	203	229	254	279	305	914	1,000
Centimeters (cm)							0.95	1	1.27	1.59	1.91	2.22	2.54	5.08	7.62	10.16	12.7	15.2	17.8	20.3	22.9	25.4	27.9	30.5	91.4	100
Meters (m)																								.30	.91	1.00

Converting Measurements

TO CONVERT:	TO:	MULTIPLY BY:
Inches	Millimeters	25.4
Inches	Centimeters	2.54
Feet	Meters	0.305
Yards	Meters	0.914
Miles	Kilometers	1.609
Square inches	Square centimeters	6.45
Square feet	Square meters	0.093
Square yards	Square meters	0.836
Cubic inches	Cubic centimeters	16.4
Cubic feet	Cubic meters	0.0283
Cubic yards	Cubic meters	0.765
Pints (U.S.)	Liters	0.473 (Imp. 0.568)
Quarts (U.S.)	Liters	0.946 (Imp. 1.136)
Gallons (U.S.)	Liters	3.785 (Imp. 4.546)
Ounces	Grams	28.4
Pounds	Kilograms	0.454
Tons	Metric tons	0.907

TO CONVERT:	TO:	MULTIPLY BY:
Millimeters	Inches	0.039
Centimeters	Inches	0.394
Meters	Feet	3.28
Meters	Yards	1.09
Kilometers	Miles	0.621
Square centimeters	Square inches	0.155
Square meters	Square feet	10.8
Square meters	Square yards	1.2
Cubic centimeters	Cubic inches	0.061
Cubic meters	Cubic feet	35.3
Cubic meters	Cubic yards	1.31
Liters	Pints (U.S.)	2.114 (Imp. 1.76)
Liters	Quarts (U.S.)	1.057 (Imp. 0.88)
Liters	Gallons (U.S.)	0.264 (Imp. 0.22)
Grams	Ounces	0.035
Kilograms	Pounds	2.2
Metric tons	Tons	1.1

Converting Temperatures

Convert degrees Fahrenheit (F) to degrees Celsius (C) by following this simple formula: Subtract 32 from the Fahrenheit temperature reading. Then, mulitply that number by 5/9. For example, 77°F - 32 = 45. 45 × 5/9 = 25°C.

To convert degrees Celsius to degrees Fahrenheit, multiply the Celsius temperature reading by 9/5. Then, add 32. For example, 25°C × 9/5 = 45. 45 + 32 = 77°F.

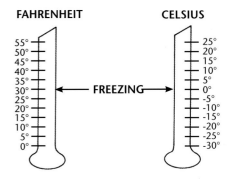

FAHRENHEIT   CELSIUS

← FREEZING →

Resources

ACG Greenhouses
888 888 9050
www.littlegreenhouse.com

American Institute of Architects
800 364 9364
www.aiaonline.com

American Society of Landscape Architects
202 898 2444
www.asla.org

Asphalt Roofing Manufacturers Association
202 207 0917
www.asphaltroofing.com

Backyard Golf
Artificial turf putting greens; Muirfield model
featured on p.508–511
770 456 5322
www.backyard-golf.com

The Betty Mills Company
www.bettymills.com

The Big eZee
Metal Kit Sheds
101 N. Fourth St.
Breese, IL 62230
800 851 1085

Black & Decker (US), Inc.
800 544 6986
www.blackanddecker.com
www.bdk.com

Brick Institute of America
703 620 0010
www.brickinfo.org

California Redwood Association
888 225 7339
www.calredwood.org

Cedar Shake & Shingle Bureau
604 820 7700
www.cedarbureau.org

Certified Wood Products Council
503 224 2205
www.certifiedwood.org

Construction Materials Recycling Association
630 548 4510
www.cdrecycling.com

Greenhouses.com
800 681 3302
www.greenhouses.com

GreenhouseKit.com
877 718 2865
www.greenhousekit.com

HDA Inc.,
www.houseplansandmore.com

Juliana Greenhouses
www.julianagreenhouses.com

Masonry Society
303 939 9700
www.masonrysociety.com

National Concrete Masonry Association
703 713 1900
www.ncma.org

Paint Quality Institute
www.paintquality.com

Portland Cement Association
847 966 6200
www.portcement.com

Simpson Strong-Tie Co.
800 999 5099
www.strongtie.com

Southern Pine Council
www.southernpine.com

Sturdy-built Greenhouses
Redwood greenhouse kits
800 344 4115
www.sturdi-built.com

Finley Products, Inc.
888 626 5301
www.2x4basics.com

Summerwood Products
866 519 4634
www.summerwood.com

Photo Credits

p. 31 Crossville Porcelain Stone
(www.crossvilleinc.com)

p. 52 (top) Kemiko Concrete Stains
(www.kemiko.com)

pp. 53 (top two) Becker Architectural Concrete
(www.beckerconcrete.com)

p. 76 Bob Firth / Firth Photo Bank

p. 90 California Redwood Association
(www.calredwood.com)

p. 94 Charles Mann

p. 98 Walter Chandoha

p. 122 Crandall & Crandall

p. 132 Clive Nichols, designer Jane Mooney

p. 141 Crandall & Crandall

p. 142 Crandall & Crandall

p. 152 Jerry Pavia

p. 156 Walpole Woodworkers
(www.walpole.com)

p. 158 Saxon Holt
(top right & middle left) Distinctive Design
(www.distinctivedesigns4you.com),
(top left, middle right, lower two) Deckorators
(www.deckorators.com)

p. 308 Jerry Pavia

p. 437 (top right) Jerry Pavia; (top left)
Courtesy of Greenhouses.com; (lower)
www.istockphoto.com

p. 502 iStock Photo

p. 506 ProSport

p. 507 (top) iStock Photo

p. 514 Brian Vanden Brink

Index